I0134557

GOD DESIGNED

366 DAYS OF INSPIRATION

J.P. OSTERMAN

J.P. Osterman

GOD DESIGNED
366 DAYS OF INSPIRATION

Copyright © 2015 J.P. Osterman
All rights reserved.

No part of this book shall be reproduced or transmitted in any form or by any means, electronic, mechanical, magnetic, and photographic including photocopying, recording or by any information storage and retrieval system, without prior written permission of the author, except for brief quotations by reviewers or in connection with critical analysis.

Requests for permission to make copies of any part of the work should be submitted to the publisher:

ITM Press at: davidcohen7891@gmail.com

Published by: ITM Press
a subsidiary of The ITM Group

ITM
Press

ISBN-10: 069255095X
ISBN-13: 978-0692550953
First Edition
Date of Publication: October, 2015

Printed in the United States of America
CreateSpace, Charleston SC

Cover Photo: © Igor Zh. | Shutterstock

DEDICATION

I dedicate *God Designed* to:

Adonai

J.P. Osterman

Acknowledgments

I would like to acknowledge the people who influenced me during the writing of *God Designed*. Thank you, Dr. Scott Wilson and Youth Pastor Jason Schack of FBC Melbourne. Sincere thanks to you, Dr. Wayne Moore, of FBC Malabar. Thanks to the ministry of David Asscherick of New South Wales, Australia. Thank you, Rabbi Alan Levine of Kol Mashiach.

A special thanks goes out to the website, *Bible Gateway*, and the *Complete Jewish Bible*, two invaluable resources I utilized for writing *God Designed*. I also extend loving thanks to my friend Chaplain Jane Shaffer, Leader of our Tuesday night Bible study. You are truly a five-star worker in the advancement of the Gospel. Also our close knit Tuesday-night study group comprised of the following Christian brothers and sisters: John Mauro and Diane Mauro; Lorraine Laws, Lisa Bertanza; Angie and John Hammond; Susan; and, Carl and Sharon Sandquist. You were inspirations with your comments and ideas.

Thanks also goes out to the Brevard Scribblers and Space Coast Writers' Guild for their encouragement. I thank all my teachers, particularly my fifth-grade teacher Sister Rose at St. Joseph's school in Hammond, Indiana; and Mr. Young at Munster High School, Munster, Indiana. I thank my cousins: Sis Groff; Linda Campbell; and, John McCarten. I thank my brother, Thomas Michael Pink, and my sister-in-law, Joan. I thank my dad, George Pink, Jr. as well.

I am especially thankful, grateful, and indebted to my family for their advice, encouragement, and patience: my husband Drew; my son Andrew; my daughter Jennifer; my son-in-law Keith; my Granddaughter Rachel; and, future generations for whom I've persistently, lovingly, diligently, and thoughtfully written *God Designed*. Thanks also to my son Jacob Eller and daughter-in-law Amanda Eller. I pray for God to bestow His blessings upon you all. Thanks again, Dad and Mom; for through you, I was God Designed. Debbie Sanchez, friend, wherever you are, thanks. In 1988, we joined Church of the Open Door, my first Christian church where my road to God and salvation began. Thanks, again, to *everyone* above. You helped me become the best I can be today to write *God Designed*. Little bits of *all* of you live in me, and now *through* me, to reach souls for God. He reigns.

INTRODUCTION

We're surrounded by signs everywhere, on billboards, buildings, the roadside, banners, Zeppelins, airplanes, sign spinners, neon signs, electric signs, car signs, signs on screens and newspaper headlines. Did I get 'em all? Probably not; however, one day I saw a sign after my own heart.

Nothing prepared me for September 21, 2014, my Aunt Mary's birthday. Feeling antsy about my next project, I've been asking God for weeks, "What direction do you want me to take in life, Lord?" Then, I spotted a counseling sign on Lipscomb Street like bright-green neon firing in my brain.

"What's this mean? Yep, I guess I'm a bit of a mess lately."

Have you ever wanted to start over? "God, please show me another direction for my life." So many times, I find myself being designed by the people, places, and things in this world that I lose sight of the little experiences God uses to fashion us for His glory.

Aunt Mary's birthday began a change of focus for me, a Holy Spirit calling. Reminiscing and laughing, we talked on the phone about life on her parents' farm in Hannah, Indiana. I didn't know that she would die March 30, 2015, eight months after her sister Elizabeth.

There's nothing like the realization of Death that'll make a person take a second look at life and what they're doing with the little and big things that happen to us daily.

Yet, Jesus is calling ... every moment of the day, hailing us in our busy lives to "Come to me, all of you who are struggling and burdened, and I will give you rest" (Matthew 11:28). I heard His call that first day of fall in Melbourne, Florida. I asked Him to help me live for Him, inspire and encourage others with His Word, and help people discern His designs for them. When Jesus walked among us, He made a profound connection with a man plagued with a serious skin ailment. The afflicted man knelt right down in front of Him. "Sir, if you are willing, you can make me clean" (Matthew 8:2). I needed a change from my own plagues and ailments, metaphorically speaking.

Driving with the windows wide open on that September evening, I basked in the balmy Florida ocean air and thanked God for His love and my life. I passed by sign-after-banner-after-ad. More neon! I whispered into the towering cumulus rain clouds, "Jesus, if you are willing, you can make me matter for you." Ideas tossed in my mind like Bingo tiles ... until, I saw that counseling sign again: The Caring Center.

"That's it!" I said to my husband Drew. "I'll focus on scripture, a daily topic, and connect them with a sign-of-the-day, because God can use *anything* to draw people close to Him. He designed us from the beginning, and He's designing us in the moments of our lives."

Well, my husband liked the idea. Since that day, I've kept my promise to God to put the best of my education, Bible studying ways, knowledge of scripture, and experiences [the best o' me!] into a daily devotional and inspirational work—actually, His work, for you. Here are a few considerations as you read *God Designed*.

I used the *Complete Jewish Bible* (CJB) for scriptural quotes. Some people like the King James Version (KJV); some like the NIV Version. Nowadays, anyone can compare scriptures and access multiple versions of the Bible via numerous online sites. I utilized Biblegateway.com to search topics and quickly find quotes. Two important differences you'll notice between the CJB and the KJV are "*Adonai*" for God and "*Yeshua*" for Jesus. "Adonai" first appears in Genesis 2:4 as "Lord, Master." He is God, Lord, and Master of our lives. How do we know Him and find inspiration from Him daily? *God Designed* attempts to do just that. As for the name, "Yeshua," Matthew launches the Savior's name right away in verse 1, "This is the genealogy of Yeshua the Messiah." When I began *God Designed*, I prayed, "God help every seeking person to seek you so they will know they are God designed." I hope I help you seek some answers with which you might be struggling.

Still, I encountered obstacles. What would I do about the dates that don't match successive years? For example, Easter, Mother's Day, and Father's Day all have different dates. Year-after-year, New Year's Day, St. Patrick's Day, Fourth of July, Halloween, and Christmas have the same dates. The answer? I wanted a book that could float through the years and remain applicable no matter what date or day. Whether the year is 2016 or 20016, you can rearrange various holidays according to how they fall on your calendar. However, I've included an eight-day bonus section at the end of *God Designed* for Easter week. Also, the sci-fi artist in me couldn't help it ... I've included a bonus 367 day. Hey, we never know where humanity might flourish in the future with God designing us, right?

I also left a *Note* page at the end of the book to jot down themes or important scriptures. Perhaps the section can function as a diary, helping you on your journey of discovery and inspiration. Always remember, you are God designed, precious to Him, and vital in this world. He listens to your *every* word.

Focusing on my purpose and mission evoked a title, *God Designed*, now in your hands as a daily devotional, book of reflections, an inspirational work, a source of encouragement, and an investigative work into the character and nature of our God Adonai. How does God work and communicate with us? I pray *God Designed* will help you focus on some of those minutes that sweep by and mount into irretrievable years. "I, *Adonai*, your God, say to you, as I hold your right hand, 'Have no fear; I will help you' " (Isaiah 41:13). He's listening. He's knocking. He is blessing us. He *is* helping through the Holy Spirit. We only need to let Him in.

You can begin *God Designed* any day. So let's turn to today's date and, begin the journey.

EVERYONE WHO IS SERIOUSLY INVOLVED IN THE PURSUIT OF SCIENCE BECOMES CONVINCED THAT A SPIRIT IS MANIFEST IN THE LAWS OF THE UNIVERSE - A SPIRIT VASTLY SUPERIOR TO THAT OF MAN, AND ONE IN THE FACE OF WHICH WE WITH OUR MODEST POWERS MUST FEEL HUMBLE.

Albert Einstein

JANUARY 1
PLACE OF HOPE

At 10^{-43} seconds "Planck" time, instantly after the clock struck midnight, another beginning *tick*ed into reality. Beginnings. I drop to my knees in thanksgiving for them. I'm always in need of a new beginning, another chance, a red starting line, a bright-yellow dawn, a new moon, a fresh goal, a different target, a blank page, a clean slate, or an open door with a shining threshold to step over after I've been standing still and waiting in a *long* corridor. What's the new beginning you want for your life? "Trust in *Adonai* forever, because in *Yah Adonai*, is a Rock of Ages" (Isaiah 26:4).

Maybe your want is simple, or maybe it's a long-drawn-out desperate longing. Every want, dream, or goal begins as a thought, a seed that needs to germinate. "The earth is filled with your love, Lord. Teach me" (Psalm 119:64).

Yes, a brand-spanking new year starts today, right now! Today is the first holiday of the year for most people; however, other countries celebrate their own transitions into a New Year. There's the Albanian New Year on March 21, Chinese New Year that falls on the day of the second new moon after the winter solstice, and the Cambodian New Year on April 13, just to name a few. What's so important about a measurement of time the experts created to track Earth's revolution and rotation?

Hope is important. "Hope deferred makes the heart sick, but desire fulfilled is a tree of life" (Proverbs 13:12). "Hope," means, "a feeling of expectation and desire for a certain thing to happen." The word is action oriented or object oriented. We can "be hoping" or "have hope;" yet no matter where we stand with respect to hope, time is passing, which means the two states of being and living out our lives in our ever-changing world are inextricably intertwined.

Albert Einstein connected hope and time: "Learn from yesterday, live for today, hope for tomorrow." Compare last year to your hope for *this* year. What did you learn from last year's experiences, and how do you hope to change because of what happened? I'm reminded of one more type of hope: the need for God to walk with me every Planck second of the year. "Adonai is all I have, I say; therefore I will put my hope in him" (Lamentations 3:24). He lives.

Lord God, as we begin this year, we long for *your* will. Amen.

JANUARY 2
FREE GYM MEMBERSHIP

We need exercise, and yesterday I read the best news ever. We just need thirty minutes of walking five times a week. Thirty minutes!

That's not hard to do, right?

You might say, *I can't do that.* Maya Angelou once said, "You want me to do something … tell me I can't do it." Now that's motivation. Here's another:

Are you a "couch potato" with an irregular, or no exercise routine? Oh well, "not hard" just flew out the window! But wait, there's good news about beginning anew at any time in our lives.

All the New Year sales, advertising exercise equipment on TV and in sporting-goods stores might entice you into some serious change—that is the change you have left in your purse or wallet is all that is left. I guess I could use a better exercise routine other than mowing the lawn, vacuuming, cleaning the floors with Clorox wipes, raking, and picking up dog hair. But first, I need to lasso in my cravings. Yeah, right. How? That hasn't worked so far.

Thought control might be the answer: fighting the hypnotizing urge for a chocolate chip cookie and my sweet tooth for ice cream when I see commercials, signs, and billboards dangling the goodies in my face everywhere. I wonder: how many commercials are there on food? American children see over a thousand fast food commercials every year, with McDonald's Golden Arches at the top of the list (Richard Feloni, "Here's How Many Fast Food Ads Kids See Each Year," Businessinsider.com; Nov. 15, 2013). Cravings and exercise appear as heavy counterweights, always repelling like two magnets trying to touch. Eat a cookie, then walk a mile to burn it off.

The Psalmist says, "Teach us to count our days, so that we will become wise" (Psalm 90:12). Instead of ineffectual thought-control experiments to change that have only left me the same, there's behavior modification. Experiencing an illness or near-death catastrophe usually gets a person motivated to change, and fast. After my stepmother died, my 86-year-old dad changed right away by contacting the local senior center and volunteering for lunch clean up duty. After two years of a solid work routine, he's now fit and healthy. Counting days really works.

Jesus, we want to live long to fulfill your plans for us, and we need your help to change. Amen.

JANUARY 3
'F' STANDS FOR *FAST*

I received an automated call from my bank, which went something like the following: "This is Fraud Prevention. We have tagged your account because of two suspicious transactions. Until we can speak to you, your account is blocked."

Have you ever received such a call?

The information felt earth shaking and nerve rattling. Who could do such a thing as steal, and steal from me? When something that catastrophic happens, we can't believe it occurred to *us*. Theft happens to others, but not—*never*—to me, right? Did I talk to God right away? Nope.

The automated caller left me only a phone number, just as I was about to enter the pet store to buy food for our dog. I scrambled for a pen and paper, and then ran back to my car, where my husband and I sat anxiously with the engine idling as we spent the next ten minutes in a twilight zone of suspended disbelief. It turned out, when I was in California, at some place where I had shopped, *someone* [miscreant thief!] had inserted a skimmer into one of the machines and lifted my card's information. Thank goodness my bank declined the bandit's best *three* efforts at an ATM to rob me of $500. *Whew.* If the illegal transaction had succeeded, we would be rafting down Torrent River toward Waterfall Junction! Unfortunately, skimmers have been problematic all over, as well as hacking attempts to steal peoples' identities. The good news is: institutions have been revving up technological precautions to thwart greedy thieves. Good triumphed over bad, at least today, and gave me a reprieve. Still, we can't escape forever.

With Christmas gone, I guess evil-doers believe that people received truckloads of gift money—all for *their* easy pickings. This makes me wonder: What if we lived in a world where everyone steals? The opposite of "stealing" is "protecting," for "stealing" involves "harm" and "injury," while "protecting" aims "to preserve" and "keep safe." Christmas is not gone. It remains with us daily in the message of what Christ did for us. "For God's grace, which brings deliverance, is offered to all people. It teaches us to renounce godlessness and worldly pleasures, and to live self-controlled, upright and godly lives now, in this age" (Titus 2:11-12).

God, help us show your saving grace to others. Amen.

January 4
Record Heat

Do you ever wonder why the people to whom you sent Christmas cards didn't write back? That question repeated in my mind this morning—a bad spirit I couldn't slap away. I think of the quote, "Let brotherly friendship continue" (Hebrews 13:10). Sometimes, friendships *don't* evolve.

I asked myself the following: "Did I do something wrong?" "Did I say something inappropriate in the card?"

If this has happened to you, I suggest you write out the questions you're asking yourself as well, and I bet you'll find the answer to be something like the following:

I didn't do anything wrong, say anything inappropriate, or gossip about the individuals. So what's the answer?

There's a saying that goes: "Don't reserve a space in your heart for someone who doesn't make an effort to stay" (Unknown). The key words there are, "make an effort." That's all a person can do to be a friend or keep a friendship. Making an effort is extending your hand of friendship, or offering support, or showing love to someone. The word, "effort," means: "a vigorous or determined attempt; exertion; energy." Theodore Roosevelt once said about energy: "It is only through labor and painful effort, by grim energy and resolute courage that we move on to better things." Oh-oh, here comes the next step when we do try everything we possibly can—writing emails, phoning, or sending cards—and the other person does not reply, either because of inconsideration or just their way of letting go of me.

The message is clear: When we make an effort but the other person does not respond, they are telling us that their own world is noisy, their energy is spent, or since we're out of sight and long gone, we're out of mind." It's okay though. We have the love and approval of our God. Even Paul exclaimed: "I want God's approval" (Galatians 1:10)! We live for Him, He lives in us, He loves us, and He always writes back in our hearts through the Holy Spirit.

"Human being, you have already been told what is good, what Adonai demands of you—no more than to act justly, love grace and walk in purity with your God" (Micah 6:8). Move on and live for today.

Lord, in times when we feel we have no friends, we need you to fill us with peace, love, and direction. Amen.

JANUARY 5
BORDERS TO DEEPNESS

Church can take place between people. Jesus once said, "Wherever two or three are assembled in my name, I am there with them" (Matthew 18:20).

I don't know about you, but I'm the type of person who likes to communicate with people more than just on the superficial level of, "How's the weather where you're at today?" My 'Circle of Closeness' begins with my husband and our son, then our Bible study fellowship, followed by church members, and then "our children" who no longer reside with us but with whom we keep in close contact. Yesterday, as we ran into the church sanctuary after I had complained in the car about how we're *constantly* over ten minutes late, I met one of our Bible study friends. She looked so exhausted; and after a few minutes of exchanging pleasantries over the holiday, I told her my observation. She broke into tears. Last year was a total bomb for her, filled with family hurts and pressures to find a job, which she now has, but which is still precarious. She's grateful for "the paycheck," but life with her stepsiblings has been wrought with emotional pain. Her stepmom died just a couple of months ago in October, and funerals can bring out the worst in people. I recall a phrase that appears true, "Why is it, when someone passes away, grief often turns into greed?" The stepsiblings abandoned my friend and quickly sold off their mom's possessions, not even allowing my friend to attend her stepmom's memorial service, a person who had been a "real" mom to her. Hurt and disbelief are like bleeding sores for her now; yet, in times such as this, friendships are born.

Most times, I believe I don't have a friend; however, whether in church or in a grocery store line, friendships can manifest as little helping miracles. "A friend shows his friendship at all times—it is for adversity that [such] a brother [or sister] is born" (Proverbs 17:17). Friendships take time and work to cultivate.

Friendships occur when we do Christ-like actions for others.

I can't believe how many people are smiling but struggling. We can listen and be present when other experience sadness and need. That's also being a friend to God. Remember, He said, "Whenever you did these things for one of the least important of these brothers of mine, you did them for me" (Matthew 25:40)! Who are the least?

Holy Spirit, we need your words to comfort people. Amen.

JANUARY 6
STILLNESS

I found unrest today instead of stillness. Are you ever caught up in an unrestful days? "Their redeemer is strong; *Adonai-Tzva'ot* is his name. He ... can give rest" (Jeremiah 50:34). God gives us rest. Have you ever cooked in the kitchen with people hovering around you like helicopters, adding their "ideas" for the perfect recipe?

"Spray the hot wings with cooking oil and then bake 'em," I said. My husband wanted the wings coated with hot sauce and then fried; and my son "needed" them baked, then dumped in a bowl, and finally stirred in with hot sauce. It's just gotta be done *his* way.

"But that'll take off all the coating," I countered.

There are sayings about too many people in the kitchen: Hunger is the best sauce, but too many cooks spoil the broth. Something out of the ordinary happens when family mixes all their advice and opinions. Chaos.

I can imagine the same scenario occurring with people *outside* my close-knit family circle whom I've invited to dinner but then afterwards they leave, to see them another time:

"The recipe calls for breading the wings, coating a lined pan with foil, and then baking them," I might say, reading the recipe.

"Okay, where's the flour, spices, foil, oil, and pan?" an acquaintance might respond.

Seems life is calmer and less emotionally charged when "peripheral" people come into our lives.

Why, and what's the ingredient for "quiet water" (Psalm 23:2)?

Psychologist Karen L. Fingerman coined the term "consequential strangers" to describe peripheral people outside our family circles. They are weak ties for us; and because the level of intimacy with them is more superficial than with close family members, our emotions and expectations are less charged, and we're more subjective than objective in our dealings with them.

"Keep yourselves under control, and fix your hopes fully on the gift you will receive when Yeshua [Jesus] the Messiah is revealed" (1 Peter 1:13). Once in Heaven, Jesus is there. We'll all mix well, without arguments. In situations where we have to mix with family, "Don't let this matter get you down" (2 Samuel 11:25), "Through the faith we share, encourage one another" (Romans 1:12).

Holy Spirit, give us patience in our actions. Amen.

JANUARY 7
PIECES

I walked into my local grocery store to find a bevy of Valentine's Day products, everything from shoebox-sized red-heart candy packs to love-enticing ceramic mugs packed with tiny stuffed animals and elegantly wrapped cellophane candy. Valentine's Day in January, really? You notice how stores ramp up sales now months before a holiday? Don't you feel like a money bank for all these companies?

Feeling disoriented, I stopped. I remembered when I was a kid. I used to spin around in circles on the Merry-Go-Round at Harrison Park. Someone would suddenly stop the ride, and I'd jump off and stagger around, trying to regain my balance. Then I'd jump back on, and we'd kick our way through the dirt, accelerating in the opposite direction. Time is going by just as fast now. Do you feel its spin? "Flowers appear on the earth. The time of singing has come" (Song of Solomon 2:12). Can you sing through the changes? It's hard.

"New Year's Day glided by so fast!" I whispered into a stack of passion-lifting Valentine's Day cards. I feel as if I'm diving off a cliff and chasing the past ... along with every other day that's appearing-then-disintegrating with the rising-and-setting sun. Transfixed in the aisle while people quickly wheel by me as if their roasts are burning in the oven, I can hardly breathe. I see future products on those shelves: Easter, Cinco de Mayo, Fourth of July ... You get the picture. As an exercise, take out a few frayed school photos and then glance in the mirror. I didn't say stare. Just notice. I can't help contemplating about God who has no beginning and no end: "I am the 'A' and the 'Z,' the Beginning and the End" (Rev. 21:6). I ask, "Does that 'A' mean the Big Bang, and 'Z' mean the continued expansion of our universe?" God has existed beyond the former and will live after the latter.

What an awesome Father, who takes us *with* Him.

I wonder if I'll ever receive an answer from Him, except for the only moment over which I can have some degree of control: now. "So long as the earth exists, sowing time and harvest, cold and heat, summer and winter, and day and night will not cease" (Genesis 8:22). Genesis and Revelation offer two types of beginnings, and God has our moments *always* in his sight.

Lord Heavenly God, as time progresses, we want to cling to You and Your promises. Amen.

January 8
Volunteer Here

Have you ever heard of a Mexican standoff?

It's a confrontation between at least three parties in which no party can proceed nor retreat without being exposed to danger. Mind boggling, confusing, right?

Have you ever been in one? How to solve it?

A few days ago, I agreed to do some volunteer work at my church, stuffing and sorting letters for one of our large ministries. Stepping into the cafeteria, I noticed I was the only person under sixty-five. A few people were already seated and shakily passing around flyers, envelopes, and labels as more excited volunteers trickled in on walkers, lumbered to round tables in oxygenated wheelchairs, or meandered confusingly around a towering information table. Everyone was waiting for someone in charge to tell them what to do and where to go. I saw one table with three people energetically fast at work collating forms and stuffing them into envelopes. They were "Speedy Gonzalez" and I was, "Huh?"

"You can stick labels on envelopes," Amy said, gesturing for me to sit next to her. "Ron is sealing them." He introduced himself, as did Beth to the right of me, and Mel next to her. Mel had a few missing teeth, and Parkinson's, but his determination was contagious as he quickly worked to assemble the inserts. Glancing around, I saw six other tables and the gothic leaflet table that appeared impossible to level; but all seven tables were manned, and white-haired eager beavers were working with ambidextrous expertise as if assembling weapons on a line for the Army. We—my A table—was going to finish first. "Love each other devotedly and with brotherly love; and set examples for each other in showing respect," Paul advices (Romans 12:10). *I don't have to race. This isn't a race. If I'm racing, trying to win, the race is in my own mind.* Whew, thanks, Paul!

I situated the envelopes just right, and then slapped a label on each finger as I lifted them off the backing, and then stick, push, swipe left, and repeat. Did we win? "Imitate God, as his dear children, and live a life of love, just as also the Messiah loved us" (Ephesians 5:1-2). We captured one another with our life stories, and the time raced by like children sliding over hills of snow.

Jesus, help us see beauty in monotony and purpose in the seemingly mundane. Amen.

JANUARY 9
PROGRESS

There are a few of God's Bible prophets who appeared weak but then finished strong.

Do you ever think you're weak? Or, maybe there are times you feel strong but you're really weak?

God's with you today. "Accept the one whose faith is weak" (Romans 14:1)

Still, even the Bible uses examples of people who were less than perfect on their journey to fulfilling God's purposes. By reading about and understanding their frailties *and* accomplishments *we* can draw closer to God. I don't know about you, but when I discover mistakes in a writing project I've worked so hard to perfect, I disparage myself with self-doubt like: "How could you have overlooked that comma after reading the chapter fifty times?!" Can you imagine King David saying, "Why did you have to look at *her* when you had everything goin' for ya?!" Or think of Hosea proclaiming in the mirror while slapping his forehead: "What else did you expect to happen after you married that lose woman Gomer?" No one punishes us more than we criticize ourselves.

Yet I'm amazed at God's compassion for his chosen servants who often strayed while inching their way to God's purposes. David, for example, not only committed adultery but also murder. God showered his graces on Gomer, the harlot who kept cheating on Hosea. He continued to bless Gomer in spite of her unfaithful adulterous behavior that must have crushed Hosea *and* God. "I will betroth you to me forever; yes, I will betroth you to me in righteousness, in justice, in grace and in compassion; I will betroth you to me in faithfulness, and you will know Adonai" (Hosea 2:19-20). If God has this much mercy and compassion for us, we need to show the same gentleness when *we* disappoint ourselves, or land outside our self-imposed goals. Leviticus 19:18 says, "Love your neighbor as yourself." God tells us in Matthew 22:39: "You are to love your neighbor as yourself;" in Luke 10:27, "...as yourself." In Romans 13:9 and James 2:8, "...as yourself." Breathe, and let's move forward in love and self-nurturing. The past is gone. Our sins are forgiven. "They are like trees planted by streams" (Psalm 1:3).

Lord God our Father, give us peace and wisdom in what we cannot change so we can move forward with our day. Amen.

JANUARY 10
WINTER RETREAT

Remember the last time you packed for a long trip? Did you take your time packing? Or did you rush around like there was an electrical outage and the clock stopped in the middle of the night?

Recently we had to jam clothes and squash toiletries into a carry-on so our son could survive comfortably for three days away from home. It's not easy bundling summer clothes for indoor swimming activities with winter-wear for frosty hikes in the outdoor expanse of a mountain retreat. And don't forget the new battery to charge your portable technology while on the ride. Oh, and remember your pillow and extra towel in case your roommates use up the ones in the bathroom.

You know what it's like to rush. Can we slow down?

I don't care how conscious I am in following a list and checking off items, I always forget to pack something I need. I'll forget dental floss or slippers. They're insignificant items, but seem very important when I'm looking for them in desperation but can't find them among all the unnecessary things I could have left home.

I have learned one important thing: Don't pack *anything* you'll cry over if you leave it or lose it.

I can just imagine what Abraham experienced when God told him that his descendants would be living in foreign lands—packed and on permanent vacation—for generations. "As the sun was about to set, a deep sleep fell on Avram [Abraham]; horror and great darkness came over him. Adonai said to Avram, 'Know this for certain: your descendants will be foreigners in a land that is not theirs. They will be slaves and held in oppression there four hundred years. But I will also judge that nation, the one that makes them slaves. Afterwards, they will leave with many possessions. As for you, you will join your ancestors in peace and be buried at a good old age. Only in the fourth generation will your descendants come back here'" (Genesis 15:12-16). Whether packing to move, or for those little excursions, know God's shepherding hand is leading us (1 Peter 2:25). His love is always covering our losses. He calms us, slows us down. "God will do battle for you. Just calm yourselves down" (Exodus 14:14). In stressful moments, God is beside you.

We want to have you *always* at our side, in our sight, and *first* in importance, Lord. Carry us in hard times, Jesus. Amen.

JANUARY 11
FLOORING INCLUDED

Ever try walking on a floor with no tile or carpet? Ouch!

There's a rough mortar, or flexible underlayment, that a builder lays down as a home's foundation, which functions as a sturdy base for years of wear-and-tear. However, over time, a pipe might burst. The ground shifts, and cracks appear. They can be repaired, maybe not easily. The fixes might also be costly, but breaks are mendable.

Yet, something *not* so easily and readily fixed is a changed friendship.

Are any of your friendships changing today, or in need of change?

"A friend loves at all times, and a brother is born for a time of adversity" (Proverbs 17:17).

What was wise King Solomon saying?

Last month I visited a city where I once lived and met a friend who I've known for twenty-six years. It's the oldest friendship I've put effort into so as to sustain the bond, even though my friend has moved several times without leaving a forwarding number or address. About sixteen years ago, I loaned her money, but I forgave the debt because, again, she was struggling, homeless, and seeking a fast fix for her troubled life. Author David Baird said about friends: "Friendship is a tree to take shelter from the storm, to find shade from the blazing sun, to climb its branches to get a better view, and to swing from when we're happy." Have you ever put so much into a relationship but received very little in return? That's the pattern I have with "my friend." Our friendship has fallen into foundational disrepair. I won't say, "defect," because "defect" implies that our friendship had serious flaws in the beginning. She and I started out as single moms in need of support and took a church membership class together. We were close and not cynical in our youthful years, and open to new people entering our intimate circles. For that reason, I will not push the "let go" button. "Some friends pretend to be friends, but a true friend sticks closer than a brother" (Proverbs 18:24). How do you fix a floor crack? Cover it with a rug? Or put work into the problem, filling it in with grout and water? After the grout dries, the tile should look like new, at least from afar.

Holy Spirit, help us spread love, joy, peace, patience, kindness, and faithfulness. Help us *be* a friend and *be* the change. Amen.

JANUARY 12
KEEP GOING, GOING, GOING

The 1973 song, "The Way We Were," talks about the emotional moments people experience but then forget. These moments are "misty" and "scattered."

Do you have lingering "misty moments?"

"Now, for a brief moment, the Lord our God has been gracious in leaving us a remnant and giving us a firm place in his sanctuary, and so our God gives light to our eyes and a little relief in our bondage" (Ezra 9:8). God is firm in our lives, no matter how our memories try to deceive us into believing anything different. He's firm. Are you the type of person who remembers not just the date when something significant happened, but the *exact* time? Freud coined the term, "the unconscious," as a mental process of which people are unaware. The unconscious part of our mind is a repository for socially unacceptable ideas, desires, traumatic memories, and painful emotions that we repress by defense mechanisms, such as displacement, where we proverbially "kick the dog" instead of expressing anger out of fear a loved one might abandon us. I say "displacement," God calls those mechanisms, sin.

Three years ago yesterday, my stepmom died, alone, in hospice. We were walking back to the house from McDonald's and received a call from my dad. She had died. A nurse was with her, although I doubt that because when we were there, no one checked her except on the half hour. We spent evenings with my deteriorating stepmom, but then my tired dad wanted to go home. Did she die at 11:35 a.m.? 10:22? As years pass, the memory is obscuring, reminding me of winter mornings when I was a child. I was the one to scrape ice off the car windows so we could see to drive.

I recently heard the story of humble Amos who told people, "I watch sheep and grow figs" (Amos 7:14); yet God called him to be a prophet. God showed him locusts (7:1), a blazing fire (7:4); and finally Himself: "I saw Adonai standing beside the altar" (9:1). I bet Amos never forgot the exact times he saw God, just as God cancels our past transgressions when we accept Christ. "For, look! I create new heavens and a new earth; past things will not be remembered, they will no more come to mind" (Isaiah 65:17). We'll be our *true* selves in eternity with Jesus. The things of this Earth, gone.

Father God, restore us, fashion us, and plant us firmly. Amen.

JANUARY 13
UNBREAKABLY STRONG

"If we can't pick up the pace so we can make it to Camp 1 in *three* hours," a lead mountain climber shouted to his team, "we'll have to turn back to the base camp. A *white out* is on the way!" Their legs and arms began churning like powerful pumping rods until they arrived at the Valley of Silence, 20,000 feet above sea level. Survival was their only thought and concern for their fellow mountain climbers.

Have you ever heard of a white out?

You don't have to be on a mountain to encounter this overwhelming and sudden shift to dangerous fog, rain, wind, or snow. "A windstorm came down on the lake, so that the boat began to fill up with water, putting them in great danger" (Luke 8:23). You could find yourself in a white out while driving down the freeway, walking down the street or shoveling snow.

A white out severely limits visibility; and the sudden bombardment of snow, rain, or fog obscures your reference point so you become directionally disoriented and confused. At this stage, you better have a compass, or you might get lost and not be found. While most of us aren't die-hard mountaineers, we can still become hit by white-out obstacles that can hamper us from accomplishing our goals or dreams. Are you experiencing a white out today? How can a person finish a goal under such conditions?

Paul encountered life-threatening hurdles that could have stopped him from preaching the Gospel. In Philippi, he suffers with Silas when a mob attacks them, judges beat both of them, and they land in prison (Acts 16:22-24). In 2 Timothy, the Romans imprison Paul, knowing death is near. His friend Demas has deserted him, and other Christians can no longer "friend hop" so as to conserve money and visit him. He faces a court of law alone (4:10-16). Yet, while Paul persevered through times of extreme suffering, his Christian communities helped him: "In Thessalonica when I needed it, you sent me aid twice" (Philippians 4:16-18). His close Thessalonian family boosted him spiritually: "Yes, you are our glory and our joy!" (1 Thess. 2:20). When problems feel overpowering, we can pray. "He invigorates the exhausted" (Isaiah 40:29). We have the power of prayer on our side—a direct line to Father God.

Jesus, when life feels so overwhelming, we need the Holy Spirit to fill us with strength and perseverance. Amen.

January 14
Yours for a Small Fee

This is the time of year for the International Consumer Electronics Show (CES) in Las Vegas. What technological innovation do you have your heart set on buying?

With everything new and titillating before us, buying technology these days is like a kid in a candy store. Have you ever felt like an uncontrollable kid in your favorite store? Our eyes become periscopes, luring us everywhere, to our indulgences. Good luck changing and gaining control, but God can redirect us.

Throughout CES, companies large and small display their innovative products in the hope they'll generate hype with the media and tech junkies, and then strike gold with the public, who'll flock to stores to purchase their latest gadgets. Wearable technology is this year's rave. Products such as *Fitbit*—that monitors your heart rate continuously—and *Narrative Chip 2*—a quarter-sized camera that snaps pictures of you as you go about your day—and *Alcatel One Touch*—that can connect with your cell phone so you can open apps or toggle settings, are just a few of the high-tech gadgets and gizmos of 2015. Oh, and don't forget the Mercedes-Benz F 015, a tempting driverless car of the future.

We live in the era of "the technology butler," wherein we can perform a multitude of tasks like open or close the curtains, or change the temperature of our refrigerators from our cell phone. People living in Jesus's time appear Stone Aged. Yet, when we research those times, we see inventions that allowed Jesus to proclaim the everlasting message of his Father's grace and salvation to the world. "Your word continues forever, Adonai, firmly fixed in heaven" (Psalm 119:89). After Jesus' resurrection, the Apostles utilized Roman technology to preach the Word. The Romans were masters at harnessing energy. They were experts in the construction of aqueducts, dams, bridges, roads, and, of course, the amphitheater. God appeared and convicted Paul on the Road to Damascus, which in those days was a well-traveled brick road. And in modern center-city trade markets, such as in the heart of Athens at the time, Paul often preached the Message of Salvation to the lost, lonely, disillusioned, and disheartened (Acts 17:16-32). The Word lives.

Father, we want to be examples to others of your living breathing word. Amen.

JANUARY 15
BURIALS AND CREMATIONS

War is everywhere now.

Have you noticed, war doesn't ever stop?

God knows war too. He called his people to fight for and keep their Promised Land: "All these kings met together, then came and pitched camp together at the Merom Spring, to fight Isra'el [Israel]" (Joshua 11:1-5); and, "The P'lishtim [Philistines] drew up in battle formation against Isra'el. The battle was fierce, and Isra'el was beaten by the P'lishtim—they killed about four thousand soldiers on the battlefield" (1 Samuel 4:2). We're in a war, and it seems war never ends. Peace appears allusive. Can you find peace in today's turmoil?

There are countless instances when the Jewish people died in some form of hostility or prejudice against Jews, anti-Semitism. In the 1940s, we witnessed that evil side of human nature in Hitler's coal stoking killing rooms. When visiting Germany in 2007, I toured Dachau, an extermination camp, which had written on the gate, *Arbeit Macht Frei*, meaning that upon entering, people could leave if they worked hard. It's horrible to give someone *false* hope.

Yesterday, people in Israel and France mourned the deaths of seventeen people killed in a wave of terror attacks in Paris. Four victims were Jewish. Imagine telling the world: "She was killed because she was Jewish." Would you believe the early Christians were considered a Jewish sect (i.e., Acts 4:22 and 5:17:22) until the middle of the second century? Nero began the persecution of Christians in 64 AD. In 524 AD in Yemen, King Dhu Nuwas murdered 20,000 Christians. If you're a Christian living in a Muslim nation, or you're Muslim and convert to Christianity, you're a criminal under Sharia Law. Yet the eternal God tells everyone: "If a person does not love his brother, whom he has seen, then he cannot love God, whom he has not seen. Yes, this is the command we have from him: whoever loves God must love his brother too" (1 John 4:20-21). People *perceive* God through religions, yet his Word tells us to love people. Human interpretations and perceptions can be so wrong. Religions are supposed to stem from the Bible and God's word, right? Let's read His words and the Holy Spirit will guide us and inspire us to the things we can control for God's glory.

Let your words shine truth on us, so we can show others You, God, and tolerance, peace and love. Amen.

JANUARY 16
KEY WORDS

Have you ever been ashamed of a secret sin that someone in your family tree committed? "Every morning [God] renders his judgment, every morning, without fail. Yet the wrongdoer knows no shame" (Zephaniah 3:5).

I have. Someone *way back* in my family line married a cousin. If you're like me, you might have even *more* than one "family secret" which people call "skeletons" buried somewhere—some even criminal—like the secret murderous man Edgar Allen Poe tries to conceal in, "The Tell-Tale Heart." What do we do about shame?

Growing up, you might have heard something like this harsh order whispered to you, "Don't talk about *that* when we visit them!" Are you still carrying those *don'ts* with you today? God has an answer for you. He can use all sorts of people—whether from our own past or Biblical—to help.

As the title of Poe's short story reveals, *nothing* can be hidden forever, and "the secret sin" can leave open wounds or scars of shame for generations. In her book, *Adult Children of Alcoholics,* Janet Geringer Woititz discusses the wreckage an alcoholic person can indelibly impress on the lives of their children. Thank goodness, God made children to be resilient, yet any habit not kicked can leave a child with lifetime of hurt or damage. "Each person is being tempted whenever he is being dragged off and enticed by the bait of his own desire. Then, having conceived, the desire gives birth to sin; and when sin is fully grown, it gives birth to death" (James 1:13-14). That's a habit. "Those who plow sin and sow trouble reap just that" (Job 4:8). I used to believe my depression was the result of God's judgment when my distant relative married that cousin.

Then I found contradictory evidence with its freeing ray of truth: "I, Adonai your God, am a jealous God, punishing the children for the sins of the parents ... but displaying grace to the thousandth generation of those who love me and obey my commandments" (Exodus 20:5-6). Furthermore, Jesus died, was raised from the grave, is at the right hand of God, and pleads for us on our behalf (Romans 8:34). Grasp these promises, and hold onto them through those undermining times when negative self-talk tries to dominate your life.

All day, Lord, we want your promises to comfort us and You to speak Your truths to us. Amen.

JANUARY 17
PLAYOFF

In a football playoff game last weekend, the Dallas Cowboys lost to the Green Bay Packers 21-26. I can't imagine Tony Romo's feelings after the loss. Prior to the game, Jerry Jones, the owner of the Cowboys, told Quarterback Tony, "You were made for this moment!" Have you ever had such a time?

Have you ever experienced a moment wherein the result would change your life? Perhaps you have entered a contest and are waiting on pins-and-needles for the organization to announce the winner. I've been there. Or, perhaps tomorrow you to take the SAT, GRE, or another standardized test to prove proficiency in a helping profession. Maybe you're standing at the end of an exam table, waiting for the doctor to give you news as you prepare for the birth of your baby.

One of my "shining moments" occurred on my first day of teaching high school as I waited for students to arrive for class. I was at the front, standing next to my stack of books while listening to my heart pound in my ears. Chattering students were easing into the building, the soles of their new shoes tapping on the shiny floor. Scanning a sea of empty chairs, I felt so excited. *I'm a teacher. I've studied years to be a teacher. This is my moment!* I believed I was stars for the first time. Maybe this is what you need today … to feel like today is special and significant. Today is significant, with God.

That day, with shaking hands, I wrote my name on the black board as perfectly as I could—yellow chalk dust shedding into the air. I was nervous, yet I had to show confidence. I had to convince my students who would surely test me that I knew English, and had the skills to direct them toward their goals. I had to earn *their* trust. Only time and factual exchanges closed the gap between skepticism and trust. You remember David. He was the youngest of eight children, the baby of the family only permitted to tend sheep. However, he asks one bold question (1 Samuel 17:26) that motivates King Saul to allow him to pick up that stone, hurl it, and kill Goliath (vs. 49-51). He changed history. He had weaknesses and suffered consequences for his actions, but he had shining moments that changed the world. Shine brightly today. You only have *this* day, today.

No retrieving the past, and tomorrow is God's mystery.

Lord, help us make *each* of our moments matter for you. Amen.

January 18
Yield to Oncoming Traffic

After you vent the facts of a bad experience to a close friend, you might hear the person say, *been there—done that*! However, if he or she has *never* had your bad experience, such as being lied to by someone you trusted, the person will not be able to relate to you and extend you a comforting empathetic hand.

Can we receive compassion from those who have never experienced our situations?

Mark Twain said, "Get your facts first, and then you can distort them as you please." A *bit* of distortion has been occurring in my life akin to what happened in Alfred Hitchcock's movie, *Rear Window*, wherein a recovering man spies on his neighbors.

Snowbird neighbors I met last year, but who are *not* here currently, are in denial over their forty-year-old playboy son. He split from his wife, has no contact with his child, and relocated here to Florida after his parents jumped through hoops to buy him a condo. My snowbird friends—upright Christians—blame his wife. They give excuses for why he can't divorce her, and they firmly maintain that "the woman" who accompanied him to Florida is *only* a friend. They're *not* cohabitating? I asked his dad last year, "That's none of my business!" *Oo*, he volunteered too much personal information that made me a bit uncomfortable. Yet, the Apostle James calls us to share our innermost worlds with brothers and sisters in Christ (James 5:16). "Openly acknowledge your sins to one another, and pray for each other, so that you may be healed." I couldn't advise, yet I stayed focused to my snowbird neighbors and listened to their sad issues.

Still, I can't believe how their "Wild Child" continues to fool his naïve blind parents. They didn't even notice him smoking down the street. I want to tell them the truth, so they can *see* the truth. Deep down, I believe they probably know the truth, but I can't force them to acknowledge it. Still, I see a sub-glacial sea of agony for these devoted Christian parents. I told them parents are *not* their children. God says: "Fathers are not to be executed for the children, nor are children to be executed for the fathers. Every person will be executed for his own sin" (2 Kings 14:6). I close my window blinds in search of sin in my own life because sin yields death.

Holy Spirit, open our eyes so we can *see* our sins, repent, and experience freedom. Amen.

JANUARY 19
SHOVEL READY

For some reason today, lyrics from the 1970 song "We've Only Just Begun" by The Carpenters kept circling in my mind. They tell an exciting story of the beginning of a couple's life after their marriage vows. "We've only just begun ... with life," Karen Carpenter sings. Unfortunately, Karen died at thirty-two of a heart attack brought on by her unrelenting eating disorder anorexia nervosa.

I too battled that illness off-and-on through my late forties. In those days, no matter how far my weight inched down the scale, the number wasn't small enough. I still saw my body as blimp-sized even at ninety-eight pounds. Truly dangerous on my 5'8" frame. I remembered thinking at the point, even when my heart lacked sufficient potassium: "Wow—I was ninety-eight pounds in third grade!" The terrible thing is: I had conned myself into believing I was beautiful in a size 2 pair of jeans when people were giving me funeral stares. All the while, I was going to church, reading my Bible, and sometimes singing in the choir. I was struggling, always recovering, and praying: "God heal me because no matter *who* counsels me, *what* I read in your word, and *what* I do for you, I'm *not* getting better. Am I really a Christian?" I *knew* I was. So what was the matter?

I didn't feel like a Christian, and God knows I wasn't showing an example of a Christian. What people in church must have thought. Yet, I never asked, nor did anyone volunteer their opinions. They just basically stayed away ... while I kept on singing ... and dwindling away.

I committed one special verse to memory in the battle raging within my mind: "The Spirit helps us in our weakness; for we don't know how to pray the way we should. But the Spirit himself pleads on our behalf with groanings too deep for words" (Romans 8:26). God loves you and me. Our universal eternal God, who sent Pentecostal flames to light on his Apostles, *loves*. He can help you win your deepest struggles: "*Adonai* your God is going with you to fight on your behalf against your enemies and give you victory" (Deuteronomy 20:4). Have life today. Live. Every moment you're alive is a new beginning. Start again, in *this* moment.

Lord, words of inexpressible gratitude are always in our hearts for your healing wonders. Amen.

JANUARY 20
MAKE YOUR MOVE

I thought all was lost in the second quarter for the Seattle Seahawks when they were down 0-16 against the Green Bay Packers. I almost turned the channel. Have you ever wanted to "change the channel" but the suspense wouldn't let you? I couldn't watch ...

Until, the third quarter when a fake kick stunned Green Bay's defense, and John Ryan threw the ball 19 yards to waiting-and-ready Garry Gilliam. *Bam*—touchdown! Seattle's roll of points continued until the Seahawks beat the battling Packers in overtime with a 16-point comeback to victory at 28-22. If you're a Packer fan, you might have felt dazed by Seattle's quick choreography and the bounce-back resilience of young quarterback Russell Wilson who had bobbled the ball a few times, but then recast himself to take his team to victory. After such a big game comes the commentary—a cadre of old pros who offer their slick-n-sleet opinions of the game and plays, with perhaps, a few of the winners to interview. In this post-game commentary, ex-quarterback Terry Bradshaw said something like this: *You gotta keep going forward because you never know when something will turn around and give you a win.* I about cried!

Have you ever agonized about giving up when you've put so much of yourself into a project, task, or career?

In a synagogue, Jesus meets a man with a shriveled hand. One more time, it's the Sabbath, a day of no work. There are antagonistic religious people there who have seen Jesus perform miracles. They're waiting for him to perform another today, so they can accuse him of lawlessness. If it were me, I'd quit. He *knows* they're accumulating reasons to kill him, but Jesus gives them a quick comeback. "What is permitted on Shabbat? Doing good or doing evil? Saving life or killing" (Mark 3:1-4)?

He heals the man. Through his example, we now receive help in our struggles to persevere in our life's purposes. A big break could happen at any moment. When you feel stuck, lost, or are facing an impossible situation, pray. "*Adonai* is a great God. ... He holds the depths of the earth in his hands; the mountain peaks too belong to him. The sea is his—he made it—and his hands shaped the dry land" (Psalm 95:3-5). Creator God holds you and sustains you.

Lord God, fill us with strength and confidence so we can make a difference for you. Amen.

JANUARY 21
YOUTHFUL RESULTS

I woke up and washed my face as usual. Reaching for my moisturizer in its standard spot under a packed medicine cabinet, I couldn't find it. We have limited bathroom counter space, and I have a tiny area to cram together my things. However, my husband doesn't want for space. That's because he's taking up all o' mine.

Do you ever feel a bit cheated, or invisible?

Then I walked into the kitchen and sat down to drink my coffee. My husband inched his wicker basket full of vitamins and diabetic supplies my way. A domino effect ensued—topple-tumble—ending with my little red pencil sharpener cracking apart on the floor. The pencil shavings scattered under *my* side of the table. You don't know me, but *uh-oh*, I about lost my wits over *my* spaces that have been disappearing like settled farmland.

What's your tendency?

I pointed at the packed basket on our little table resembling a Legoland city. "I can't even set down my toast!" I fumed.

He apologized, "Okay, ya, I know you need space."

Still, every time I walk into our master bath, the office, or the kitchen, I feel my burning grudge spread over my usurped landscape. Apology accepted? Not really.

Maybe you've experienced the same situation but with a roommate or guest. Letting go of grudges and daily grievances isn't easy.

I have to look to God for help. God has this incomprehensible capacity for mercy and forgiveness after we sin. He doesn't hold grudges. "He has not treated us as our sins deserve or paid us back for our offenses, because his mercy toward those who fear him is as far above earth as heaven. He has removed our sins from us as far as the east is from the west" (Psalm 103:10-12). I wonder: How far above earth is heaven could his mercies extend? The distance is at least intergalactic!

"The stars fell from heaven to earth" (Revelation 6:13). He also forgets our sins so we can be free from guilt, "as far as the east is from the west." Travel the equator and you'll *always* end up going east or west. What a grudgeless awesome God we have.

Jesus, shower your grace upon us today so we can extend mercy and forgiveness to others. Amen.

January 22
Enhancements at a Minimum Cost

At my house, we can get into an argument over salt.

"That's too much salt!" I tell my son who's twisting and turning the grinder over his steak, fortifying it with Dead Sea sheen.

"No, it's not too much," he snarls back at me, directing the shaker to his dad's steak.

Wind-crunch-wind.

"And next time, get me a thick steak." He gestures two inches with his fingers. "I want one *that* thick."

"Dream on," I tell him, "'cause you can only buy those at a specialty meat market, and I'm not paying twenty-five dollars for a steak!"

Have you ever wanted a relationship in your family seasoned?

Salt has significance to God. He commanded his people: "Everything in Isra'el which has been consecrated unconditionally is to be yours. All the contributions of holy things which the people of Isra'el offer to Adonai I have given to you, your sons and your daughters with you; this is a perpetual law, an eternal covenant of salt before Adonai for you and your descendants with you" (Numbers 18:14-19). Jesus tells us, "You are salt for the land" (Matthew 5:13-16). We *need* salt. Salt seasons our foods, and salt was a priceless commodity in desert lands where an ocean appeared as a meager mirage for many indigenous peoples. Salt has been on Earth since the beginning. Imagine our world void of salt. We'd die.

When you're dehydrated, doctors recommend you drink a beverage containing electrolytes, which include sodium and chloride—*salt*. A little morsel can save you. Many morsels make a difference. Earlier today, I made potato salad. With tender care, I added eggs, parsley, mustard, pepper, mayo, onion and celery to the diced potatoes. After a first taste, I about spit. I forgot the salt. Salt is a seasoning, probably the most important one. In the world, you are a special seasoning designed by God. Thus, when He says, "an eternal covenant of salt," he's telling us we are bound to Him and He's bonded to us, like sodium and chloride. We're "molecules" with God. We need Him to survive. We need our Holy Spirt connection with him, which can then transfer onto others as salt.

Lord, give us patience as we try hard to love others in times when we're livid with pepper. Amen.

JANUARY 23
LIFE WAY SOLUTIONS

Have you ever tried to *make* someone *do* something? I'm reminded of a story I once read.

After a football game ends, a woman asks her husband, "Can you take out the garbage?"

Licking sweet-n-sour sauce off his fingers and pushing away his plate full of chicken bones, he replies, "Oh, yeah, right after the commentary ends."

A half hour later, she asks: "Bill! The commentary's over. *Please* take this garbage out."

"Oh, yeah, yeah, I forgot, Julie, be right there."

Half an hour later, Julie takes the white bag out of the can, walks over to couch potato Bill, and tips the bag of smelly trash into his lap.

After Bill's brief rant-n-rave through which she believes she has the upper hand, he stands up, shakes off trash, and says, "I'm hittin' the shower, Julie, so I can't take out the garbage."

I can just see Julie fuming with anger and hurt as she sweeps up the mess, Mr. Cleans the floor, puts the garbage back into the trash bag, and hauls it to the curb, alone.

Bill wasn't *ever* going to budge. I can just imagine her huffing and saying, "He wasn't that way when I met him. What the heck happened?"

Garbage can come in many forms and smelly scents, yuck. "A wise man's heart leads him rightly, but a fool's heart leads him astray" (Ecclesiastes 10:2).

I'm reminded of the prophet Elijah who stays at a hard-working widow's house. We never know her name, but she's a questioning woman who waits on Elijah hand-and-foot, until her child dies: "What do you have against me, you man of God? Did you come to me just to remind me how sinful I am by killing my son (1 Kings 17:8:24)? We can hear her vent her frustration as she tries to make herself worthy of God's attention. She's done everything, and finally, God shows himself to her by raising her child from the dead.

We have God's love through Christ's resurrection. No more proving is necessary because *we* are his loves. Imagine Jesus enfolding you with his loving arms. That sacrificial love incinerates *all* garbage.

Heavenly Father, we work so hard for your purposes. Please continue to guide us. Amen.

JANUARY 24
SLOW FOR CURVE

I'm the kind of person who *likes*—no, wants—fast results. Can you relate? For example, my front fences have been black at the bottom with mold since we moved here over a year ago. The black's inching upward. Every time I drive away from the garage I've been saying, "We need to get new boards," or "We need to hire a fence company to at least build a new fence," or "I need to pull out all the boards, buy new ones, nail 'em in, and *abracadabra* new fence!" Those blue-eyed dreams swirled down the shower drain like the suds after a good shampooing. What did I finally do?

I mixed a concoction of half-chlorine (liquid pool chlorine) and Simple Green, funneled it into a sprayer; and then using a bristle brush, I sprayed all that black [*stuff*, I'll say for niceness] off the bottom of the fences. It goes like this: *spray spray, sweep sweep*; spray *spray, sweep sweep* ... .

I thought I'd had victory. No. Have you ever felt you've won or reached perfection, only to discover you haven't?

There's a funny thing about bleach. When you bleach one section of anything and not another, you have two tones ... maybe multiple tones.

Rr, I dislike it when things don't mix well together to provide the fix I'd expected. Can you relate? What do we do? Paul says, "Love one another. Whoever loves his fellow human being has fulfilled the Law" (Romans 13:8).

I remember the story of Joshua who had to confront seven tribes because their leaders couldn't decide on the land they wanted. He orders them: "Go; walk through the land; and describe it; then come back to me, and I will cast lots for you here before Adonai in Shiloh" (Joshua 8:1-18). They did as instructed, "surveying it by cities, dividing it into seven regions and writing the results on a scroll" (Joshua 8:9). Before Joshua could do anything with the land God had given them (8:3), every leader had to become part of the team and sign on with God's plan. Joshua "caste lots" over the land in front of God (v. 10); and everyone received what God intended for them to own. An easy solution that showed them the whole picture. God's Word will give us the clarity and victory like that.

Lord, we pray for insight and clarity so we can see a whole picture. Amen.

JANUARY 25
BEAUTIFUL SAVINGS

We live in a universe of unseen particles and forces, wherein laws, like gravity, ground us. If you weigh 138 lbs. here on Earth, on Mars you'd tip the scales at 50 lbs. 10 oz. Now, unless scientists make some serious adjustments to suit technology, people will be bouncing everywhere all the time up there on Mars. Essential particles, like radiation, we can't see except through detectors and the process of elimination, much like the Large Hadron Collider just proved the Higgs Field, a vital force in the universe that scientists detected by smashing protons and locating its position among the Standard Model. If not for the Higgs Field around us right now, electrons would move so fast, never be able to settle into molecular states, and we'd not be here. Here's another example: Quantum theory dictates that electrons exist in multiple places at the same time. Multiple possibilities are everywhere around us ... but they only become reality when we chose.

What options are you struggling with today?

I had just dumped the last little batch of pistachios onto my TV tray, and my husband grumbled. Swirling them like open oysters for the green pickings, I noticed so many unshelled nuts, perfect salty dregs. Possibility 1: eat; 2: divide the best in half and share; 3: save them all.... You get the picture. After he said, "I don't want any;" I chose number one.

I'm reminded of Esther in the Bible who is forced to be part of the Persian King Ahasuerus' harem. Her cousin Mordecai tells her about a plot to assassinate the king, so she tells the King and stops the conspiracy. She could have let him die. Then another Persian noble wants everyone to bow to him, but Mordecai doesn't. He bows only to God. Because *one* person disobeys, Haman wants the king to grant him a Jewish genocide! Esther sidesteps a deadly edict: unless the king summons you, you can't appear before him; but brave beautiful Esther sneaks in and saves everyone! "Who knoweth whether thou art come to the kingdom for such a time as this" (Esth. 4:13-14)? What precious choices do we have before us that when taken, will cement us?

We are *cemented* to our creator.

Good Shepherd, guide our steps today. Continue to shape our souls for your glory. Amen.

JANUARY 26
INTERACTIVE CAPABILITY AVAILABLE

Every Sunday morning, I hop onboard a type of run-away train with my family. Which type of person are you? The one who is on time, or always late?

Every Sunday, I'm ready for church. They're not. I fume, and feel embarrassed when we walk into the service late—like ten to fifteen minutes late. Today, five minutes after I had told everyone, "we leave in *fifteen* minutes at 10:30," I sat in the car and read the comics. Another five minutes ticked by. I return inside, where my son was eating noodles and my husband was *finally* dressed. Still, I knew we were going to be *so* late, and I stomped: "I'm *so* sick of this! Never again. You have to start getting your act together 'cause I'm tired of people glaring at us like we're interrupting the whole service."

Have you had a, "I'm never going to again" experience?

Years ago, I had another: "I'm *never* going to date again." When you make those "never again" oaths with yourself, you feel yucky inside, your stomach churning and your mind swooning with the previous bad experience that you just know you'll "never" again. Does the self-proclamation work?

No. We're human. Swearing off __ doesn't work. Something happens, and the live-and-learn experience fails. One more time, we jump on the carousel of doing what we did in the past. Emergency intervention, God. We'll always be trying, but we need God *with* us.

Before Emperor Nero beheaded Paul in 68 A.D. (and thereafter committed suicide), Paul wrote a letter to Titus, a young pastor he had put in charge of the church in Crete. In that Letter, Paul instructs: "In everything set them an example yourself by doing what is good. When you are teaching, have integrity and be serious" (Titus 2:7). "Setting an example" is serious business.

James Madison once said: "The happy Union of these States is a wonder. Their Constitution a miracle; their example a hope of liberty throughout the world." Combined with yesterday's paraphrased quote from the book of Esther, "Did you ever think that your previous bad circumstances brought you to this moment to do this great task," I glean strength to face those staring eyes because my family hasn't matured to master priorities. Just be dressed to go. Today, you can be prepared.

Lord, we praise you for giving us wisdom and patience. Amen.

JANUARY 27
JEALOUSY

Have you ever felt jealous of someone?

In Act III, Scene iii of *Othello*, William Shakespeare says jealousy can kill you. "It is the green-eyed monster which doth mock the meat it feeds on." Jealousy feeds on, and laughs at, the person who is jealous. What do we do?

As a child going to bed, I had monstrous fears of critters lurking under the bed or in the shadows. Only the light would relieve me. "You, God, are my lamp. God lights up my darkness" (2 Samuel 22:29). God lights up those frightening corners s so we can see what we're exactly jealous of. Are you jealous of someone? God can help.

We've all been jealous, which means, "feeling or showing suspicion of someone's unfaithfulness in a relationship," or "fiercely protective or vigilant of one's rights or possessions." We end up coveting people and things when we're jealous. Jealousy eats us on the inside so we can't function on the outside. We need security from God. In today's internet world where it's easy to remain anonymous, some people are freely cheating on their significant others and spouses. There's a problem. Hackers are exposing the names of those cheaters. Marriages and relationships are falling apart. God designed marriage to be sacred and to the death. We all need to count on our spouses because in this life everyone changes.

In Numbers 5:11-31, God deals with marital faithfulness. If a spouse is believed to be unfaithful, the husband and wife must come before God in the Temple and drink the water of embitterment and cursing (Numbers 5:24). The priest is to say, "May this water that causes the curse go into your inner parts and make your abdomen swell and your private parts shrivel up! The woman is to respond, 'Amen! Amen' " (5:21-22)! The word *amen* means *yes*. We need to submit to our God for His discipline when we sin. "Let him [her] submit absolutely; there may yet be hope" (Lamentations 3:29). God never intended us to be intimate with person-after-person. "Anyone who divorces his wife, except on the ground of fornication, makes her an adulteress" (Matthew 5:32). Any kind of cheating is sin. "You [God] have rescued me from death, my eyes from tears and my feet from falling" (Psalm 116:8). We end with our knees bent at the cross of Jesus, ultimately our only real security.

Lord, remove our tears and let us know you in our souls. Amen.

January 28
Eggs to Fish to Beef: Your Super Store

Have you ever seen someone give another person something, or be overly friendly with them and not you? Dejection, right?

Today, as the wind whipped pine trees behind my yard like switches, I stepped outside to the front yard where I spotted a neighbor at another neighbor's door, offering her a cutting of flowers. "That person's *never* been that way with me, and I gave them a Christmas gift. I thought we were friends. I'd sure appreciate one of those beautiful cuttings." What did I do or not do?

According to Dr. Steve Taylor in his book, *Out of the Darkness*, "Psychologists call slights 'narcissistic injuries.' They bruise our egos, making us feel belittled, insignificant, threatened, and unimportant. People with heightened narcissistic tendencies will lash out and hurt others. Ultimately, all types of slights boil down to the same basic feeling: being devalued or disrespected. Paul tells us, "Imitate God, as his dear children" (Ephesians 5:1). Are you feeling devalued or disrespected today?

I *never* thought *I'd* be on the Narcissistic spectrum. Yet Dr. Taylor says we *all* are a bit Narcissistic. "Our vulnerability to slights seems to point to fundamental insecurity inside us." The cure? We need to acknowledge we've been hurt, and then change our expectations of people, places, and things. *Whew*, I'm not alone.

Everyone has insecurities. Hey, I've gone to talk to neighbors and not included the above-mentioned one in the conversation.

God engineered us to function in community and made us to be social (Genesis 32:33, Genesis 48:4). "Adonai said, 'I have seen how my people are being oppressed in Egypt and heard their cry for release from their slave masters, because I know their pain' (Exodus 3:7)." And through salvation in Christ, we *share* God's promises: "the people of Isra'el ... were made God's children ... and from them, as far as his human descent is concerned, came the Messiah, who is over all" (Romans 9:4-5). Through the Holy Spirit, we have a heavenly hope of rich glories beyond what neighbors and our families offer (Ephesians 1:18). *Whew*—God in my soul. He's in your soul too today, engineering so many possibilities for you. Offer them to others as well in your testimony about how our Lord saved you.

Father God, we want to experience you in the moments we perceive a slight in my life. Amen.

JANUARY 29
TEMPERATURE DROPS

We had a strong debate in last night's Bible study of Revelation.

Oh, let me interrupt. I just ate a fortune cookie and accidentally read the fortune. Oh no!

God says: "These nations ... listen to soothsayers and diviners. But Adonai your God does not allow you to do this" (Deut. 18:14).

Have you had that experience where you accidentally sinned?

Saul disobeys God by consulting a medium, and God proclaims to him through Samuel's spirit: "The Lord has left you and has become your enemy. The Lord has done just as he said he would. He has torn the kingdom from you and given it to your rival, David" (1 Samuel 28:16-19). I can't imagine a life void of God. He sustains me, strengthens me, provides for me, and comforts me. He's pure love—the love you and I need every second of our day.

I tell God, I'm sorry. "Lord, forgive me for opening that note and reading it 'cause I was distracted and on auto-pilot." I think of the woman with an uncontrollable problem who begged Jesus to help her. "The woman, quaking with fear, threw herself down before him and confessed in front of everyone why she had touched him and how she had been instantly healed" (Luke 8:47). Lord, your mercies endure forever and I praise you for your forgiveness, Amen. Now, back to the debate in last night's study.

After Jesus resurrects Lazarus, the strict Jewish leaders panic. "This man is performing many miracles. If we let him keep going on this way, everyone will trust in him, and the Romans will come and destroy both the Temple and the nation" (John 11:47). One man sticks up for Jesus. He knows Jesus is Messiah. "You people don't know anything! You don't see that it's better for you if one man dies on behalf of the people, so that the whole nation won't be destroyed ... but so that he might gather into one the scattered children of God" (John 11:49-52). No human can resurrect dead people. I'm sure those Pharisees interviewed the doc who pronounced Lazarus dead and who had no idea how he came back to life, except through Adonai via Jesus. In those moments when we sin, and a little bit of death apprehends us, Jesus is our Savior who died for those sins. Ask for forgiveness. He gives forgiveness freely through His cross

Lord, thank you for a spirit of certainty that shines now-and-then so that we can evangelize to others. Amen.

JANUARY 30
STOMACH FOR IT

Here in Brevard County Florida at the Kennedy Space Center, this is the time of year for mourning ceremonies. You've had a mourning ceremony in your community as well, I'm sure. At some point, such an honorary ceremony has taken place in every city, honoring those who died, and the helpers who gave their lives, perhaps on 9/11.

How can our grief transition to hope?

On January 27, 1967 *Apollo I* caught fire at Launch Complex 34, killing Gus Grissom, Edward White and Roger Chaffee. I remember the day. I was nine, in fourth grade, and the time felt like the first hours after J.F.K. died. Then, on January 26, 1986, *Challenger* exploded, killing astronauts Ellison S. Onizuka, Greg Jarvis, Judy Resnik, Michael J. Smith, Dick Scobee and Ron McNair. Christa McAuliffe was a teacher who died with them. Lastly, on February 1, 2003, seven more brave astronauts lost their lives while re-entering Earth's atmosphere. *Columbia* experienced trouble and disintegrated over Texas and Louisiana. They were pioneers who transcended the bar at the time so others could advance farther into space, including David M. Brown, Rick Husband, Laurel Clark, Kalpana Chawla, Michael P. Anderson, William McCool, and Ilan Ramon. You recall those sad moments, right? "In laughter the heart can be sad, and joy may end in sorrow" (Proverbs 14:13). Cheering can end in grief.

The last space-flight disaster is more vivid in my mind because my half-sister called me at 3:30 a.m. with bad news. "Joyce, Mom's dead, and the astronauts just died, too." In that sleepy daze, I thought I had died.

I wish Jesus were here now to raise people from the dead as he did often when he was alive. "The blind are seeing again, the lame are walking, people with *tzara'at* [a skin disease that can take many different forms] are being cleansed, the deaf are hearing, the dead are being raised, the Good News is being told to the poor" (Matthew 11:5). We all focus on Jesus resurrecting Lazarus, but he resuscitated *many* people after they were proclaimed dead. T.O.D.? Think again. "Also the graves were opened, and the bodies of many holy people who had died were raised to life" (Matthew 27:52). We will have new bodies when Jesus returns. Today, we can have hope and move on from our grief. We'll see loved ones again.

Lord, help us mourn over those gone too early. Amen.

JANUARY 31
ALL YOUR SPORTS NEEDS HERE

I've been preparing. Are you the type of person who likes to be prepared?

I'm prepared. I found *three* packs of tender beef ribs on sale for $10 a pack. Heck if I spend that kind of cash for *one* package. My husband and son will eat twice that much, and now I've spent $30! I buy one garlic-and-herb pork tenderloin for $7. That's good enough, because...

I'm ready! I bought Velveeta cheese to mix with hot-n-spicy diced tomatoes for dipping with tortilla chips. I thought I was ready, until my husband asked, "Did you buy avocadoes and Cilantro for the dip?" I guess we believe we're fully prepared when in fact we're not. Then what?

Gosh, I can't seem to do everything that everyone expects me to do. So, I told him everything we've got in order to be ready: dip, chips, lettuce, meat, and scrumptious Little Debbie chocolate cakes wrapped in plastic. What are we ready for that I've been working so hard to buy delicious food so we can suck the juices off our fingers while rooting for our favorite team? *The* Super Bowl. It comes every year around this same time, and here's a secret. If you want to go to one of the crowded theme parks, Super Bowl Sunday is the day to rush the gates and get on all the rides you've been dreaming about. Get ready. There are no lines. You can relate to wanting life easier, right? God sure can. Without sin, life becomes easier and softer.

I've read the Book of Daniel and his prophesies about the End Times. I'm working hard to understand the complicated symbols and signs in Revelation. But nothing has frightened me more than the Book of Zechariah, particularly, the verses depicting the energy that will ultimately destroy Earth. "Adonai will strike all the peoples who made war against Yerushalayim [Jerusalem] with a plague in which their flesh rots away while they are standing on their feet, their eyes rot away in their sockets, and their tongues rot away in their mouths" (Zechariah 14:12). This looks like a nuclear annihilation--complete obliteration of everyone and everything by nuclear war. Who can prepare for this? No one. All we can do is believe on Jesus and trust him. "Trust in *Adonai* with all your heart. Do not rely on your own understanding" (Proverbs 3:5).

Father, let us do our best to do your will. Amen.

FEBRUARY 1
RALLY CRY

"He secures justice for the oppressed" (Psalm 146:7)

They're smiling ... but not for very long 'cause they're going to prison for a *real* long time. Ten years in the slammer. Yes! However, I don't think the sentence was justice enough. I'm sure you've felt the same way when someone isn't paying a high enough price for the crime he/she has committed. We want more justice. Do we get it? What if we don't?

The judge also ordered them to pay $9 million in restitution to their victims. Who were they and what did they do?

A few months ago, I wrote about two con men posing as investors who robbed people to pay for their lavish life styles. There was a TV show a long time ago: "Life Styles of the Rich and Famous." But those hard-working people who vaulted to upper class status didn't leave a jagged stinking trail of devastation and grief on their way to success. These frauds are sociopaths. Listen to what one is quoted to have said: "We're not bad people. We're good people who got into a bad situation" (Price, Wayne T., "Scheme Leads to Decade in Prison," *Florida Today*; January 31, 2015, 1B). Doesn't that make ya wanna just scream?!

Let's examine the words, "got into". Think of some phrases: "got into hot water," "got into trouble," and, "the blizzard got the roses." You might be able to conjure up more of these twins: *To acquire as a result of action or effort; to become drawn in, entangled, or involved; and, to overcome or destroy.* This isn't passive. "Got into" is action.

I recall what Jesus does with our sins when we accept him. He castes them as far away as the east is from the west, to be remembered and counted against us no more. Even if these two frauds come to accept Jesus Christ as their savior, and Jesus removes their guilt (He 10:19-22), they will need to make restitution. "For doing such a thing, he has to pay back four times the value of the lamb—and also because he had no pity" (2 Samuel 12:5). Samuel was talking to Nathan the prophet, and Nathan told him in return: "You are the man" (v. 7). David paid dearly. It's important for us to keep our lives straight and assess our daily actions. We all do little harms that ripple consequences. However, He forgives, always.

Lord God, we never want greed to infect our life. Please, cut off its source when it does. Amen.

FEBRUARY 2
EDGING FORWARD

With one minute left in the Super Bowl, Seattle Seahawk, Ricardo Lockette, jersey number 83, dashed to the 1-yard line.

Victory must have appeared like a halo around the football that quarterback Russel Wilson had just thrown to him ... about to land in Lockette's hands when ... New England Patriot, jersey number 21, Malcolm Butler leaps between the ball and Lockette, intercepts the ball, and crushes Wilson's drive for a sure-thing victory.

Imagine, just 1 yard away from the goal line.

"Who among you is wise and understanding? Let him demonstrate it by his good way of life, by actions done in the humility that grows out of wisdom" (James 3:13).

There are moments when we know we're going to lose, right?

The camera panned to Seahawk coach Pete Carrol's unreadable face—his blue-green eyes free of tears, shock or disappointment. If the camera would have focused on me, you would have seen my mouth open in a gasp, and my hands hit my cheeks. So close ... yet no win. I've been in that situation: from being a finalist in a swim meet and neck-to-neck with another swimmer, to racing after the garbage truck with a bag of trash in my hand. Have you, *almost*?

What's the answer? You're almost winning ... then you lose.

Leader Moses committed a major transgression: "Because you did not trust in me ... you will not bring this community into the land I have given them" (Numbers 20:12). After a long trek to Israel, Moses stands on Pisgah, a summit of Mt. Nebo, and God shows him the Promised Land. "This is the land concerning which I swore to Avraham, Yitz'chak and Ya'akov, 'I will give it to your descendants.' I have let you see it with your eyes, but you will not cross over there" (Deut. 34:4). Thereafter, Moses dies.

Where does he end up?

"Eye hath not seen, nor ear heard, neither have entered into the heart of man the things which God hath prepared for them that love Him" (1 Corinthians 2:9). We all experience win-lose moments that even after the passage of time still linger in our minds: some big, some trivial. Yet they all pale to our *eternal* destiny, the one and only true line of victory.

Father, "Abba!" In the little-and-big losses when we cannot see *your* big picture, help us. Amen.

FEBRUARY 3
FIERY

A few days ago, I took part in a "Book in a Day" conference. The collaborative novel we were about to write, *Love and Rockets*, appeared easy and stress free. I arrived forty minutes early to secure my perfect seat and ideal location. *I can do this*, I kept convincing myself. Just smile, keep your mouth shut, listen, be encouraging, and *don't* be honest. "*Adonai* gives wisdom; from his mouth comes knowledge and understanding (Proverbs 2:6).

We've all had times when our honesty landed on sensitive ears. There are no take backs after our words exit our mouths.

While teaching me how to drive, my dad once said to me, "Joyce, you go backwards better than you go forwards," and I snap better pictures under water than I do anywhere on the surface. So, you get my personality. I like imaginary worlds and function with imaginary characters far better than I mix with surface Homo sapiens. *But I'll try hard here*, I kept telling myself. I left the large sci-fi group and joined the screenplay group of one, yes, *one* person was there, so I quickly set up my laptop and we collaborated to write a short play, really a tribute to his wife. I don't write romance. I do *not* have steamy scenes in my novels. Thus a few times, my discomfort resounded a little too loftily, with boisterous laughter—my interpretation—as I displaced my shame in order to stretch my boundaries, expand my abilities, and try something new.

Growing sometimes stings like touching fire; and being around people who seem so smart, successful, like falling.

Lot must have known the feeling. His name means, *veil* or *covering*. Most of my life, I've been veiled, especially around people. Lot's uncle was Abraham, and they parted ways when Lot settled Jordan, a land "like the garden of the Lord" (Genesis 13:10). Wow—a place like Eden. Where does Lot settle though? Near Sodom. You wanna reach into history and crack 'im on the side o' the skull! What were you thinking? He really went outside his comfort zone, perhaps to better fit in with people? To learn? Become enculturated? God burned Sodom. Sometimes, we need to stretch ourselves while guarding ourselves from expanding in the *wrong* direction. Prayer and trust: *always* our internal spiritual meter attuned with God's touch.

Lord, guide us to what would be good for us, and *keep* us from what's bad and evil. Amen.

FEBRUARY 4
MUSIC STORE

One of my favorite narrative poems is T.S. Eliot's *The Love Song of J. Alfred Prufrock*.

J. Alfred, really? Poor guy, and Eliot's poem expounds on the narrator's dismal enculturated crucible. J. Alfred is bogged down in the propriety of high-society existence.

"What is the overwhelming question?" I've always asked while reading this poem

I believe the answer is: "to say what I really mean." Do you tell people on a daily basis what you *really* mean? Your heart? Can you? What happens to you on the inside when you're not honest?

So many times, ideas flow through my mind like cars flying at 90 miles-per-hour on the freeway. So many times, even when I take a chance and say what I mean, people misinterpret what I say. Has that happened to you? Have you arrived at the point where you realize we all have our own unique individual realities? We see things, people, and places from our own *individual* perspectives.

How does the world function in all this chaos?

Most times, it doesn't.

Think of Cain and Abel, sons of Adam and Eve. Have you ever been disappointed in your children, co-workers, or people you manage? Abel was a shepherd; Cain was a farmer. Cain presented God with "some of the land's produce" but God had a problem with what Cain "believed" was sufficient. Something with Cain's offering was wrong, and God told him: "If you don't do what is good, sin is crouching at the door—it wants you, but you can rule over it (Genesis 4:7). Obviously, Cain doesn't get the message of self-control, and the competition between Cain and Able doesn't end well: "When they were in the field, Kayin turned on Hevel his brother and killed him" (Genesis 4:8). Can you and I rule over sin? No, but through Jesus our Savior, we can! "From that time on, Yeshua began proclaiming, "Turn from your sins to God, for the Kingdom of Heaven is near" (Matthew 4:17). Never stop confessing. Never stop being yourself. "Wounds from a friend are received as well-meant, but an enemy's kisses are insincere" (Proverbs 27:6). In the sincerity and gentleness of Jesus Christ, we can be honest.

Lord Jesus, we are growing older by the second, and we need your saving hand. Amen.

February 5
Reasonable Rate of Return

"Get up! You have to go to school!" I try jostling awake my son Andrew [Andy] for the second time.

"Go away—*ahhhh* … lemme me aloooone!"

Have you ever heard of Behavior Modification?

Sometimes, we need a little self-behavioral modification. But Jesus's way.

The "altering" of undesirable behaviors has ingredients of classic conditioning and cognitive behavioral therapy (CBT). All our actions are acquired through a process called "conditioning." In classic conditioning, if you want to change a bad habit, you substitute another to replace it over time. Some people who quit smoking chew ice. In CBT, to change a bad pattern, you sort through your belief system and begin countering faulty messages. Thus, if a person wants to quit eating so much, CBT would explore the person's past, discover the root causes of his/her overeating, and then begin countering those messages with alternative self-talk. "I'm substituting food for telling you how I really feel." So the beginning of an eating program might be to begin telling "that person" how you really feel. I've used a chart system with stars and monetary rewards to change my son's behaviors. Still, there's no reprieve from his *daily* morning venting on our ear drums. Some mornings, I cry.

Do you ever cry in defeat? "Everyone who does what is true comes to the light, so that all may see that his actions are accomplished through God" (James 3:20).

I'm reminded of Isaac's sons. Jacob is a contemplative in-door type of person and Esau is a hunter (Genesis 25). One day after Esau comes home exhausted, he is so desperate to eat that he asks his chef brother for a choice red stew. I guess he felt *so* hungry and exhausted that he believed he might die. Jacob wants Esau's birthright in exchange … since he's gonna die anyway, right? The kid was smart! A birthright gives the first born son all the authorities and responsibilities of the father. Did he learn another way to live in this world? Esau experienced more hard-knocks-of-life before he grew up and shaped up. In the end, he and Jacob reconciled. Good triumphed over betrayal. Love won over dishonesty.

Lord, when we want to take the easy way out, show us that expediency will only hurt us. Amen.

FEBRUARY 6
BEL-AIRE HEIGHTS

In Bible study, we shared stories of angels manifesting in our lives. "He will order his angels to care for you and guard you wherever you go" (Psalm 91:11).

Have you ever encountered an angel of help when you were confronted with harm? There was one horrific time in my life that's never completely healed … that's left me with adrenaline-pumping neurological consequences. Still, I told my story to the group.

In April of 1991, after I arrived home from a late-night class, I put my daughter to bed and then heard musical notes playing on a figurine over my mantle. I hadn't turned the base. I felt overcome with fright, and an eerie feeling.

Knock, knock.

I checked the time, after ten! Slowly, I approached the door, which I had locked and chained. After he identified himself, I realized he was one of the men I had paid to move me into this house in January. In my daze and shock, a voice welled up from the depths of my being: "Go away. You're *not* allowed in here." That bought me time to call for help, but not enough time for the police to arrive before the intruder severed my electricity and then cut my phone line, which also disconnected me from my the police. I ran to my daughter. As I tried lifting her out the window, I turned around. The intruder was holding up a pipe, ready to strike me with it. I remained brain-frozen, yet alert as I worked to stall for time. When he pulled a knife on me, I believed he was going to kill me. Then I noticed squad cars with their reds-and-whites cyclin through the window. Yes! Then, Intruder forced me to open the door. I cried: "This is *not* a family matter! He's going to kill me!" As police burst inside my house, Intruder dragged me down the hall while yelling, "I'm going to slit her throat." Trapping me in the bathroom, he rummaged for a razor. The police broke through in time, and I saw a gun barrel at my forehead. Numbness takes over in violent events. I believe God's invisible touch saving us from *feeling* a painful horrible death. An officer pulled me out, and led me to the free-tasting sweet air. The Holy Spirit was that deep voice inside me, rescuing me, but also trying to direct Intruder on another path.

Jesus, thank you for your angels and your saving Holy Spirit who never gives up on people until the exhale their last breaths. Amen.

February 7
Healthy Dose

Today is the 38th day in the year with 327 left to go.

Remember the list of resolutions you penned down in your diary, typed into your computer, or announced to the universe in the firm belief you would remember them?

I'm thinking about one of mine: to *not* allow my feelings to dictate my reality. I have that tendency to allow my emotions to permeate my actions. My self-talk is automatic. Here's an example. "I feel embarrassed about what I said; and I *believe* you think I'm an embarrassment; so, I better not show up and be a part of the group again." This could be any group for me, church to professional. Some groups, a person just drops and never returns, without being missing or missing "them." *Ships passing in the night*, the phrase says. But one can't continue long on that moving walkway without *completely* disconnecting from society and experiencing *profound* loneliness. A hermit is a person who *voluntarily* lives in such seclusion, sometimes to pursue spiritual connections with God. St. Jerome said he was visited by angels, and Sarah of the Desert led a strict life of asceticism (deprivation of all worldly pleasures) to ward off a demon. Mostly, these lone wolves and eccentric loners don't live happy lives. Think of Howard Hughes. He died alone and insane. *We* want to live. "Live lives worthy of the Lord and entirely pleasing to him, being fruitful in every good work and multiplying in the full knowledge of God," Paul says (Colossians 1:10). Let us please Him.

The opposite happens when I fight my natural tendency to be ruled by my feelings, and instead kick the self-absorption in pursuit of making a positive difference in the world and in the lives of others.

"He who pursues righteousness and kindness finds life, prosperity and honor" (Proverbs 21:21).

The word, *pursue*, means: *follow, chase*; and, *continue or proceed on a path or course*. And *prosperity* means, *success, comfort, wealth, security*, and, *well-being*. Thus, we can conclude: "He who follows and chases what is right and kind in the world, finds life, prosperity, and honor." I have to pursue. We can pursue, Jesus. It is action on *my* part, in the world, with others, and for others. Just keep moving forward … even when we don't always "feeling" driven to pursue.

Lord, divert us from self and too much over-thinking so we can be in tune to others. Amen.

FEBRUARY 8
YOUR JEWELRY DESIGNER

Remember your first love?

Most first loves, or crushes, I've heard people recount didn't turn out well or last. As I assess the relationships I've had, I notice patterns drifting through the ocean of relationship behaviors.

Have you ever seen a school of fish? While living in Hawaii, I used to dive, and marvel at the behavior of all sorts of fish. When one fish moves in a school, they *all* gravitate in the same direction. During an ell attack, they scatter like breaking glass, confusing the eels. Safety in numbers; survival of the fittest. Our behavior patterns tend to follow patterns if we open ourselves up as observers to watch subjectively.

I liked swimming at the YMCA in Hammond, Indiana. During the summer of 1968, I met "Michael L." We began a nightly swim meet competition. We would laugh, and he paid attention to me. I felt affirmed and special. After all the physical abuse from my mom, emotional neglect from my dad, and name calling from my peers over my last name, Michael L. treated me so opposite. When he gave me my first kiss, I felt … reborn, and I could finally breathe. Then, as quick as our budding friendship began—in between the *Hawaii Five-O* night-time shows of those star-swarming summer nights—Michael L. suddenly began a tight friendship with another girl, who I perceived as athletic and fun. I felt crushed. Thereafter, I never believed myself worthy of someone just loving me for me. Worse yet? Jesus says, love your neighbor as yourself (Leviticus 19:18; Matthew 19:19).

That word "as" means, "to the same degree or amount," and "in the way that," and "that the result is." When we're not loved, esteemed, or pronounced worthy by our first examples—our parents—we'll search for those basic needs beyond the perimeter of our homes. We will also be emotional cripples in life, incapable of giving love, and thus loving our neighbors. However, Jesus's love heals. That's the great gift of Him *mastering* our lives. "I bless *Adonai*, my counselor; at night my inmost being instructs me" (Psalm 16:7). His love heals us, so the abused and neglected *can* change and love others. "The Counselor, whom the Father will send in my name, will teach you everything" (John 14:26).

Lord, help us continue to learn to love as you embrace us. Amen.

FEBRUARY 9
NO JOB TOO HARD

I opened the door to let my dog Sparky into the back yard when I spotted a wild animal

Have you ever seen something wild and became afraid? I did. I pulled Sparky back and called inside to my husband: "There's something rooting in the grass! What it is?"

Everyone came running as I watched the beige-plated animal with the long snout searching and scratching through my lawn.

"That's an armadillo," my husband replied.

"I'll have the dog shoo it away," I said, walking to the screen door. The animal hadn't noticed me, and I was mere inches away from it, albeit behind the safety of the screened-in patio.

"No," he waved me back. "It could have rabies or something."

In no way did I want Sparky attacked. A neighbor told me that if you sneak up on and startle it an armadillo, it will jump straight up into the air, which if true, would freak me out.

I continued to watch the armadillo's snout burrow in my grass, until my lawn had holes in it the size of Nebraska. Its cuteness wore on me like skunk spray. I opened the screen door. I didn't care if it attacked. Have you ever been so mad that you didn't care about the consequences? "My anger has been fired up. It burns to the depths of Sh'ol, devouring the earth and its crops, kindling the very roots of the hills" (Deuteronomy 32:22). That's anger. "Out! Scat! Away!" All the while, I tried patting down the dirt the critter had excavated. I guess it was looking for acorns? Grub worms?

The beautiful can turn to the unexpected ugly. I'm recalling the times Jesus preached. He must have had high expectations of changing *everyone's* lives (Matthew 4:25; 7:28-29; Mark 10:1; John 2:23; John 11:46-50). Yet, not everyone liked him (Matthew 8:3; 9:11; 12:2; 12:140; Mark 11:27-28; John 11:46-53). When he was praying and fasting in the desert, Satan appeared next to him, trying to tempt him from his purpose. I can just imagine the Enemy's slow coax: "Come on, you can *be* and have *everything*." A pure moment of communion with God high-jacked by ugliness (Matthew 4; Luke 4). No bad surprises with Jesus, only eternity (Hebrews 2:16). What temptations do you have rooting around in your spiritual soil? Jesus can fix 'em.

Father, when we endure trials, we pray for your wisdom; and not to turn ugly, seek revenge, or withdraw. Help us endure, Lord. Amen.

FEBRUARY 10
SERVICING YOUR GROWING NEEDS

"Tell Dad I can fix it!" my son cried after our internet connection suddenly severed. We couldn't get the connection back even though our usernames and passwords were syncing with the main hub.

Frustrations can often hit us like calamitous stinging snowballs at *any* time. Most often times, frustrations occur at the most inopportune times.

My husband had the door locked because our son kept crying: "I can fix it." *Pound-pound.* "I know what I'm doing!"

I thought my guts were gonna wrench out of my belly button. "Just leave Dad alone. When he gets tired, then he might listen to you, believe you, and let you inside the office with him to help."

All I kept hearing from the computer room and out of my husband's mouth were: "Get out, now!" and "Quit banging on the door!" and "You keep this up—"

Have you ever believed you could *do* something but no one would allow you to do it?

My son *really* believes he can solve the problem. I had a friend who tried going into business for herself several times. They all failed. *I* have tried a few careers only to quit when I realized they weren't for me. Still, at the very beginning, I believed I could ... just like that little engine: "I think I can (*chug-chug* up the hill), I think I can." Are there any "I think I can" or "I know I cans" in your life? How are you doing with them? No matter what the stage, God can.

We were always taught and we keep hearing: you can be anything you want to be if you just work hard and believe in yourself. I'm not saying that's not always true. However, what happens when we don't attain our goals, and are left with devastation and failure from trying?

The psalmist gives us a promise from God, "I call to God ... who is accomplishing his purpose for me" (Psalm 57:3). Jesus said about himself: "The passage from the *Tanakh* that says, 'He was counted with transgressors,' has to be fulfilled in me; since what is happening to me has a purpose" (Luke 22:37). *Everything* that happens to us—our attempts and failures—*have* purpose. Hold onto this great truth even in despairing times, and you will gain strength. Bye the way, my husband and Andy cooled off to Andy's computer in a snap.

Lord God, as we question the direction of our lives, we count on your guidance and peace. Amen.

February 11
More about People

"We have to drain the pool now," I said after a heavy rainfall. "It's close to overflowing." We don't have an automated system for measuring the pool level, and adding or draining water. So if there's too much rain and someone doesn't lug the hose to the curb—like a lumberjack hauling wood—and begin emptying the pool water into the street, we would have a flood in the back yard. Have you ever had a situation that felt as if it was life-and-death? "A gentle response deflects fury, but a harsh word makes tempers rise," wise Solomon once said (Proverbs 15:1).

The opposite happens to us during hot weather. We need to drag the hose to the *other* side of the house, tap into the water supply there, and fill the pool from that hose bib. I just get tired of everything being so complicated and emergency-like. Don't you?

Complications arise when you least expect them, when you're often not prepared for them, and when you *don't* want them. I call these times: learning from life's curve balls.

We all have black-and-white issues, all-or-nothing scenarios, or situations we have to monitor constantly. If we don't, we could have a catastrophe on our hands. I'm even thinking of the relationships in my life. Sometimes, it's so hard to know when to add a little love, when to be less rigid, or appear hard as granite.

Paul tells us: "I may speak in the tongues of men, even angels; but if I lack love, I have become merely blaring brass or a cymbal clanging. I may have the gift of prophecy, I may fathom all mysteries, know all things, have all faith … but if I lack love, I am nothing. I may give away everything that I own, I may even hand over my body to be burned; but if I lack love, I gain nothing" (1 Corinthians 13:1-3). What's love? "Those who do not love, do not know God; because God is love. (1 John 4:8).

As Americans we see love as: a profoundly tender, passionate affection for another person; a feeling of warm personal attachment or deep affection, as a parent for a child, spouse or close friend. If I withhold any of the above characteristics, "I am nothing." We can all agree that Jesus commands, "Love God and neighbor." Love is a journey of overcoming black-and-white thinking and *loving* people.

Holy Spirit, continue to change our hearts to show God's love in our lives. Amen.

FEBRUARY 12
REVEL IN VALENTINE FLOWERS

I rushed to my computer and launched NASA's live-streaming website. "The Falcon 9 is scheduled to launch at 6:03!" I love going outside to my front yard and watching satellites launch.

Ten minutes, and counting ...

You've felt that nerve-tingling excitement for an historic event in the timeline of your life. It's a special and significant pinch in the fabric of time that changes you forever. You're never the same, as the day you met Lord Jesus. He changed you into a new creation.

I rushed around ... taking the laundry out of the dryer, shoving wet clothes in the dryer, turning on the bar-b-q, and making sure my cell phone had enough charge to withstand a possible ten-minute manipulation. My outdated phone always dies if I have to keep switching it on after the password activates. But this time, I have a newer iPhone version at $399! Outside I ran, focused hard, and waited. My neighbor and I said hi, and gave me pointers on how I could take a video. Shoot, a video? I have a hulking video camera in my living room that I use to take YouTube uploads ... now all I need is this slim-lined sleek cell phone. Worth every penny—

Falcon rises ... bright and high like a shooting star streaking into the stratosphere ... with a white contrail and white bullet nose.

Listen ... now comes the sonic *boom, boom, boom.*...

I tried hard to steady my phone as my neighbor gave me tips on how to zoom in and capture the best footage. I just kept breathing, thanking God and feeling blessed, considering we just received news about our son's best friend. His 13-year-old sister discovered she has stage-4 skin cancer.

I'm consistently faced with the beautiful and the shockingly unexpected. It's like I'm always fluctuating on a high wire, and trying desperately to steady myself. I can't. I need our Lord. I recall what God says: "I will have to keep shocking these people with astounding and amazing things, until the 'wisdom' of their 'wise ones' vanishes, and the 'discernment' of their 'discerning ones' is hidden away" (Isaiah 29:14). Our accomplishments in everything medical and technical amazes me, while the limits of our humanity prod me to seek Him in everything I do and plan in my life. He's in the big events as well as the small situations that take us off guard.

Lord Jesus, we pray, infuse us with hope in our trials. Amen.

FEBRUARY 13
CHILLY DAYS

We've all had disagreements. Disagreeing with people doesn't feel good though, right? I guess it depends what you're disagreeing on. Our tendency to disagree started at toddlerhood, when we stomped to get our own way in "Gimme-Gimme" land. God had different plans for giving. "Every moving thing that lives will be food for you. Just as I gave you green plants before, so now I give you everything" (Genesis 9:3).

We've all had arguments, and fights. But *fighting* hinders relationships. What's the difference?

A *disagreement* broken down means: "dis" (suffix) "apart" or "having a reversing effect." "Agree," means, "harmonizing in opinion or feeling." The suffix, "ment," at the end of a word indicates state, condition, or quality. Thus, a disagreement is the condition of *not* agreeing, but a disagreement is *not* an argument.

An *argument*, however, is: *a process of reasoning; a debate, a verbal opposition,* and, *an oral disagreement.* Let's take this up a notch. Have you ever had a *fight* with someone? If you *fight*, you're in a battle, a struggle, or an angry argument or disagreement. There's heat in the form of energy you give off in a *fight*. People murder during fights, but not disagreements. Why? Evolutionary theorists say we're born to fight to survive, and "selective perception" describes our human condition that makes us *see* and interpret the world in our own unique ways. What does God say about fighting? I don't know about you, but I always benefit from his help, wisdom, and loving intervention.

If you ever *hurt* a person while fighting, God has this payback written in stone. "If two people fight, and one hits the other with a stone or with his fist, and the injured party doesn't die but is confined to his bed; then, if he recovers enough to be able to walk around outside, even if with a cane, the attacker will be free of liability, except to compensate him for his loss of time and take responsibility for his care until his recovery is complete" (Exodus 21:18-19). God wants us to control ourselves, and to be concerned about others: Luke 6:31. People = self. "Treat other people as you would like them to treat you," Jesus says (Luke 6:31). Wow would the world change, right? *You* can be that change today.

Lord God, we pray for self-control and *your* intervention during heated discussions. Amen.

FEBRUARY 14
HEARTS A GLOW!

"Joyce, will you come here and check out this toe 'o mine?" my husband Drew calls to me.

I slowly approach his toes. *Rgh!* Two are fungal infested. I can't bear looking at them without my stomach turning a bit. *Oh my gosh, no not again, gross.*

Have you ever felt that way? It can make you want to leave the situation, not the person though, right?

Still, I inch my way over to his right foot on the stool, where I see a gray-black area. "Yep, it's full 'o fungus," I replied. Three months ago, I had taken a toenail nipper, with alcohol pads, peroxide, and cotton swabs, and surgically removed his toenail, ripe with black fungus. Fungus under the nail looks like thick black pencil lead from the 1960s. Every moment, I keep thinking, *oo, yuck, disgusting.* I keep cringing and recoiling as if I'd swallowed a tapeworm and realized the infestation had invaded my intestines. Sorry, I know this is Valentine's Day, and no one wants to hear a story about fungus, worms, and surgery, but that's what love has come to mean to me.

"Do you take this woman [man] to be your wife [husband] for as long as you live?" You know the vows the preacher speaks at the wedding ceremony. People make vows all the time. Can you keep the vow you make no matter what? That's the issue ... the grit and grime of everyday life. God respects marriage and commands people to remain faithful to their spouses.

"Suppose a man marries a woman and consummates the marriage but later finds her displeasing, because he has found her offensive in some respect. He writes her a divorce document, gives it to her and sends her away from his house. She leaves his house, goes and becomes another man's wife; but the second husband dislikes her and writes her a *get*, gives it to her and sends her away from his house; or the second husband whom she married dies. In such a case her first husband ... may not take her again as his wife, because she is now defiled. It would be detestable to *Adonai*, and you are not to bring about sin in the land *Adonai* your God is giving you" (Deut. 24:1-4). "You are permitted to all men" is a *get*. How utterly cruel. It's sin. True love means staying put, even with fungus. You *can*.

Jesus, we long to love others as you loved people, and to be holy and authentic in this world. Amen.

February 15
Immunizations and Boosters

If you receive a vaccine against a particular disease, you *will* become immune.

For years, however, some people have been refusing to vaccinate their children. A month ago at a theme park, someone with measles infected people who hadn't received the vaccination. You'll be right to predict what happened. The exposed people took the disease home with them after their vacations and exposed others who hadn't received the measles shot. Fear. We all have it. Sometimes we let it rule our lives, and sometimes we step through its chilly door. Is fear stopping you from doing what's right for others today? God can give you strength. "He strengthens the bars of your gates. He blesses your children within you" (Psalm 147:13). God is our spiritual bar.

Famous talk-radio host and author, Laura Schlessinger, once said: "This is all you have. This is not a dry run. This is your life. If you want to fritter it away with your fears, then you will fritter it away, but you won't get it back later." The unvaccinated—primarily children—have parents who opted out of the shot because they *feared* their children might acquire autism from the mixture, a hypothesis shortly disproved almost right after dangerous this false claim appeared. Google, "the measles," and see the severe side effects of this horrible illness that are inflicted upon innocent children like a life of deafness. Why do we believe we're invincible? What happened to considering the lives of others beyond ourselves?

There is a magnificent behemoth in the Bible, an amphibious leviathan God made: "What strength he has in his loins! What power in his stomach muscles! He can make his tail as stiff as a cedar, the muscles in his thighs are like cables, his bones are like bronze pipes, his limbs like iron bars. He ranks first among God's works" (Job 40:15-19). If you ever manage to confront this Loch Ness monster, you'll never forget the fight and never do it again (v. 32). You can't capture it, kill it, or annihilate its species. It's fearful on its approach. Yet, there are things only God can eradicate. He gives us a way to fight these behemoths. One of them is immunization shots. Live well, live long, and love others.

Lord, when we become stubborn with our brothers and sisters, knock us in the head with your word. Let us see the light, and help us to change. To be true ambassadors for you. Amen.

FEBRUARY 16
SAVINGS WITHOUT WAVERING

After saving a valuable computer file, you *will* experience something like the following at some point....

I tapped the *camera* icon on my iPhone. Then, I double-tapped the file icon responsible for storing my photos and videos. It has my granddaughter's one-month-old video and the Falcon-9 launch. I hold onto these photos like a food pantry, retrieving my treasurable slices of life during stressful times. The memories help me.

What do we do when we know everything we've been working on is lost?

"Oh my God, help!" I tapped the icon again.

Nothing.

"They're all gone!"

My husband had synched our iPhones with "The Cloud" yesterday, obviously erasing *everything*.

In threatening situations, neurons in the brain send response signals through the hypothalamus, amygdala, and hippocampus to our cerebral cortex, our throne of logic. "How could you have deleted everything?!" I was having a heart-attack pumping moment as our verbal flame throwing began.

"I'm sorry! I made a mistake!"

Breathe, I think. You had better heed your Mainframe cerebral cortex because you can't retract what you say at this point.

Suddenly, I remember I have another source. *Ah*, I have another phone at home. I might have to track down the launch, but I'll recover the rest. We both remain silent, chewing our sour grapes.

King Manasseh hated God and did everything wicked to strike Him out of Israel's history books. "He shed so much innocent blood that he flooded Jerusalem from one end to the other" (2 Kings 21:16; 2 Chronicles 33:2-11). But when Manasseh was in distress, he abjectly humbled himself before God and prayed for forgiveness. God forgave him, and restored him to his kingly position. "He understood that Adonai really is God" (2 Chronicles 33:12). We all need God's expansive capacity for forgiveness. After we spun out of control, we forgave each other, and realized again that our relationship had been fortified through the tumultuous event.

Forgive us Lord when we are "Like a city breached without walls is [me, when I] lack self-control" (Prov. 25-28). Amen.

February 17
Take the Next Step

Have you read anything about Kayla Mueller lately? A worldly angel exemplifying sacrifice, 26-year-old humanitarian Kayla lost her life to ISIS terrorists. It's been days since *USA Today*'s poignant tribute to her [2/11/2015, 2B], and I've managed to hedge in my grief. Remember Kayla? Remember the martyr? "How blessed are those who are persecuted because they pursue righteousness! The Kingdom of Heaven is theirs," Jesus says (Matthew 5:10). Heaven is theirs … wow. Still, we miss Kayla.

In her home city of Phoenix, Kayla was an angelic presence and bottomless well of strength as she helped the homeless and assisted victims of domestic violence to forge ahead in the world. Moved by the human suffering of foreign refugees fleeing war-ravaged areas, Kayla ventured selflessly to Turkey and Syria, where a terrorist group kidnapped and then imprisoned her. Where could Kayla have acquired such a reservoir of giving?

How did she teach people to fish instead of just dispensing food? Innocence, and love, and perseverance are angelic. Kayla.

In the early 1960s, psychologist Lawrence Kohlberg postulated six stages of moral development ranging from obedience-and-punishment in infancy, to the highest stage of universal principles that transcends mutual benefit. In other words, Kayla's behavior stretched beyond the stage of where most of us exist daily, one example being, immunizing children so they don't spread diseases. Mutual benefit is "other" focused but not life-sacrificing behavior. Kayla ventured down a Universal Road of Principles and Beliefs, and she is now living among other champions who died in their endeavors to ease human suffering, such as Martin Luther King, Jr., Abraham Lincoln, and John Kennedy. *USA Today* printed a handwritten letter from Kayla, letting us in on what made her tick. "I remember mom always telling me that…in the end the only one you really have is God. … I have come to a place in life where … I have surrendered myself to our creator because literally there was no one else." A beautiful light extinguished too soon in this chaotic world, goodbye angel. God values *each* person, it's that simple.

How can Kayla inspire us today?

God, help us meet others *right* where they're at and as they are, as Kayla did. Amen.

FEBRUARY 18
TAKING LIFE TO NEW HEIGHTS

Our well used Formica countertops are getting worn, embroidered by knife cuts, and dotted with coffee stains. They definitely need updating and renovation.

Is there anything in your life in need of renovating? The process isn't easy.

Change *doesn't* come easy. "I wish I could be present with you now and change my tone of voice. I don't know what to do with you," says Paul (Galatians 4:20).

For the last week, we've been interviewing "granite fabricators," craftsmen who measure countertops, determine square footage, give clients their perfect sales pitch, and then present their potential customers with quotes. We had our countertops replaced before, but Florida is different in the way "dealers in stone" sell their products. It's all wholesale, and we can't purchase the granite directly, only through a fabricator. Gosh! This is enough to make me pull my hair out, and trust is at an abject low. The first he'd written a novel. The second was better, but higher priced. Let me tell you, there is a difference between 43 sq. ft. and 53 sq. ft. If their price is $25 per sq. ft., then miscalculating could cost us hundreds of dollars.

Your situation might be a suit, dress, furniture, jewelry, antiques, or a flight into space. Regardless, one must always get quotes on everything, and listen to your intuition if that little voice inside of you screams: "This person isn't right for me!"

Several times in the Bible, measuring exactly was crucial. Abraham tells Sarah to make a meal for angels. "Quickly, three measures of the best flour! Knead it and make cakes" (Genesis 18:6-8). You want to make sure that if you're feeding angels, they like what you've cooked for them, right? You do your best, because God's happiness is your utmost concern. They're important, and what they're about to say is paramount. Measuring cities is important (Numbers 35:5), and you can't cheat people using faulty measurements (Leviticus 19:36). One of the most important and exacting measurements is Ezekiel envisioning the rebuilding of Jerusalem years after the Babylonians had decimated everything (Ezekiel 40-48). We can measure well.

Lord, we long to please you in our thoughts, words, and how we treat people. Help us see our weaknesses and change. Amen.

FEBRUARY 19
IN THE QUEUE

What's on your bucket list?

There's a contest I didn't like losing although I was never aware of such a competition. A Dutch nonprofit group called Mars One has selected its first round of 100 winners out of 200,000 applicants to colonize Mars. Out of those, the group will pick 24. It's a dream I've had since I saw John Glenn orbit Earth on February 20, 1962.

Mars One has a slogan: We're all going to die, but it's important what you do before you die.

Yeah—'cause the Martian colonists traveling the seven months to arrive there and then settling there will know their journey is a one-way ticket. They'll be living there in modules, I presume around Gale Crater, and dying there. Bringing them back would be too expensive.

How would *you* cope on Mars, with its' different atmosphere, low gravity, and lack of Earthly conveniences?

Will God be there?

Jesus once proclaimed: "The time is fulfilled, and the kingdom of God is at hand. Repent, and believe in the gospel" (Mark 1:14-15); and, "I must preach the good tidings of the kingdom of God to the other cities" (Luke 4:43). *Kingdom* as Jesus says is, *basileia*, meaning: *reign, rule, authority*, and *sovereignty*. In other words, Jesus was God who walked among us to *show* God to his creation, *us*. "Those who see me see the One who sent me" (John 12:45), and he gives us who have *not* seen him a special blessing: "How blessed are those who do not see, but trust anyway!"

Doubting Thomas had to touch Jesus' wounds to believe he wasn't hallucinating because after his resurrection, Jesus could appear in different forms (John 20:14; Mark 16:9; Mark 16:12; and Luke 24:36). People also *saw* Jesus "carried up to heaven" (Luke 24:51). "Some people, without knowing it, have entertained angels" (Hebrews 13:2). Therefore, where faith in Jesus exists, Jesus will be. "Adonai is close to all who call on him" (Psalm 145:18). Even on Mars, people will have and know Jesus, God and the Holy Spirit. There will be religion and culture. God meant us to worship Him and express ourselves through art and hobbies.

Father God, let us always be aware that no matter *where* we step, you are there with us. Amen.

FEBRUARY 20
BUILDING AN EVENT

In the Austin marathon a few days ago, a female runner from Kenya who was in the lead, suddenly collapsed 450 feet from the finish line. Hyvon Ngetich had fatigue and exhaustion pinching on her face, but motivation and a spirit of finish inside her, drove her forward. She crawled on her bloody hands and knees staining the pavement with her palms.

Can you picture a face desperate to arrive at any cost to the finish line?

There's something inside us that likes to cheer in prayer for someone so desperate not only to win, but also to accomplish a goal or a dream. We root for the underdog—our tendency to rally behind the person at the bottom who appears to deserve being on top but can't due to unexpected circumstances.

The evil person sabotages; however, the encourager rallies people forward in life. The encourager wants success for the person trying so hard. Hyvon made it. Running 26.2-miles, Hyvon placed third with a time of 3:04:02. Yet her drive and determination also motivated the Austin Marathon Director, John Conley to give Hyvon the same award money as the second place winner. John was that amazed and emotionally moved by Hyvon's enduring spirit.

What does it take to make a champion?

Who roots for us most in life when we believe we can't see the finish line? God, and here's your proof: "Beloved friends, if this is how God loved us, we likewise ought to love one another. No one has ever seen God; if we love one another, God remains united with us, and our love for him has been brought to its goal in us" (1 John 4:11). Here is the directional arrow, and this same flow moved from Hyvon to John and then to us so we could see an example of pure love. Love directs us to help others. Love is selfless and is fueled by empathy—putting oneself in another's place. If you simply love in the behavior of helping someone, you fulfill everything God asks of you: "Don't owe anyone anything—except to love one another; for whoever loves his fellow human being has fulfilled Torah [law]" (Romans 13:8). Love.

Father, when we feel we can't give more, help us give more. Amen.

FEBRUARY 21
BREAKING RECORDS

I remember the first TV show that ended when I was child: *The Mickey Mouse Club*. I recall the music, each character, and cartoons from Walt Disney's creative mind. Remember TV shows from your childhood?

As my life inched upward on the Age Scale, I saw the endings to *more* TV series I had become attached to: *Bonanza*, *Star Trek*, *Happy Days*, and *Wings*, one of my favorites. The show *Lost* confounded me sometimes. The plots became so entangled, and new characters kept popping up while old ones died. I think I experienced a breakthrough in dynamics, however. In life, we all experience breakthroughs that change our behaviors and thinking. "At last, you will start thinking about what has happened to you" (Deuteronomy 30:1). I began pondering my writing and realized that I can introduce characters, and kill off characters in the middle of a series—as long as they're *not* the *essential* main characters—and a story can succeed, upgrade, and remain appealing. Still, at the end of *Lost*, we learn the characters have been dead all along. The series writers concluded with an island, which was just a place to "work" for a place of redemption, a place where they could do things differently, relieve their shame, and earn the right to enter Heaven.

We live in a culture where rights, freedoms, and liberties are championed. And as we experiment with those mediums in which we navigate our world, we step on peoples' toes, and can create some big rippling damage. What's your Achilles' heel? The mistake you wouldn't tell your best friend!

The Bible is peppered with the worst of shameful sins. We know Cain killed Abel. And Lot's two daughters had a child with their father (Gen. 19:36). But there was a Judge, and leader of Israel named Jephthah, who made a devastating vow to God. "If you will hand the people of 'Amon over to me, then whatever comes out the doors of my house ... I will sacrifice it as a burnt offering" (Judges 11:30). Guess who greets him after battle? His only daughter. After two months mourning her situation, Jephthah kills her as promised (11:39). Today, young Jewish women go "to the mountains" (v. 37) to grieve over Jephthah's *unnamed* daughter. Jesus has *us*.

Lord, we praise you for your forgiveness of our worst sins ... freeing us so we can spend eternity with you. Amen.

FEBRUARY 22
SUNRISE AND SUNSET VIEWS

Do you ever get so tired, you feel like you can't take another step?

Think of the moment you wake up every morning. Is the sun rising? Or is darkness all around you. Are you stumbling to the bathroom? Or are you groping everywhere, trying to focus to make coffee, wake up, and then commute to work and make money? I remember times when I slept in my clothes! I wanted to savor every sleeping second I could before my telephone would *ring, ring, ring* me to consciousness. Then I'd pop up, answer it, and wipe the sleepers outta my eyes. The same routine, day-after-day. I longed to have different days. I was burning out.

Are you burning out?

Here's what burn out looks like, followed by refreshing showers of relief from Jesus.

"Burn out" is long-term exhaustion, and diminished interest in work. I'm sure when you picked your profession, you were enthusiastic, like Icarus who believed his winged invention would soar him to freedom and change the world. I felt that way once, and studied hard to be a teacher. I believed so much in advancing humanity in a positive direction by introducing young people to the creativity of the most distinguished writers, such as Hemmingway, Willa Cather, T.S. Eliot, Rainer Maria Rilke, and Sophocles, only a *few* of my favorites. Work ... it's part of God's plan, but so is resting, and taking care of yourself, and rejuvenating. Play time!

We read "don'ts" in the Bible, but God has a lot of "dos" too. "Whatever work you do, put yourself into it" (Colossians 3:23). You're putting "yourself" into your job, and you know how dedicated you are to making a difference. I recall what Patrick Jane, a character in the TV show, *The Mentalist*, said, "Everyone makes a difference." Remember to rest and not to burn out. Jesus says, "The water I give him will become a spring of water inside him, welling up into eternal life" (John 4:14). We go to Him, give Him our burdens, and He quenches and revives us. How refreshing He is.

"It is a Shabbat of complete rest for you" (Leviticus 16:31).

What's fun for you today? Write it down, then experience a bit of fun and rest today.

Lord, give us a spirit of play, as children play, so we can further your purpose in the world. Revive us, precious Jesus. Amen.

FEBRUARY 23
CAFETERIA, GYMNASIUM, ADMINISTRATION

Have you ever wanted to make a good impression on someone?

I remember dating. What extravaganzas were those first dates, *whew*.

If you're a guy, you're concerned about the amount of money you make, your job, and the *perfect* restaurant to take her to. You *know* those will be important, and she'll be asking you all sorts of questions about what you *do* during the day.

As a woman, you're focused on wearing the right outfit, matching it with pretty shoes, and primping and priming while perfecting your makeup. Every second of prepping feels like an exciting burn. Or maybe the experience is more like eating Mexican food. The Tabasco is delectable. Except for the slow tongue sting ... eye squinting and dragon scorching, *ouch*.

Either you want more, or you might need to take a break from the dating scene.

Dating is a ritual really, as are job interviews, attending classes for the first time, and showing up at a new church. There are times, however, when you become lost behind your Mask of Impressing People, and you become dangerously close to succumbing to peoples' expectations of who you *should* be rather than your *authentic* self. Paul Laurence Dunbar wrote a poem, "We Wear the Mask," and T.S. Eliot wrote one of my favorites, "The Love Song of J. Alfred Prufrock." J. Alfred's always asking: "How shall I presume?" We become so thick-masked, that we need plyers to pry off all the layers of dishonesty for authenticity. *No one* can return to the womb.

However, the Lord knows the real you.

When you go to your special praying zone, just talk to him. Tell Him where you're at in life, and what you're doing. Tell Him what you've done (any sin?), and how *He* affirmed your innermost being by creating you, and how much you want to do some things differently. He's listening, with *infinite* love. "Then your light will burst forth like the morning, your new skin will quickly grow over your wound; your righteousness will precede you, and *Adonai*'s glory will follow you. Then you will call, and *Adonai* will answer; you will cry, and he will say, "Here I am" (Isaiah 58:8-9). Remember John 3:16, and *let* Him love you.

Father, thank you for standing all around us. Amen.

FEBRUARY 24
OSCAR PARTY

Well before Christmas, the Academy of Motion Picture Arts and Sciences (AMPAS), begins lining up contenders for The Oscars, which honors cinematic achievements of the film industry. They judge "who's the best" in 24 categories, for example, best picture, and best art direction. People around the globe start watching....

The Oscars challenge the nominees to promote their films while working with famous fashion designers so they can look their best for all the media as they strut down the Red Carpet to the Dolby Theater. Then there's writing a reward speech, and a congratulatory speech to write for the victor. I'm sure the nominees are also conjuring up what they'll say to people if they lose.

Imagine spending January 31 to February 22 in that type of psychological tug-of-war.

Is waiting or pondering over an outcome unnerving you, today?

The writer of Proverbs says: "Grace and truth are for those who plan good" (Proverbs 14:22).

What is planning good?

Well, *my* plans *always* change, because I cannot control people and Nature. You've heard of John Steinbeck's book, *Of Mice and Men*. George tells Lennie: "Someday we're gonna," and, "Someday we're gonna have." Their dreams splinter as they mix with a climate of dysfunctional people. Robert Burns wrote a poem, "To a Mouse," that shakes us to our souls: *The best laid schemes o' mice an' men Gang [go] aft agley* [awry]." What are you planning? Is God involved? "If you entrust all you do to Adonai, your plans will achieve success" (Proverbs 16:3). Wow! But I know I just said that *my* plans might not come true? What a head scratcher. Let's look again: Entrust all I do to God = my plans succeeding. My plans succeeding = entrusting everything I do to God. Thus, God is in charge, and His plan will always succeed as I follow him. "I know what plans I have in mind for you, says Adonai, plans for well-being, not for bad things; so that you can have hope and a future" (Jeremiah 29:11). He has our welfare at heart, listens to our desires, and cares about our future. Close your eyes ... pray ... and say a healing Bible verse. What's He whispering to your soul?

Father God, as we walk through uncertainty while navigating through this stress-filled world, we need your guiding hand. Amen.

February 25
Chips, Three for One

This morning we were driving to an appointment and pulled up next to a car in which a woman driver was smoking a cigarette. She had the window cracked open, smoke billowing out of her lips, and then she flicked the butt out the window. It landed on our hood!

Well, I always keep a little notebook out and ready to write in, so I began penning a storm. She was next to my passenger side, and I believe I gave her a scare. I bet she thought I was taking down her license plate number to report her for littering. In her case, the old proverb, *let the chips fall where they may*, might procure her a juicy fine. In Washington, a litter bug could pay a fine of $1,000. Or, perhaps she just didn't think before flicking her trash out the window.

Sometimes, that happens to us, right?

We "do" before thinking. It's like we're on autopilot with some of our actions.

I thought that raw side of human thoughtless had ended for the day, until we picked up our son from school. We stopped when a girl dropped her shoe. She began yelling at my husband, accusing him of almost running her over. She was with a group of friends who began cheering her on. I told my son: "Some people have chips on their shoulders, are *really* burdened, and angry at the world."

The shoulder is often the place where people set their heavy burdens (Genesis 24:15); however, the shoulder can be so much more consequential in our Bible readings.

After the flood, Noah becomes a drunk (Genesis 9:21-23), and his sons are so ashamed of his stupors, they put cloaks on their shoulders, walk backwards, and cover their drunk naked father. We bow our shoulders in prayer, and the sacrificial ram's right shoulder is consecrated to God (Exodus 29:22-27). The high priest's shoulder contains beautiful worship jewels (Exodus 28:5-7); and when we sin, Jesus sweeps *us,* his lost lambs onto his shoulders, carrying us to his fold (Luke 15:4-6). Even governments will be on his shoulders (Isaiah 9:6), and he has "the key of David's house on his shoulder," our key to heaven (Isaiah 22:22).

He carries our each-and-every hurt. Jesus has the broadest shoulders ever. He handles our pains, hurts, cries, and heartbreaks.

Lord God, keep from the delusion that our actions have no consequences. Amen.

FEBRUARY 26
OVERCOME THE URGE

Have you ever wanted to give up? Are you contemplating giving up on something or someone today? "Stay alert," Paul suggests, "stand firm in the faith, behave like a *mentsh* (Yiddish for *Mensch: a person of integrity and honor*), grow strong" (1 Corinthians 16:13).

Other extensive synonyms for "give up" include: "bail out," "leave," "abandon," "throw in the towel," "fold," "drop like a hot potato," "walk out on," "surrender," "cave in," "buckle under," "bow out," and "pull out." These synonyms for "give up" are just a few. I don't think I've ever seen such a little phrase pack so big a punch.

I "gave up" once, and regretted my actions. While living in Hawaii years ago, several situations struck me head on. I felt like a half-dead canary with weak wings, trying to fly free from an increasingly confining cage. I left everything and everyone.

I wonder how the homeless people everywhere around us wind up on the streets. I could have been one of them, if not for a monthly paycheck I was receiving. Why did I "bail," "walk out," "give up," and "throw in the towel?" I'll tell you, so perhaps you might *not* "throw in the towel" and make a big mistake. In one year, my mom died, my husband's job was going south to the point where he was displacing his anger onto me, and my son was diagnosed with ADHD and Asperger's. Oh—I forgot. My daughter—a teenager at the time—had your standard high-pitched never-ending rebellious personality. There are times when you feel you just can't take it anymore. Even though you're going to church, and standing out in the rain crying for Jesus, God, and the Holy Spirit to help you, you're so overwhelmed and emotionally exhausted that you ... leave. I broke down in hysterical crying, and left for a few months. I kept in close contact with my husband, children, and dog; but I was severely underweight and needed to recover. Recovery comes at a cost.

Joshua's harsh words struck us and burned our lives. "When you violate the covenant of God, which he ordered you to obey, and go and serve other gods and worship them, then the anger of Adonai will blaze up against you" (Joshua 23:16). We lost everything in our mistakes. Yet, we remained with God, who reunited us.

Merciful and compassionate Lord, we praise you for taking us back. Your example allows us to reconcile with others. Amen.

FEBRUARY 27
DRAMA TO THE RACE

Have you ever noticed how some people have the capacity to love more? They become our inspirations.

Loving people are all around us. We need to see them, that's all. Then, watch them. We can learn from their loving actions.

Today a pastor, Jason S., and another worker from church came to our house to give us an estimate on removing some brush and adding mulch. My husband wants two, large pepper shrubs dug out. "I don't think they do that sort of hard labor," I told my determined husband. "They're just teens who are coming together to earn money for summer camp, not professional landscapers." I've been worried about the cost. I also want to be fair, and *more* than fair. My son will be one of those hard working teens participating in this Saturday's Mulching and Weeding Day. The pastor was so accommodating on what he will charge. We don't get paid until Monday, and we can't afford over $100. I'm sure you might know what it's like to have every dollar budgeted and every payday notched.

Yes, some people have the capacity to love more. I wonder if a person's love can be quantified. Gary Chapman offers an online "The Five Love Languages" assessment. There's a "Love Style Quiz," by Milan & Kay Resources, and a "Love Indicator Assessment," by Love for Successful Women. Is your mind spinning with all these available assessments? Wondering where you're at on the love scale? I noticed my tendency to measure my ability to love on the scale of 0 – 10 based on how I see others love. The categories are "behaviors," "intentions," "mouthing," and "apathy." Pastor Jason today showed his caring/love by showing up. That's a 10. In*ten*tions (oh, pun on "ten") are the people who say they're going to show and do show up. "Mouthing" is "I will," and "I did," and "I'm going to do." You know what *apathy* means? Love means, I *want* to improve. I'm willing to improve and change. "I love you, Adonai, my strength" (Psalm 18:2). God defeats David's enemy, and David drops to his knees: "I love you God!" Let's do that, now, and love.

Won't it be a blessing when people see love working in us and making a difference in this sometimes, *unloving*, world?

Father God, we praise you, worship you, love you, and put you first. Amen.

FEBRUARY 28
DIGITAL AGE

I have an old video camera containing short movies of me reading stories I've written. I tried uploading them to a site, and the site spit back a "Processing Reject" message. *Rr!* I can reformat documents, but movies? Nope. I have *no* idea about the difference between an MTS file and MP4 file. I used to be tech savvy twenty years ago when the internet first boomed. Now, I'm lost.

Do you ever feel frustrated and lost with ever-evolving technology? Do you need a change in direction?

Changes in media production have changed from the days when you simply pointed your video camera, recorded, and then played the VCR tape. I learned. It took me the whole day, but I discovered online software, downloaded it, and then dropped files into the program that converted my MTS videos to MP4s. I then uploaded them to my author page. *Whew.* That was a load o' change for me in one day. What change are you experiencing that's leaving you feeling anxious and disoriented? For me, I survived. But don't you want *one* thing, or *one* person, to remain constant so we can count on stability and *never* be surprised like a doe startled by car lights in our lives?

Sometimes, I cling onto God's word so tightly that I feel my soul squishing. "God is not a human who lies or a mortal who changes his mind. When he says something, he will do it. When he makes a promise, he will fulfill it." Those words came out of the mouth of Bil'am (or Balaam), one of five kings who were barriers to the Jews acquiring the Promised Land. Another king, Balak of Moab, orders Balaam to curse the Israelites. Riding on a donkey to fulfill the order, he encounters the Angel of the Lord. His donkey speaks, thus converting Balaam (Numbers 22), who then pronounces a blessing on Israel—so opposite of what their enemies wanted. Now that's a drastic change—a total switch from evil to good. God makes changes happen. In the most unexplainable or senseless acts, He changes circumstances *and* us.

God told the prophet Malachi, "I, Adonai, do not change" (Malachi 3:6). When you feel whipped about by chaos, or reeling from the constant changes this life inflicts, cling to his promise. He does not lie. He's constant. He's your awesome unchanging God.

Lord, we praise you for your awesome ability to calm us down during difficulties and trials. Amen.

February 29
Unique Offerings

You're a "make up" baby!

If you're born this date, wow are you special.

In a Leap Year, there is a Leap Day, *your* special birthday, which falls on February 29, 2016. Not everyone will like the extra day because it'll mean one more day before they get a paycheck. Yet others *will* like your special birthday because it might offer them an extra vacation day, or additional interest on their stocks or investments. See? You did it. You're special.

Did you know that 10 days were dropped in 1582 to make room, for you?

Your special day created arguments. A February 30 actually existed in Sweden and the Soviet Union. Measuring exactly our rotation on our axis and revolution around the sun has discombobulated time keepers and calendar makers until January 1, 1927. That's the day Turkey, the last country to do so, *finally* adopted our modern Gregorian calendar. God is involved, with *you*.

In the universe, where our Earth's precession is concerned, your birthday is designed to keep the calendar year synchronized with the astronomical or seasonal year. God so perfectly designed our revolution around the sun, and people have managed to measure that movement exactly by adding your day as a make-up day on the calendar. You're the extra-ordinary, and God designed for purpose.

Can you imagine the complexity of our calendar? Each nano-second is the glue to time ticking, and measuring our days and years. "A word at the right time, how good it is" (Proverbs 15:23)!

You are special. *You* deserve a special prayer. Then again, Jesus counts us each special to Him. So please, share the prayer:

"Lord God, aren't you the God in heaven?" King Jehoshaphat prayed. "You rule all the kingdoms. You possess power and might, and no one can oppose you. ... We will cry out to you in our troubles, and you will hear us and save us" (2 Chronicles 20:5-12). Jehoshaphat was special. His name means, *Jehovah has judged*, and he lived in the Valley of Jehoshaphat, which will one day be the place where God will gather all nations for judgment (Joel 4:2). Time: *tick, tick...* What special little action will you *do* today, your special day?

Lord, Father, thank you for your blessings in what *we* may see as misery or misfortune. Amen.

MARCH 1
PARTY CITY PRODUCTS

Selfishness likes to hide in weird twisted folds of our personality. We can't see its beginning, but hopefully we can smooth it out and stop selfishness from spreading its life-sucking tentacles in our lives.

God' word illuminates those indiscernible areas with His truth. Like sour medicine, truth is mind puckering, but so freeing and healing. Do you need a tablespoon of Truth to attack Selfishness today?

This morning, our son's friend who had spent the night didn't have lunch money. My husband told me to get $20, $10 for our son and $10 for his friend. "Why do we have to pay for him?" I asked. I know my son's friend is poor, but excuse me. We're *far* below rich, and above the poverty bar.

Have you ever been there? Given so much with nothing in return, or wondered if you're going to receive anything in return? How much do you give and put out in a relationship? Living this way becomes gauging *everything* with a measuring stick.

Okay, you can see my shade of selfishness. My thoughts were spinning like a hamster on a wheel as I conjured up ways to halt my selfishness. *Well, we received a tax refund, but didn't give to the church, so this is like an offering. And we didn't give hardly anything to people at Christmas, so now's compensation time, so just fork over $10 cheapskate,* I thought.

The Holy Spirit suddenly illuminated my selfishness and pickiness. $10. That's ten $1s. My husband likes to tell the story of a rich man who bargains with God to take his gold to Heaven. After death, the man approaches St. Peter with his gold bars, and St. Peter says, "Oh, I guess we could always use more pavement bricks."

"Charity edifies," Paul says (1 Corinthians 8:1). The word, *charity* means, *the voluntary giving of help to those in need.* The word, *edify*, means, *to teach (someone) in a way that improves the mind or character.* Many times, I have received God's provisions and unwarranted charity; and many times, it made me kiss God's holy ground in my middle class status. "God has heard your prayer and remembered your acts of charity" (Acts 10:31). Wow. God sees. His word is sunshine to the shadows of those parts of our personalities we *cannot* see. I'm glad for His selfless and sacrificial love into my soul.

Lord, soften our hearts, and give us spirits for charity worthy of you and Heaven. Help us love. Love helps us see. Amen

MARCH 2
THREE WEEKS TO SPRING

After God's lesson yesterday on selflessness, I realized $10 was no big deal. There comes a time when you just can't change on the yellow-brick-road of old attitudes and behaviors. I simply had to "do" and let my feelings grate. It's what God instructs. "Moses did this—he acted in accordance with everything God had ordered him to do" (Exodus 40:16). And James says, "What good is it, my brothers, if someone claims to have faith but has no actions to prove it" (James 2:14)? Thanks to the kindness of others, I got most of that money back. So when the church offering plate came 'round, I realized: "Let the money go again."

Have you ever thought: What I let go of, God might return to me in another way?

There is an actor, model, and singer by the name of Nicole Richie. Her father is the 1970's pop-icon Lionel Richie. In the mid-2000s, Nicole and her BFF Paris Hilton partied until the wee hours of the morning, spent lavishly, and bulldozed people with their reckless behaviors. Jail, rehab, and court appearance were their norms. The paparazzi never deprived spectators of Richie and Hilton's foibles and vices. Sickened by the same-old-same-old, I quit watching *Entertainment Tonight*. I found myself thriving on the gossip, and comparing my "goodness" to their "wickedness." Years later, these two are opposite from their bad-girl personas. Perhaps they finally asked the question most people ask when they stand at the precipice of change: "Who do I want to be 'cause I'm sure not happy now!"

Their behaviors remind me of King David. Famous and right with God, he sins terribly, finds himself at pain's cold thick door, drops to his knees, and prays. "Whom do I have in heaven but you? And with you, I lack nothing on earth. My mind and body may fail; but God is the rock for my mind and my portion forever" (Psalm 73:25-26). Do you remember the poor woman in Mark who gives *everything* in the offering plate? Jesus was watching her. His disciples were busy somewhere, but he calls them to witness her worship. She's the most beautiful person in the Temple. A week later, Jesus dies, for her and for all humanity. I want Jesus. He changes us.

God, when we hold on tightly to money, we pray: "Help us see and give to others in need." Amen.

MARCH 3
STRAW POLL TIME

Have you ever needed an item, but were also determined to find the best deal and the best price?

We've been driving from place-to-place—and searching internet sites—for garbage disposal push buttons to insert into our new granite sink top. It's not fun. We've been sales-rep schmoozing, and telephone hopping with so many clerks that we almost wanted to forget about installing new kitchen countertops and suffer with the stains and age-rings of our current off-white ones.

In the commotion, I prayed: "Jesus, you do it. Please, you do this, because I'm going nuts!" "All the many believers were one in heart and soul, and no one claimed any of his possessions for himself, but everyone shared everything he had" (Acts 4:32).

Yet shopping around for bargains doesn't stop with *things*.

I've shopped around for churches, meandering from Pentecostal, to Baptist, to Catholic. At one church, I began feeling comfortable, until a Sunday school teacher's anti-Semitic pronouncement that the Jewish people were guilty of killing Jesus. I ran out without hearing the service! Didn't we *all* kill Jesus? I mean, aren't we all responsible because we're sinners? If he *hadn't* died for our sins, we couldn't spend eternity with him *and* one another in Heaven! Before his conversion, Paul committed horrible sins in the name of religion; for example, ordering Stephen's stoning (Acts 7:58; Acts 9:2). Yet he had Christian relatives who no doubt had tried several times to turn him to Christ. "Greetings to Andronicus and Junia, relatives of mine who were in prison with me. They came to trust in the Messiah before I did" (Romans 16:7). He planted over fourteen churches—I believe one in Athens, not mentioned in the Bible. In Acts 16, we acquire an understanding of the Holy Spirit's influence, leadership, and shepherding of Paul as he moves throughout the area to advance Jesus Christ. He sees a vision, and follows God's instruction (v. 10). He meets Lydia, who becomes a great help to him (v. 14), and the Holy Spirit frees them from a terrible prison (v. 30). Thereafter, many people believe! There's no church hopping when people have one united purpose: to tell people in *need* about the saving power of The Cross. You can stop hoppin'.

Father God, we ask you for more confidence as we share with people how you changed us, our testimonies. Amen.

MARCH 4
HAIRCUT SUPER STORE

A famous TV personality on Fox News' *The Five*, Greg Gutfeld said something that's stuck with me. "Look for the beautiful in the one you love, and the ugly in the one you lust."

Considering the over twenty divorces occurring since January among the rich and famous of Hollywood—from Rosie O'Donnell to Stephen Collins—the love market sounds risky at best, and downright long-term frightening. And these Hollywood icons are our examples through wide-spread media coverage. Their marriages, divorces, scandalous behaviors, tumultuous relationships, and sex lives are the shark bait for Hollywood gossips.

Did you know, statistics show the median length for a marriage in the US today lasts 11 years? Prior to the end of "no fault divorce," a spouse had to give a sound reason in court, for example, adultery or cruelty. Now, a person just needs to say, "irreconcilable differences," or "incompatibility." *Shazam*, you're free! Can you believe that?

Are we *really* ever free--and fully escape--the people we leave? The people in our past and everything we've shared with them?

God says differently. When His words intersect with what people want, people often turn from God to do what they please. Firstly, God tells us who He is. "My thoughts are not your thoughts, and your ways are not my ways. As high as the sky is above the earth are my ways higher than your ways, and my thoughts than your thoughts" (Isaiah 55:8-9). He has a truth for us to follow. Secondly, God designed marriage. "A man should leave his father and mother and be united with his wife, and the two are to become one flesh" (Genesis 2:24). And, "no one should split apart what God has joined together" (Matthew 19:6); and, "I hate divorce" (Malachi 2:16). I guess we need to appreciate what we have now because we won't have marriage in Heaven. "When people rise from the dead, neither men nor women marry—they are like the angels in heaven" (Mark 12:25). Thirdly, we are to honor marriage as a society (Matthew 19:6). Perhaps this could be the fix for us if we are experiencing marriage troubles. Look to people who are succeeding in their marriages, who love each other in spite of their faults and weaknesses, and who are surviving their interpersonal struggles. That's building history.

Father, we need your intervention when marriage appears hard and our relationships seem impossible to endure. Amen.

MARCH 5
HIGHER THAN NORMAL

Did you ever wonder if Jesus needed encouragement?

Since Easter is approaching, I'm contemplating Jesus' final week on Earth and trying to put myself in his situation. All the while on Earth, Jesus has known He is going to die; and in his final seven days of life, all four Gospel writers set Jesus' omniscience as a center piece for his divine nature. "My Father, if possible, let this cup pass from me" (Matthew 26:39)! In Mark 14:36 we read: "*Abba*! [Dear Father!] All things are possible for you. Take this cup away from me!" In Luke, Jesus prays, "Father, if you are willing, take this cup away from me" (22:42); and in the Book of John, Jesus tells Peter: "This is the cup the Father has given me; am I not to drink it" (18:11)? He's praying, for encouragement.

We've all had (or will have), "last weeks." Everything from a last week on a job, a last week in class, a last week before school lets out; and, perhaps, the worst of all, the last week of life. What would you do if someone told you that you have *one* week to live? We see in Jesus ways we can approach "our lasts" as we move through life.

In the above scripture, Jesus holds fast to his Father God. "Abba," and, "My Father." He also continues his job of teaching in the Temple and instructing his disciples. He knows he won't be with them soon, and they'll need to carry on His mission (Mark 12). In the Temple, Jesus calls their attention to a poor widow who gives everything she has as worship (verses 41-44). "Yes!" he says in verse 43. His exclamation is powerful, and an encouragement to Jesus who will soon sacrifice his life for her, and us. Then there is the woman who anoints him with perfume (14:3). She is so humble, in abject sin and sorry. He hasn't been encountering those types in a while. Wouldn't you ask if in a similar situation: Why should I die for people who have rejected me? Just a few verses up, we see what could be discouraging for Jesus. "The very rock which the builders rejected has become the cornerstone" (12:10). Jesus continues to flood the world with Tanakh prophesies which *He* is fulfilling. Thus He shows humanity He *is* Lord, Savior, and Messiah. Let us always be watchful for the little encouragements that come in many forms. Everything comes from Him. Nothing escapes Him.

Father God, we need your encouragements daily, and we cling to them as spiritual food. Amen.

March 6
Employee Hand Washing Mandatory

My church provides Sunday bus service for the elderly. For the past few months on my way into church, I've seen a man whom I've come to know as "Tom" standing alongside one of the buses and staring at the pavement. "Hi, are you okay?" I ask.

He had a shy boyish expression. "Oh, yeah, I'm fine." His face reddened.

"Can I get someone to help you?" I pointed at the doors and ushers. "There's a water fountain inside where you can get a drink."

"No thanks." He turned away quickly, tapping his tie.

I noticed he was sweating. "How about coming inside at least?"

He shuffled his feet and gave a skeptical glance at the church. "Oh, I can't go in there. I just can't." We introduced ourselves, and all I could do was tell him that I'd never met anyone mean inside church, only welcoming. A few Sundays later, I saw Tom again, but this time sitting inside on a bench just outside the sanctuary. I reintroduced myself, and pointed out to him the beautiful choir music and the pastor's sermon topic. He fiddled with his tie, but still remained planted like a root to his seat. What I noticed was that no one was just sitting with or talking to Tom. Obviously, he has some type of affliction, whether physical, mental, social, or spiritual.

Have you ever noticed, we live in a sanitized society? Do you have the need to be sanitized? From others?

We have hand-sanitizer dispensers everywhere, toilet bowl sanitizers, sterile gloves, stores devoted to soap selling, Clorox disinfectants, and eye-stinging Lysol antiseptics.

Do you like people, sanitized?

Several times Jesus touches people with skin ailments: "A man afflicted with *tzara'at* [any type of severe skin disease] came, kneeled down in front of him and said, 'Sir, if you are willing, you can make me clean.' Jesus reached out his hand, touched him and said, 'I am willing! Be cleansed' (Matthew 8:2-3)!" And Matthew 11:5-6: "People with *tzara'at* are being cleansed ... and how blessed is anyone not offended by me!" As we become more like Jesus, we can approach and touch those on the periphery of society and make a *real* difference in the world. They can be inspired by us.

Lord, help us shed our views of perfection and our demands for everything excellent. Amen.

March 7
Your Search Is Over

A major spokesperson announced that its search engine might add a knowledge bank to the sites we visit. For example, if you search for "global warming," the site will spit back statistics on the validity of global warming based on what "they" discern as the science of the day. This search engine has *total* control over reaping statistics. We all use search engines like Google. I use them as research tools.

Control is a powerful tool. *Whoever controls the truths controls the world.* Scary huh? I often question what we're hearing on the news. Are media reports true? Are they distorted based on the reporter, narrator, or TV station in control? What can we believe?

In light of the recent Brain Williams scandal, wherein he finally admitted he told a few lies to advance his own agenda, I have to question what reporters tell us. Doubt can affect our inspiration and confuse us. Jesus tells us not to ignore our gut feelings when we believe the facts might be wrong. "Why are you so upset? Why are these doubts welling up inside you" (Luke 24:38). We've seen control roar its ugly face throughout history. A dictator convinces people to adopt a certain belief (worldview), and then those people launch a campaign to persecute, imprison, or annihilate those who *don't* conform. Today, we have such murderous dictators such as Abu Bakr al-Baghdadi, the leader of ISIL, Kim Jong-un in North Korea, and Abubakar Shekau of Boko Haram in Africa. *All* have viciously murdered people in the advancement of their beliefs.

Enemies come in many forms. Moses knew his enemies—both in Egypt and in the Promised Land. "The enemy said, 'I will pursue and overtake, divide the spoil and gorge myself on them. I will draw my sword; my hand will destroy them' (Exodus 15:9)." But God destroyed those enemies. "You blew with your wind, the sea covered them, they sank like lead in the mighty waters. You reached out with your right hand: the earth swallowed them. In your love, you led the people you redeemed; in your strength, you guided them to your holy abode" (Exodus 15:10-13). From our smallest of struggles to the grandest of our problems, God is victorious. El Taqeph, God of Strength, and El Sali, God of my Strength (God My Rock) can defeat any enemy. We only have to turn to Him and trust him.

Father God, we turn to you to fight all enemies without and within. Amen.

MARCH 8
EXERCISE COURSE

One of my favorite authors is Sr. Arthur Conan Doyle. His famous main character, Sherlock Holmes, often says while solving crimes: "How often have I said, that when you have eliminated the impossible, whatever remains, however improbable, must be the truth" (*The Sign of Four*, "Sherlock Holmes Gives a Demonstration," Chapter 6)? I've encountered a situation wherein the facts don't add up to solving the problem. I remember one Holmes' story wherein the criminal uses a pulley to enter the building to commit the crime. Then, there is always the trick door in the old haunted mansion through which the criminal gains access to all the rooms to commit murder. Sometimes, we face what we believe are insurmountable problems, and we rack our brains to figure out solutions.

What's ailing you today that your mind is twisting and your thoughts are contorting in a heated effort to solve "the impossible problem?"

My palindrome is still: *who* are we ever going to hire to renovate our kitchen counter? Compared to other problems though, like finding a surgeon to perform a life-saving operation, my jigsaw is light. Large or small—snub cube to truncated icosahedron—the improbable and impossible *are* probable and possible for God.

Dark Matter and Dark Energy? God knows what binds elements and the forces of nature. "By his knowledge the deep springs burst open and the dew condenses from the sky" (Proverbs 3:20); and, "O the depth of the riches and the wisdom and knowledge of God! How unsearchable are his ways" (Romans 11:33)! Do you believe God made the universe? "He determines how many stars there are and calls them all by name" (Psalm 147:4). You might say that's impossible. Many scientists maintain that the universe began with the Big Bang. God promised Abraham, "I will most certainly increase your descendants to as many as there are stars in the sky or grains of sand on the seashore" (Genesis 22:17). I saw a show on the cosmos, wherein the narrator says there are more stars in the universe than grains of sand on Earth. God said that to Abraham over 4,000 years ago. Who is *really* teaching whom, huh? "With God everything is possible," Jesus says (Matthew 19:26). He is our inspiration, hope, and comfort among so many stars.

Lord, we long to remain humble and teachable. Amen.

MARCH 9
50 YEARS LATER

The only way we can possibly know which directions to take in the future—whether the year is 2015 or 21,015—is to learn from the past. Can you pinpoint a situation, wherein you learned from a past mistake? It's easier than making the same mistake twice, right?

We see peoples' actions and their lingering effects ripple through to today at one particular infamous site: Selma, Alabama, at the Edmund Pettus Bridge. From its inception, the U.S.A. condoned slavery, until January 1, 1863 when Abraham Lincoln signed the Emancipation Proclamation that freed all slaves. Free? Yes. Equal? No. Henceforth, African Americans would be persecuted by those adverse to change. In a demonstration of protest for lack of voting rights, on March 7, 1965, Martin Luther King, Jr. marched with about 600 people across the Edmund Pettus Bridge. What bravery, and what comradery. Three people died; many beaten bloody. John Rankin was a high school junior on that day known as Bloody Sunday. "We weren't treated right. We didn't have the right to vote. We didn't have the right to go to any restaurants. We couldn't get the type of jobs we were qualified for." Another march took place on March 9, with one purpose: to march as a people to the courthouse in Montgomery, Alabama so they could rally for their right to vote. Stories of these participants are filling our history books so we *don't* repeat the past.

We all have a history, but is there a behavior you keep repeating? When will we learn *not* to continue raking ourselves over hot coals?

Who knows *how* people ever justified slavery. Our consciousness has progressed to the point where we *know* the practice is unconscionable! Paul sent a slave, Onesimus, back to his Christian master, Philemon; but the letter is a call to service, not slavery. In several books in the Bible, there are verses devoted to slavery: Leviticus 25:44-45, Exodus 21:2-6, Exodus 21:7-11, and Ephesians 6:5. What's changed? When Jesus relinquished his glory in Heaven to live among us, God changed the very fabric of our reality. "Brothers, you were called to be free" (Galatians 5:13), and, "Always be humble, gentle and patient, bearing with one another in love" (Ephesians 4:2). We fail horribly at being masters over anyone.

Lord, we pray to remember your great sacrifice, Jesus, who saved us, procuring for us eternal life with your son, Jesus. Amen.

J.P. Osterman

March 10
Spring Time Preparations

This afternoon, I took the solar cover off my pool, skimmed it, and stepped into the 88° water. Wow. Floating feels indescribable. The only thing left for me to experience would be outer space.

Have you ever seen the surface *from below* the surface of the water? The blue is the deepest shades of transitioning blue, and the sun is a wavering ball of white light, like a nightlight in the blackness of darkness. Try it sometime. Find a pool, weight yourself down somehow, and then briefly—I say briefly because you don't want to run out of air—glance up with your eyes open, or while wearing a mask. See the undulating surface? The light?

If you dive at night, you won't see any light, only your flood light with its determined rays guiding you in the dangerous world. At night, underwater, it's like being in outer space. The blackness is all around, and the cold, and unseen particles and microscopic critters lurking all around. In the perilous vastness where God didn't create us to exist you need a buddy. Yet, we love exploring. Maybe where *you're* going today, you'll step out of your comfort zone and explore … with a heart for Jesus, to love and serve. It's not easy, right?

God knows the places where we might get eaten up alive. "God created the great sea creatures and every living thing that creeps, so that the water swarmed with all kinds of them … and God saw that it was good" (Genesis 1:21). *Everything* and *everyone* He made is good.

God even knows the long deep canyons on Mars, objects in the Oort Cloud, every galaxy cluster, black hole, and quasar. He's vast and omniscient. Hey, He might one day direct us beyond our Milky Way to exist on an exoplanet He's already created. He might be creating one for us now. He loves us that much, that deeply.

He loves you. So if you're having one o' those awful days … and you don't know how you're *ever* going to make it through, pray like Elijah prayed, who was also in your situation: "*Adonai* … let it be known today that you are God, and that I am your servant, and that I have done all these things at your word. Hear me, *Adonai*, hear me, so that this people [I] may know that you, *Adonai*, are God, and that you are turning their [my] hearts back to you." (I Kings 18:36-37). Just look up from the bottom, and start your day over. Simple.

Lord, you know the universe. We are filled with awe that you know and love us your creation *every* moment. Amen.

MARCH 11
DENTAL LAND

I spent fifteen minutes yesterday afternoon out in the sun, swimming for the first time this year in my pool. Have you ever experienced a day when everything from the weather to your friends and family were running smoothly like a well-oiled machine? No hiccups, arguments, or thunderstorms. Just bliss, until—

Snap. My front tooth broke. "*Yee*-ouch!"

"Life happens," people say. I began crying.

"That's three teeth in a row missing," I wept to my husband.

Remember those years when you lost your baby teeth? I recall tying one end of a string to my loose tooth and the other end to a knob on an open door. My dad would then shut the door—*slam*—and out popped my tooth for the Tooth Fairy's to swap for a quarter that night. No quarters anymore. These are the beginning of my golden years when teeth fail and options end at Denture's White Wall. Implants? Ya got $2,000? When I get to Heaven, I'm going to ask God: "Why didn't you make human teeth the way you formed sharks' teeth? When *theirs* fall out, they grow new ones." Reclining in the blue patient chair with blinding white light over me, I kept wiping tears off my cheeks with my stained tissue as I waited for the clerk to bring me my treatment plan. *Pray, and trust Him.* I prayed for the dentist and for his assistant. I prayed that the cost would stay low. But when you're in that dentist's chair, you're at *one* more place in life where you're vulnerable, and in the hands of someone with knowledge and skill in their field. You need the person. *Pray, and trust Him*, I kept thinking, and wondering, Are you hearing me, God? "*Adonai* my God, pay attention to your servant's prayer and plea, listen to the cry and prayer that your servant is praying before you today" (1 Kings 8:28). I kept searching the Bible for His answer, and I received one. "You will receive everything you ask for in prayer, no matter what it is, provided you have trust" (Matthew 21:22). Jesus said these words right after he dried up a fig tree void of fruit. He was hungry, but the tree was barren. I guess the same thing happens with teeth when they fail. I'll just continue praying and trusting, 'cause I'll be receiving fake teeth that will be better for me. I guess we can always look at the bright sides of life. At least, they're not wooden anymore.

Jesus, fill us with trust and faith. Dry our tears. Amen.

March 12
Light Designs

On December 14, 1977, a culture-altering movie appeared, *Saturday Night Fever*. This slice of life drama takes place in the City that Never Sleeps, New York City. The main character is a spoiled, immature man living at home with his unhappy family. He's miserable with his job, a womanizer hunting for the perfect woman, and disillusioned with life in general. One famous song from the movie, "Stayin' Alive," pretty much sums up Tony Monero's life. *Life goin' nowhere/Somebody help me/Somebody help me, yeah/I'm stayin' alive.* We can live to "stay alive," or we can live out our lives by letting God direct us. Have you been just "stayin' alive?"

You don't have to anymore.

God is your *perfect* Director and can break through any wall of stagnation or disillusionment. He can give you freedom to make new plans based on His loving desires for you. He also gave you free will.

One of God's names, Jehovah-raah, means, The Lord My Shepherd. A shepherd is a leader who tends and rears sheep; or one who guides, directs, steers, or escorts people in a particular direction. In Genesis 4:2, Abel is a shepherd: a *keeper* of the sheep. Abraham and the prophet Amos were shepherds. Shepherds first saw Jesus! In Latin, the word for *shepherd* is *poimén*, meaning, *to feed the flock*. The word, pastor, comes from *poimén*. Jesus, the first pastor, tells Simon Peter: "Feed my lambs. Shepherd my sheep. Feed my sheep" (John 21:15-17)! Are *you* convinced *now* that God is shepherding you? *You* have gifts and talents to navigate among people in this lost world. "God's free gifts and his calling are irrevocable" (Romans 11:29). When I was young, I loved playing teacher to my stuffed animals. For years as a young adult, I taught high school. "There are different kinds of gifts, but the same Spirit gives them" (1 Corinthians 12:4), and, "We have gifts that differ" (Romans 12:6). For the past several years, I've devoted myself to writing. This book I committed into the hands of Our Father, Jesus, and the Holy Spirit to minister to people in need of spiritual direction, and to point the lost to Christ. So if you're unhappy in life, or with your job, or with a relationship, pray. Ask God to be your shepherd. Seek out a church Shepherd or spiritual mentor to guide you and feed you as you grow and change in service to our Lord. You *can* change course. Be led by Him.

God, we will be compass needles in your steady hands. Amen.

MARCH 13
SPRING FLORAL ARRIVALS

There is a legend about an Attentive Gardener who can't stand the sight of anything dead or dying. He (*or she*) spends almost every waking moment tending his beautiful flowers, many times on his knees, plucking out, picking, hoeing, and digging out everything wilted, dead, spotted, or brown. At night, he searches for ladybugs to eat the nutrient-sucking aphids, and worms to replenish the soil. He's attentive to every detail of trimming, pruning, planting, weeding and irrigating his garden that life passes by him, uneventful. One nippy Jack Frost fall day, he collapses from exhaustion and loneliness. Knowing the Attentive Gardener cannot hurt them, fairies materialize and glide him gently to his deathbed made of tough weeds—*nature's unreached potential*—surrounded by colorful roses canopied with baby's breath. Surrounded by weeping fairies, the Attentive Gardener prepares to exhale his last breath and says, "As I depart this earth, let me *forever* half remain with my garden." After he dies, long green stems sprout from his body, rooting at the center of his garden. Rare blue orchids sprout and bloom, and a hedge of thorns surround them, protection from discovery.

Have you ever been so preoccupied with your own little world you can't see the whole picture?

The Attentive Gardener had that problem. He (or she) could have delegated work, connected with people, and looked at life from multiple viewpoints. He didn't have to live with his head in the flowers. I'm sure his floral arrangements were beyond exquisite; yet, if we're always focusing on *one* area, for example, being a workaholic, we never try something new that could bring joy, growth, and fulfillment. Our purpose becomes obscured, *really* corrupted. Peter, the Rock Apostle, cautions us. "God's power has given us everything we need for life and godliness, through our knowing the One who called us to his own glory and goodness. By these he has given us valuable and superlatively great promises, so that through them you might come to share in God's nature and escape the corruption which evil desires have brought into the world" (2 Peter 1:-4). Our desires can quickly evolve into corruption, *decay*, surrounding us with a garden of loneliness and sin, all dead ends and a wasteful life. God can re-cultivate our gardens. We only need to look in His word.

Father, help us *always* live out your big picture. Amen.

March 14 "This is Your Life"
Introduction to tomorrows One-Act Play

We talk to God in prayer, but what if He would appear before us during one of those sessions? We'd be able to have a *real* dialogue with Him. Wouldn't those moments be earth shaking and life altering? What questions would you ask God? I thought I would take today and tomorrow to explore an actual conversation I'd have with our Master Maker, "I Am That I Am," the names He tells to Moses. YHWH He is in the *Bible*.

In a play, the writer needs to set the scene, name characters, perhaps provide a description, and reveal a bit of background information. Where might *you* meet God if He'd appear to you? I'll set the scene right here, in my dining room where I type these devotionals. I'll insert my name inside the brackets tomorrow, but you can insert your name as you read along, or write your own mini-conversation with God. It could become one of your prayers.

What might God look like? *Oo*, this is going to be difficult because we *never* get a glimpse of God. In Genesis 1:1, we see His power: "God created the heavens and the earth." Adam and Eve see God, and He tells Moses in Exodus 6:3: "I appeared to Avraham, Yitz'chak and Ya'akov as *El Shaddai*, although I did not make myself known to them by my name, *Yud-Heh-Vav-Heh* [*Adonai*]." Thereafter, God rarely appears. But wait! We have Jesus as God's perfect reflection. He says, "I and the Father are one" (John 10:30). They must resemble each other, as *we* look like our parents because throughout Matthew, Jesus refers to God as "my Father" (Matthew 26:29). And one day in the future, people everywhere will see Him: "The Son of Man will come in his Father's glory, with his angels" (Matthew 16:27). The best description of "Jesus from God" appears in John 8:42: "I came out from God; and now I have arrived here." When Jesus walked among people, healing them, and raising the dead, those people were gazing at God's face, staring into his caring eyes, hearing his perfect-pitch voice, and touching the Creator. As we read the gospels, we get a glimpse of God's reality-altering miracles through Jesus his Son. See His stunning awesome face, now? "Even if you don't trust me, trust the deeds; so that you may understand once and for all that the Father is united with me, and I am united with the Father" (John 10:38). His Holy Spirit is here.

Thank you Father for your blessed wisdom. Amen.

MARCH 15
"THIS IS YOUR LIFE"
A ONE-ACT PLAY

I pray each day before I begin writing this devotional: "Lord God, wonderful Creator and Father, I worship you and bless your holy names. I thank you for every atom you have ever created, for Jesus' death on the cross that saved me; and I praise your magnificence in this universe. Most of all, I am sorry for my sins, and those things I should have done that I didn't. Please forgive me. Do you?"

I wait for an answer, even though I know I'll never see God in this lifetime, but then suddenly—God appears through a stream of blinding white light with perfect facial features—every person's face who's ever existed on Earth.

God: Hi, Joyce.

Joyce: (I drop to the ground, kneeling, panting wildly, and crying): God?! (I want to pass out, I'm hyperventilating. I look up and see His eyes, always changing color as they continually exude the features of every person He's ever created.)

God: I Am That I Am, Joyce.

Joyce: (I can't waste time. I must ask Him important questions 'cause I know He's not gonna stand around here forever.): Can you stop the killing that's happening around the world right now, God?

God (*hovering in the white-undulating light—behind which angels are mirroring behind him*): Joyce, people kill people. I did not create people as puppets to obey my every commandment. I endowed people with free will. Yet, out of their evil acts, everything will work together for the good.

Joyce: Why am *I* here? Why did you put *me*, here, with the parents who raised me, 'cause they really sucked. You know what I've been through? What happened to me? I could have been so much more.

(I know my mistakes. They've been many, but I've confessed them all; and now all that's left of me is sitting here, daily, writing this devotional. Is it good, enough? He knows. He's been helping me, through the Holy Spirit.)

God: Yes, I know every second of your life, everything that has happened. You are my daughter, Joyce.

Joyce (I'm crying, and facing my deepest moments of hurt, almost reliving them. Yet I know in my soul that God knows them as well; after all, Jesus experienced the biggest rejections of all.): Then why didn't you stop all my mom's abuse, and make my dad care about me. Neither one of them ever spent much time with me. If they had, maybe I could have turned out so differently! (So many children die or are crippled because of all sorts of evil abuse. I feel a bit mad at God right now.)

God: You are precious to me, Joyce. As I create everyone, I already know their names, and instill every potential within them. Your life matters, Joyce. The life of every child matters to me. One day, [*with a stern voice*] I will demand from every human being an accounting for the life of his fellow human being. (His light begins fading, fast, as He's lifting off, back to Heaven. I know He's referring to Genesis 9:5, so one day, He will be my parent, and will cradle me in His eternal arms.).

Joyce: (That's what He means when He spoke through Jesus and said: Love thy neighbor.) When is Jesus coming back? Because when He does, Eden will return like Heaven on earth, and suffering, pain, and misery will all go away.

God: Joyce, just paying attention to what I say, and clinging to me, for that is the purpose of your life until I can one day actually embrace you, and then give you a much bigger and better job than what you're doing right now.

[He's almost gone … faded into space/time in front of me—His brilliance only a flicker.)

Joyce: Okay, God … and Bye God. I love you!

#

Even though my father and mother have left me, Adonai will care for me.   -- Psalm 27:10

Father God, thank you for your Holy Word and the saintly examples who lived out your many purposes. They are with you now and sharing your glory, as we will one day, Father. Amen.

MARCH 16
PALM TREE VARIETIES

One of the worst cyclones in the Pacific's history, Cyclone Pam, hit the Island of Vanuatu on March 15, 2015. It generated sustained winds of 168 mph and wind gusts as high as 198 mph. Thousands of homes, schools and buildings were damaged or completely destroyed, 3300 people were displaced killing several as it completely crippled the island of Vanuatu's infrastructure.

As Pam packed a wallop of a punch and altered the landscape, so can our emotions be as devastating. They can be hurricane force—Category 1 to 5—and beyond. When our emotions cross the tipping point of self-control, we tend to behave off-kilter and make spontaneous and irrational decisions that leave destructive wakes pummeling the people near and dear to us. Do you now-and-then feel like your emotions are hurricane level? What to do?

Remember when Joseph's envious brothers plot to kill him? "They hated Joseph still more for his dreams and for what he said" (Genesis 37:8). Joseph was talented, and Jacob's favored baby boy. This story of sibling rivalry should caution us about having favorites in our lives, and how people who are not favored can become bitter and angry. Joseph's brothers behave impulsively as their hatred for their brother escalates: "Look, this dreamer is coming! So come now, let's kill him" (37:19-20). In a fit, they strip him and throw him in the empty well. However, God has different plans for Joseph. He brings along a caravan of merchants to whom the brothers sell him. Joseph finally ends up in Egypt enduring various hardship experiences. We feel pity for him, but by age thirty-seven, he has two children. "Yosef called the firstborn M'nasheh [causing to forget], 'Because God has caused me to forget all the troubles I suffered at the hands of my family.' The second child Joseph called Efrayim [fruit], 'For God has made me fruitful in the land of my misfortune' (41:51-52)."

How can we stop what feels like hurricane emotions that could sweep us down a road of destruction? "It is in the name of the Messiah, Yeshua Ha-Notzri. There is salvation in no one else! For there is no other name under heaven given to mankind by whom we must be saved" (Acts 4: 10, 12)! Urges are powerful, but when we obey God's commandments, we can win over our emotions.

Lord, battle our impulses so we can submit to you. Amen.

March 17
St. Patrick's Day

Green is everywhere … and spring is bustin' out all over. Do you see the flowers bursting back to life where you're at?

Growing up in northern Indiana, I couldn't wait for winter to end and March to slip in like a lamb. The dismal subzero nights and fingertip numbing days of January and February would be finally *over*. Tiny green stems appeared daily to stretch out of the thaw-cracking earth, reaching for the sunlight. Soon, lilacs would be blooming—my fragrant favorite. I could sit for hours along the windowsill, watching snowdrifts melt into soft mounds, their disappearing waters gurgling down storm drains as gray-salt slush ponds drizzled off the scratchy pavements and driveways as if being rubbed with a fast-acting detergent. The sun is higher in the sky. The days longer; the nights shorter. Then would come St. Patrick's Day, usually my first coat-free day of the year. I'd spend a few chilly hours at the park on the swings and merry-go-round. Always, I'd hunt for four-leaf clovers among the sprouting grass and dandelions. I could never find any. I think Grandma McCarten used to challenge me to search for them on purpose so I'd let her do her spring cleaning. Grandma, are you cleaning somewhere in God's green heaven today? Sure she is.

Not all spring days were happy. I recall one sad day—April 4, 1968—the terrible day James Earl Ray assassinated Martin Luther King, Jr. I was ill and home from school. I cried that day. Today, however, I'll celebrate St. Patty's Day by eating corned beef and cabbage, just like my Grandma Anne McCarten used to make. But we must have days when we commemorate those special saints, like St. Patrick, who risked their lives to advance Christ. Stephen was stoned to death (Acts 7). Saul tries killing David whom God had chosen to rule Israel (1 Samuel 13:11-14). Haman—King Xerex's high official—plots to kill *all* the Jewish people until brave Esther intervenes, saving them (Esther 7). Lastly, there are *thousands* more martyrs, and some Christians being martyred right now. The most senseless was that of John the Baptist, Jesus's cousin. He spoke out against Herod's affair with his brother's wife, and she orders his execution—his head on a platter. Such sin sickness. We need Jesus' sweet breath of spring today as our Sun is rising and setting.

Father, give us courage to proclaim your Word and glory. Amen.

MARCH 18
CHARGED PARTICLES

Are you in the mood for a renovation? Look around you. See anything that might be in need of changing? How about a change in behavior or personality you might need to make? Wow, but oops. I guess I hit a sore spot, huh? *Those* types of changes are hard and difficult to make, like nail biting hard. I know, 'cause I've been forced to make some pretty hard changes lately. They don't come easy.

The contractor we hired has been busy renovating my kitchen. He had to cut off an old fashioned bar behind the sink, add under-cabinet light fixtures, and insert new electrical boxes. His plans sidetracked when the kitchen ceiling light didn't share the same circuit as the connection on the opposite side of the kitchen. Plans changed. I had been trying to adjust to the missing bar and different switches, but this unexpected glitch in our plans disappointed me. We had wanted dimmer switches; but because of the different connections and block wall, the contractor couldn't give us the hardware we wanted. So, we have to live with full-power LED lighting on *that* kitchen side. Drats. If I had faced this same circumstance years ago, I might have thrown a little fit. I might have gone into the bedroom and went bombastic on the pillows, or screamed into a bowl of water. Now, I didn't. I just went with the flow. Hey, life's too short, and at least I have the kitchen remodel, and a dimmer light on one side that'll be great when I make coffee in the mornings when I can barely see and the LEDs will be blinding.

Can you see how far God has stretched you through the changes in your life? He's caused you to grow into the beautiful inspiring person you are right now.

We know we haven't arrived at perfection, but now-and-then, we need to acknowledge our progress. It's been won for us, through Jesus and the Holy Spirit. Amen.

In rebuilding the Temple after their Babylonian captivity, the Jewish people began trusting God again: "The leaders of the Judeans made good progress with the rebuilding, thanks to the prophesying of Hagai ... and Z'kharyah the son of 'Iddo. They kept building until they were finished, in keeping with the command of the God of Isra'el" (Ezra 6:14). Let us always be in the process of self-renovation, not perfection, with God as our builder.

Lord, thank you for growing pains that refine us. Amen.

MARCH 19
SAVINGS CATCHER

After I buy groceries and take my receipt home, I enter certain code numbers from the receipt onto a website that gives me a *little* return on my future shopping at Walmart.

Are you looking for a return on some investment you've made?

One receipt doesn't do much, but added up over time, I now have $25.38 in my on-line Savings Catcher account. Still, I'm trying to figure out exactly *how* to glean my rewards money because collecting it appears blurred in a network of gift cards that I haven't found lying around the house or in one of my very old card stashes. I will though … figure it out, but what's more important is that I keep aligning my receipts, entering them regularly on the website, and shopping at the same place to keep up the good routine.

In our lives, we tend to put in the same amount of hard work with the friends we decide to attach ourselves. However, if we aren't discriminating with who we "hang out with," we risk losing precious time and behaving like many non-Christians lost in sin with no trust and focus in Jesus. How do we keep aligning with people who have our same mindset, and why?

These past few days, the Israeli Prime Minister Benjamin Netanyahu has been in a tight race against an opponent who wants to foster closer relations with opposing Palestinians. The Prime Minister has been adamant: Israel must stand firm against the Iranians who want nuclear weapons. His hardline rhetoric and gutsy actions—appearing at a joint session of our Congress—are those of a prophet. To diversify for Israel would be like those ancient times when they disbanded from God to blend in with their enemies. The Book of Isaiah tolls a warning bell that ripples a message through time to *us* today. "For you have forgotten the God who saved you, failed to remember the Rock of your strength; so you plant pagan-style gardens and set out vine-cuttings for a foreign god" (17:10). Pagans do not know God (1 Thessalonians 4:5). I'm not saying we should stay away from people who are not Christians, because how else can they come to Christ if we don't talk to them? "You are light for the world," Jesus says (Matthew 5:14). Together as Christians we are individual lights on a beautiful chain who shine, sparkle, and throw Jesus's words of salvation as growing sowing seeds to the world.

Lord, guide me where you would have me do your work. Amen.

MARCH 20
TIME TO SOLVE

In high school, I wanted to be an opera singer or teacher. I took two years of voice lessons from a former singer at the Met, and one semester I assisted a Catechism teacher. Do you know what can crush a dream? Have you ever had a dream, crushed?

I suffer from stage fright. Whenever I'd walk on stage to sing with ensemble groups, the lights would blind me, but then I would stare down the hundreds of faces waiting for us to sing. I believe I lost consciousness at times. The next day when our music director played the recording of our performance, you could hear me blast the high notes outta the auditorium. Darn. In my later years, I joined church choirs and praise teams as I worked on kicking my stage fright issue. Now, however, in my late fifties, and having survived another move, I decided to do something different for Christ.

Have you ever just wanted to change directions? I prayed, and observed people, and discovered—

Handbell choir. The director, "Linda," is starting me in a children's handbell class. Praise God I can read music or I'd be lost. With every note I ring out to Him, I ask, "Lord, please make this sound beautiful as I play for you beside these your precious children." God loves music. In his worship ceremonies, people praise him with song and all types of musical instruments, even homemade instruments. "David and the whole house of Israel celebrated in the presence of *Adonai* with all kinds of musical instruments made of cypress-wood, including lyres, lutes, tambourines, rattles and cymbals." (2 Samuel 6:5). There's dancing in worship ceremonies as well. "As the ark of *Adonai* entered the City of David, Mikhal the daughter of Sha'ul, watching from the window, saw King David leaping and spinning before *Adonai*" (2 Samuel 6:16). David's wife Mikhal isn't thrilled about his dancing, however, and she's filled with "contempt" at his behavior, really shame and disgust. David doesn't divorce her, but he does choose God over her: "In the presence of *Adonai* ... I will celebrate *Adonai*! I will make myself still more contemptible than that, and I will be humiliated in my own eyes" (2 Samuel 6:21-23). So make a joyful noise to the Lord. It's soul praise, your stamp of God's uniqueness in this world. He loves your voice, your song, your unique spirit. Sing to Him today.

Lord, give me music and lyrics to sing your praises. Amen.

MARCH 21
PLATINUM TOUCH

Have you ever tried contacting people who don't answer your calls or emails, or won't phone you or email you back?

Or, do you have Facebook, post info, but "your friends" or "family" don't respond? After a few futile attempts at reaching them, you keep asking yourself in the mirror: When do I stop? Why won't this person answer?

I can't stand automated receptionists who put us through a series of options and make us listen through endless numbers on a loop of extensions for which I have trouble writing the names and numbers fast enough. It's almost impossible now-a-days to get a real live person on the other end of a call. Leave your number at the *beep?* Have fun waiting … until Pluto veers toward our Sun.

However, when God talks, someone's always listening. One such powerful God appearance occurred to Joshua after the Jewish people crossed the Jordan River—which God dried up for them to cross. Then they arrived at the Promised Land. Still, you have to imagine how insignificant Joshua must have felt, and totally unprepared to take Jericho. I can picture myself there, standing alongside him, whispering a heart-felt prayer to God. "How are we *ever* gonna take that gigantic place, Lord, 'cause we have no battle training and have grown up for forty years wandering through the desert?" Suddenly, Joshua raises his eyes and looks. In front of him stands a man with his drawn sword in his hand.

"I am the commander of *Adonai*'s army. I have come just now" (Joshua 5:13-15). Is this an angel? Perhaps Jesus? God.

Joshua falls face down to the ground and worships him. "What does my lord have to say to his servant?" We kneel in desperate times.

The commander of God's army answers, "Take your sandals off your feet, because the place where you are standing is holy." He tells Joshua the results of the battle for Jericho even though Joshua has no idea how to attack the place. "I have handed Jericho over to you, including its king and his warriors" (6:1-2). We don't have the Commander of God's army always right before us, but we do have the Holy Spirit. He's our never-failing communicator to our always attentive God who is on all sides of us right now.

Father, we only need your presence when people fail us. Amen.

MARCH 22
CREATIVE NETWORKING

My husband loves to tell stories from the past ... over and over. Whenever we're among people and I hear him say, "I've got an interesting story related to that;" I know one of the same ole stories is coming. I could yawn to hear about one of his Silicon Valley business ventures, or an old boss, or a repeat of one of his boyhood trips. I don't yawn. After seventeen years of marriage, you become accustomed to your partner, his/her ways, needs and wants. Shoot, I'm sure there are *plenty* of things about *me* that drive him batty. Like my tendency to leave microwave lids on the stove where he believes someone will come along, forget about the lid, and turn on the stove. Oh, well. However, it was after one of his *looong* tales that I commented: "Strange how the people we talk about and think about have *no* idea we're talking or thinking about them." We laughed through the epiphany of discussing the possibility that someone from our past, important or not, *could* be talking or thinking about us "in the moments of our lives." That might be happening to you now as well. We affect others. They remember us.

We can read several stories in the Bible where characters have no idea they're being discussed, and possibly targeted. Zimri plots to murder King Baasha, and he succeeds in usurping the throne (1 Kings 16:9-10). We see Envy dig its ugly green claws into the backs of other characters as power hungry people plan wicked deeds. Saul plans to murder David (1 Samuel 23:9). And God tells Isaiah to disclose to Achaz, King of Judah, a grand scheme to kill him and divide the Nation of Judah (Isaiah 7:1-12). Remember how important Ahaz is? He's the father of Hizkiyahu [Hezekiah], one of many vital forefathers in the long line of Jesus's lineage (Matthew 1:9). There is another plot that turns out positively, however. Joshua orders two spies to survey Jericho. The spies are nearly caught, until Rahab hides them, saving them from capture. She has heard of God's mighty deeds in saving His people from the Egyptians and Amorites. She's a foreigner, but a Believer.

Because of her faith, God sanctifies her. Because of her help with the Scarlet Cord, Joshua defeats Israel's enemies (Joshua 2). Some narrations are indelible, while others from our past remain alive by our words or actions.

Lord, thank you for your promise of binding us to you forever.

March 23
Easter Egg Hunts Coming Soon

After having two hand bell lessons with children, the director approached me with a blue folder. Her expression was warm but serious. "It's the church's policy that anyone working with children has to fill out these forms."

The navy-blue folder appeared like a dark cloud. So many thoughts spun in my mind: from self-chastisement for getting involved, to realizing people will finally discover everything "in the system" about me. *I have nothing to hide!* "Okay, I'll fill 'em out."

"Can you give them to me by Sunday?" she asked.

Wow, Sunday's just three days. "Okay," I replied, opening the folder containing stapled forms, policies, and guidelines while working with children. *These look like bricks on the Great Wall of China.* "I'll give this to you Sunday." Then she was quickly gone.

When I sat down at the dining room table two days later and pulled out the forms, I noticed *three* separate forms: one to a federal agency, one to a private company, and another release form for the church's records. Each form wanted my social security number, driver's license number, "aliases" [Wow, I'm a spy or something?], previous volunteer experiences working at churches, and work history. It made me think, gosh, what would they do if they *couldn't* track down, or access, all my numbers?

What are *your* numbers? Do you know them by heart? I can't tell you my cell-phone number. Could we exist without numbers?

Numbers. We're just numbers in this world.

I've heard of people who have become so sick of "being a number" and feeling insignificant that they left society to live off the land in the desert, the Appalachian Mountains, or some anti-government commune in some "Wilderness Territory" which must becoming scarce by now. Who ultimately know us, *not* by a number? To whom are we really connected? "It is God who sets both us and you in firm union with the Messiah. He has anointed us, put his seal on us, and given us his Spirit in our hearts as a guarantee for the future" (2 Corinthians 1:21:22). God has named us, anointed us, and put His seal on us. With a special oil, and new Spirit infused *indelibly* inside us, we are in His constant view and presence. We can talk to Him. He knows us. You can look to Him for encouragement.

Thank you, Lord Jesus for your forgiveness and love. Amen.

MARCH 24
ASSEMBLY REQUIRED

Have you ever walked in another person's shoes lately? Put yourself in another person's experiential world to participate in life from his or her perspective?

Last night we dropped our son off at church for a "Homeless Experience" activity. To prepare, we found a giant box and several small boxes at Walmart out of which my son could piece together and tape "shelters." Then he bought a little bag of candy to share with his pals, some Silly String for a fun activity, and a large pack of teriyaki jerky that he stuffed inside his sleeping bag. "I *need* these! I promised my friends," he maintained.

"With all this cushy stuff you're taking," I began, "how will your experience be a *true* homeless experience? I thought you're supposed to learn a lesson about life. I don't think the homeless have all this food that you and your friends will be eating all night." I gestured at the cardboard boxes. "And what if it rains? I think it's going to rain, Andrew. Then what?"

"Then we'll go inside church," he replied.

I forgot about his allergies! "Take your eye drops. Oh—and sinus and aspirin pills—"

"Mom," he interrupted, "it's only *one* night."

Now I ask you: Did all the participants *really* learn what it's like to live on the streets—or alley—and homeless?

No matter what we do to replicate someone else's life and experiences so as to "walk in their shoes," we can't. We can't live in someone else's skin.

God can ... and He did, through Jesus His son. He's walking in *your* shoes today and every day. "No one has gone up into heaven; there is only the one who has come down from heaven, the Son of Man" (John 3:13); and, "Yeshua [Jesus] the Messiah is Adonai" (Philippians 2:11). God wanted to walk in our shoes, and He sent part of Himself to do just that: "We do see Yeshua—who indeed was made for a little while lower than the angels— now crowned with glory and honor because he suffered death, so that by God's grace he might taste death for all humanity" (Hebrews 2:9). He knows our experiences, each difficulty, every temptation, and what we're enduring. We cry to Him, and He hears.

Father, during our pains in life, thank you for holding us. Amen.

March 25
Final Trek

Do you know what an "anachronism" is? If something is *anachronistic*, it is *a custom, event, or object in a period to which it does not belong.* In other words, something is out of place and time. Three years ago under a parking lot, British archeologists found the bones of King Richard III. For the past several days, those medieval bones have been trekking through the British countryside toward Richard's final resting place, now a bucolic farm that once resounded with clashing swords where the King died in battle in 1485. The horse-drawn carriage transporting Richard's remains through popular cities and modern cheering crowds is anachronistic, especially with the knight on horseback directing the funeral procession.

Do you have anything around where you live or work that you'd consider an anachronism? And because it's an anachronism, you couldn't use it even if you tried? A while ago, I dropped off an electric typewriter at the Goodwill store. I can't buy ink ribbons or correction tape. I also have a laptop that can't connect to the internet because Microsoft is revamping Internet Explorer into a new operating systems.

Do we ever feel out of place and time as something "new" surfaces to make our lives easier, softer, and less complicated than our yesterdays?

In the *Complete Jewish Bible*, the word "time" appears 972 times. One of the first appearances of "time" is in Genesis 3:8. After Adam and Eve sinned, they must have felt so out of place, so separated, and so disconnected from God. "They heard the voice of *Adonai*, God, walking in the garden at the time of the evening breeze. The man and his wife hid themselves from the presence of Adonai God, among the trees in the garden." *Eden* means *pleasure*. They had pleasure no more. Yet, we can feel the evening breeze. You know the kind of gentle blowing wind that's like a wonderful balm on your skin after the long hard day. I don't believe Adam and Eve are even aware of their surroundings at this post-sin point. They are concerned about hiding, getting away, and escaping. Sin puts us out of place and time with God. Yet Jesus and His grace and forgiveness whip us back into God's outstretched loving arms. Magnificence is our Savior. He loves you and is always welcoming

Thank you, Lord that your mercies are always new. Amen.

MARCH 26
STEP UP

When I was two years old, I used to run fast, trip, and then stub my toes on the sidewalk. *Ouch*—my bloody big toe. It didn't help when my mom or dad tapped the orange iodine stick on my cut, making the jagged sore burn and throb even more.

Remember those times when you didn't quite step right, and then tripped, stumbled, or fell? Maybe your spiral happened at a roller skating rink, while water skiing, or playing ball. Wherever you fell, I'm sure your miscalculation of space and distance smarted.

In our personal lives, we can stumble on a bad decision, sin, miss a goal, lose an opportunity, or misjudge someone. The famous mystic monk and poet, Thomas Merton, once said: "We stumble and fall constantly even when we are most enlightened. But when we are in true spiritual darkness, we do not even know that we have fallen." Thomas Merton died when he stumbled out of a bathtub and was electrocuted by a fan. Yet he left spiritual encouragements for us on our Christian walks.

Having been saved by grace, we have our eyes and ears open to God's truths. When we stumble over our desires and sin, we can repent and be restored. When we were lost, we were unaware of our sin sicknesses.

Are you on the lookout for stumbling blocks?

We will fall *and* stumble, but God turns our stumbling points into stepping-stones. I'm reminded of the time when David brought the Arc of the Covenant (Jehovah of hosts who is enthroned upon the Cherubim) to Jerusalem. David transports the Arc on an oxcart and orders non-Levites to guide the Arc from Avinadav's home. The ox stumble, Uzah touches it to protect it, but then God kills Uzah. They had taken pagan advice from the Philistines who had the Arc in long-term storage. David transgressed the Law. He's angry for a time, but he recovers. Blessed are we when we acknowledge our mistakes. As we take baby steps over stumbling stones, our God refines us. "Even some of those with discernment will stumble, so that some of them will be refined, purified and cleansed for an end yet to come at the designated time" (Daniel 11:35). We have confidence that one day we will be completely refined, and shine, with God and His glory.

Lord of Hosts, Father God, Holy is your name. Amen.

March 27
Promotional

My cousin John and I often discuss our common genealogy. My mom, Mary, and my dad, George, met at John's parents' wedding. John's mother, Theresa, was my dad's sister. His dad, Robert, was my Grandpa Harold's brother. Yes, confusing. Now try charting it all out, which John and I frequently do while debating names, dates, and professions.

One evening, John exclaimed: "Your Grandpa Harold was a boxer."

"Naw—he was a painter," I returned. "I never heard of him boxing. He was so thin. I bet his opponents pummeled him!"

John laughed. "That's why he quit boxin' and took up paintin'."

I remembered that conversation when my husband and I learned about a boxing match. On May 2, fiery-fisted punching-bag-breaker Manny Pacquiao is scheduled to fight face-wrecker, mule-kicking Floyd Mayweather, Jr. Part of me wants to order the fight on Pay-Per-View, until my husband reminded me, "Remember when we paid for the last fight?" It cost over $50, and Antonio Tarver defeated Roy Jones Jr. in the second round. We felt definitely cheated.

Still, "being a spectator" reminds me of how people who are *not* Christians watch us. They notice how we respond to difficulties and how we deal with life's curve balls and side-ways challenges. Your time is not a waste because you are always on display in our world. As Christians, we *will* suffer. Paul did, as an extreme example, to model endurance and grace *for us*. "Conduct your lives in a way worthy of the Good News of the Messiah. ... Stand firm, united in spirit, fighting with one accord for the faith of the Good News, not frightened by anything the opposition does. This will be for them an indication that they are headed for destruction and you for deliverance. And this is from God; because for the Messiah's sake it has been granted to you not only to trust in him but also to suffer on his behalf, to fight the same battles you once saw me fight and now hear that I am still fighting" (Philippians 1:27-30). How else can the lost repent and accept Christ, except by watching you and me as we lean on Jesus when uncontrollable circumstances of this world, Satan, illnesses, or diseases afflict us? Together—united in Christ—we glean knowledge and help save souls for Christ.

Jesus, help us be the light and salt to lead people to you. Amen.

MARCH 28
UN-BUILDING

Hailed an architectural ingenuity in 1961, the Glass Bank once shimmered in the Cocoa Beach skyline. Its builders christened the surround-sound Bank, with palm-tree tropical ambiance, as a hub for the space age. It included Ramon's Rainbow Dining Room, a Sky Room, and the Sky Walk, the latter an observation area where one could marvel at rockets and pioneering astronauts launching into the abyss of space exploration. Frank Wolfe, one of the occupants, even built a windowless penthouse at its top, and the bank quickly settled into a 1960s Space Coast trademark like the Founding Fathers once gathered at Boston's Green Dragon Tavern. Then a series of misfortunes began pummeling Frank Wolfe's Glass Bank. Two bad hurricanes in 2004, the economic downturn of 2008, and legal problems left the glistening beacon bleeding air through jagged holes and graffiti-stained cement beams. Then appeared the relentless black mold, almost as bleak and desperate as Frank Wolfe's attempt to keep his Wonder of the Space Coast alive. Frank just couldn't leave, and he took his life at the Base of his creation, his Soul Nest. In the end, before the Glass Bank's demolition, barely could we discern, between brown boards and nails, the bright blue words of a fitness center: Atlantic Nautilus. Strange how even one of Jules Verne's namesake masterpieces couldn't keep alive the Glass Bank.

Can you point out any archeological splendors that are now rust buckets or dilapidated relics of the past where you're at? Do you appreciate it, or want the wrecking-ball to take it down?

Jesus predicted the rise and fall of nations, kings, and natural wonders. In Passion Week, he began drumming into peoples' minds that the things of this world don't last. Setting our hearts and souls on fallible people, changing places, and eroding objects will only leave us directionless. "As some people were remarking about the Temple, how beautiful its stonework and memorial decorations were, he [Jesus] said, 'The time is coming when what you see here will be totally destroyed — not a single stone will be left standing!' (Luke 21:5-6)." In 70 A.D., Roman General Titus completely destroys and burns the Second Temple to the ground. Jesus concludes his Passion prediction with, "In your patience possess ye your souls" (Luke 21:19). Our souls are everlasting, so let's touch people and lives.

Lord, give us insight for what is truly important. Amen.

MARCH 29
NEVER FAIL

"Let no harmful language come from your mouth, only good words that are helpful in meeting the need, words that will benefit those who hear them" (Ephesians 4:29).

Sometimes, the day gets long. We get exhausted. Have you ever said to someone, "Just one more word from you and I'm gonna scream?"

In John, Chapter 16, Jesus breaks bad news to his disciples. "They will ban you from the synagogue. In fact, the time will come when anyone who kills you will think he is serving God" (verse 2). We are people who tend to act on our perceptions. We do or say what we "believe" or "have learned" is right, whether it's from our parents, our teachers, our colleagues, or just plain society in general. Not everyone is receptive to us. We might not even be acting on the truth, only what we *believe* is true. The ensuing friction can create frustration. Frustration can snowball into irritation, which can result in a meltdown, outburst, and "harmful language." I've often heard the axiom: Broken bones heal, but the wounds a word opens can fester forever. We don't forget harmful words.

Yesterday, our son said, "I want to buy a vaping atomizer." My husband and I exchanged shocked glances. "What's that?"

Our son explained how e-cigs work.

"No way!"

"But I want one. I'll sell my bike," our son responded firmly.

"Then, when I get a job, I'm movin' out," he exclaimed.

When Jesus tells his disciples, "I am going to the One who sent me," they must have felt puzzled. Then Jesus says: "In a little while, you will see me no more. Then, a little while later, you will see me" (verse 176). I would have scratched my head in confusion. Maybe, I might have flipped my top—had it up to my ears with His parables. Do you think they ever got mad at their God-sent teacher? Said horrible things and then regretted it? "A time is coming," Jesus begins, "indeed it has come already when you will be scattered, each one looking out for himself. And you will leave me all alone" (verse 32). The ultimate pain is loneliness. I haven't sent a harsh word yet to my son. He's in God's hands and will one day be making his own decisions for his life. Sometimes, we gotta let people fall.

God, help us control ourselves and see your plan. Amen.

MARCH 30
ON THE BRINK

Behind my back yard beyond the preserve, I often hear the faint barking of a dog. "*Ruff, ruff … ruff, ruff*"….

Just because a sound is distant doesn't mean it's not annoying. "Rejoice in *Adonai* your God! He is giving you the right amount of rain in the fall. He makes the rain come down for you, the fall and spring rains. This is what he does first" (Joel 2:23). Rain can be a good thing and a bad thing. You notice that? How do we deal with petty annoyances?

It's rained so hard at my place at times that I've had to run outside in the pounding drops, drag the hose to the curb, and drain the pool. I've had to change clothes twice. Can you relate to those times when annoyances feel like attacks?

The Israelites were attacked by various enemies multiple times, and God used amazing methods to help them win battles. When the five kings of the Amorites and all their armies attacked the City of Gibeon, God wouldn't stand for it. He spoke to Joshua with orders to change the celestial sphere. "'Sun, stand motionless over Gibeon!' Joshua shouted God's directive into the sky. 'Moon, you too, over Aijalon Valley!' So the sun stood still and the moon stayed put until Israel took vengeance on their enemies" (Joshua 10:12-13). These are drastic reactions to a full-scale assault on an annoyance. And I don't believe God is going to thunder down on all the annoyances in our lives. However, He can bring us tolerance, patience, and forbearance in times when annoyances are pushing us to the brink of tears or wrinkling our day. Rain is a metaphor in the Bible for relief. *Relief* comes from God as, *a feeling of reassurance and relaxation following release from anxiety or distress, help,* and *sustenance.* God is our spiritual nourishment. The Holy Spirit is continuously speaking to Him on our behalf, pleading our every situation to Him, conveying to Him our grievances, and lifting up our annoyances to Him. "The Lord is good, a refuge in times of trouble. He cares for those who trust in him" (Nahum 1:7). How does he help us when we feel irritated beyond belief? "When my cares within me are many, your comforts cheer me up" (Psalm 94:19). He comforts us. We only need to speak to him in prayer. "Throw all your anxieties upon him, because he cares about you" (1 Peter 5:7). Annoyances never last forever.

Father, give us peace when annoyances seem intolerable. Amen.

March 31
Behind the Scenes

Have you ever noticed how people, like money, can sometimes be counterfeit?

The word means *fake*, *bogus*, and, *phony*.

While leaving a church event, I bumped into an acquaintance who had changed her hair style. "You look beautiful! Who styled your hair 'cause I'm thinking of getting mine cut."

She beamed with a proud smile. "I did it myself." She pulled up her hair, and with her fingers gestured, *snip, snip, snip*.

I marveled at her inspiring authenticity. "Amazing!" I imagined doing the same thing, risky for me, though. I recalled when I was in middle school and cut my hair short—the popular bob style. My face appeared blimp-like. My self-esteem swirled down the drain until my hair finally grew back. I had put so much emphasis on my looks—so important to teenagers. At the time, my family was attending a church where the reverend read a little Bible verse and then pontificated for on sin and shaming consequences. What I needed—as we do every day—is God's hand of encouragement, love, and acceptance. We are as His creations. We need confidence from Him to become salt, light, and shining lamps. "You are salt for the land," Jesus says (Matthew 5:13). "You are light for the world," He also says (Matthew 5:14). He also cautions us. "Take care that the light in you is not darkness" (Luke 11:35)! When we separate ourselves from His word—part from Him—we turn from what's important to Him to pursue what the World would have us do and look like. Didn't Satan entice Eve and Adam that way? "Did God really say, 'You are not to eat from any tree in the garden' (Genesis 3:1)?" That's like someone on the playground asking, "Did your parents *really* say you can't open the door to every stranger?" What enticements we encounter when we move away *from* God. Satan is "the deceiver of the whole world" (Revelation 12:9). He tricks, fools, dupes, misleads, deludes, and beguiles. If we listen and fall for his lies, we're gone.

Paul uses affirmations. "The grace of the Lord Jesus the Messiah, the love of God and the fellowship of the Holy Spirit be with you" (2 Corinthians 13:14). We have the grace from Jesus. We have God's love every minute. We have fellowship with the Holy Spirit. We only need to ask for a heart to know Him (Jeremiah 24:7).

Lord God, enlighten our minds and guard our hearts. Amen.

APRIL 1
INSOMNIA

Did you get enough sleep last night? Or, is there a concern, worry, fear, problem at work, or a relationship keeping you awake? Then again, some people can't sleep because they're giddy about tomorrow.

Still, unwanted energy is at the heart of lack of sleep, right?

When sleeplessness strikes, we toss and turn, or fidget or stare into black space. Some people count sheep. I focus on the smoke detector's red laser light.

Sleep comes from God. He can help us ... sleep.

After God had created Adam, He realized Adam needed a mate. "God caused a deep sleep to fall upon the person. While he [Adam] was sleeping, God took one of his ribs and closed up the place from which he took it with flesh" (Genesis 2:21). When we sleep, pronounced changes and healing happen in our bodies. God designed the night to be for rest, and the rejuvenation of our bodies, minds, and souls. Furthermore, when we sleep, we dream. Sometimes our dreams tell us things about ourselves and our lives. In Genesis 41, Pharaoh has dreams that Joseph interprets as premonitions from God. They come true, and Joseph vaults to fame in Pharaoh's court. This fulfills God's plan for Joseph, his estranged family, Egypt, and the Israelites. God is always awake and in charge, caring for us and guiding our future for His glory.

There is one person who always appears to have God's favor; that is, until he walks away from God and has fretful nights—David. "Look, and answer me, *Adonai* my God! Give light to my eyes, or I will sleep the sleep of death" (Psalm 13:4). The opposite of *light* is *darkness*. David is pleading for clarity. In times of indecision or when we sin and are left mulling over the consequences, it's troublesome to go to sleep and get sleep. After repenting, David feels God's presence throughout the night. "I lie down and sleep, then wake up again because *Adonai* sustains me" (Psalm 3:6). God strengthens and supports us physically, mentally, and spiritually. "He provides for his beloved, even when they sleep" (Psalm 127). No matter what's keeping you wide awake, God is *always* awake and carrying your issues. David taught his son Solomon well. "When you lie down, you will not be afraid. When you lie down, your sleep will be sweet" (Proverbs 3:24). Feel relief and sleep. Rest in Him.

God, bless us with the sleep we need to heal exhaustion. Amen.

J.P. OSTERMAN

APRIL 2
LIVE AND LEARN

My stepmother liked collecting plaques with special sayings on them. One of my favorite contains Dorothy Law Nolte's poem, *Children Learn What They Live*, in which one of my favorite lines is, "If children live with acceptance, they learn to love."

Jesus always implored us to love. Love is God's Law. "You are to love Adonai your God with all your heart, all your being and all your resources" (Deuteronomy 6:5).

God also commanded, "Love your neighbor as yourself" (Leviticus 19:18). I've sometimes asked the question, how can I love my neighbor if I have trouble loving myself? Do you sometimes have trouble with self-love? It's not selfishness, self-obsession, pride, or self-absorption. What is this love?

"In your love, you led the people you redeemed. In your strength, you guided them to your holy abode" (Exodus 15:13). He designed you and me—from an eternity past, to today, and to your offspring in the future. How wondrous is our loving God! "Only *Adonai* took enough pleasure in your ancestors to love them and choose their descendants after them — yourselves — above all peoples, as he still does today" (Deuteronomy 10:15). Love redeems, sacrifices, and leads the beloved to what is good for them.

Paul tells us, "God demonstrates his own love for us in that Jesus died on our behalf while we were still sinners" (Romans 5:8). We were so separated from God, yet Jesus became a sacrificial lamb for our sins (John 3:16). That's love, when someone will die for you. "Don't see that it's better for you if one man [Jesus] dies on behalf of the people, so that the whole nation won't be destroyed" (John 11:50)? What else might *love* be? "... God is love" (1 John 4:8). Paul also tells us what love is in how Jesus manifested love. "Love is patient and kind, not jealous, not boastful, not proud, rude or selfish, not easily angered, and it keeps no record of wrongs. Love does not gloat over other people's sins but takes its delight in the truth. Love always bears up, always trusts, always hopes, always endures. Love never ends" (1 Corinthians 13:3-8). When we struggle to love, we need help. "The fruit of the Holy Spirit is love" (Galatians 5:22). We love as we remain in His word and He feeds us with love. You are His fruit. How beautiful. How glorious. He cares ... He loves you.

Father, help us go out into the world to love today.

APRIL 3
SPECIAL DEAL

Sitting in the dentist's chair, I asked the blue-clad dental assistant, "I bet you see people at their worst and at their best."

Her brown eyes rounded. "Yeah, you could say that."

Later, I check into Radiology. My mammogram had revealed an abnormality. Feeling low, I remarked to the radiologist, "I'm sure you see people at their worst times and best times."

She laughed. "Yeah, that's about right."

Doctors, teachers, mechanics, deli workers, baristas, and store clerks are only a few specialists who help and serve people at their lowest and highest points in life. Do *you* stop and realize the importance of what we do and say?

Jesus knew *everyone* at *every* stage of experience. Isaiah foretold whom Jesus would serve. A person's looks, money, or success didn't matter to Jesus. He spent time with the worst-of-the-worst and best-of-the-best. He touched and loved everyone at his or her highest and lowest peaks in life. "It was our diseases he bore, and our pains from which he suffered. Yet we regarded him as punished, stricken and afflicted by God. But he was wounded because of our crimes, crushed because of our sins. The disciplining that makes us whole fell on him, and by his bruises we are healed" (Isaiah 53:4-5).

What do you do when you believe you're at your worst? Spend time in front of the mirror? Shop? Visit the plastic surgeon? Maybe you talk to a barista or surf web sites. You might think, *If people can't see me, then they can't know me when I'm at my worst. I'll just pretend.* Really? Is what you do at your worst moment making ya feel better? When you're at your worst, who is there *for* you and *with* you?

We can know that Jesus sees us and knows us at our worst times and as we endure our hardest trials and stresses. "I want compassion. ... I didn't come to call the 'righteous, but sinners (Matthew 9:13)!" Jesus means you, at your worst. Take his comforting, loving hand. Rise up to do your best even while you're at your worst. Paul also offers words of friendship for you. "Don't throw away that courage of yours, which carries with it such a great reward. ... Having done what God wills, [that] you may receive what he has promised" (Hebrews 10:35-36). You're never at your worst when you're with Jesus, who believes you're the best 'cause you're His.

God, we want to know you, love you, and serve others. Amen.

April 4
Language App

The famous talk show host, Larry King, once said something profound about listening instead of talking. "I remind myself every morning: Nothing I say this day will teach me anything. So if I'm going to learn, I must do it by listening" (brainyquote.com).

Which do you do more of, talk or listen? I don't know about you, but I'm inclined to leave a conversation when someone keeps focusing on "I," "me," and "my."

How can we become inspired to monitor and improve our listening skills? What's the benefit?

Solomon understood the importance of listening. "Someone who is already wise will hear and learn still more" (Proverbs 1:5). Being *wise* entails listening more, and developing a hunger and thirst to learn more. Nonstop talking—conversation hogging—projects the opposite and shuts people down. The word, *wise*, means "intelligent, clever, learned, knowledgeable, enlightened, sensible, prudent, discriminating, discerning, perceptive, rational," and "logical." This word is a diamond surrounded by gold strings. From the start, Jesus was divinely wise. "On the third day, they [his parents] found him sitting in the Temple court among the rabbis, not only listening to them but questioning what they said" (Luke 2:46). When we listen to people, we learn about them so we can ask *them* more questions about *them*. We show them care and respect. Who doesn't want to be looked in the eye and listened to? Relationship building happens when we listen. People become inquisitive about us and begin asking *us* questions. "There is coming a time. In fact, it's already here, when the dead will hear the voice of the Son of God, and those who listen will come to life" (John 5:25). Jesus wants us to listen. Listening makes "the dead come to life." How? "It is written in the Prophets, 'They will all be taught by Adonai.' Everyone who listens to the Father and learns from him comes to me," Jesus says (John 6:45). Since we bonded with Jesus through the Holy Spirit, God listens to us and teaches us daily. Inspiration is, "drawing in of breath." Jesus gave us The Breath. "'As the Father sent me, I am also sending you.' Having said this, he breathed on them and said to them, "Receive the Holy Spirit'" (John 20:21). We only need to listen to Him, learn from Him, and help others know Him.

Father, help us listen, which is really love, and obey you. Amen.

APRIL 5
GALLERIES

In Florida, waddling ducks cross the roads, winded turtles stall in the streets, and graceful sand cranes peruse drivers. Today, I saw a woman rescue a turtle from the middle of the street. It was flailing and obviously upset she had interrupted its trajectory. Thank goodness she did or it would have ended up squished meat. Unfortunately, the turtle didn't recognize the helping hand, didn't see her grand scheme, the Big Picture of his salvation.

Do we grimace, complain, or retaliate passive aggressively when people try to help us even though no one can see God's Big Picture?

I recall the parable of the Good Samaritan (Luke 10:25-37). A man asks Jesus, "Who is my neighbor?" Jesus commands us to love our neighbors as ourselves. In other words, do to others as you'd have others do to you. Simply summarized, the parable is about a traveler heading to Jericho. He's robbed, stripped naked, beaten and left for dead. Bad things happen to people, right? Sometimes, we need a little help. Other times, we need a lot of help. This stranded guy needs *big* help. The road's long, barren, and desert. A priest and Temple worker see him but pass by. They know what's happened but lack compassion, right? Or, maybe they think he deserves what's happened. Or maybe they don't believe he's worth helping. We find people thinking that way today about some groups, don't we? Meanwhile, the hurting guy gets hungrier and thirstier. Now, the Jewish people at that time considered the people in Samaria outsiders. Their old leaders Omri, Ahab, and Ahab's wife Jezebel had erected temples to God and the false god Baal. Yet, in this parable, a Samaritan stops to help. He preps and bandages the stranded man's wounds. He puts the guy on *his* donkey. The Samaritan walks the rest of the way to Jericho. He pays for his room and board and tells the innkeeper to charge all the expenses to *his* account. Wow, what's the Big Picture? God's love, help, and care for you and me. Imagine this world if *each* person could do as Jesus commands. "Of these three, which one seems to you to have become the 'neighbor' of the man who fell among robbers? He answered, 'The one who showed mercy toward him.' Jesus said to him, You go and do as he did (Luke 10:36-37). If we can do *one* helpful thing, a ripple effect will add to God's Big Picture for the world. We just might not see it.

Lord, help us realize our importance in peoples' lives. Amen.

APRIL 6
A NEW ID

I attended another book fair where I had a table in front of the entryway. I set up all my books, business cards, a banner, and brochures. You get the picture. I was determined to sell, sell, sell! When people entered the conference room and turned left, I'd call: "Hi--hello!" When they'd veer right, I beckoned, "Hi! Do *I* have a book for you!"

He or she would *generally* begin walking my way.

"You want to take a trip to Mars?" I asked, holding up my novel *Cosmic Rift*. I can read people's interest as their eyes squinted with a "no" expression, or their shoulders rose in apprehension. "How about short stories?" I'd quickly scooped up my new compendium and fanned the pages. "I just published this book, *Commuter Collection*. It contains most of my short stories—some award winning—for the past thirty years." Thus I'd try keeping their attention by telling little blurbs about each of my books, a few times even reading paragraph one. Many times, they'd walk away with my business card, brochure, or bookmark. No sales. No interest many other times. You've experienced the same in some area of your life, surely. What to do?

Another author at another table commented, "You're the only one calling people in and to your table." Yes, I was energetic, eager, focused on their eyes, and always positive even when they left my table. Surprise though when a few returned and bought a book.

Recall go-getter Peter? On the Sea of Galilee, he spots Jesus walking on water. "Jesus spoke unto them, saying, 'Be of good cheer. It is I. Be not afraid.' And Peter answered Him and said, 'Lord, if it be Thou, bid me come unto Thee on the water.' And He said, 'Come.' And when Peter had come down out of the boat, he walked on the water to go to Jesus" (Matthew 14:27-29).

Would you have had such a faith to leave the safety of your situation and walk on water? Yet Peter's most triumphant moment with our Lord is when Jesus tells him how expansive the Kingdom of Heaven will be under his direction. "Thou art Peter, and upon this rock I will build My church. The gates of hell shall not prevail against it" (Matthew 16:18). Sisters and Brothers, we are bricks in Peter's rock. Your gifts and talents can build Christ's church. You are needed, in words and deeds. Be inspired through Jesus

Jesus, help me be an encouraging difference for you. Amen.

APRIL 7
WHIPLASHES

Have you ever seen a fish fight to swim off a fishing line? Deep below the surface, the fish is circling madly through the dark water. It's tugging hard on the line to struggle free. The tension on the pole is taut while the catcher pulls hard to reel in the prey.

Sitting in my backyard and praying today, I heard a light helicopter noise—no, humming. Looking up, I saw a large dragonfly trapped in a spider's web. I had seen the web a few days ago in the pine trees beyond the fence, but I never suspected a spider could be so gargantuan to weave an eight-foot-long web. The dragonfly was no spider's match. Flying frantically in circles to free itself, it altered the web into one, long, thick white string. Could *I* set it free? My stomach ached as the dragonfly gyrated, stopped, and then dropped limp, dangling in the air. I ran to the garage, grabbed my telescoping pruner, ran back to Dragonfly, leaped into the air, and cut Dragonfly free. It was like playing tetherball. Then, *wham*. Dragonfly hit the ground. I didn't solve the problem. The web had morphed into a straightjacket on the shiny green insect. For seconds, as I contemplated how to help, we stared each other down—me gazing into Dragonfly's bulbous eyes—and it fighting for freedom. Then I yanked the white thick fuzzy string ... *zzzz*, off Dragonfly flew into the preserve. I hope Dragonfly's all right now and not some bird or lizard's dinner. At least I managed to unravel its straightjacket and give Dragonfly another chance at life.

We all need more chances, right? Do you find yourself needing *more* chances? I need multiple chances.

God frees us. He plucks out our transgressions to give us *innumerable* chances for a relationship with Him. "Blessed are those whose transgressions are forgiven, whose sins are covered over" (Romans 4:7). God forgives and forgets our sins. "I have forgiven, as you have asked" (Numbers 14:20)." Until we die, He will. Are you afraid your sin is too great for God to forgive you? No, Brothers and Sisters. Just as Dragonfly's rope was thick and his weak body inching upward to the spider's fangs, our sins are never too heavy for God. "For this is my blood, which ratifies the New Covenant, my blood shed on behalf of many, so that they may have their sins forgiven" (Matthew 26:28). *All* sins He plucks to oblivion. You're free.

Thank you Lord for forgiving all my sins. Amen.

APRIL 8
TAKE STEPS

If God appeared in front of you and asked, "You get *one* miracle, so what do you want?"

Money is out.

Never once did Jesus give someone money outta thin air. Remember His declaration about money? "As soon as he could convert his share into cash, the younger son left home and went off to a distant country, where he squandered his money in reckless living" (Luke 15:13). That's the Prodigal Son, who had so much money and desires that he went on a mass spending spree. Then Jesus gave us another warning. "You can't be a slave to both God and money" (Matthew 6:24, Luke 16:13). Why would a miracle of money be like drinking poison? Paul tells Timothy: "The love of money is a root of all the evils. Because of this craving, some people have wandered away from the faith and pierced themselves to the heart with many pains" (1Timothy 6:10). I guess if you need a "miracle" for money, you might have a distortion of desire, craving, or love. Jesus didn't want to change the world with money, right?

God instigated miracles to persuade people in high places to change. God tells Moses, "When Pharaoh says to you, 'Perform a miracle,' tell Aharon to take his staff and throw it down in front of Pharaoh, so that it can become a snake" (Exodus 7:9). One of God's names is Adonai Nissi. "Moshe built an altar, called it Adonai Nissi [*Adonai* is my banner/miracle]" (Exodus 17:15). Who ultimately performs miracles? "Adonai, God! You gave signs and performed miracles in the land of Egypt which continue to this day, also in Isra'el and among other people; thus you made yourself the reputation you have today (Jeremiah 32:17-20). Miracles are hard to come by, yet Jesus had compassion on desperate people like Nicodemus. "This man came to Yeshua by night and said to him, 'Rabbi, we know it is from God that you have come as a teacher. No one can do these miracles you perform unless God is with him' " (John 3:2). Ultimately, John tells us the vastness of Jesus capabilities. "There are also many other things Yeshua did ... I don't think the whole world could contain the books that would have to be written" (John 21:25). Wow, what John must have seen. Hold onto John's belief Let faith take you to Jesus and trust He's working in your life.

Lord God, help us know you today as never before. Amen.

APRIL 9
NUCLEAR DEAL

Have you ever wondered what goes on behind closed doors? What's going on in secret with you?

I heard several quotes about closed doors and expanded them into one: Sometimes, the strongest people are the ones who smile through their pain, cry alone behind closed doors, and fight their battles in solitude. That's pretty lone wolfish, wouldn't you say? To always force a smile instead of crying now-and-then, to have no one to whom you can tell your difficulties and hardships, and to lack a friend or confidant. The great news? We are *not*--ever--alone. God never lets us sit and cry in the dark. He knows everything we do, and what is done to us, in secret. You could be in a sub at the Mariana Trench, or exploring Valles Marineris on Mars, or passing Pluto. We have God, El Roi, the God who Sees.

Hagar gave God that name in Genesis 16:13, after she ran away from Abraham and Sarah to forge her way through the desert to escape a life of servitude. To be a concubine for Abraham and then successfully turn up pregnant with his *first* son, Hagar must have felt the full weight of Sarah's jealous wrath. She also had to have felt used, lonely, and gossiped about. She must have experienced abject abandonment, felt uncared for, and unrecognized in her enslaving situation. However, God noticed. Out there in that dry desert sand, The Angel of God appears to her. His light must have been overwhelming. He tells Hagar she will have a son, and directs her to name her child, "Ishmael [God pays attention] because *Adonai* has paid attention to your misery" (Genesis 16:11). What a relief Hagar must have felt. God cares ... God *sees* the world through my eyes. Walking back home, Hagar couldn't believe God hadn't struck her dead. "Have I really seen the One who sees me [and stayed alive]" (16:13)? Not once does God or one of His angels appear to us humans and they remain the same. Hagar changed. God tells her, "*Adonai* has paid attention to your misery." In other words, God has been watching *everything*. Then He tells her the best news. "I will greatly increase your descendants; there will be so many that it will be impossible to count them" (16:10). Sometimes, we need a God shot to go on with the day. "The eyes of the Lord are in every place, watching the evil and the good" (Proverbs 15:3). He sees.

Father God, wrap us now in your tender arms. Amen.

April 10
Service Beyond Local

Have you ever swatted a piñata? Did little candies, trinkets, or tiny toys rain down on you?

Today, I smashed open a God piñata.

For the past several weeks, I've been spending time outside in prayer. Recalling helpful scriptures, I've been praying to Him about my teeth. The extraction appointments I've had with a new dentist has been morphing into tornado size proportions. I wrote my concerns down and offered them up as prayers at my church *and* Bible study. Trying to forget a pending life-changing procedure isn't easy. I need several upper teeth pulled. The last time I'd seen myself without those vital choppers was in a picture of me at six months old. Sometimes, we have pity parties, and then we begin taking on projects, shopping, or having wine—*whatever* to keep our minds occupied so we don't have to think about radically changing. I recently met a woman who had a mastectomy, and another woman who is suffering with Irritable Bowel Syndrome, and another who's trying *everything* to quit smoking. Then, when I believe I might not stop crying as Extraction Day approaches, I see an old man with his legs amputated above his knees. He's pushing a cart full of groceries while driving his wheelchair. And I'm complaining about *teeth*?

Extraction Day is here. The blue dentist chair is raised high with sealed instruments in a silver tray. One bit of advice: Do *not* look at the Novocain vials. Sitting down, shaking and shuddering, I open my hands. *God, you are El Roi, the God who Sees. Help me, please.*

There comes a time when relatives need to leave the pre-op room, and you're alone, staring into that blinding surgeon's light, and the operation is—*tick, tick*—seconds away. Sometimes, God finds us at the end of ourselves. "Before they call, I will answer. While they are still speaking, I will hear" (Isaiah 65:24). He knows where we're at. Before we even pray, and as the doctors are preparing to speak to us while perusing our charts, God's wth us. "The ways of man are before the eyes of the Lord, and He ponders all his paths" (Proverbs 5:21). Guess what? The dentist hummed the Christian song, *10000 Reasons (Bless the Lord)* the entire time he was preparing my teeth and extracting them. God piñata busting blessings. My fears evaporated!

Father, thank you for your mercies that stop us from shaking and shuddering as we trust in you. Amen.

APRIL 11
WHO YA GONNA CALL?

"I just can't do this anymore!"

Have you ever said that? Given up? Or do you want to quit a project, job, or relationship?

Our son has a degenerative eye condition. Today we had another attempt at the ophthalmologist's office to fit him with very expensive, corrective contact lenses. Now, this was the second time we'd been working with him on this goal so he could insert and take out the lenses on his own. Failure.

"I can't do it anymore," Andrew kept saying.

The doctor and two assistants encouraged him. "Yes you can."

I tried holding his upper lids open, and we kept directing him to keep both eyes open and just ... yes ... just lift the contact lens a little higher ... and keep both eyes open ... now, focus....

Andrew kept missing his corneas. Looking up, looking down, or blinking kept the contacts from positioning correctly. There's nothing like a deep breath, in between tries, that will help you when you want to quit trying something and give up.

I kept praying, and asking God for help. "Jesus, you are radiance of the *Sh'khinah*, the expression of God and you uphold everything that exists by your powerful word" (Hebrews 1:3). *Shekhinah* means *dwelling* or *settling*. Are you settled in Him?

I realized God was there with all of us in these difficult, hard, and frustrating moments. I kept appreciating the doctor's time, and the time she had set aside for Andrew in which she could have made much more money servicing other patients. Humility and gratitude come when we are at our desperate moments sometimes, and feeling quite powerless to change other people. After all, I couldn't *make* my son insert his contacts in the manner in which everyone was instructing him. What to do when you're taking that driver's test, LSAT, SAT, or proficiency test for the umpteenth time? When you want to quit?

"The Lord said, I am watching, and I will certainly carry out all my plans" (Jeremiah 1:12). Almonds taste bitter at first, but with age they sweeten. God has a plan for us; so as we work to bring our goals to fruition, let us keep trying. "Everything in the heavens and on earth is yours, O Lord," David says. Show up and try again.

Holy Spirit, give us a spirit of patience and endurance. Amen.

APRIL 12
STRAIGHT UP

Years and years ago, when I was attending church regularly, and singing in a front-and-center worship team and choir, I wouldn't wear *anything* I didn't buy at Neiman Marcus or Macy's. I had to maintain a look, you see, and invoke a persona to impress people.

However, please don't be so hard on me, because we all at times suffer from *Selfi-mania*.

Could the condition be affecting you?

It's a term I coined for: being so into *me* and tryin' to impress *you* with my false mask that I forget the truth about how God sees me. I had to have perfect teeth, be a size 8, and memorize the songs perfectly. I had to perform, had to ... *fizzzzzle* ... *crash*.

Have you ever asked yourself the question, What if I *can't* live up to someone else's high expectations? Maybe you're working hard to get promoted, or trying to impress people so they'll include you in their club, team sport, or association. The intensity to perform is like a pressure cooker *hissing* and rocking on its valve.

What is the truth we need so we can float back down to reality, and become genuine in spite of trying so hard and stressing over becoming recognized and super human? Brothers and Sisters, God designed *truth* as a stress-release valve so we can see ourselves through His eyes and take comfort in His approval.

Are you in need of relief? His relief? God is rest and relief.

Jesus knows. He prayed to His Father, also our Father, so we can have peace and be ourselves in a demanding world where other people expect us to achieve and perform. "I will ask the Father, and he will give you another comforting Counselor like me, the Spirit of Truth, to be with you forever. ... You know him, because he is staying with you and will be united with you" (John 14:16-17). Where is our comforting Counselor who is *always* with us and united with us? "Identify with ... the Spirit of God [who] is living inside you" (Romans 8:9). The Holy Spirit, the Spirit of God, is our helper, and nothing can ever separate us from His love (Romans 8:38-39). God's Spirit is "living in you" (Romans 8:11). *Living* means: *in actual existence, in use, flowing freely, as in water*, and, *the means of maintaining life*. With God, Jesus, and the Holy Spirit living within us, we no longer need to pretend to be someone we're not. He—*He*—loves us.

Father, I need you, *oh*, I need you, every moment. Amen.

APRIL 13
CALL FOR CHANGES

Crawling on the tables and countertops—and scuttling in jagged lines across the floor—ants just won't leave no matter how diligently I've been spraying outside and inside. I've been crushing 'em, Clorox wiping 'em, and sanitizing their pathways. Nothing works. Now, I think they've tasted my arms and are considering me for a treat. I can't settle down *anywhere* without seeing at least one scout ant. I have a case of the creepy crawlies. Or, maybe it's just my imagination making me examine my ankles now and then.

Have you ever had something, or someone, make *your* house *their* home? Getting rid of the unwanted is hard, and a struggle.

Bad habits are just as cruel. I don't know one person who doesn't have one, and who can just command the nasty intruder to leave, and then *bam*, the habit's gone. Have you ever noticed that when you have a problem, you begin asking people whether they've ever experienced the same situation? Bad habits ... they're relentless. They like to sneak up on me, like resilient ants marching in a line of permanency into my life. They overthrow my common sense, and become part of my personality as I start lubricating my difficulties and hardships with their easier softer ways.

Ah, the Lord just convicted me here. He's the little voice in the Denial Section of my busy mind. He's calling my bad habit what it really is: sin. Sin's got me. Sin is like the unwanted ants I'm working so hard to track down until I can exterminate every last one.

But how? Crying and self-chastising does not eradicate a sin.

The first source is God's word. He is your help today as well. Since we're no longer of the world, we have another place to search for help and advice in our struggles against bad habits and sin. Immediately, I open up to Peter. "He [Jesus] himself bore our sins in his body on the stake, so that we might die to sins and live for righteousness—by his wounds you were healed" (1 Peter 2:24). Meditating on Jesus and his suffering on the cross, we know what He did to help you and me as we confess our sins and habits. Jesus is our Changer, and He eliminates habits, because if a habit has infiltrated far into our minds and bodies, there's nothing we alone can do to stop it. By his wounds, we are healed. He is the Divine Power, penetrating healing light into our afflictions.

Lord, help us. We *on our own* cannot stop our habits. Amen.

APRIL 14
GIFTS FROM GOD

There are two Bible characters with unusual names and a history. One is Mephibosheth. As Saul's son, Mephibosheth was hung with six other of Saul's descendants because they had planned to exterminate all the Gibeonites, favored by God (2 Samuel 21). The Gibeonites leave all seven of them hanging on top of a large hill—for everyone and God to see. They become bird and animal food in retribution for a mass murder under their ancestor Saul. In secret, Mephibosheth's mother, Rizpah, protects their dead bodies from that horrible desecration. "Rizpah daughter of Aiah took sackcloth and spread it out for herself on a rock. From the beginning of the harvest till the rain poured down from the heavens on the bodies, she did not let the birds touch them by day or the wild animals by night" (2 Samuel 21:10). We're talking maybe weeks that Rizpah is out there in the wilderness, with a sackcloth for her residence of repentance, swiping at birds and beating back wild animals with sticks, stones, and branches. She's determined to protect the bodies of her children and relatives from desecration and desiccation. Seeing Rizpah's bravery, sorrow, and strength, David has compassion on her and buries them. Meanwhile, he's also formed a protective relationship with Saul's grandson Mephibosheth, who is the son of David's dead friend and ally Jonathan. This Mephibosheth was crippled in a terrible fall when he was five and is "lame" (2 Samuel 9). David wants to reward *any* relative of Jonathan's—the man who could have fought against him to be King of Israel when Saul went berserk. He didn't. He trusted God's choice for the kingship of His people.

Do you see God's compassion at work here? God's mercies are extending through his Holy Spirit in every area of your life today. I see another name for our awesome Divine Lord of the Universe: Jehovah Rachum, The Lord of Compassion. "If he cries out to me, I will listen; because I am compassionate" (Exodus 34:6; Exodus 22:26-27). God repeatedly tells us this everlasting truth: "*Adonai* descended in the cloud, stood with him [Moses] ... passed before him and proclaimed: '*YUD-HEH-VAV-HEH*!!! *Yud-Heh-Vav-Heh* [*Adonai*] is God, merciful and compassionate'" (Exodus 34:5-6). When you take a stand, He is with you.

Father God, thank you for not casting us aside in our sinful moments when we are lost and need you the most. Amen.

APRIL 15
DESTINATION

Have you ever asked the question: How am I *ever* going to make it to my destination? Forage through the airport chaos and wait in long lingering lines to endure the security scrutiny and pat downs? Then at my destination, pinpoint the rental car booth? Then drive into a strange dark area while squinting at the street signs to locate the hotel/motel? Then I need to make it through the meeting, reunion, funeral, or convention.

How will I ever?

Whether planned or not, we have days like today, Tax Day, when ya just gotta get through the day, in baby steps, go through the motions and pay your dues. Paul says about taxes: "This is also why you pay taxes. The authorities are God's public officials, constantly attending to these duties" (Romans 13:6). He gives us a coping mechanism for the things in life that you and I must trudge through until the next time when we're faced with the *next* big thing and we ask, "How we I ever make it through?"

Take a second, and breathe. Recall Joseph? His brothers throw him into a well. He's sold to Egyptian merchants and then bought by Pharaoh's Captain of the Guard, Potiphar. In a day, lavished Joseph changes from being the apple of his father Isaac's eyes to poverty, disorientation, and abandonment. Ever had the rug pulled out from under you? Joseph sure did. Yet, in that foreign land of no escape and enforced slavery, God is with Joseph when he cries, "Adonai, how will I *ever* make it through this and get my life back?!"

God answers his prayers. "*Adonai* was with Yosef, and he became wealthy while he was in the household of his master the Egyptian. His master saw how *Adonai* was with him, that *Adonai* prospered everything he did" (Genesis 39:2-6). Several times, people notice Joseph's tight bond with God and his unwavering obedience to do the right thing. He couldn't have gone far in Potiphar's place if he had been a thief, adulterer, liar or hypocrite. God blesses Potiphar's entire household. Just when Joseph believes all is well in his new surroundings, and that he can make a comfortable life managing Potiphar's estate, *wham*. He's confronted with another "how will I ever" yet God stands with him. In our messes, God saves us, reeling us in, to Himself.

Father, please guide us to the right choices for you. Amen.

April 16
Expertise and Collaboration

I heard of a new job title today. A Penetration Tester is a computer hacker who purposely works to infiltrate companies' software for threats. They use legal and illegal means to put code dents into a company's website so that employees and executives can quickly take countermeasures and save their software, hardware, and portable devices from corruption. After all, no one likes his or her information stolen or sold. It's a vulnerable feeling to know you've been victimized that way. To *always* live in "protective mode" for fear of becoming a target or having your identity stolen appears to be the new normal way of living. It's so frustrating, as if we don't already have enough scenarios where we—especially women—have to look over our shoulders and behind shrubbery after dark, or—as a man—trying to be always essential, needed and irreplaceable on the job. Boundaries exist everywhere, from interpersonal relationships to the systems we work on, communicate into, and link together through our "Location Settings."

Are you aware of your boundaries?

Sometimes I can be an *emotional* Penetration Tester, and I'm *not* a hacker. Even though I'm not aware of what I'm doing, I might cause an argument or say something that irritates someone. I accidentally push a boundary, and then, the person retaliates. This morning while he had the car in park at a drive-through window, my husband was app pecking. Then he had to leave immediately so the next customer could approach the window. He put the car in reverse. "Ah!" I squeaked and jumped. I had embarrassed him in front of the clerk. Have you ever said something you didn't mean to say, and penetrated someone's wall of comfort, or challenged their comfort zone?

"Now what can I do to make things right?" you might ask.

Jesus's disciple Peter said, "Keep loving each other actively because love covers many sins" (1 Peter 4:7). Shouting, screaming, or seeking revenge are not loving. They penetrate to our cores and damage.

There's also another saying: Watch what you say because you can't take it back, so better not say anything at all. Sometimes, it's hard to keep your lips closed and do the *loving* thing. After a minute, things between us were back to normal. Love heals.

Holy Spirit, we need a cool-calm mind in heated times. Amen.

APRIL 17
FRESH BLOOMS AND SPRING PLANTS

I saw a t-shirt today, sporting the saying: Bloom where you're planted. It's an uplifting encouragement.

We all have talents, gifts, and strengths. We are vital in this world. What we do matters.

Bloom. It sounds like *boom*, right? What a powerful positive word. I think of my granddaughter, Rachel, who daily makes little developmental strides. She's blooming. And there are people at my church who work tirelessly to advance the youth and help distressed and needy people. They are always blooming. If they could change into greenery, I couldn't begin to imagine their splendor.

What's blooming in your life today … or lately … or tomorrow?

The action-oriented word, *bloom*, means, *to be in flower, blossom, open*, and *mature*. A few days ago I bought a burp-less cucumber plant in a biodegradable pot. I guess the soil is genetically designed to fend off insects? I transplanted it into a raised planter in my backyard. Every day I peek at the stalks that look like green toothpicks with little pairs of green leaves at the top. The little sprouts shoot up an inch a day. Amazing, huh?

Don't you wish everything you did could turn out that way? Blooming into an explosion of brilliance? I think of my writing, because today my husband finally discovered a rejection letter for one of my favorite short stories. "The Mons Genius," one of my sci-fi stories has *not* bloomed but tanked.

However, as a Christian, writing this devotional, I am daily growing in love for our God, Jesus, and the Holy Spirit. They are at work in me to help you, and me, on our journeys through this complicated and chaotic world. I'm reminded of the Parable of the Sower. The story is in three of the four Gospels: Matthew 13, Mark 4, and Luke 8. God telling us this story is important to our growth as Christians. How? The seeds that fall into rich soil produce grain a hundred, or sixty, or thirty times as much as had been sown (Matthew 13:8). Find your niche, and bloom. Guess what? That niche might be a total surprise in your life, as this book is to be, enriching me, and hopefully helping you. You have been given a secret, "of the Kingdom of Heaven" (Matthew 13:11). Dig your roots deep. Grow … bloom.

Lord, help us advance you in this world. Amen.

April 18
Drop in the Bucket

The state of California has been in the middle of a severe drought, and its 38.8 million residents have been paying a heavy price while trying to conserve. On April 1, Governor Jerry Brown did a little arm twisting, issuing a statewide mandate to cut water use 25%. However, California agriculture, sometimes called the "Bread Basket" of America, gulps down 80% of the water supply, so Brown's being a little lenient on farmers. Have you seen current photos of places that used to brim over with water? The land looks like a flat cracked tar bed, as the dirt exhales its last breaths.

Are you in a drought? Are you suffering from a dry spell in a relationship or a career?

It happens, drought and dryness in our lives that leave us thirsting for something more to sooth an inner parchment. Dissatisfaction and boredom spread. You just want to plop down on the couch and munch on any junk food you can grab. Or, just sleep.

"Wait—don't," I said to myself. What do we do when a dry spell strikes, and we feel like blowing desert heat is baking our inner worlds? "Trouble produces endurance, endurance produces character, and character produces hope," Paul says (Romans 5:3-4).

I recall one bad drought that struck Israel after people turned away from God to worship false gods. That's not what we've done though to deserve *our* droughts, right? After all, we don't have control over others who might be the causes of our droughts. Someone fires us, or calls off a relationship, or gets angry and refuses to speak to us. Droughts come in all sorts of forms, not always our fault. Yet we can turn to Him. He has the answers. He will relieve our emptiness and fill us with spiritual fruit. "Can any make it rain? Can the skies, of themselves, send showers? Aren't you the one, *Adonai*, our God? Don't we look to you? For you do all these things" (Jeremiah 14:22). God relieves our suffering through the Holy Spirit who moves to act through others to help us in our times of difficulties and struggles, or just when things aren't going the way we expected. Then, drought sets in. Remember the Good Samaritan in Luke 10 that sees a half-dead man on the road? "He was moved with compassion," and helped him. In our dry spells, we can also turn to believers for help, comfort and encouragement.

Lord, help us confide in others about our feelings. Amen.

APRIL 19
FOR YOUR HEALTH

Sometimes, during the middle of working in the yard, vacuuming, watching TV, or observing my husband and son, I stop. A deep anxiety I've been calling, the Rumble of Life's Brevity, shoots through me in mini-shocks. It's my mind shuffling through how quickly the days are passing, how yesterday is still lingering and tingling on my skin, and who in my family has died and is still alive. Next week, I'll leave to fly north to help lay my aunt to rest. The Rumble is more frequent now. *I* can't stop it. Have you ever stood still to feel Time just waft over you?

It's a theme we encounter every day on TV shows. In an episode of *The Middle* ("Food Courting," S6 Ep 20), the father takes his son out for a beer to transition him—a rite of passage—from boyhood to manhood's sought-after 21. The father has a revelation. It was yesterday that I was sitting in your seat ... 21. Now, feel the Rumble of Life's Brevity. Can reality be anxiety filled? You bet. "People, even rich ones, will live only briefly. Then, like animals, they will die" (Psalm 49:13). But wait. The Rumble is only an illusion.

I can't imagine anyone not believing in God, and praying, and holding onto Him in the penetrating moments when the rumble of how short life is, spreads over them like cold air. It's like lying down in the snow. However, we're not innocent laughing children making "Snow Angels" waving our arms and legs in the flakey ecstasy of a carefree existence. Even though things weren't all that good growing up for me, I remember giggling. Do you?

In Ecclesiastes, Solomon reminds us how we like to keep busy so we can't feel time shifting and sifting. "I wisely applied myself to seek out and investigate everything done under heaven. What a bothersome task God has given humanity to keep us occupied" (1:13). Is that all we're doing? Just keeping ourselves occupied?

I encounter Jesus in the tingling rumble that moves through my temporal body. "The message about the execution-stake is the power of God," Paul tells us (1 Corinthians 1:18). The power of God resurrected our Savior Jesus. He conquered death, giving us a glimpse into the glory we will one day have with him. "The dead will be raised to live forever, and we too will be changed" (1 Corinthians 15:52). Let us live out our purpose today, beyond the Rumble.

Father, we long to see you, but first, know your will. Amen.

APRIL 20
NOT CHANCE

Recall those nights when you were a child, when the nightlight was on but you wanted to check under your bed for living things like ghosts or monster? The closet door was closed, but it still loomed large, and opening? Sometimes, I recall holding my pillow, clutching my covers, and whimpering. Then my aunt would come in and tell me that my guardian angel was standing next to my bed and protecting me. Do you experience one of those nights now, when worry, anxiety or fear are monsters about to pounce on you? "You granted me life and grace. Your careful attention preserved my spirit" (Job 10:12). Remember, God cares.

Perhaps, if we can deconstruct these destructive moments that make our hair turn gray, God will help us *re*construct those moments into pulverized dust so we find *peace*, not fear. Redefine those monsters, and call them out for what they are. Their new definitions will relieve the sting and allow us to let go of the hold they previously had on us and the damage they've inflicted on our lives. In the Complete Jewish Bible, the word, "worry," most often is action-oriented, appears 22 times, and means, *"to give way to anxiety or unease; allow one's mind to dwell on difficulty or troubles."* Jesus says about worrying: "Don't worry about your life. ... Can any of you by worrying add a single hour to his life (Matthew 6:25-34)? Worry appears to be the stepping stone to anxiety. Jesus implies that "being worried" might take minutes off your lifespan. Anxiety might be worse. Psychologists have names for anxiety when it impedes our social, emotional, and physical well-being: Anxiety Disorder and Panic Disorder. In the Bible, "anxiety" appears 7 times. People who are anxious react without thinking. In Joshua 22, several tribal descendants breach a boundary and build an altar to God. Trouble ensues. Fear can be the worse, immobilizing a person. "Fear" appears 345 times, it can be a good thing or a bad thing. "This place is fearsome," Jacob says in Genesis 28:17 after he wrestles with the angel. Then fear can be a barrier. "There is no fear in love. Love that has achieved its goal gets rid of fear" (1 John 4:18). Jesus gave us the solution to our anxiety and fear: "Don't be anxious. ... Rather, seek his Kingdom. ... Have no fear" (Luke 12:29-32). Let us now truly breathe, and live in Jesus our God. No fear.

Holy Spirit, give us the gift of complete faith in you. Amen.

APRIL 21
MONOPOLY

You've played Monopoly at some time, right? Do you recall keeping an eye on your opponents throughout the game, sizing them up, trying to figure out their next moves? That's part of the excitement. If we could predict another person's next move, the anticipation and fun would be gone. Except for those people who like winning at all cost and find ways to win. That's called cheating, right? Can we cheat at life?

It's a heart issue. Sometimes we become so caught up in playing games with people that we might as well walk around the world wearing a rubber suit and painted face. Once a week, I meet with people with whom I've been sharing more about myself than "how's the weather" and "you look nice." We're divulging personal information that's uncomfortable to share, for example, troubles we're experiencing with our families, bosses, and neighbors. Just when I believed I was beginning to know one person well and could trust her, *bam*, something I said in confidence returned to me, hurting me. We can never see a person's heart. We cannot peer into souls to know the other person's motives, intentions, or perceptions. We don masks, always, that function as barriers and impenetrable boundaries, shielding us in Skin Armor. We're not transparent and clean in our dealings with people. Most times, we're not even clean with ourselves. We cheat. Then, we are cheated, however. The solution?

In the Old Testament, the word, *clean*, appears 166 times. God likes *clean*: clean meat for sacrifices, clean food, clean water, clean clothes, and clean skin (Leviticus). *Clean* means: *free from dirt, marks, or stains; morally uncontaminated; pure; innocent.* Are we all of those today? I have good food and water, and unstained clothes and unsoiled hands. Yet inside, I do have a few sinful thoughts that I don't tell tell anyone. David illuminates this tendency to mask our inner worlds when he writes the Psalms in prayerful contemplation to God. "Who can discern unintentional sins? Cleanse me from hidden faults" (19:13). David knows that life is a heart issue not a ritual washing away of outer stains. "Create in me a clean heart, God. Renew in me a resolute spirit" (Psalm 51:12). Maybe we can be a bit more transparent to our fellow Christians today after confiding our inner worlds to God. He already knows them, but loves to hear us.

Father, we long to be honest with you in our prayers. Amen.

April 22
Fasten Your Seatbelts

Have you ever been at high altitude and then, *shake jolt*, turbulence strikes the plane at 33,000 feet? Everyone gasps and clutches their armrests. Then, *ding*.

"Ladies and Gentlemen," the pilot begins, "due to some minor air turbulence, I've turned on the, *fasten your seatbelt* sign. So please return to your seats if you're up and about in the cabin and fasten your seatbelts. For those of you seated, please remain in your seats, with your seatbelts fastened. Thank you."

It makes you wonder, what's coming next? What can possibly go wrong next? If that's your mode of operation today, God can take control of your day. Put Him on autopilot. How?

At times, we're surprised, or downright shocked when turbulence rocks our worlds as it often does when a plane encounters unstable currents. What can we do besides holding onto the first thing we can grab, and panicking? Fear is a God-given instinct that engages our fight or flight mechanism in turbulent situations. However, we also have more resources we can grab hold of when life's unsuspecting situations jolt our lives and rattle our nerves.

In the Book of Daniel, King Nebuchadnezzar of Babylon has a turbulent and troubling dream. When his wise men (magicians, astrologers, enchanters, and astrologers) can't interpret his dream, he orders their execution. Even the King's captive wise men, like Jewish Daniel. I don't know who is more turbulence-affected here, the King or these wise men running for their lives like stepped on ants. Daniel takes action. He approaches the King and asks for more time. Then he runs to his friends, and they pray for God's mercy and guidance. That night, Daniel has a dream. "God opens people's ears and seals the matter with a warning, to turn a person away from his action and protect a man from pride" (Job 33:15-18). God gives Daniel the interpretation of the King's dream, and Daniel praises God for saving *all* their lives. "Praise be to the name of God for ever and ever. Wisdom and power are his" (Daniel 2:20). God reveals mysteries and provides solutions (Daniel 2:27). Daniel could have run, but he takes God's countermeasures. He turns to his brothers in the faith for help, and they call on perfect God who holds every answer to every problem. Let us do the same when turbulence strikes our lives.

Lord, we need your presence in every waking second. Amen.

APRIL 23
THIS COUPON GOOD FOR ...

I'm staying with my cousin John as our aunt is a few days away from being interred alongside her husband's remains.

Ticking time is in slow-motion one hour, but fast-fleeting other hours. John and I are also catching up on family news, shopping, and meeting and his friends. John, my brother Tom, and I are bloodline close, almost brother and sister related, because my dad and mom met at his parents' wedding. Now, the closeness is paying off for John and me as we move out of our comfort zones into vulnerable territories to accommodate each other and help each other prepare for our Aunt Mary's services. We're trying! You've been there, right? When you needed someone's help because you might not have enough money or resources to do it all alone?

I pause now, tearfully, and submerge myself in God's word. "Ever since the creation of the universe his [God's] invisible qualities—both his eternal power and his divine nature—have been clearly seen, because they can be understood from what he has made" (Romans 1:20). Our Lord God, Heavenly King, Father Almighty, powerful Creator, Omnipresent Master, loving Protector, and all Seeing Father created *everything*. He designed and created you and me, every star, the seas, every atom, and Sequoia trees. He is our help and vital resource, spiritually feeding us. Know those truths in the depths of your soul today. "Help" appears in the Bible 249 times. It means, *assistance, aid, support, succor, advice, guidance*; and, *appeal for urgent assistance*. I kneel, clasp my fingers together, and pray. "Lord, blessed Light, please give me wisdom in speaking and courage as I walk in unfamiliar places, interact with people I haven't seen in years, and pay my last respects to my loving aunt. I'll miss her until I see her again with you. I need you, Father. Help me. Amen."

John and I have been shopping and rearranging spaces for me to put my suitcase, sleep, and set up my laptop at his farm house in Three Oaks, Michigan. We've been barbequing and searching for a torch to light the ten-year-old charcoal he's been stockpiling, along with fixing a few things. John's five cats won't come near me. They look at me with those glassy wide eyes, stand still—startled—and then run like ... well frightened and confused cats. God never runs. Extend your hands, and feel his Holy Spirit Breath, inspiration.

Lord, we meet you everywhere. Amen.

APRIL 24
CAFFEINATED

My cousin John needs to fix his truck so we can arrive safely at our aunt's memorial. He's been securing the bumper while I thread him the galvanized wire into two holes he drilled through his fender. He suddenly stops. "Oh, I forgot. I need oil for the differential."

"Where's the oil?" I ask. "I can get it."

"In one o' the barns," he gestures in the direction of a large shed, a few coops, and several self-erected huts. Now, you don't want to go into one those places alone. Are there spaces you won't enter alone? God is with you.

We drop everything and walk through a shed stuffed with jagged metals and broken machinery. John finds the oil, and we return to "fixin' things." Ten minutes later, he stops *again* with a puzzled expression. I'm trying not to feel scattered, but he's the inventive type who can easily conjure up quick fixes to a problem in a split second. He's learned to survive that way because he manages his farm all alone. Furthermore, repair technicians charge minimum fees to diagnose a problem. John can't afford that. So before his parents died, pretty much the entire McCarten side of our family taught John how to think fast on his feet and *MacGyver* through tough problems. What are the problems you need to resolve fast? God is resolving them for you. "Have no fear, little flock, for your Father has resolved to give you the Kingdom" (Luke 12:32)!

You might recall the TV show, *MacGyver*. He's a trouble-shooting scientist who uses his encyclopedic knowledge to solve complex problems with every day materials. That's my cousin John. Although his life's never being threatened, he saves *everything* for fear he, "Might one day run out and need what he's collected." At his core, he really *is* afraid for his life.

Are you holding onto anything as if you might run out one day?

Moses confronted Pharaoh about one of the worst hoarding nightmare of all: amassing people for slave labor. He just wouldn't let the Israelites go. Yet he was no match for God who orders through Moses, "Let my people go, so that they can worship me" (Exodus 9:2). God tells him that nine times, giving Pharaoh nine opportunities to surrender. We can surrender too ... just stop when we feel anxious about what might happen in the future, and pray.

Lord, we always need to put our survival in *your* hands. Amen.

APRIL 25
THE LORD WHO HEALS

Jehovah-rapha, Healer Lord, we need you.

I need Him. *You* need Him.

In every area of our lives, *we* need Jehovah-rapha. When heartaches wrench our eyes in tears and illnesses become kilns to our bodies, sealing in the intruding aches and pains, we need Our Lord Who Heals. Sometimes, He lets time do the healing; sometimes, doctors. He's healing you in some way today. Can you glorify Him?

For me today, I need Jehovah-rapha because I can't stop remembering my wonderful Aunt Mary who died. At times, she was like a mom to me, an example of endurance, especially when I had troubles being a mom. Now, I'm left with those precious memories.

There's something about a church where every type of depiction and celebration of life is captured in stained glass, water fountains, furniture, accessories and Jesus' presence *everywhere.* As I walked into the church to attend her farewell, I greeted mourning relatives whom I hadn't seen in years. I notice a *bride's room*, a baptismal fountain at the sanctuary entrance, and, just right of the altar a large cement picnic table with two life-sized sculptures—most likely Mary and Joseph—seated at the bench. Obviously, they're meant to teach children about the approachability of our Lord, communion, and our need for family and friends. I saw every stage of life represented in that church, even in the choir's presence, whose members were elderly. Adults were working. Ceremonial singing becomes a purpose, which gives the elderly value, even if the singing is for a funeral. The Lord Who Heals is always dealing with us as He directs us to act for His various missions and purposes. Today, everyone in the church was focused on one blessed objective: to say goodbye and pay tribute to my Aunt Mary, comfort the mourning, and encourage us survivors with the words of Jehovah-rapha. He will heal.

One day, we too will be with Him and, "Stand before God our Father at the coming of our Lord Yeshua with all his angels" (1 Thessalonians 3:13). One day, "God, through Yeshua, will take with him those who have died" (1 Thessalonians 4:14). Jesus conquered death, so "Those who died united with the Messiah [him] will be the first to rise ... and thus we will always be with the Lord" (1 Thessalonians 4:16-18). Know this, brothers and sisters, and heal.

Jehovah-rapha, we need your healing touch always. Amen.

APRIL 26
VARIOUS TREATS

"I can't clean these contact lenses 'cause I don't have the right solutions," our son Andrew said after we told him to insert his contact lenses in his eyes as his doctor prescribed.

He's supposed to wear special expensive contact lenses every day for four hours. He's finding every excuse why he can't, even losing the ingredients the ophthalmologist gave us. So now we're off to the store. Then he says he needs a soda. "It keeps me calm so I can steady my hands," he maintains. Eventually, Andrew will run out of excuses for sidestepping the doctor's orders. Excuses for stalling.

Are there important projects you're shoving off today? Do you procrastinate? Sometimes I do. What steps can we take to get moving and accomplish a task or embark on a goal?

You remember the Bible story of the Roman Centurion (Matthew 8:5-13; Luke 7:1-10) who has a sick-and-dying servant? He goes to Jesus. "A Roman army officer came up and pleaded for help" (Matthew 8:5). This humble man will do anything for Jesus to heal his servant. "Sir, my orderly is lying at home paralyzed and suffering terribly" (8:6).

Why should Jesus care? He cares for everyone.

Jewish elders tell Jesus that this Roman officer helped build the synagogue, "He loves our people—in fact, he built the synagogue for us!" (Luke 7:5). The exclamation tells us this Centurion's plea is important to Jesus. Now, in our time, the Centurion is an example of faith. Faith is the first ingredient in the vital mixture of belief in the power of God to help us. He is our Jehovah-rapha, our God Who Heals. We talked about Him yesterday. As Jesus kindly treated the desperate pleading Centurion, Jesus is listening to your needs now, and engaged and present with you. Faith is ingredient one. What's ingredient two? The Centurion tells Jesus: "Sir, don't trouble yourself. I'm not worthy to have you come under my roof. ... Instead, just give a command and let my servant recover" (Luke 7:6-7). In Matthew 8:8 he says, "Sir, I am unfit to have you come into my home." Humility and need are ingredients two and three in the recipe for healing. "Asking," ingredient four, is hard, because *asking* means *acting*. Do you need to move on with a task today? Ask Him for help, now. He is listening and attentive.

God, please give us humility to extinguish our pride. Amen.

APRIL 27
THRIFTY

Yesterday I had a table at a book expo. I spent $10 for gas, traveled forty miles to the sales site, and had to buy water because of the parching humid weather. I had high expectations, of selling at least few books. Nothing. I might as well have named my six-by-four table the; *Letdown Flat.* I kept waving people toward me, but they were only interested in eating at the diner at the end of the strip mall. Time-and-again, when stragglers would walk my way and peruse my books, I'd pitch them my stories—all eight novels—one a collection of short stories, some of which I expanded into novels. No sale. Disappointment settled over my body, like wilting flower petals.

Have you spent many years learning and training for a specialized position, only to experience disappointment when people don't buy what you're offering, selling, or pitching? Maybe prospective employers didn't like your interview, or perhaps your boss is disappointed with the job you're doing. You're trying your hardest and doing your best, but that's not good enough.

How do we handle a disappointing performance?

I wanted to blame God. "I'm doing *all* this, and using my gifts that *you* gave me. For what? Nothing's working out. Why did you make my mind work this way when I'm not producing any results?"

Money is the result of working, right? I feel angry, then I become self-denigrating and cry, and then I feel like a failure.

I think of Solomon who was the wisest most intelligent person who ever lived. "I [God] am giving you a wise and understanding heart, so that there has never been anyone like you, nor will there ever again be anyone like you" (1 Kings 3:12). Wow, imagine being the wisest person ever. I'd take that! Yet, God didn't give it to me, drats. We do have our DNA, and gifts and talents (1 Peter 4:10).

Sitting still, I pictured myself standing before Solomon. "Should I continue? Through all this disappointment?" We know in our hearts the answers to our questions when we remain still and pray, because the Holy Spirit speaks to us. "The Spirit himself pleads on our behalf with groanings too deep for words" (Romans 8:26). My answer came. I hold a key position in a writers' group. When it's over, if I haven't made progress, I will do something else. We need to give ourselves time and leave the results to God.

Father, you are in control, even in our disappointments. Amen.

April 28
Advanced Degrees

The website, USA.gov, offers a complaint letter template that will help you write a letter of dissatisfaction to a person or company. I've seen soft complaint letters and harsh ones. I like to take the soft approach when complaining about a product or service. I recommend not using harsh language, crass words, and name bashing. Those will only irritate the reader who might ball your letter up and toss it into the trash, leaving you in suspense.

Do you need to complain about something today?

I did. I wrote a play, and hired an editor who extracted most of the stage directions in parentheses. Stage directions inside parentheses and usually italicized are the typical format for plays. Without stage directions, directors are lost, and actors are suspended somewhere in the air and talking like androids. So, if I want an answer as to why my editor redacted all my stage directions, I need to tread softly in a letter and not hurt her. There are consequences when we unleash unrehearsed criticisms onto others. Also, we can't retract our words.

How do we complain rightly by God's rules?

I'm reminded of the complaining that the Israelites unleashed on God during Moses' time. "The people began complaining about their hardships to *Adonai*. When *Adonai* heard it, his anger flared up, so that fire from *Adonai* broke out against them and consumed the outskirts of the camp" (Number 11:1). "Complaining," here means an "accusatory grumbling." Moses prayed for forgiveness. "That place was called Tav'erah [burning] because *Adonai*'s fire broke out against them" (11:3). If we allow our complaining to get out of control, we accomplish nothing. If we release our unbridled frustrations onto someone else as the Israelites did in Exodus 14:11 and 16:7, they will only boomerang back at us with *twice* the amount of energy. Jesus recommends a nice private conversation between you and the person who has wronged you. If the person does not respond in kind, one day God will decide how the complaint ends (Matthew 18:15-20). We must do our best to tell people our dissatisfactions in a loving manner. Then God will at work in the situation and in the lives of those we perceive have wronged us (Ephesians 4:31-32).

Father God, help us persevere and show you at all times. Amen.

APRIL 29
RESONATING MESSAGE

By now, you've probably experienced some type of cruelty, or cruel treatment at the hands of a powerful person. Perhaps someone bullied you as a child, a co-worker is backstabbing you, or a neighbor spread false information. Maybe you have a megalomaniac boss who is a slave driver, or someone has disparaged you with racial slurs. The list goes on, but the cruel treatment has left you hurt, worn down, anxious, or depressed. Martin Luther King, Jr. once said about cruelty, "The ultimate tragedy is not the oppression and cruelty by the bad people but the silence over that by the good people" (www.brainyquote.com). The worst type of cruelty is witnessing it and saying nothing to stop it, or failing to teach people about its victimizing consequences. That's the lesson for us and our path to healing. We can tell others of our painful experiences and listen to people as they tell their stories so *they* can heal.

Are you hurting today, a victim of cruelty?

God saw it. He knows. "Do what *God* sees as good and right" (Deuteronomy 12:28).

Perhaps years have gone by, but you still can't shake the memories that keep stacking up with each slight. Those bricks are set in mortar now, stopping you from becoming all you can be for God, and a barricade to peace and joy. I've been there, endured name calling from third grade through high school until I married and my name changed. Kids called me every cruel name that rhyming with Pink. How do I still counter the ill effects from those formative early years that at times now cause me to distance myself from people?

In Exodus 6:6-8, Moses works hard to encourage the enslaved Israelites by delivering God's powerful message of promise. "I am *Adonai*. I will free you from the forced labor of the Egyptians, rescue you from their oppression, and redeem you with an outstretched arm and with great judgments. I will take you as my people, and I will be your God. ... I will bring you into the land which I swore to give to Avraham, Yitz'chak and Ya'akov—I will give it to you as your inheritance. I am *Adonai*." Through God's son, Jesus, we inherit every good and perfect promise from God. Jesus told the hemorrhaging woman in Mark 5:34: "Daughter, your trust has healed you. Go in peace, and be healed of your disease." Live.

God, we pray for healing when bad memories invade. Amen.

APRIL 30
SPEAK OUT

After Bible study, a few of us women were finding it hard to stop the study and continued talking as we entered the elevator. We were so engrossed in discussing God's generational curse in the Old Testament that we didn't push the *down* button. Instead, we found ourselves facing the men. We laughed for minutes

However, we weren't joking about the hammering consequences for rejecting God. What heavy consequences?

Here are a few verses where God specifically tells us to teach our children to worship Him, reject idols, and trust Him in *all* areas of our lives. "You are not to bow down to them or serve them [idols]; for I, *Adonai* your God, am a jealous God, punishing the children for the sins of the parents to ... those who hate me" (Exodus 20:5).

The ancient Egyptians who enslaved the Israelites had over 2,000 gods, mostly depicted in animal form, like the goddess "tauret" that had the body of a hippo, the lower jaw of a crocodile, and the head of a cow. The ancient Egyptians showed this pregnant goddess actually nursing a pharaoh. They erected worship temples of mud and reeds all along the Nile and estuaries, and they had a deity for *everything* from beer to indigestion. They displayed their ornate gods in woven symbols, jeweled headdresses, household accessories, and jewelry. When you visit a museum and inspect their relics, you'll see how enmeshed all those ancient cultures were to their gods, for example, "baal shamin," in ancient Syria.

However, Our Lord Jehovah, the one true God, showed Himself to Moses and His people before freeing them for the Promised Land. "*Adonai* descended in the cloud, stood with him there and pronounced the name of *Adonai*: "YUD-HEH-VAV-HEH!!! *Yud-Heh-Vav-Heh* [*Adonai*] is God, merciful and compassionate, slow to anger, rich in grace and truth; showing grace to the thousandth generation ... but causing the negative effects of the parents' offenses to be experienced by their children and grandchildren, and even by the third and fourth generations" (Exodus 34:5-7). I think of my life before Jesus. I was selfish, self-centered and focused on my rights. Now, I serve Him, and leave a *giving* legacy to my children and the world.

Perfect Yahweh, you are awesome, and burn false gods (1Kings 18:20-39). Amen.

GOD DESIGNED

MAY 1
TEPID

Every day after I get up in the morning, I step outside and dip my toes in the pool. I like testing the water to see if I need to start the solar panels and warm it up. Then you're probably like me and need a cup or two of coffee, tea, or an energy drink. Do you remember testing yours this morning, so you don't burn your tongue or choke on any of your drink's effervescence? Oh, the testing isn't over yet, friends. Before going to work or school, perhaps you strike a conversation with a stranger, or an acquaintance at a convenience store or gas station. Don't we test people as well, to gauge their degree of friendliness or "stability?" Hey, these days, you never know who might unravel, like the unstable James Holmes who went on a shooting rampage in a Colorado movie theater, killing 20 people.

We're always testing people, and confronted with events over which we have little control. I'm reminded of the blind man Jesus healed in John 9. We never learn his name. He's simply "a man blind from birth" (v. 1). After Jesus directs him to healing waters, telling him, "While I am in the world, I am the light of the world" (v. 5), everyone begins testing not only the healed man but also their senses. This blind man—who now can see—has been unable to navigate his environment since birth. He's needed *constant* assistance from family and neighbors. Thus, the skeptics begin a quest to discover what happened that miraculously caused him to see. The guy simply reiterates what happened, that Jesus ordered him to wash his eyes with mud in the Shiloach Pool and then he could see. Seeking answers like frazzled detectives, his dumbfounded neighbors take the healed man to the Pharisees (v. 13). It's the Sabbath, and work is not permitted. Jesus healed. Who is this Jesus? Is he *really* from God as he claims? However, he worked on the Sabbath, a holy day, so he *can't* be from God because God wouldn't allow such a violation. The Seeing Man says Jesus is a prophet, and people are frightened to admit something else. "Judeans had already agreed that anyone who acknowledged Yeshua as the Messiah would be banned from the synagogue" (v. 22). To test *those* strict fundamentalists with the truth would render a person an outcast, excommunicated from community and the base of survival, the temple. The Seeing Man trusts Jesus for his future provisions as he kneels and worships Him.

Jesus, let us trust *you* to meet our *every* need always. Amen.

123

May 2
Have the Advantage

It's been over a week since I've been home from my Aunt Mary's memorial and I still haven't kept a few promises I made. "I'll send you these photos I took," I told some relatives, showing the pictures on my iPhone. But I also asked *them* to email me their addresses so I could send them the pictures. They haven't. Then there are a few more things I said I'd do but haven't, yet:

"I'll copy my family's DVD and mail it to you," I told a cousin.

"Give me two weeks," I later told my cousin John, "and I'll mail you copies of all these family records." We visited *four* cemeteries, where I took pictures of tombstones, and then we picked up birth and death records at the offices. Even if I send the copies to him, I don't know where he's going to put them because he's got one heck of a stuffed house. Still, a promise is a promise, and a commitment is a commitment, right?

Have you lately promised someone you'd do something and haven't fulfilled it? It can be disconcerting when people tell us one thing but do something else, or don't follow through on their word. Then you wonder, *What's the right way to remind them without offending them or hurting their feelings?*

All of us have been on both sides: Promising and not delivering, and waiting for someone to follow through on a promise. I'm reminded of the mother of James and John who asks Jesus, "Promise that when you become king, these two sons of mine may sit, one on your right and the other on your left" (Matthew 20:21). Jesus knows there's no way they can, "drink the cup," he's about to experience, for it is His death, by which he will become a living sacrifice for our sins. When we believe *in* Him, a promise is instantly fulfilled, holiness and Heaven. Paul said, "With all kinds of people I have become all kinds of things, so that in all kinds of circumstances I might save at least some of them. I do it all because of the rewards promised by the Good News, so that I may share in them along with the others who come to trust" (1 Corinthians 9:21-23). God will *never* break His promise to give us Heaven. "Whoever approaches him must trust that he does exist and that he becomes a Rewarder to those who seek him out" (Hebrews 11:6). We are His, always.

Father God, as you fulfill your promises, help us fulfill our commitments to others. Amen.

MAY 3
WEB DESIGN

Have you ever had one of those days? My "bad day" is today. First, I turned the water on to fill the pool, but when a neighbor stopped by to chat, I forgot to shut it off, so the pool nearly overflowed. Second, I didn't correctly budget for a tree service; so when the landscaper handed me his bill, I had to leave, keep his workers waiting, and then skedaddle to the bank. Third, a cold seized me like a supernatural vacuum sucking out my vital energy, leaving me sneezing, my throat scratchy, and my body achy.

Have you ever wondered how to re-set a day? I need some Resurrection power to restart mine! Jesus *is* our re-start power.

Recall the man who probably had the worst day *ever* in the history of humanity? Lazarus. He had been in his tomb four days (John 11:17). I wonder: How long was he dead before they wrapped him in his burial linens and laid him in the tomb? I figure at least a day, right? That means Lazarus was dead and his soul out-of-body for five to six days. He has mourning family members who *know* Jesus' divine power, and they're angry because they *know* Jesus could have saved him. He breathes new life into Lazarus. Lazarus' sisters are Mary and Martha, Mary being the one who pours expensive perfume on Jesus' feet in John 12:3. The same Mary and Martha who invite Jesus to their home, and Mary is so captivated by Him that she sits at his feet to soak up his every word; but she doesn't help Martha.

Martha complains: "Lord, don't you care that my sister has left me to do the work by myself? Tell her to help me!" Now wouldn't you say Martha is having a bad day here? I'm sure you've felt like her at some point, doing your work, other peoples' jobs, and trying to get them to change but they don't. Bad day.

"Martha, Martha," the Lord answers, "you are worried and upset about many things, but few things are needed—or indeed only one. Mary has chosen what is better, and it will not be taken away from her" (Luke 10:38-42). Ouch. God rules though, right, telling us to just go with the flow of our bad days and change our attitudes. Like Peter, Martha is one of the few people who tell Jesus to his face: "I believe that you are the Messiah, the Son of God, who is to come into the world" (John 11:27). Relax, breathe (*ahhhh*), and re-start.

God, thank you for your Holy Spirits energy within us. Redirect our days and ways, infuse us with renewal. Amen.

MAY 4
THE RECEIVING WINNER

When you apply for a job, you've probably filled out an application and were asked to give your prospective employer a resume. What would you write on your resume to market yourself? The first items should be your name, address, and phone number, your contact you so employers can call you. What comes next?

Believe it or not, most people get writers block trying to figure out what to put on their resume. What would Jesus write on His resume? Okay, besides Son of God, Savior, Miracle Worker, and King of Everything?

God put Jesus in charge of *everything*, so one highlight, or heading, would read: "My Father has handed over everything to me. Indeed, no one fully knows the Son except the Father, and no one fully knows the Father except the Son and those to whom the Son wishes to reveal him" (Matthew 11:27). He *is* the *I Am* in Exodus 3:14 and John 6.

What would His job description be? "Father, the world has not known you, but I have known you" (John 17:25). He is our Master, reigning over the Earth, our solar system, and the universe...oh, and everything *beyond* the universe that science is detecting but we can't yet understand. And He *loves* you, His creation!

Are we kneeling now? Jesus is awesome, our "everything."

Another heading Jesus might include on His resume would be: "I will return in absolute glory." We see evidence of His return. "He comes in his Father's glory with the holy angels" (Mark 8:38). To the interviewer, Jesus might ask, "Are *you* ready for a job in Heaven? Are *you* prepared for life after death with me?" Jesus tells us, "God is spirit" (John 4:24). We can't see "spirit," yet God is here with us. God's Holy Spirit interacts with us on the deepest of levels. "The Spirit himself bears witness with our own spirits that we are children of God" (Romans 8:16). You can add another heading to your resume for Heaven: You are a child of God and known deeply to God. "For the Spirit probes all things, even the profoundest depths of God" (1 Corinthians 2:10). The biggest item on your resume? God is *in* you. "Don't you know that you people are God's temple and that God's Spirit lives in you" (1 Corinthians 3:16; John 17:26))? Let us pray in thanksgiving to our King.

Father God, we bless you and always worship you. Amen.

MAY 5
ROYALTY

Today we learned the name of the baby girl born to the Duke and Duchess of Cambridge. They named her Charlotte Elizabeth Diana, in honor of her grandfather Prince Charles, great-grandmother Queen Elizabeth and her departed grandmother Princess Diana. The media has been inundating viewers with baby Charlotte info. One reporter predicts that by the time Charlotte turns five, the British fashion economy will quadruple, as Charlotte will set the standard for clothes. Everywhere, little girls will want to look like "a princess."

Do we ever dress like someone else so people will like and accept us?

American culture is definitely prince-and-princess oriented, and obsessed with the British royalty. It's pretty much always been that way, hasn't it? Recall Cinderella who vaulted from rags to riches, and Prince Charming who kissed his Sleeping Beauty. We want to live "happily ever after." Their carefree, famous, elite existences mesmerize us like binding enchantments. Yet, another person besides Shakespeare cautions us about coveting the lives of the rich and famous. I think of a warning quote: *The higher you fly the farther you fall.* The story comes from ancient Greece around 40 B.C.E., by Diodorus, who writes about Icarus. Icarus wants to fly off his island of exile so badly that he has his father Daedalus invent strong wings of wax. Icarus doesn't listen to his father's warning: don't fly too low or the dampness will clog your wings, and don't fly too high or the heat will melt them. *With pride comes a fall*, another saying goes. Icarus pummels into the sea when he flies too high, and the sun's blistering rays melt his wax wings. Tragedy. We see such tragedies in the Bible in prideful characters who don't listen to God.

Do you recall Jesus' parables of the rich man and the beggar Lazarus in Luke 16? The story really is about repenting of our pride and selfishness. I once believed the great lie: "If I can look just like *you*—in body shape, size and clothing—and have what *you* have, I will be liked and happy. Wow, was I wrong! Whenever I slip back into that old thinking of focusing on my appearance, I am in sin; for I am not being, and living, through Jesus's eyes. "Unless you repent, you too will all perish" (Luke 13:3). When we walk falsely among people, are we really living? Let's just *be*, and let Him sculpt our beauty.

Jesus, help us *be* authentic just as you *designed* each of us. Amen.

MAY 6
SOBRIETY

"When someone asks you for something, give it to him [or her]; when someone wants to borrow something from you, lend it to him [or her]" (Matthew 5:42). Those were Jesus's words.

Can we *really* do what He asked of us? Dig *deep* into our pockets and give?

While at the last church service, a pastor confronted us with giving. Our church started a Micah 6:8 ministry which asks us parishioners to do the following: "Human being, you have already been told what is good, what *Adonai* demands of you—no more than to act justly, love grace and walk in purity with your God."

We are to "act justly" as in Isaiah 1:17. We are "to learn to do right; defend the oppressed; and, take up the cause of the fatherless." The pastor was about to ask the congregation to give money to house the homeless and orphans in the homes our church bought across the street. Suddenly, he introduced a guest speaker, another pastor, who preached on Matthew 7:7-11 and James 4:2-5. I didn't expect this type of surprise sermon that deviated from our scheduled series. Do you ever feel uneasy with a sermon? "Their inhabitants, shorn of power, are disheartened and ashamed, weak as grass, frail as plants, like grass on the rooftops or grain scorched by the east wind" (Isaiah 37:27). I twitched in my seat and felt uneasy because the need for money was real. The pastor's sincerity touched my heart. Children are being abused and neglected. In the 1960s, I was one of them.

"Uh-oh," I thought. "He's going to ask for money. What do I do? There's *no way* I give 10%!" Yet, people are in desperate need. Jesus calls us to help them and be His examples in order to bring people to salvation. "I am not ashamed of the Good News, since it is God's powerful means of bringing salvation to everyone who keeps on trusting, to the Jew especially, but equally to the Gentile" (Romans 1:16). People are suffering. We can help in any way we can if we have the means. "Give us the food we need today" (Matthew 6:11). Jesus sees our hearts and asks that we care. "I needed clothes and you provided them. I was sick and you took care of me. I was in prison and you visited me" (Matthew 25:36). We give because we are saved, and we care about souls. It's written in our hearts to love.

Father, change our attitudes about money and possessions so we can give more. Amen.

MAY 7
TREATING PEOPLE

I saw a couple in the middle of an argument at the grocery store. "You can't buy—

We *can't* afford," a man kept telling a woman as they walked quickly through the store. I remained about twenty feet behind them, but I had my iPhone ready for recording. I kept waiting for her to say something, but the short brown-haired woman kept her head lowered and her stare fixed on the linoleum.

"You didn't budget—" he yelled, but then quickly shut his smoking lips.

A meat worker dressed in a white blood-tinged apron passed them. "Excuse me, can I help you find something?"

I had stopped and was perusing soups for lunch, but my ears were itching as I eavesdropped. You would think I was bored or something that I didn't just turn around and leave. As the couple, suddenly calm, dismissed the worker and walked on through the store, I couldn't help but watch the short woman with the brown hair cower a bit behind her strutting husband. I had always seen his face through shifting perspectives, but never her face.

Sometimes, silence is the loudest cry. Are you keeping silent about something going wrong in a relationship, or within yourself?

You've heard the phrase: *Smiling on the outside but dying on the inside.* Is that you today?

God sees. God knows! He's *Jehovah-jireh*, our Lord who provides. The "jireh" comes from Genesis 22:14, meaning, "to see," actually, "to foresee." When God provided a ram sacrifice in place of Isaac (Genesis 22:13), God had already read Abraham's heart. He had already provided the ram as a substitute for Isaac, just as God knows our hearts and provided his Son Jesus as a sacrifice for our sins. You are known to Him, and Jesus is the perfect sounding board for our conflicting, and at times, hurtful experiences. Our souls are His territory, open books to Him. "When you are praying, do not use meaningless repetition...for your Father knows what you need before you ask Him," Jesus tells us (Matthew 6:7-8). Yes, we can *always* be in prayer, even when we are outwardly silent. "God, you know my distress, so please help me."

To you, Jesus, is the victory. Every victory, and the glory. Father, thank you for blending into our thought worlds. Amen.

May 8
Comparison Shopping

"I wish I could be doing more for God's Kingdom," I often tell myself. Or, "I should be doing more with the gifts God has given me." I aspire to be like a Kay Arthur, Joyce Meyer, or Beth Moore. Instead, I self-criticize. "All I'm doin' is writin' these books."

Do you ever think of yourself as being "less than" simply because you're not doing something exceptional, or not accomplishing enough for God with your time and money? I must admit, people with money in our churches tend to be the ones who give the most and accomplish the most. Compared to them, my tithing must look like 2 small coins! Still, now-and-then, I get a call from someone at my church's radio station asking me to volunteer. I'm always looking for ways to be a part of a ministry. However, stuffing letters and sponge-sealing envelopes? Really? I have a master's degree in education. Most times, I have to tell you, I feel God telling me, "You're a waste."

Have you ever thought that way?

No sooner does that sinful song, "You're a Waste," start playing in my mind, does the Holy Spirit intervene. *That's a lie.*

Whew—thanks, God. I quickly do a search on the word, "help," at the online website Biblegateway.com, because *helping* is what we do when we volunteer. Yes, at this point, I'm also in need of a bit of "help." When we *help* people, we involve ourselves—in our unique ways—in the *entire* Body of Christ. This is the point where my mind's broken record stopped, giving me gasps of fresh relief I can pass onto you. "Under his [Jesus'] control, the whole body is being fitted and held together by the support of every joint, with each part working to fulfill its function; this is how the body grows and builds itself up in love" (Ephesians 4:16). Paul's instruction is telling us that each person is vital in the job that Jesus directs us to accomplish for his "whole body," the church—not the building we go into to worship on the Sabbath, but the entire body of Christians. What is our One Mission, our Calling? To spread the Gospel and tell people about the Jesus who saves all people from *eternal* death. "God, the Father of all, [who] rules over all, works through all and is in all" (Ephesians 4:6). His spirit is telling you something right now. Answers do come when we pray.

God, help us go right to you instead of just spinning. Amen.

MAY 9
FULFILLMENT

What are your dreams? What's your deepest desire? Next big goal? If you say you don't have any, I'd ask: "Are you dead?" We all have dreams and wishes.

I have an acquaintance from church, Donna, who has been the co-leader of a group for years. She mentored a young woman who has a dying four-month old baby girl born with a severe disability. Donna is naturally distraught, her thoughts always redirecting to how she can help her friend and the baby. "I wish I could do something!" Donna can't save the baby's life.

I have another friend who continues on a path of homelessness. No matter the start-up businesses she opens, her consultation services, or the paid speeches she delivers; "Susan" always manages to lose everything and living friend-to-friend. Her dream? For years it's been, "to get out of my ruts and make a business a success."

We all keep trying and striving. I'm reminded of the story of Zakkai (CJB), or Zachaeus (NIV) the Tax Collector in Luke 19:1-10. Zakkai was a "chief tax collector" and "rich." That meant he'd go around and bully people into paying their dues and back taxes, demanding a little extra to stuff his own pockets with a nice chunk of other peoples' money. He's "short" and can't see over a crowd of people encroaching upon Jesus for healing and teaching; but he longs to know Jesus, the living God. Obviously, he has believed in Jesus for some time. Now, he wants to meet Jesus, desperately. We can just imagine his dream because we all share it. "I want to touch Him, Hear him and say hi." Imagine Jesus appearing today!

Jesus is our dream giver. When we become desperate or frustrated to know what He wants from us, or His will for us, He alone can comfort us and direct us. He sooths the lonely, the exiled, the vanquished, and the disconnected. Zakkai climbs up a sycamore-fig tree, and we can imagine his words: "Jesus! I'm here! I just wanna see you! Just look at me!" What do you suppose he's feeling?

"When he [Jesus] came to the place, he looked up and said to him, 'Zakkai! Hurry! Come down, because I have to stay at your house today" (Luke 19:5)! Today, Jesus is calling *your* name.

Jesus is answering *your* dreams. He inhabits *your* House, your heart. So *many* spiritual gifts He has waiting just for you. Choose.

Jesus, thank you for accepting us, and fulfilling dreams. Amen.

MAY 10
CONCEPTS AND IDEAS

While volunteering at church this morning, I sat with two elderly men. We exchanged small talk on vacations, our spouses, and retirement. After a few hours of working on repetitive tasks, we began feeling a bit lame-brained and began talking about our families.

"I have a sister," Len began, "but her husband left her a long time ago for another woman. He had *problems*."

I felt sad. He appeared still affected by her loss. "I'm sorry."

After silent moments, Sam on my left said, "Well, I guess some men have problems with that."

I know for sure that God and Jesus *don't* approve of people breaking their wedding covenants (divorce, fornication, and adultery), but I couldn't pinpoint the exact verse in the Bible from memory where God commands a one-woman-one-man permanent union. So I offered an excuse for men leaving wives and children. "I guess men blame evolution, and insist that their DNA compels them to be with as many women as possible so as to spread their seeds."

We all laughed, while also realizing the situation isn't funny. First, we believe God created man and woman. We're not monkey spawned. Second, we know God said: "a man is to leave his father and mother and stick with his wife, and they are to be one flesh" (Genesis 2:24). Third, the word "wife" appears in Genesis, and the term must imply God's desire for a man to be a *husband* and a woman to be a *wife*. "Adam made love to his wife Eve, and she became pregnant and gave birth to Cain" (Genesis 4:1). Has someone ever left you? Has someone given you an excuse to break his or her covenant of marriage, and moved on? Maybe he or she left you with the full responsibility of children, and you are feeling distraught, overwhelmed, and burdened…or perhaps, blaming God. God didn't intend marriage as an in-and-out doorway, and that people should say marriage vows and then leave. "'I hate divorce!' says the LORD, the God of Israel. 'To divorce your wife is to overwhelm her with cruelty,' says the LORD of Heaven's Armies. 'So guard your heart; do not be unfaithful to your wife'" (Malachi 2:16). We are to love, *commanded* to love. As humans, we function on trust, hope, and love. They are our psychological and spiritual water; and of the three, "Love [is] the greatest" (1 Corinthians 13:13).

Father God, help us love others as *you* love us. Amen.

MAY 11
MOTHER'S DAY

In almost every store I enter, bouquets of colorful flowers dot the aisles, even in home building warehouses. Flowers are typical presents for Mother's Day as about two-thirds of gift givers purchase them for the big day. They're an easy and inexpensive gift to whip into your arms, because *everyone* has a mother, and most children want to show her even a simple appreciation.

I've been watching stories lately of people whose Mother's Day experiences are like touching a red-hot rack, healing after the blisters, and then living with black scars. One woman on the news told a reporter how she survived terrible abuse at the hands of her mother, and a Vietnamese man showed a picture of himself as baby at an orphanage on the day Saigon fell, April 30, 1975. I remember that time. Americans were shuffling, yanking, and cramming men, women, and children into boats, helicopters, and airplanes for freedom. The Vietnamese man is part of a group of orphans returning to Vietnam searching for their mothers. They also long to know: "Who's my father, and why did he give me up?"

We know that feeling, that desire to know why, especially after hurtful things happen to us, right? Most times, in the midst of hurting, we just want to be heard, and know the listener cares. Good moms have a tendency to do just that. I recall one of the best moms who did everything to protect her child, Moses' mother Jochebed (Numbers 26:59). A fearful and malicious king of Egypt orders his people: "Every [Hebrew] boy that is born, thrown in the river" (Exodus 1:22). Moses' mother concocts a wild plan, risking her life to save him. Now, Jochebed was also the king's slave, so when the king's daughter joyously finds Moses floating in the river, she hands him over to Jochebed to nurse him. *Moses* means *to draw out*. This king's daughter realized that Moses' survival was the result of a direct intervention from God, with understanding from God's word given to *Moses* in 2 Samuel 22:17: "He reached down from on high and took hold of me; he drew me out of deep waters."

God knows our aches and pains, for his spirit pools at the depths of our souls. Maybe, that's how you feel now, drowning in hurts because you lacked a good mother or caretaker. However, He's drawing you out of that sorrow to lift you up to Himself, for new life.

Jesus, we now thank you for every good thing. Amen.

May 12
Hope Happening

A friend of mine has been going to college part time for years and finally graduated this week. Today, we attended her party, and we talked about why she and her husband haven't been in church and missing from our Bible study. She's been working hard. She has gray circles under her eyes and she walks with a tired gait. Before Christmas, she hired on with a new employer. Her job hasn't turn out as planned, but she's at least somewhat satisfied with her work. She has children and a husband. Needs. Everyone has them, and when we take on responsibilities, we have to give of ourselves and cut back on activities that are not on our priority list. Are you stressed like my friend? We talked about stress turning our hair gray; and our derrieres are widening from sitting, how we eat-on-the-run, and don't exercise. Are you feeling the pressures of life yet?

Jesus is our calm in the storm. "He took me and pulled me out of deep water," David tells us (Psalm 18:17). When the stresses and pressures of job, family, and difficulties darken our spirits and pull us far from God and His word, we can return to Jesus in prayer. He gently nudges us back into His fold. God is our Shepherd, Jehovah-raah, and our loving Father, Jehovah-shammah, the Lord who is Here and Everywhere—with you and me, now. "Save me, God! For the water threatens my life" (Psalm 69:2)! Did you know there are studies proving that too much work, stress, and little down time to recuperate *will* take many years off our lives? Demands of daily living can be like deep-vast waters through which we'll eventually drown. However, God is our life preserver. You've seen one of those. It's inflated to the fullest with oxygen—life saving—and red and white. It's easy to spot when someone throws one overboard for us to catch and cling to for dear life. That's God. Give Him each stress, now.

Do you need saving today? What kind of life preserver are you looking for? Your *inflatable* might be an hour's worth of church time. Or story time, or music hour with your family or a friend. Maybe you need something simple: A home cooked meal, a hot cup of coffee or glass of ice-cold water, or just plain silence listening to the wind or rain. God comes in simple beautiful forms as rest to our senses. "Rescue me from the mud! Don't let me sink" (Psalm 69:15)! So inhale His breath of life. Rest stress-free.

Father, we love you and worship your holy names. Amen.

MAY 13
DEDICATION CEREMONY

We're going to have a dedication ceremony next Sunday at church. What's that? The word, dedicate, means, to devote to the worship of a divine being; specifically, to set apart (a church) to sacred uses with solemn rites, and, consecrate, devote, give up to. In Deuteronomy 11, God tells Moses His expectations in a covenant, the most important rule being, "To love Adonai your God and serve him with all your heart and all your being" (v. 13). He then concludes His list of dos and don'ts with a directive for parents. "You are to store up these words of mine in your heart and in all your being ... teach them carefully to your children, talking about them when you sit at home, when you are traveling on the road, when you lie down and when you get up ... so that you and your children will live long on the land. Adonai swore to your ancestors that he would give them for as long as there is sky above the earth" (verses 18-21). Have you experienced this type of intense dedication of your body, soul, and mind to our God who sanctifies? He makes us right, and dedicates us to Himself when we believe in Jesus. As Christians, we adults then dedicate ourselves to Him in baptism. From our moment of salvation, there's no separating from Him, no un-salvation. We are sealed. Stamped *His*. Jesus'. "You who heard the message of the truth, the Good News offering you deliverance, and put your trust in the Messiah were sealed by him with the promised Ruach HaKodesh [Holy Spirit]" (Ephesians 1:13).

Try asking people the question: Have you dedicated your life to Jesus Christ? Some might ask you back: What for? This is what dedication is all about: our purpose. As Timothy's grandmother, Lois, and his mother, Eunice, raised Timothy in the Jewish faith in obedience with Deuteronomy 11, so we need to read God's word and try our best to obey him according to Deuteronomy 11. If anything else, dedicate yourself to Him right now. It's an easy prayer, even at times when I must *re*-dedicate myself to Him, which happens when I miss His perfect command to love Him and others. Still, in the midst of sinning, He never un-seals us. Seeing parents dedicate their children to our Lord symbolizes our commitment as Christians to raise our children to God's covenants through Jesus Christ.

Lord God, put your light in the form of your holy Word into our hearts and minds. Amen.

MAY 14
ONCE UPON A TIME

"Mom, I don't want to go there," our son Andrew exclaimed after his dad told him where I wanted to eat lunch on Mother's Day. The morning was typical: trying to drag him out of bed; my husband setting out several outfits for him; Andrew retorting with *urgs, uggs,* and *grunts*; and, finally, offering him *four* choices for breakfast. Who says a special day designated for celebrating *will* be happy?

Are you having expectations for others and how they'll treat you today? I guess we should ask one question first though, *What do we expect?* Sometimes I have to stop and ask this question and do a little self-examination. If I don't, I can become irritated or snappy when my expectations aren't fulfilled. I recall a quote someone told me: *The higher my expectation, the higher my level of discomfort when it's not fulfilled.* It was a time when I felt disappointed because someone didn't say *thank you* for a party I had given her, but simply went on with life until the next time she needed something. See? Here's one of my expectations: When I do something nice a person should at least say *Thanks.* That seems reasonable, right? However, I'm sure you've encountered situations where you were nice, courteous, or even generous, and the other person didn't respond; for example, opening a door for someone and the person didn't even nod. Sometimes a simple gesture would suffice, right? We don't always receive kindnesses after being polite or thoughtful. Then we're left disappointed, which can layer over with bitterness and cynicism, the last two becoming life-altering like black mold on our personalities. What to do? We're often reminded of Paul's advice: "be kind to each other, tenderhearted; and forgive each other, just as in the Messiah God has also forgiven you" (Ephesians 4:32). His advice might not always work when we're wading in "Disappointment River!" Sometime, I need more. What now? "Sadness can improve a person," Solomon writes (Ecclesiastes 7:3). Disappointment can improve us? Now *that's* a new one. How? "Don't be overly righteous or overly wise; why should you disappoint yourself" (Ecclesiastes 7:16). Solomon, the Wise One, shows us the origin of disappointment. Instead of setting our eyes on God and letting Him handle others' behaviors, we can change our expectations of "righteousness," how I *believe* others should act, and look to God.

Father, help us see others through Christ's eyes. Amen.

MAY 15
EXPECT ATTACKS

Our son Andrew has a problem. "I found two sites on the internet saying the terrorist attack on 9-11 was just a hoax ... a movie," he said as we were driving to the store.

His dad and I began an assault on his faulty belief. "What sites!" I turned around in my seat until the belt nearly choked me.

"Get off your phone now!" his dad ordered, turning a sharp corner. "That's a bunch of malarkey. You can't believe *half* of what you watch on the internet and you *know* that!"

After parking the car and feeling defeated like two gerbils losing a hamster wheel race, we gave up when we realized the problem.

Maybe you've experienced *denial* in some area of your life where you don't want to look at evidence running contrary to your beliefs. "People are paradigmatic people," begins Dr. David Ray Griffin, Ph.D., professor and author. "They have a paradigm. They say, this is the way the world works and I am convinced that this is the way that the world works. 9/11 doesn't fit into that paradigm. So, I don't have to look at the evidence" (www.consciouslifenews: September, 2014). What is a *paradigm*?

We live by paradigms. They're engrained since before birth even, as processing codes in our brains—impulses we *each* create about the world and by which we navigate through life, relate to people, and perceive experiences. Our Christian faith is a paradigm, thank you Jesus, because now our souls and *everything* we do are interfacing with God's holy paradigm through His Holy Spirit. Okay, so here's the definition of, "paradigm:" *a typical example or pattern of something; a model; pattern, example, template,* and, *prototype.* It's like a pair of glasses through which we see everything. If contradictory information flows into us that doesn't fit our paradigms, we experience anxiety and denial, at least at first. Jesus talks about this type of blindness throughout the Book of Matthew. "Though seeing, they do not see; though hearing, they do not hear or understand" (Matthew 13:13-15). Jesus is the light, the evidence we need to crack through our Denial Dam, to the truth, accepting the truth, and changing our faulty paradigms. What do we need to change in ourselves, our minds, our behavior today so we can *see* troubling events differently? Then we can respond differently.

Father, help us act as you guide us and *renew* us today. Amen.

MAY 16
WIRING

Have you ever found yourself distracted? Starting one task only to become multi-directional like a wobbling compass? This morning is one of those mornings for me, so I prayed, asking God to create in me a calm heart and focused mind. Researching various versions of the Bible at the website *Bible Gateway*, I discovered antonyms (great opposites) for "distracted" according to 1 Corinthians 7:35 as follows. "Undistracted" means: "undivided devotion (AMP);" "to live right and to love the Lord above all else" (CEV); "without impediment" (DRA); "without giving your time to other things" (ERV); "undivided" (ESV); "without separation" (GNV); and, "free of complications" (MSG). I believe we get the picture of what *distract* does not mean. The word *distract* comes from the prefix, "dis," meaning, "apart;" and the Latin root word, "trahere," to draw or drag." Later, the verb evolved, "to pull in different directions, prolong, plunder, squander." Are you prolonging the *one* thing you *need* to do because of distractions? Squandering time by being *distracted*, with your thoughts or actions dragging you to other things?

We need to become grounded, as an electrical grounding wire safely directs wild currents to one place.

We need to go back to the beginning, before all that compass flickering began taking over the moments of our day, prolonging confusion and thus creating a cycle of distractions. We need solid ground, and a firm footing. In Genesis, we're reminded of what God started with when he created everything. "God formed a person from the dust of the ground and breathed into his nostrils the breath of life" (2:7); "Out of the ground *Adonai*, God, caused to grow every tree" (2:9); and, "from the ground *Adonai*, God, formed every wild animal and every bird that flies in the air" (2:19). Can you feel God's calmness breathing into you right now? His word calms us, steadies our thoughts, grounds us, and directs us to His perfect purpose. The ground is where we kneel to Him in prayer; and *one* place his Holy Spirit settles in us, and Jesus' hand comforts us. "Let your good Spirit guide me on ground that is level" (Psalm 143:10). He breathes a steady flow of change, peace, and focus as He guides us to alter our distracted ways.

Father, we need to seek *you* for solid ground so you can renew us and work through us today. Amen.

MAY 17
CEASE FIRE

There's an expression that goes: *Fool me once, shame on you; fool me twice, shame on me.* I liken the saying to a feedback loop. Like me, do you ever put yourself into *negative* feedback loops? A feedback loop is "a circuit that feeds back some of the output [energy] to the input of a system." That's a *positive* feedback loop, since only some of the outgoing energy is returning, thus yield positive results. A *negative* feedback loop keeps re-cycling, yielding no results, like trying to adjust a thermostat to a temperature that *just won't* adjust. Your bad feedback loop might divert your attention to the alcohol aisle even though you know you can't drink. Or you might have an inappropriate magazine app, or shopping, gambling, junk food, or dating app; and you keep visiting the site, hoping this time you'll be able to manage your behavior without over-indulging. Then comes the hangover in a downpour! Your attempt has failed, one more time, and you end up suffering. When's it gonna stop?

I joined an instrumental choir as they were finishing final touches on a performance. I can read notes, but I had never played those particular instruments. I'd need a miracle to play to *their* standards after only *six* sessions. The leader replaced me, without telling me. I discovered I was out when someone simply stepped in my usual spot and the director began practice without including me. I felt rushed. The negative feedback loop? I was so eager to do something for God, so I accepted her invitation to help. I didn't think through the situation. How could I possibly live up to the group's performance standard after having only *six* lessons? Still, I fumed ... squishing inside the crack of anger and hurt. I should have known better than to put myself in a situation where it was only logical that I would be replaced. I have that tendency to act—jump right in!—without thinking. When I was small, my dad would tell me, "Joycie, you *never* think!" Did my *fast-acting* start with that Drill Sergeant instilling me with a self-fulfilling prophesy? I stopped and thought of Jesus. He puts himself in the *worst* negative feedback loop *ever* when he *purposely* travels to Jerusalem. "Isn't this the man they're out to kill" (John 7:25)? He knows He's Calvary bound (Matthew 16:21; Mark 10:33; and Luke 18:32), yet He knows the other side of death: eternity with God for us who accept Him as the true Messiah.

Father, help us change, and *become* change for you. Amen.

May 18
Impact

On May 18, 1980, at 8:32 a.m., a catastrophic force unleashed a volcanic eruption killing 57 people. The 110,000-acre explosion on Mount St. Helens killed approximately 7,000 big-game animals, annihilated their lush habitats, and reduced the mountain's height by 1,314 feet. How extensive was the damage? There are 5,280 feet in a mile, so that explosive force erased a ¼ mile off the top of Mount St. Helens into the atmosphere as ash, steam, and debris that then drizzled down on cities as far south as 2,000 miles to Oklahoma. What devastation is left of the remaining area is now named, Ring of Fire. Explosions of this magnitude are powerful—their release changing lives, even the Gross National Product.

Feel like exploding? What could be the consequences?

Two months prior to the mountain popping her top, scientists recorded more than 2,800 earthquakes and saw a bulge on the mountain's left side. Those are called warnings, yet about 57 people didn't listen, and remained at their homes and businesses. Some of whom merely "scoffed" at the concern for their safety. They wouldn't listen to the experts warnings. A pyroclastic flow engulfed the upper areas, destroying a lake and burying the site under 150 feet of volcanic landslide debris. Each of those 57 people could have avoided their horrific entombment if they'd *listened* to the experts and just let go of their unbelieving death-wish grasp on their property.

Are you *staying* in a potentially explosive situation where someone is mistreating you? What is the Holy Spirit telling *you*?

Our minds and bodies are always giving us warning clues as to when we need to pay close attention to our escalating or festering emotions, or ask for help when we become boxed in by someone's abusive tendencies. There's a theory hypothesizing that we all get caught up into a cycle called the Victim-Persecutor-Rescuer cycle, people at some points in a relationship relate from one of those three perspectives. What to do? We need to listen to our warning signs. *Warn* appears 91 times in the Complete Jewish Bible. "Hear, my people, while I give you warning! If you would only listen to me" (Psalm 81:9)! *Warn* means, *alert, caution, advice, prepare*, and, *signal*. Notice the exclamation points. Taking immediate action, on impulse, leads to evil outcomes. Things get worse, never better, without God.

Father, help us in all areas of our lives to help ourselves. Amen.

MAY 19
FORCED INTERACTIONS

Earlier this evening I received a call out-of-the-blue that left me feeling a bit rumbled. The conversation went something like this:

"Hi! It's me, Marlene, from our Thursday group."

My memory of her *clicked*. "Oh, yeah, hi." She left the group weeks ago, *hmm*.

"My son Matt has a *big* essay due Monday, and someone from the group told me you'd be the *perfect* person to help him write it. Can you please help Matt? He just doesn't know where to begin, and I *really* want him to meet some of my Christian friends so he can see examples of what a good Christian is." As she spoke on, a river of information coursed through my brain as I tried recalling my Friday schedule: an entire morning of writing, one meeting, and an afternoon meeting. I wouldn't be home until 3:30 p.m., and then Sharon said Matt had an important appointment he couldn't cancel at 8 p.m. Wow—what short notice.

"Okay, but I can only help him for an hour," I told her. Later, I received an email. Matt is *so* thrilled that I'll be helping him. In the aftermath of the whirlwind, I felt manipulated by Marlene who seemed to know human nature and that people will agree to a spur-of-the-moment request if they can't get a word in edgeways. Have you ever been taken by surprise by someone trying to slip their job onto your shoulders, or a colleague needs your help but doesn't tell you the truth behind their request? I thought through the haystack of Marlene's information to the heart of her issue. That Matt doesn't live with her makes her feel unfit. She was using my skills as a former teacher and author to impress Matt. I don't know all her motives, but they're between her and God. I did as promised, helped Matt, and learned something more about myself. "*Adonai* your God is right there with you, as a mighty savior" (Zephaniah 3:17). I survived the teaching experience while seeing a glimmer of Marlene's motives makes me want to hunt for my own selfishness and dishonesty when relating to others. "That our conscience assures us that in our dealings with the world…we have conducted ourselves with frankness and Godly pureness of motive—not by worldly wisdom but by God-given grace" (2 Corinthians 1:12). I can't; He can. We *can* be teachable.

Lord, help us see when we wrong others. Amen.

MAY 20
ONWARD

Like graduating from a school or program, moving to a new location can feel like standing at the shore of a rapid river. Have you ever seen the rapids, a place in a river between a smooth flowing stream and a wild cascade? They're tough-rough waters.

When I was a teenager, my parents, brother and I vacationed out west; and after touring Yellowstone, we took a river-raft ride on the Snake River. The black raft bounced us—tossed-and-turned us—every which way, but the guide was expert at steadying our course. Wow, were we all frightened at times. Have you ever been at a scary or confusing transition in your life?

The switch from one stage-of-life to another can be calm-and-smooth, or it can be bumpy, jagged, and frightening, depending on how well we're prepared for the change.

That's how I feel about moving. Beginning when I was only 4 years old up until today I've moved over 35 times, frequently starting over with school, church and various groups. Beginning anew and making friends was easier when I was in middle school than in my middle adult years when igniting lasting relationships becomes much harder. Now, I belong to a church and a Bible study group; however, I do not have any close female friends like the girls I used to hang out with in high school. Back then, we'd call one another several times a week, see one another daily, and have weekend slumber/birthday bashes. Now, I meet with people outside my family once a week, and *occasionally* we talk during the week. So different, huh? What are your friendships like now-a-days? Are you happy with the particular group you're affiliated? Now imagine having to move and losing your "network." Many times in life, we find ourselves caught between opportunity and survival, forced to move, or change. It's hard!

In Judges, we see the Israelites constantly caught in a cycle of love-hate with God. In Judges 4, Prophet Deborah was Judge over Israel. She advises Barak, a warrior, how to defeat an enemy that's been "cruelly oppressing" the Israelites for twenty years" (Judges 4:3). But God was their banner: *Jehovah-nissi*. With a "tent peg and a hammer," God moves through the cruel situation to save His people (4:4-23). Moving can be a good thing sometimes when God's involved in your move. He's our Raft Guide through the turbulence.

Lord, help us see our circumstances through your eyes. Amen.

MAY 21
OPENING NIGHT

Do you long to be magically transported to *Tomorrowland?* It's a mysterious but fantastic place in space-time where you can fly on hovercraft, receive instant food from a sci-fi kitchen, call up virtual experiences, and interact with androids. Or maybe you'd like to be Spiderman, Super Girl, Wonder Woman, the Six Million Dollar Man, Bionic Woman, a Marvel Ant-Man, the Hulk, Elasti-girl with rubberized physiology, or an X-Men character?

When the *Avengers* opened last week, it raked in $200.3 million the first weekend, domestically, making it the largest grossing superhero movie ever. More such films and TV shows are in the works because people can't wait to be carried into a magical superhero world where good triumphs over evil and villains. Superman and Spiderman—X-Men and X-Woman—the Fantastic Four, the Avengers, and, *oh*, we can't forget Batman and the Arrow. Superheroes. They're champions of us ordinary folks, make right everything that's wrong with society, expose corruption, and save the victimized. Feel wronged lately? Feel like you need some justice, maybe even a little payback, after someone in a powerful position hurt you, insulted you, gypped you, demoted you, injured you, or maybe even arrested you unjustly? That's why we like superheroes. We experience a catharsis when the bad guys and gals lose, get tossed in the pen, and get what they deserve. We can't be vigilantes, but at least we can see justice prevail in a show or movie, through a writer's eyes. We're left with a bit of hope that maybe the fictional realm of Movie-dom might transfer to *real* life, change people, and make the world a better place.

We feel insignificant, really. You know what? We are insignificant, to "the World." However, we're important to God, *Elohim.* He is the Creator, who formed, fashioned, and crafted you and me. "Just as you don't know the way of the wind or how bones grow in a pregnant woman's womb, so you don't know the work of God, the maker of everything" (Ecclesiasts 11:5). He molded our DNA and knows us by name. "Let them praise the name of *Adonai*; for he commanded, and they were created" (Psalm 148:5). God knew us *before* creation! "Before I formed you in the womb, I knew you" (Jeremiah 1:5). When we seek Him, He answers His creation.

Lord we want to know you more about you each day. Amen.

MAY 22
FITTEST CITIES

"Peacemakers who sow seed in peace raise a harvest of righteousness," James says (3:18). I haven't had much success at being a peacemaker lately. Can people call you, Peacemaker? A peacemaker is a person, group, or nation that tries to make peace, especially by reconciling parties who disagree, quarrel, or fight. We've all been in those types of situations, right? When we end up spectators at a school fight, when an employee argues with a boss, or when a disagreement escalates in a courtroom or business meeting. Fights and arguments can be stomach churning, head aching, and downright intolerable; and most bystanders merely scoot back, unsure of what to do, and withdraw. It's a bit like rubbernecking as you pass a car accident. Part of us wants to see while at the same time we're afraid. Afraid to step in. Afraid to speak peace.

Is your family experiencing a bit of chaos today? Are you, like me, in need of a peacemaker? James gives us a suggestion. We need to "sow seed in peace." When I was a little girl spending much time at my grandparent's farm in Hannah, Indiana, my grandmother would take seeds and gently press them into tiny dirt-filled plastic containers—from egg cartons to long black planters. She'd begin her planting work in February; and in March, she'd transfer little shoots of vegetables into larger containers. In all their green glory, they'd fill to almost overflowing a long, white porch table until May, when we'd gather all the relatives and carry them to a large garden about two-hundred-feet from the white farm house where we'd delicately plant them in the tilled earth. One person would gently hoe while another dirt-smudged person would place the hand-sized plant into a little hole in the soil and then tap down dirt around the seedling plant. Another person would then follow with a hose and sprinkle the bowing stalk with water. It is peacemaking. Have you ever experienced times when you could invent a peacemaking activity? I remember times when my brother and I would fight and argue, always irritating my dad and grandparents. But we *didn't* fight or argue when we were planting, hoeing, watering, weed picking, and finally harvesting those vegetables, cooking and eating them. Our grandparents raised "a harvest of right," and we experienced peace. In any situation, we can sow peace and reap blessings. Today, sow.

Father, help us be the peace we want in this world. Amen.

MAY 23
ANTHEM

"To look out at this kind of creation out here and not believe in God is to me impossible," John Glenn, the 77-year-old astronaut said while circling the Earth onboard *Discovery*.

Have you ever just stood under the stars, or lay on a soft blanket on a balmy-breezy cloud-drifting day, or touched the clasped fingers of a newborn baby, or marveled at so many colliding coincidences that you had no other option but to declare, "There *is* a God."

During the almost 9-day STS-95 mission in outer space, John Glenn became an experimental guinea pig for studies on geriatrics; and because he was the sole astronaut on the *Friendship 7* mission in 1962, scientists could compare his results and form conclusions. Of course, we're only studying one person, which is like drawing conclusions on an outlier! Still, John Glenn is an adventurer, pioneer, and mission-oriented person, something along the line of Moses, Abraham, and the prophet Isaiah. They were one-of-a-kind and God chosen, and each of those intermediary pillars of divinity had supernaturally infused instruments to help them lead people to belief and trust in God. How? How can we see God working in our lives?

Moses had his "staff of God" (Exodus 4:1-5; 7:12; 7:17; 17:5; 17:8). With his staff of God's power, majesty and might, he changed wood to a snake, water to blood, parted a great sea, and made water flow out of a rock. Abraham believed God's promises, and the Lord established his covenant through him. Abraham then gave the people God's promises and everlasting covenant: "I will make of you a great nation, I will bless you, and I will make your name great; and you are to be a blessing. I will bless those who bless you, but I will curse anyone who curses you; and by you all the families of the earth will be blessed" (Genesis 12:2-3; 22:18). Isaiah had divinely inspired visions showing him the many prophesies that Jesus would fulfill (Isaiah 11:1-3). "He [Jesus] will not judge by what his eyes see or decide by what his ears hear, but he will judge the impoverished justly" (11:3-5). These leaders give us inspiration and encouragement in those moments in our sorrows, aches, and pains. Through our belief in Jesus Christ our Savior, we can call on God's divine staff, his every promise, and the Holy Spirit to help us (Hebrews 13:5-6). What can *anyone* do to us when God is completely on our side?

Father God, we thank you for your infinite grace! Amen.

May 24
Better Than...

I keep saying, "This is *better* than we had in Texas!"

Maybe you can say a similar thing because you're happy where you're at instead of a place you can't stand, or people you can barely tolerate.

Have you ever had *to stay* in a situation you couldn't leave?

Enduring the intolerable felt suffocating. At times, I had to struggle to change my attitude. Isn't that what we have to do when we're stuck somewhere, or with someone, like in a temporary job with a mean boss? We had better find new coping strategies fast, and think of new ways to re-interpret what we believe is a dire situation.

In October 2008, we had to leave almost everything behind in California and start over from scratch. We bought a for-sale-by-owner house in Texas and moved in on March 12, 2009. It felt like I'd made a moon landing! Notice how I remember the exact day 'cause we were scared and traumatized after years of having good jobs, homes, and a middle-class life style that in a matter of days evaporated in the 2008 market crash. It was like water on a sizzling skillet. Sizzling water dances in pops-and-leaps, evaporating into the room's gases. That's how I felt, as if I might disappear—after losing almost everything and leaving California for the unknown Texas wild-west terrain. Except, we had hopes and dream. We believed my husband might find another job, so we could reclaim our middle class status. It never happened.

Then God brought us to Florida, to a comfortable home that now meets our every need. Swimming in our mid-sized pool next to our nice covered patio, I like to backstroke, and look with gratitude at the blue sky while exclaiming: "Thank you, God because this is *so* much better than what we had in drought-drowning Texas." Guess what? Texas has been getting rain for the past two years, and all my "stuck" days have made me appreciate what I have. I don't pout-'n-pine over what we lost, although I do miss the plush Hawaiian-fabric covered sofa sleeper we abandoned in California. "God, thanks for what you gave us, thanks for what you took away, and thanks for what you left us with. Amen." He knows what He's doing for us. "Trouble produces endurance, endurance produces character, and character produces hope" (Romans 5:3-4). Yeah, we have hope.

Jesus, we need to trust in your perfect timing. Amen.

MAY 25
OPPOSITION

I don't know why—whether it's genetics or environment—but my fingernails grow-and-grow for two months out of the year into pleasing shapes. The rest of the time, they break at the pink, hurting, and leaving my fingers looking stubby weird. I feel witch-like! And if you'd see me some mornings with the arthritis settling into a few of my joints, without my partial on my gums, at my bleakest fingernail moments, and with my frizzy graying hair, you'd run away scared even though my clothes are clean and I've washed. We live in such a youth-oriented culture.

What do you consider your worst physical attributes?

Do you repeatedly make yourself aware of them? This is the most important question: Do you let what you consider undesirable dictate your happiness, value, worth, and self-esteem?

"You were called to be free," Paul says (Galatians 5:13). Free from what? To be, how? Existing "youth-oriented" doesn't help!

In astronomy, there's a term for when the Earth passes between the sun and a planet—called *opposition*—stemming from the word, *opposite.* You'd think the Earth would be blocking the planet and light; but in reality, our Earth acts like a lens, creating a *surge* on the planet, thus illuminating all the cracks that are usually obfuscated in shadows to enhance the planet's brilliance as well. What cannot be seen, suddenly shines! Did you ever stop and think, maybe *I'm* seeing myself *so* wrong? In 2 Corinthians 12, God tells Paul: "My power is brought to perfection in weakness." *Weakness* means, *lacking strength, fragility,* and, *a quality or feature regarded as a disadvantage or fault.* If our aging bodies, illnesses, and imperfections could talk back to us, we might hear: "Everything is so wrong with me, making me weaker and less than the best-of-the-best." However, our weaknesses manifest, illuminate, and display God's perfect power to people around us. We are then truly free to allow everything we've been trying to hide, shine; and then we can exclaim: "God is working through me." We become visible vessels of hope, like opposition occurring, between God and those who live in darkness. Always, we are valued. How important you are! F. Scott Fitzgerald once said, "What we must decide is perhaps how we are valuable, rather than how valuable we are" (knightstavern.org). God decides our value, our not culture.

Father, help us show people your work through us. Amen.

MAY 26
THUMBS UP? THUMBS DOWN?

You've seen the two-way mirrors detectives use to interrogate suspects on TV shows. They're special glass through which suspects can't see who is watching the interrogation, as on *NCIS*. Those two-way mirrors can be compared to the personas we use as we interact with people.

What are you showing to people? What are you hiding?

For me, it's so hard to be authentic when I know I'm keeping events in my life secret. I feel like one, giant, walking lie. How can I keep deep-dark secrets? I've moved and changed churches *so* many times. Once, I *was* honest and told a congregation about several of my past sins. Most of those people had been married only *once* and had strong opinions about divorce. "'I hate divorce,' says *Adonai* the God of Israel" (Malachi 2:16). I understand, because I hate divorce too, really. I made mistakes. I have regrets. Thereafter, that congregation treated me differently as people distanced themselves from my current Godly husband and me like the sun to Jupiter! Since then, I've kept my mouth shut. I use restraint and don't tell people my *entire* life story. I call it "selective self-disclosure." What would Paul, Murderer First Class, have said? I persecuted the Messianic Community of God" (1 Corinthians 15:9), he tells us. Do *you* judge? Are *you* ever judge and jury? "The way you judge others is how you will be judged," Jesus says (Matthew 7:2).

I'm not always open and honest. My grandparents were Old Country Hungarian, and they were ashamed of me. After having a child at 18 and another at 19, I divorced. I married someone else, and had another child. I divorced again. I had problems. The largest was the fact I was lost and without Christ. Apostle Paul could relate to me I'm sure. *Years* later, after accepting Jesus as Lord and Savior, I married a wonderful Christian man; but my first two children haven't spoken to me since 2006. How do you explain that to fellow Christians? You don't. I can't. It hurts.

In life, pain can well out from a soul's vast depth in floods, flashes, and cycles. Yet Jesus relieves suffering. "If anyone is united with the Messiah, he is a new creation—the old has passed; look, what has come is fresh and new" (2 Corinthians 5:17)!

Lord, help us gracefully accept the consequences of our past actions. Help us see ourselves as New Creations in Christ. Amen.

MAY 27
GRIST TO THE MILL

Standing in line at the grocery store this afternoon, I couldn't help but eavesdrop on two business women having a quick conversation. I gleaned they didn't work together at the same area, but encountered each other regularly throughout the week. They appeared educated, with senior-level jobs, and upper middle class, based on the costly foods they set down on the conveyor belt.

Don't you think it's strange how we quickly draw impressions of people just as quickly as we change our opinions? It's like our tendency called *pareidolia*, where we give weird unexplainable shapes—like nebulas—names, for example, the "man on the moon" and "the face on Mars." Viewed up close though, we're so wrong. Here's a bit of their conversation I overheard:

"Can you believe Frank is cheating on her?" Woman 1 asked.

"But he's married with two kids," Woman 2 replied. "Last week, Dana broke up with him."

"Wow he sure did find a rebound right away!"

"Speaking of rebounds, did ya hear what happened to Beth Sykes?" Woman 2 asked.

"No, what?" gasped Woman 1.

"She thinks her boyfriend Ray might secretly like … *men*."

"What? I'da *never* suspected *that*!" Woman I said. The conversation stopped when I exhaled loudly, and they realized an outsider was listening. Gossip. After hearing it, I formed an opinion about these people, like believing aliens are secretly mining Europa in all the weird shapes a satellite is transmitting to us.

Do you ever do it? Add grist to the long line of gossip? Our sins caste long shadows….

Sometimes we can find ourselves gossiping without being aware of it because everyone else is announcing "the news," and we're comfortably fitting in, right? However, later, after I meet those people face-to-face and get contradictory information, I'll have a hard time *changing* my mind. That's the problem with gossip. It's a little murderous, don't you think? "Each of us should please his neighbor and act for his good, thus building him up" (Romans 15:2). We are to *build up* people, even hold them up, and do positive acts for people. That's how God works through us to draw people to Christ.

Lord, help us intervene in false worlds of gossip. Amen.

MAY 28
MEMORIALS

This is the time of year for Memorial Day, a holiday commemorating the men and women who died serving in the United States Armed Forces. Wise leaders founded America on Godly principles. "We hold these truths to be self-evident: that all men are created equal; that they are endowed by their Creator with certain unalienable rights" (*Declaration of Independence*). In war are opposing worldviews and beliefs. We fought Hitler and his Nazi machine during World War II. In the Vietnam War, we fought the spread of communism. In Iraq, our men and women died to free an oppressed nation. Now, we are on the threshold of going to battle against ISIL, a genocidal group of Islamic psychopath terrorists who are committing human rights atrocities on a staggering scale that have beheaded babies, filmed acts of rape against women, and crucified men and women who weren't from *their* own bloodthirsty brand of Islam.

J.R.R. Tolkein said something about war. "War must be, while we defend our lives against a destroyer who would devour all; but I do not love the bright sword for its sharpness, nor the arrow for its swiftness, nor the warrior for his glory. I love only that which they defend" (*The Two Towers*). What have soldiers died defending?

No *one* person, or group of people, can determine our worth, value, and rights. Hitler tried to annihilate all Jews. Various communist leaders like Stalin and Mao Tse-tung killed millions. ISIL believes they are a key agent of the coming apocalypse. They're ransacking cities, obliterating archeological treasures, and butchering men, women, and children as they twist a peaceful religious doctrine into an ensemble of unstoppable war machines. And they're heading our way. Some people say attacks on American soil are imminent. "We hold these truths to be self-evident," we believe. We live in God's country, we believe, and we're fighting for His principles. He made us. *He* pronounces *each* individual valuable, vital, and important. Our soldiers enlist and die to preserve these rights given *by* God. "All those gathered here will know that it is not by sword or spear that the Lord saves; for the battle is the Lord's, and he will give all of you [the enemy] into our hands" (1 Samuel 17:47). Let us honor and remember all who died for *our* American way of life.

Father God, you are Jehovah-nissi, our Lord our Banner. We lift you high! We thank you, and ask for your help in battle. Amen.

MAY 29
THROW IN THE TOWEL

Christopher Columbus said, "You can never cross the ocean until you lose sight of the shore." Can you imagine the Great Discoverer at the helm of the *Santa Maria* on that exciting day of August 3, 1492? He believed in a direct trade route from Spain to China and India, and he was determined to map one out. Have you ever felt that type of self-determination, or belief in a dream, that you'd do anything, and go to any length, to prove you're right? "No shore or body can stand in my way," right? On October 12, 1492, Columbus landed on a small island in the present-day Bahamas. He discovered America! Wait. How can you discover all those islands and land that have existed all along? Today there's also proof the Vikings first stepped in Newfoundland and "discovered" America.

Is anything *really* ever discovered? Are not places and things, like warp drive, already in existence, and just waiting for the right person to come along and make them tangible? E-MC^2 has been around since God created the universe, right? At 55, Columbus died in Spain from a progressive inflammation and a degenerative emotional state because he never did receive his promised wealth and official recognition. And after disappearing into the shadows of fame, Albert Einstein died from an aortic aneurism after *years* of failing to discover his Theory of Everything. Still, those famous men changed the world. One step, and Columbus changed the world. One equation, and Einstein set the world on a course to harness nuclear energy. What great changes are you capable of actualizing? If you believe you're too old, you're wrong. Thanks to medicinal "discoveries." However, even if we can't do something Earth shattering, a smile can change someone's day. Have you discovered your smile lately?

Solomon said, "Looking over all of God's work, I realized that it is impossible to grasp all the activity taking place under the sun; because even if a person works hard at searching it out, he won't grasp it; and even if a wise person thinks he knows it, he still won't be able to grasp it" (Ecclesiastes 8:17). He was the most intelligent person ever; yet, he never had it all. One of his conclusions about life? "Whatever task comes your way to do, do it with all your strength" (9:10). Our steps alter our courses in a discoverable way!

God, help us see outside our boxes to discover new avenues thinking, learning, and relating to others. Amen.

May 30
Lost in a Labyrinth

Driving home from the Social Security office, my husband stepped on the accelerator to make it around a large truck. The truck sped up. My husband "floored it" to the stop sign. Wow, did that driver get angry. He raced up so close to our bumper, we couldn't see his front fender. Meanwhile, I felt whiplashed. "I guess the driver wants to be the first to the stop sign," my husband said.

Unclasping the door handle, I noticed the driver had finally backed off after we turned the corner. *Whew.* "I guess it didn't occur to him that we just needed to speed up so we could turn safely. Such a simple reality." Earlier in the day, I had to flick another of my neighbor's cigarette butts off my driveway. What's he thinking? Why not use an ashtray? Early morning, I saw another neighbor's dog pee on my front bushes that I've been nurturing so to obscure the green electric box at the corner of our lot. *Urrgh.* Do you ever feel like you're navigating through peoples' misguided thoughts? They're like potential land mines that we're forced to dodge daily. That's what we're really doing as we go through life, maneuvering through peoples' actions, which are *really* just results of their belief systems. Sometimes, life's a bit like a bumper car ride at a fair. You strap in; but you better hold on for dear life 'cause even if you try driving at the edge of the track for safety, you're gonna get rammed. I wish we could virtually connect with people in their cars or homes—be a little pop-up avatar appearing alongside people to ask them where they're coming from so we can understand one another better, right? Can't happen. At least not yet. So, what now?

Jesus always ran into enemies, and people bent on taking him *down.* Judas was one, "who betrayed him" (Matt 10:4). Satan was another. "The Spirit drove him out into the wilderness, and he [Jesus] was in the wilderness forty days being tempted by the Adversary. He was with the wild animals, and the angels took care of him" (Mark 1:12-13). Like us, Jesus was forced to navigate this sin-stricken world where people are often looking out for themselves. "They hated me for no reason at all" (John 15:25). Yet, like us, Jesus received angelic help from God, as we have the Holy Spirit. "Keep safe the great treasure that has been entrusted to you, with the help of the *Ruach HaKodesh*, who lives in us" (2 Timothy 1:14).

Father, give us help and patience in difficult times. Amen.

MAY 31
BUFFET STYLE

I'd like to continue yesterday's topic: navigating through peoples' belief systems, which, of course, everyone has one. It's hard work walking through a labyrinth, always knowing the starting point but searching for the end. Unless we live like Wolf Man alone in a forest, we're constantly interacting with people who are always reacting and responding to everything *we* say and do. Where will you go that'll be *different* today? *You* might have to navigate through *several* belief systems. For me, the hardest days are when I say something that someone misinterprets. Ever have one of those "what-did-you-just-say-or-mean" moments? The experience is like walking through Homonym land. "It's aero in shape but approaching fast."

"Who's shooting an arrow?"

Imagine going through the day acting on homonyms and talking like that. No thanks. In reality, we do just that sometimes. Jesus understood as He encountered people who were so opposed to him that they couldn't alter their minds when they saw the true altar for the forgiveness of their sins. "Once again the Judeans picked up rocks in order to stone him" (John 10:31). Yet, He healed people who shed their pride and asked him for help (Mark 6:1-6). He didn't heal everyone.

Jesus did not like *hypocrisy*, the appearance of holding moral standards while not acting accordingly. "The scribes and the Pharisees sit on Moses' seat, so do and observe whatever they tell you, but not the works they do. For they preach, but do not practice" (Matthew 23:1-2). Several times, Jesus calls the Sadducees and Pharisees hypocrites (verses 13 and 23). He compares their outsides to beautiful whitewashed tombstones, but their insides are "bones and all uncleanness" (verse 27). Needless to say, *they* began seeking revenge. "They picked up stones to throw at him; but Yeshua was hidden and left the Temple grounds" (John 8:59). With enemies abounding, and proclaiming God's Word while navigating through their life threats—seen and unseen—God protects His Son. So do the angels. "Don't you know that I can ask my Father, and he will instantly provide more than a dozen armies of angels to help me" (Matthew 26:53)? It's okay to wander inside a labyrinth. God is always right with us. Psalm 23.

Lord, help us when we struggle to make sense of others. Amen.

June 1
Lightning-Quick Responses

Has an irritant ever spilled on your hands while you cleaned house, or landed on your skin while fertilizing your lawn? The red blistering effects can sting, burn, or itch for days.

Once I sawed sap-bubbling branches off an invasive pepper tree behind my fence. A neighbor noticed me carrying out the long stems to the curb and stopped me with a warning: "Those pepper trees are from the same family as poison ivy, so their sap could give you a bad reaction." Definitely, I thanked him! After working, I returned to the cool inside, where I see my husband all day long. For a time, we used to work back-to-back in our office, but then I moved to the dining room table to work and type. Why? Being *too* close to someone *all* the time can be like an irritant.

In Ephesians 6:4, Paul advises, "Fathers, don't irritate your children and make them resentful; instead, raise them with the Lord's kind of discipline and guidance." In Colossians 3:21, "Don't irritate your children and make them resentful, or they will become discouraged." The word, "irritate," must pack a powerful punch for it to leave such devastating consequences. "Irritating" someone makes them "resentful" and instills "discouragement."

Feeling intrigued, I'm compelled to do a little more research. When words become so abstract that my mind can't render them in ways I can effectively apply them, I look those words up and then form a Biblical application. "Irritate" means, *to make (someone) annoyed, impatient, or angry; mad, sore, or fed up.* How can a parent *irritate* a child—make him or her *so* annoyed, impatient, angry, mad, sore, or fed up—that the child grows up resentful and discouraged? I guess the answer is: Do we know any discouraged resentful people? I think of a few famous people who exhibited those characters and are dead. Marilyn Monroe always seeking love in the arms of men she married and then divorced in bitter conflagrations. Singer Michael Jackson was always "plasticizing" his face, and constantly embroiled in family frays. Writing about those two and their childhoods biographers uncovered family strife, unavailable parents, and at times, abusive parents. The righteous live a life of integrity; happy are their children after them" (Proverbs 20:7). We *can be* a healing salve in the lives of those who are discouraged and resentful.

Lord, help us encourage seeking, hurting, lonely people. Amen.

JUNE 2
REPEAT, REPEAT, REPEAT

Okay, I'll tell you some of my faults—at least those I'm aware of today—if *you* write down yours. Well? What are you waiting for?

Okay, I'm not able to *see* you, so you have the advantage. However, I can give you a start. Benjamin Franklin wrote, *The Autobiography*, a introspective attempt to categorize what he considered to be the ten most important virtues. He analyzed his thoughts and behaviors, compartmentalizing his weaknesses and strengths. I consider Ben to be one of the first cognitive behaviorists. He kept a daily journal with an hourly schedule, wherein he'd list all his activities and then extrapolate weaknesses. Ben was determined he could eliminate his weaknesses and become fully virtuous. I say he was *trying* to attain perfection, wouldn't you? Number 1 on his list was *Temperance* because he was trying not to eat "to dullness" and drink "to elevation." In other words, he was trying to curb his overeating and excessive drinking.

What might be on your list of priorities for change? Oops, I guess I turned the tide and put *you* first because I really didn't want to reveal my list of faults according to Ben.

There's another saying: What would Jesus do? In all situations, we can pause and ask ourselves that question. However, Jesus was *out* of our culture, right? I'll answer the question in a bit, after I keep my word and give you a brief list of my faults in order of importance. 1) Anxiety, because I'm terrified of about every social situation and stammering when I speak; 2) Making passive-aggressive comments about my husband; 3) Martyr, because I do everything and let you know it; 4) Procrastinating on cleaning the grill; 5) Complaining; 6) spouting off at the mouth [a bit like Ben's *Silence* virtue]; 7) [I'll steal one of Ben's] *Moderation*, avoiding extremes; and, 8) [I'm stealing another of Ben's] *Tranquility*, keeping the peace and fostering peace. "But who can discern their own errors? Forgive my hidden faults" (Psalm 19:12). We can go to Jesus in humility and with a desire to change. My goal? I want to become blameless and pure in God's eyes, and "shine" among those who are lost in sin (Philippians 2:15). How else can they see our Jesus except as He manifests to them through the Holy Spirit who's inside of us? We can show we have become new creations, and are *refining*.

We can talk to you and ask for help at *any* time, Jesus. Amen.

JUNE 3
RUMBLING SUMMER SALES

*Rumble…rumble…*earthquake. I've been through a few when I lived in California. Everything rattles, the floor vibrates, the ground outside wobbles, and buildings sway. Thereafter … dead silence … *everywhere*, as you and Nature regain balance. Have you been through a seismic disturbance? If not, maybe you've experienced a roof-pounding hailstorm, wind-lashing tornado, or rain-splattering hurricane? When you're trapped inside uncontrollable severe conditions, you're on guard, your senses are keen, your brain and reflexes are adrenaline charging, and your social media skills are amplifying to amass information to survive and help others.

All sorts of storms can trickle or rumble through our lives. Bad school grades, a little argument, a nasty divorce, a disintegrated friendship, getting fired or laid off work. Storms take us off guard.

Frederik Douglass was a freed slave who had endured severe beatings under his master. On July 5, 1852, he spoke at a civil rights gathering, which he titled: "What to the Slave is the Fourth of July?" In this speech, he discusses chaotic experiences that sweep through our lives, spinning pain and change: "It is not the light we need, but fire; it is not the gentle shower, but thunder. We need the storm, the thunder, and the earthquake." After a storm, have you ever stood still to watch the world? Smell the rain, inhale the fresh air that's washed away all the pollution, and smiling at the rainbow birthing a prism of sharp colors across the sky. There's surrender to life's upheavals when we realize we're different, *because* of the storm.

God knows what He's doing. Recall the epic Flood and the 100 years Noah spent working on the Ark? In that 100 years of fending off wacky abusive town folk and evil Nephilim giants (Genesis 6:1-5), Noah was the laughing stock of towns! Never was there a drop of rain let alone belief in his flood forecast. Yet, Noah was the first weatherman. He had to have been testing the air daily while building that Ark under God's instructions and then rounding up all the animals. What's been your life storm? As with Noah, we'll experience times when we believe we're right but are wrong, or *made* to believe we're wrong when we're right. But wait! God was designing the sun's light and its rainbow that started its journey from the core over a hundred-thousand years ago to your window.

Father, we need you on sunny days *and* stormy days. Amen.

JUNE 4
LANDSCAPE

Do you know what a tightrope is? It's a long taut line connecting two distant points. What is a tightrope walker? One who walks grand distances, like across Niagara Falls or over dangerous ravines like the famous Ecuadorian highwire walker Jorge Ojeda-Guzman. Sometimes, life's difficulties are just one long tightrope line. Have *you* ever walked a tight rope?

I have; I *do*. However, we're not alone in our struggles and fears.

Every night—maybe due to his Asperger's and meds—my son can't sleep. He naps after school and then wakes up after I go to sleep. I hear him playing his online games. I hear him screaming when he loses, yelling when he believes he's been cheated, and happy when he's victorious. Meanwhile, I toss and turn ... walking the tightrope between sleep and heart-pounding awakenings. After enduring hours of it, I just can't stand all his screaming and yelling. I feel as if I'm walking my own tightrope between persevering and wishing God would "just take me home." Ever hear someone say that to you, especially when they're enduring a severe illness? We have them ... times when we feel like we're walking on a tightrope. What do we do? "God causes everything to work together for the good" (Romans 8:28). Grab hold of Jesus' hand!

Have you ever heard of a coping mechanism? Doctors Susan Folkman and Richard Lazarus wrote a book: *Stress, Appraisal, and Coping*. Coping means to be constantly changing our thoughts and behaviors to manage specific external and/or internal demands that we perceive as "taxing." What's *taxing*? Not paying the government, but *physically or mentally demanding, burdensome, hard, tough, back-breaking,* and, *punishing*, to name a few. When we're walking a tight roping over life's turbulent waters and feel like we're falling, we can encounter Christ. "When they cry out to me, I will hear, for I'm compassionate" (Exodus 22:27). What a deeply-loving coping mechanism from our Lord God, our Jehovah-shammah, our God who is keeping time with our every beating heart. He doesn't leave. Pray, right now, and feel his comforting healing hand. He has a "crown of love" over our heads, right now (Psalm 103:4); and Jesus has compassion on us because we are His helpless sheep (Matthew 9:36). As we walk a tight rope through difficulties, He's always there to catch us if we fall.

Lord God, how we so love you. Amen.

JUNE 5
TALLER AND GRANDER

Have you ever felt desperate to get rid of something?

I have two, robust tall oak trees that are stressing me out. They're making my hair turn grayer by the month. Are you faced with what *seems* to be a minor problem to others, but to you the difficulty is at times waking you up with the night sweats?

The oak on the right side of my house has knotted destructive roots that are beginning to butt against the foundation. The wind blows the tree's leaves into hard-to-reach gutters over my swimming pool enclosure. How can I get the courage to step on the roof to sweep off piles of leaves? Maybe I can fabricate a special pole to help me. Nope. Meanwhile, the tree in the front yard has been an oasis for multi-generational squirrels that keep *rickety-rackety pitter-pattering* across my roof and solar panels. Never mind all the raking and sweeping I have to do in March when that blasted tree sheds all its crispy leaves. I pray, "God please give us a way to take 'em down."

Then I look around. I need to make *so many* improvements. Work is *never* done. Have you felt that way lately? "The Lord is close to the brokenhearted and saves those who are crushed in spirit" (Psalm 34:18). Sometimes, the tasks we need to accomplish in life can appear *crushing*, like faulty cabin pressure at high altitudes. I remember deep-sea diving. I had to unplug my hurting ears. Then, there isn't enough time, or people to help us, or financial means we need. We can become disheartened and anxious. "Whoever gathers money little by little makes it grow" (Proverbs 13:11). So, I've been saving, and I have a fix-it list of priorities that little-by-little I cross off as I accomplish them. Solomon was right about one thing though: "Money is the answer for everything" (Ecclesiastes 10:19). It's sad to admit, but the saying is true: *Money makes the world go round.* Those who have it can buy their way out of these minor problems. Yesterday, my neighbor said he wishes he could win the lottery and hire people to do all the work around his house! "Be merciful to those who doubt; save others by snatching them from the fire; to others show mercy, mixed with fear" (Jude 1:22-23). When others unleash their burdens, we can listen, and encourage them with our successes. As I save, I gradually make home repairs. I try to encourage others, and be a Godly example.

Father, we long to show your peace to the world (Matthew 5:9).

JUNE 6
AFTERMATH

As I approached a deli counter to pick up my order, a customer was in the throng of an angry outburst. "I was first but then *you* served them *first!*" the elderly man ranted.

Glancing fearfully at one another and the deli workers, a few of us quickly stepped back. I pointed at the patient woman who had been slicing my salami. "Sir, she's been helping me for a while—" I showed him other packages she had given me earlier. "—And this is the last one." I laughed, trying to subdue his volcanic fury. "I lived in Hawaii for five years," I continued, "so I learned patience as we all lived on *"Island time"* just taking things as they come."

"I've, been, here, waiting…." The rude dude just wouldn't stop!

"Thanks, Ma-am," I told the amazingly patient worker, patting her hand as she handed me my pound of lunchmeat to help Rusty Fussy Gus. I left fast, while wondering how often, and easily, some people invade our comfortable 3-foot boundary that's an imaginary bubble around us. We walk among people while maintaining those boundaries, and we trust that our fellow humans won't cross it. I marveled at how spectacular the two, deli workers behaved. *Whew—* I wonder if I could have handled the same situation with such grace; so on my way out, I stopped the manager and said: "The deli workers are amazing. They do a *spectacular* job even when disgruntled customers are abusive toward them." She thanked me.

People need to know when they've acted bravely, or are performing above standards. We all deserve a compliment now-and-then. "He builds his upper rooms in heaven and establishes his sky-vault over the earth. He summons the waters of the sea and pours them out over the earth. *Adonai* is his name" (Amos 9:6). God is in the *building* business; and through us, He builds up, encourages, and uplifts people and their discouraged or frightened souls. Sometimes in life, we encounter people whose thoughts are twisting-and-turning or wild-and-weird, morphing those people into Space Invaders, or Rage Warriors who intrude into our personal spaces. I witnessed such clashes a few times, and the experiences weren't fun. *"Adonai* will do battle for you. Just calm yourselves down" (Exodus 14:14). Those workers maintained a calmness demeanor. They were an example to me, and now to you.

God, touch our mouths with your words (Jeremiah 1:9). Amen.

JUNE 7
FRINGE

Have you ever felt threatened by a classmate, neighbor, colleague, competitor, or Nature? We can't *affect* Nature, so we have to examine our relationships with people when we feel threatened.

Here's my history of "feeling threatened." From 1993-2001, a neighbor's gardener kept "blowing" all the neighbor's grasses onto my driveway so that after I arrived home from teaching, I'd find piles of grass and debris. Was I ticked off. And threatened. From 2002-2006 when I lived in Hawaii, the neighbor on my right kept taking my bird feeders and cutting down my roses to keep her sliver-of-an ocean view. Another threat. Now, the neighbor on my right keeps giving me sarcastic comments even though her house looks like a mold-and-mildew "elephant in the room." I'm prayin', and wavin' *hi* ... but it doesn't mean I'm feelin' any better 'bout my threat level.

Have you ever wondered, What's wrong with me that I should be so bothered? What's at the root of "feeling threatened?"

John gets to the core of this type of "threatened" feeling. "There is no fear in love. On the contrary, love that has achieved its goal gets rid of fear, because fear has to do with punishment; the person who keeps fearing has not been brought to maturity in regard to love" (1 John 4:18). Ouch. *I'm* the problem! *I'm* "immature" in regard to "loving" people. How? We are to show love to others, just as they are, so they can see Christ emanating from us. "Since we have received an unshakeable Kingdom, let us have grace, through which we may offer service that will please God" (Hebrews 12:28). Jesus served people. What a high price He paid for our eternal lives that one day we'll have with Him. Now, we live in "certain hope of eternal life;" and, "God, who does not lie, promised that life before the beginning of time" (Titus 1:2). With that special hope we're living, how can we be afraid? In the fabric of eternity—time that will proceed after our deaths—we take comfort in knowing Jesus is beside us as people we meet throughout our day test us with the question: Is that person [insert your name here] *really* a Christian; and if so, how are they different from everyone else I know? It's like a Jesus meter we're displaying from 0 to 10: 0 being, "[Your name] is no Christian," to a 10 being, "[Your name] is a true example of Christ and I want that." Then, you'll inspire them to want Jesus.

Father God, give us a spirit of self-control and patience. Amen.

JUNE 8
OFF THE BEATEN PATH

Many times, we'll have to stand on the sidelines and watch someone else accept a victory trophy, clutch the prize, kiss the Big Award, or swoop up a coveted promotion. We can't always win or be included. What have you won over the years? Lost? What groups have you been included in, or excluded from? Or, maybe you've been a runner up. Is second, third, or honorable mention good enough? Perhaps people are attending to your nemesis—a constant competitor you just can't stand, a brown-nosing colleague, or someone who manipulates to make his or her life "easy." Perhaps they're prospering as you're wonder, *why*, and pray, "God—this is so unfair!" We can't always be "included" or "be in the lime light."

We do live for God. "In God I trust" (Psalm 56:4). We're about humility. "Do nothing out of selfish ambition or vain conceit. Rather, in humility value others above yourselves" (Philippians 2:3). We are always to show love. "Let his banner over me be love" (Song of Songs, 2:4). We're here to foster peace. "I tell you, love your enemies and pray for those who persecute you, that you may be children of your Father in heaven" (Matthew 5:44-45). If love means shutting our mouths when we lose, or watching people we don't like receive accolades or attention, we *must* retreat into the shadows of our disappointment and accept our "second," "third," or no honorary place. It's okay. God's alongside us, ushering us through our disappointments. "He has made everything beautiful in its time. He has also set eternity in the human heart" (Ecclesiastes 3:11). God has eternity *with you* set permanently *with Him*. "Whoever drinks the water I give them will never thirst. Indeed, the water I give them will become in them a spring of water welling up to eternal life" (John 4:14). What "water" is Jesus talking about? In Genesis 1:2, God hovers over the waters. Then God says, "Let there be light." Water is here since the beginning and Jesus was there since the beginning. He tells us, *I am eternal life*. "Believe him [God] who sent me and have eternal life. You will not be judged but cross over from death to life" (John 5:24). You might not be fourth, fifth, one-hundredth, fifty-millionth, or on someone's fame list. Yet, we *are* God's.

You are *First Place* to Him, always, and every second of the day. He hugs us in the very air we breathe.

We worship you for your gift of salvation, Lord. Amen.

J.P. OSTERMAN

JUNE 9
ORDER OF IMPORTANCE

A *mezuzah* (Hebrew מְזוּזָה meaning *doorpost*) is a piece of parchment paper inscribed with God's commandment from Deuteronomy 6:4-9 and 11:13-21. The Jewish prayer "Shema Yisrael" begins, "Hear, O Israel, the LORD our God, the LORD is One." The parchment must be handwritten in indelible ink with a special quill pen by a special scribe, a *sofer stam*, who then rolls up the prayer and seals it inside a narrow case. The Jewish people then affix this prayer at the entryway to their homes and businesses. God's Chosen People are a tight community, like pillars, supporting one another. Do you have such a Christian group? Do you need one?

Isn't it comforting to have someone you can turn to and talk to—or just vent—when you're experiencing family turmoil, an illness, a burden, a financial hardship, an indecision, or disappointment? In the early Christian church, persecution was rampant; so followers of Jesus had to mark their doors with symbols, called iconography, so worshippers would know whom to trust. Do you ever wonder whom you can really trust with your secrets and distresses? Sometimes, I'm not sure who I can trust, yet I know I don't want *everyone* knowing my sins. In my church after the sermon, there's an altar call when the pastor invites newly saved people to the front who want to join our church, pray, or confess a sin. Once, a traveling pastor preached and several people "came to Christ." When our pastor asked them to come forward, no one did, even though they raised their hands. Why? Might it be our shame and guilt? "What will people think of me?"

God tells us, "When anyone becomes aware that they are guilty in any of these matters [sins], they must confess in what way they have sinned" (Leviticus 5:5). Confession is important. Everyone's in the same boat because we're all sinners and fall short of God's glory. David confessed his sins plenty of times. "I confess my iniquity; I am troubled by my sin" (Psalm 38:18). There's something about our *troubling* sins, that after we tell Jesus, we receive healing. We can turn to and trust a Christian friend. "Confess your sins to each other and pray for each other so that you may be healed. The prayer of a righteous person is powerful and effective" (James 5:16). Jesus is our shepherd and best friend. He puts people in our lives to listen.

Jesus, we receive your healing and now have peace! Amen.

162

JUNE 10
SWIM SUIT READY

Here's an important life lesson the Bible teaches: "A gentle response deflects fury, but a harsh word makes tempers rise" (Proverbs 15:1). Have you ever started a day determined to apply what you've learned in the Bible, but then a situation happens, and the day changes to bad, with your family or friends ending up mad?

"What went wrong?" I asked my distraught self in the mirror, because I had to leave an argument or else I woulda pulled out some of my hair! "The grace he gives is greater" (James 4:6). So what did I do? "Anyone who knows the right thing to do and fails to do it is committing a sin" (James 4:17). Sometimes, it's best to walk away, re-center, and collect our confusing thoughts so we can return to the person in a calm and collected state. By now, you're probably wondering what the argument was about. Here goes....

"Have you tried on that bikini top I bought you yet?" my husband asked me.

"Yes, it fits fine, much better than that skimpy one you bought me last year that I wouldn't be caught dead in at the beach," I huffed.

"What? You would have looked *fine* in it," he scoffed.

"No way! Half my flesh would hang out if I'd wear that—that *thing*." The faded one-piece suit from five years ago fits the best.

"It did not," he began. "You're just too self-conscious."

"There's nothing wrong with being concerned about how I look," I snapped. An analogy occurred to me. "What if I bought you one of those Speedo swimsuits and asked *you* to wear it?"

He grimaced at the thought. All I could do was wait. He's a large man, so quite a bit of flesh would roll out over Speedo elastic. "Okay," touché he sighed, "I get it."

Whether or not to wear a bikini is a question many women struggle with, but for a Christian woman, the issue takes on additional implications. God calls women to modesty and not draw attention to themselves. "Likewise, the women, when they pray, should be dressed modestly and sensibly in respectable attire... Rather, they should adorn themselves with what is appropriate for women who claim to be worshipping God" (1 Timothy 2:9-10).

Father God, help us understand that each person is responsible for their own actions and that our bodies, belong to God and are to be used for His glory, not our own. Amen.

JUNE 11
UNIVERSAL PLEA

With most of my small group of friends, I'm not able to *really* confide in, tell them what's going on in my heart, or how I feel deep down in my soul—or what I'm thinking.

Have you ever felt an emotion or recalled memories so deeply that you can't express them?

Only God, Jesus, and the Holy Spirit can read and understand the deepest cracks and crevices that appear as wrinkles and expressions of what we've been through while walking on this whirlwind of an Earth. Sometimes, our experiences are joyous and breath taking; other times, sorrowful and painful. And there are those moments you want to take time to contemplate those memories, meditate on God, or practice mind exercises, like how to play tennis, what you plan to say to a disgruntled employee, or how to resolve a conflict. They're Mind Events—personal to *only* you. However, *are* we alone—and isolated—in our thought worlds? We might *feel* alone, believe we're experiencing a solitary world, or lost in an imaginary experience. But are we, really?

"If I climb up to heaven, you are there; if I lie down in Sh'ol, you are there" (Psalm 139:8). What is "Sh'ol?" Actual hell? Or is hell the consequences we must endure after Jesus has forgiven us of our sins? Sometimes people continue to become lost and mired in the shameful sins of their past. Getting lost this way happens to me now-and-then because God didn't equip our brains with an erase button as we'd delete a TV show off the DVR.

"As water reflects the face, so one human heart reflects another" (Proverbs 27:19). Have you ever encountered a person who reflects your heart? Our hearts are comprised of our joys, loves, loses, survival experiences, sorrows, turmoil, and triumphs. We are never alone, forced to suffer in solitude, or experience joy alone. We are Christians. We have a family. If you're part of a church whose members don't accept you as part of their family, it's time to leave. "Encourage each other, and build each other up" (1 Thessalonians 5:11); and, "Bear one another's burdens—in this way you will be fulfilling the *Torah's* true meaning, which the Messiah upholds" (Galatians 6:2).

We can listen and love.

God, help us build community and gather as family. Amen.

JUNE 12
DISCOVERY

I have a challenge for you to try one day. In a swimming pool, find a way to weight yourself down so you can look from the bottom up, from about 10 feet below, toward the sun. If you physically can't, you can use your imagination. Your mission is to see the sun from a different perspective. It's fun. What you'll see is such a different Sun than what we're used to. You can actually *look* at the Sun.

In Hawaii, I used to dive. I joined dive clubs and obtained Padi certificates, such as Photography Diver, Rescue Diver, Deep-Sea Diver, Wreck Diver, Nitrox Diver, Drift Diver, and Boat Diver. Why? There's nothing like being 60 feet under water, exploring another world, establishing neutral buoyancy, rolling onto your back—which would be like floating in air—and looking at the bright-yellow wafer-round Sun and the undulating surface waves. I've always been on a search for God. Have you ever wanted to see God, hear His voice, touch Him? "I came that they may have life and have it abundantly," Jesus said.

What does "have life abundantly" mean? This may sound trivial and unnecessary, but what does *life* mean? The existence of an individual human being or animal, and, the condition that distinguishes animals and plants from inorganic matter, including the capacity for growth, reproduction, functional activity, and continual change preceding death are the definitions for "life." Life is existence, and a condition of being that is different from plants and inorganic matter like the elements on the Periodic Table. If we have "life," we are growing, can have children, can move, and change up to the point when we die—the ultimate change. "Before the mountains were born, before you had formed the earth and the world, from eternity past to eternity future you are God. For from your viewpoint a thousand years are merely like yesterday or a night watch" (Psalm 90:2). God is Jehovah which means essence, being, Time, and, space-time. He is omnipresent—in outer space, the far reaches of our universe, and within you and me, right now. That is how important and loved we are! "Adonai, I am awed by your deeds. Bring your work to life in our own age, make it known in our own time" (Habakkuk 3:2). His creation "work" is alive in us!

Breathe His oxygen that's surrounding you … inhale Him.

Jesus, we love you more each day. Amen.

JUNE 13
SCHEDULE TODAY!

In my closet, I have several purses. One for each season. A few even match outfits. A couple of purses I can use for the beach, and two "clutches" can only carry a tube of lipstick, a key, my ID, and a bank card. Some purses I unpacked long ago—thrown out the used Starbuck's cards, even some gift cards from closed stores. One, small dazzling silk purse with a delicate chain is a black evening clutch that can blend in with my black dress when I attend funerals. How many purses, wallets, or fanny packs do you have? As I reach into one old frayed purse, I nearly poke myself with a broken pin, and smoosh a stale peppermint. I want to throw this purse out, but I can't.

Grief is like purses and the junk inside them. On some days, and in some seasons of my life, my grief is heavy with memories and the burdensome emotions attached to those memories like that baked-in peppermint candy at the bottom of that black evening clutch. Then, I feel distant from God, wondering if He's still listening to my prayers for forgiveness. "I waited patiently for *Adonai*, till he turned toward me and heard my cry" (Psalm 42). Sin has a way of causing all sorts of grief—from the little consequences of my "little" infractions to my Bermuda Triangle of sins. The latter ones feel harder for God to forgive. Do you have any peppermint-sticking grief that you just can't pick off your soul, or for which you believe God isn't forgiving? "I am exhausted from crying, my throat is dry and sore, my eyes are worn out with looking for my God," David once prayed in Psalm 69. Remember what he did that it took the prophet Nathan to wake him out of his denial? "You murdered Uriyah the Hittite with the sword and taken his wife as your own wife; you put him to death with the sword of the people of 'Amon" (2 Samuel 12:9). What grief David must have experienced, realizing he had sinned so horribly, his anguish reverberating today in Psalm 69. Our grief can be the same; yet, we have a perfect answer that'll unstick it from the bottom of our pursing souls so we can move forward with our day. "When the Lord saw her, he felt compassion for her and said to her, "Don't cry" (Luke 7:13). Now hear Jesus's comforting words cutting through any lingering sadness you have today. He heals our grieving hearts.

Father, we can count on your for forgiveness and healing. Amen.

JUNE 14
SKULL AND CROSSBONES

Do you have a difficult parent, or relative, who is ornery, flighty, or aloof? My friend Vicky has one. "Joyce, my dad is toxic poison. It's a good thing I live on the east coast and *he's* on the west coast."

That was hard for her to tell me. She had just learned that her 87-year-old dad will be shacking up with a gold-digging woman for the *fourth* time. His behaviors continue to slide into abject sinfulness, leading to psychological and spiritual consequences for his offspring. He never calls her, but she's always calling and visiting him. "It's all about him," Vicky said. "Everything revolves around him, his looks, and maintaining a hassle-free, carefree uncomplicated life." He doesn't care what Vicky thinks, and he's not concerned about a Godly legacy for her children. He doesn't give a second thought to the damage he's done, or how Vicky narrates his stories. "I've spent my life trying to please my neglectful, unavailable, and abusive Dad."

Then she cried. I sat beside her, consoling her. Father's Day is approaching. "There's no way I can pick out one of those loving Father's Day cards." What does one give such a dad for Father's Day? What do you do when you can't respect your own dad? Vicky is facing a nightmare. Furthermore, it's been hard for her to believe her spiritual God—Elohim Father—loves her since she didn't have a loving human father.

What do we do when we don't have that example? I've at times, I've suffered. I've hurt. Are you hurting because of family members? If you aren't, how do you tell one of your parents that they're not "an example?" Should Vicky "tell off" her dad? His eternal soul is at risk for hell! "They have lost all feeling, so they have abandoned themselves to sensuality, practicing any kind of impurity and always greedy for more" (Ephesians 4:19).

I use the Lord's Prayer (Matthew 6:9-13)? This is how I pray it, to our Dad who matters. "Father, you are in Heaven and here with me now. You are complete holiness, and the universe displays your glory. Your Kingdom *will* come, and your will *is* being done, *now*, as my life unfolds before you. Give me what I need today, and forgive my sins as I forgive others. Please, protect me from sinning, and keep me from Satan. No matter what happens, I *will* trust you *and* believe in you, *and* proclaim you to everyone. Amen."

God, *you* are Father. One day we will see you. Amen.

JUNE 15
EQUIPPED AND RIGGED

I have three stuffed animals on my bedspread out of a giant bag we gave to Goodwill that my son originally won playing the claw machines. Have you ever played a claw machine that's at the entryway to restaurants, in motel fun zones, in grocery stores, and at entertainment centers? You insert $.50, and then the machine comes to life with lights and music. Now, aim the rocking, squeaking open claw at the stuffed animal (or bauble, decoration, etc.), maneuvering it quickly over the item you want before the red countdown ends. Then release the claw, hoping it'll grab onto the object of your heart's desire. If by chance the claw latches onto it, you quickly must lift the animal out of its tight bundle, race it to opening, and hope it drops into the chute so you can capture your prize. Sounds easy? Nope.

The game's rigged. I heard on average it takes up to twenty-five tries to win, with failure resulting anywhere from point A to J, and at anywhere from $.50 to $1.00. Add it up, and you could be out $25.00! What a rip off, but there's something about us that just won't let go of what we want. Some people have kicked the machine, some shake it, and a few people have tried crawling up to the lodged prize only to get stuck. Do you every find yourself stuck? Focused on one thing to the point where you can't let it go and your goals suffer? When will we just … let "it" go, and concentrate on what matters?

I'm reminded of the parable of woman who has ten drachmas, loses one, and then searches *everywhere* to find it (Luke 15:8-10). Strange that Jesus uses a woman to be the subject and not the man of the house, the actual breadwinner would have been responsible for the money. In Biblical times, the word *drachma* meant *to grasp*. It's the amount of "money" a person can hold in his or her hand. If you had a drachma—or fist full—of gold, you would be rich. The woman loses one. This woman's role is to be in *complete* charge of her household. As God puts Jesus in charge of shepherding us, *she's* in charge of everything. "What woman … won't light a lamp, sweep the house and search all over until she finds it" (v. 8)? When she finally finds what she's lost, she calls everyone to celebrate. "There is joy among God's angels when one sinner repents" (v.10). Every day, we long for things that ultimately won't do us one iota of good. Every moment we repent of a sin, an angel sings.

Father, help us to let go of things that don't matter. Amen.

JUNE 16
SLOWING DOWN

"It's hotter in Florida than Texas," I told my husband this morning, feeling sweaty even though the inside temperature was 77°.

"No way!" he argued. "Don't you remember feeling relieved at night when the temperature would hit eighty?" I remembered that baking summer of 2011 when there were 111 days in a row with daytime temperatures over 100°. I thought I'd melt and die. Still, my morning complaining went on … as my pool pump surged on, and the shadows outside my back sliding door indicated shade and coolness from our nice patio covers, and the dark distance rippled a bit from the tropical breezes blowing. Where's the gratitude?

Do you read the newspaper? Here are a few facts I discovered in today's paper. In 2010, nine months after an earthquake hit Haiti more than 8,000 people died of cholera as relief aid *disappeared*. In war-torn third-world countries, people are suffering and dying from racial and religious persecution. In desperate attempts to procure new lives, for example, refugees fleeing Libya for Italy risk being swallowed up in disastrous shipwrecks or returned back to Libya and then imprisoned in reeking, urine-soaked, lice-swarming detection centers. I'm sure those people often look up into the cracked ceiling, crying: "God help me!" That's what I prayed for them who, like my grandparents, left Hungary for a new life.

Often times, it takes going through a horrible taxing event to appreciate what we have in the moment, to celebrate God for helping us surmount our difficulties, and to worship Him in gratitude. Did you know that the ancient Jewish people had a thanksgiving choir (Nehemiah 12:38)? After the Babylonians returned the land they had conquered back to the Jewish people, the people celebrated their rebuilt city of Jerusalem. It was a party of the grandest scale that went on for days worshipping God—God the Healer, the Provider, the Victor. "The singers sang loudly, directed by Yizrachyah (Jehovah will shine)." With joy they offered great sacrifices that day. … The women and children too rejoiced, so that the celebrating in Yerushalayim could be heard far off" (Nehemiah 12:40-43). Have we *purposely* thanked Him today? "Offer thanksgiving as your sacrifice to God, pay your vows to the Most High" (Psalm 50:14). A simple, *thanks*, is paying Him back.

Lord, thank you for providing us with our daily needs. Amen.

JUNE 17
BETTER HEALTH

Sometimes, it *all* comes together perfectly....

The perfect movie, the recipe that turns out lip-smacking good, the hottest date ever, the most-excellent sunset, the ideal job with the *best* salary, the day we never want to end, and arriving at the "top o' the mountain" (whatever your "mountain" might be). Sometimes, we might reach the highest point where everything smells, tastes, and feels grand, high, happy, "I made it—I'm here—I arrived!"

Wait for it ... just wait....

You've seen the ball drop on New Year's Eve. You've been on the fun Rotor ride, until the floor drops. Do you feel the bottom dropping today because of something you've done or said?

Adam and Eve had it all. "They were both naked, the man and his wife, and they were not ashamed" (Genesis 2:25). Then they ate *that* fruit. Then came abject shame! "The eyes of both of them were opened, and they realized that they were naked. So they sewed fig leaves together to make themselves loincloths. ... *Adonai*, God, made garments of skin for Adam and his wife and clothed them" (Genesis 3:7-21). I guess they didn't get the sewing thing right 'cause God had to teach them, right? Then follows Cain and Abel. God was pleased with Abel who was always so happy with God. Still, God tries to help jealous Cain. "Why are you angry?" He asks Cain. "Why so downcast? If you are doing what is good, shouldn't you hold your head high? And if you don't do what is good, sin is crouching at the door. It wants you, but you can rule over it" (Genesis 4:6-7). Happiness ends when Cain kills Abel. Can we *rule* over *our* sins so we can keep our lives always happy and perfect? Isn't it sin—our sins and the sins of others—what makes our lives miserable? "Just stop sinning," someone will tell us. We can't be perfect. Yet Jesus was perfect for us. That's the great news for today. Savior Jesus catching us when the bottom falls out from under our lives.

God told Adam and Eve at their highest happiest point in life: "You are neither to eat from it [the fruit of the tree in the middle of the garden] nor touch it, or you will die" (Genesis 3:3). You'd think threat of death would have stopped them. Nope. "Courage, son [daughter]! Your sins are forgiven" (Matthew 9:2). What a wonderful Lord we have who still secures Heaven for us sinners one day.

Jesus, we long for the day when sin will exist no more. Amen.

JUNE 18
DECEPTION

At age 2, 30% of children lie; at 3, 50% lie; and, by 7 and 8, 100% of all children will lie. These statistics come from an experiment conducted on children and lying by Dr. Kang Lee, a Developmental Psychologist at the University of Toronto (Lee, K., Talwar, V., McCarthy, A., Ross, I., Evans, A., & Arruda, C.; 2014. "Can Classic Moral Stories Promote Honesty in Children?" *Psychological Sciences*). Do a search on *lying*, and you won't believe the websites you'll find, as follows: *Do you know when someone is lying to you? The Signs that someone is lying to you. How to make someone admit they're lying to you.* To test for the truth, we need concealed lie detectors, right? I've told little white lies now-and-then. Like Dr. Lee says in his research, "We lie because we have exhausted all the options, so lying becomes our best way to handle a difficult situation" (*Through the Wormhole: Why We Lie*, narrated by Morgan Freeman, June 3, 2015; Season 6, episode 6).

Do you lie? What's the last lie *you* told? Why? According to both these sources, all people lie—from the little white lie, to the point where that's all someone can tell—lies—and their entire world becomes one giant lie. We can become diseased, "dis" "ease" with reality, so lie. In the news, the feds just charged former House speaker Dennis Hastert of covering up a decade's old misconduct. He paid his victim over $3.5 million in hush money. He was someone, everyone thought he wasn't. *Digital deception* can run along the same sinful gauntlet. Because people can't see us on social-media sites, it's easy to portray ourselves as someone else, to lie.

"I am he who knows," God says (Jeremiah 29:23). A *lie* is: *a false statement made with a deliberate attempt to deceive* (noun); fib (verb); and, *intending to convey a false impression* (verb). God also says, "Do not steal from, defraud or lie to each other" (Leviticus 19:11). Where does lying come from? "Satan ... from the start he was a murderer ... there is no truth in him. When he tells a lie, he is speaking in character; because he is a liar—indeed, the inventor of the lie" (John 8:44). However, Jesus is truth! He always told the truth and still teaches us God's truths (Matthew 22:16; Mark 12:14). Truth might be hard to handle, but knowing the truth is freeing (John 8:32). What was Jesus profound truth in John 8:58? "Before Avraham came into being, I AM!" He was God in the flesh, and touches people today.

Jesus, when we are lied to, help us return *you* to them. Amen.

JUNE 19
CAMPAIGN SEASON

Are you tormented lately by what you can't have, a job you can't secure, the person you love who doesn't love you, the person who won't listen to you, anxiety, or depression?

Demons come in many forms, Brothers and Sisters. "Yeshua [Jesus] went all over the Galil [Galilee] teaching in their synagogues, proclaiming the Good News of the Kingdom, and healing people from every kind of disease and sickness. Word of him spread throughout all Syria, and people brought to him all who were ill, suffering from various diseases and pains, and those held in the power of demons, and epileptics and paralytics; and he healed them" (Matthew 4:23-24). What demons are attacking or tormenting you?

Jesus can help us. We only need to ask Him for relief. "They brought to Yeshua all who were ill or held in the power of demons, and the whole town came crowding around the door. He healed many ... and expelled many demons, but he did not allow the demons to speak, because they knew who he was" (Mark 1:32-34). Demons flee Jesus when those who believe in Him call out His name to drive those intrusive, hateful, spiteful, divisive demons to Hell. "'Away with you, Satan! For the *Tanakh* says, *Worship Adonai your God, and serve only him.*' " The name of Jesus drives out the Devil whose purpose is to destroy our precious relationship with Jesus. "We are not struggling against human beings, but against the rulers, authorities and cosmic powers governing this darkness, against the spiritual forces of evil in the heavenly realm" (Ephesians 6:12). Look around you. What do you see? Just people and objects? Wrong. There are beings, rulers, authorities, and cosmic powers governing "this darkness." What's this current darkness?

Not light! *Not* the love and goodness God intended from the beginning. "I am the light of the world; whoever follows me will never walk in darkness but will have the light which gives life," Jesus tells us (John 8:12). From the beginning, we see God's light breaking the horizon, which is now transferring *into* this world *through* Jesus. "The city has no need for the sun or the moon to shine on it, because God's *Sh'khinah* gives it light, and its lamp is the Lamb [Jesus]" (Revelation 21:23). *Shi'khinah* means *glory*, and *glory* means *eminence, splendor, grandeur, majesty, greatness,* and *beauty.*

Jesus, we long for your presence every second of today. Amen.

JUNE 20
ERASER READY

Waiting is like playing Monopoly. You sigh and groan when your opponent, for minutes on minutes, contemplates the next move. You fidget. "Come on! Roll the dice! Just move!"

"In him [God, Jesus, and the Holy Spirit] we live and move and exist. Indeed, as some of the poets among you have said, 'We are actually his children'" (Acts 17:28). *You* are His child.

Let's look closer at the above words and delve into their awesome meanings. The preposition, *in*, means, *expressing the situation of something that is or appears to be enclosed or surrounded by something else.* We are encapsulated everywhere by God. "In" the Divine Trinity, we move and exist. Have you ever dived *into* a pool, lake, or river? You're *surrounded* by water. Before your birth, comforting water enveloped you in a perfect warm secure bath, just as now, every element of God's vital oxygen is pressing in on us, keeping us alive.

Can you right now take a calm breath? Inhale the elements He created, just for you? He loves us that much.

"Here, I'm standing at the door, knocking. If someone hears my voice and opens the door, I will come in to him and eat with him, and he will eat with me" (Revelation 3:20). Did you know that in Heaven, Jesus will be serving us? "He will put on his work clothes, seat them at the table, and come serve them himself" (Luke 12:37-38)! He will one day, serve, *you.* We are loved and special to Him.

Continuing on, the word, *will*, means, *certainly* and *without a doubt.* Jesus *will* inhabit the soul of *anyone* who asks Him to enter. Where does He enter? "God is greater than our hearts, and he knows everything" (1 John 3:20). What is greater than our hearts? "Please do me this favor in the Lord; refresh my heart in the Messiah" (Philemon 1:20). Our minds are as important as our hearts, for they are the powerhouses of all our decisions. "Dear friends, keep in mind the words spoken in advance by the emissaries of our Lord Yeshua" (Jude 1:17). Jesus enters our minds and hearts.

We *move* on Earth because our atmosphere is closed off from the vacuum of space, and we "exist" *surrounded* by Elohim, Lord Creator. He always presses around us. "Keep asking, and it will be given to you; keep seeking, and you will find; keep knocking, and the door will be opened to you" (Matthew 7:7). Ask for your needs, now.

Father, you are our every breath. Amen.

June 21
Summer Solstice

Daylight Savings Time (DST) really began with the Uniform Time Act of 1966. Changing from Standard Time to DST, Congress meant to conserve energy from the last Sunday of April to the last Sunday of October. However, *everything* changed. Retailers like to make money around Easter, and the candy industry lobbied to keep Daylight Savings Time until November to allow for safe Trick-or-Treating (lots of candy sales).

The "time saver" was meant to conserve energy, but didn't, because people then had enough time after arriving home from work on the long summer days to go shopping. So, we're expending gas energy. The government should help us, right? Government doesn't always do that—or should I say, the people enacting the laws. "In the same place as justice, was wickedness ... in the same place as righteousness, was wickedness" (Ecclesiastes 3:16). We elect them, yet sometimes, politicians fail us. "I turned away and thought about all the kinds of oppression being done under the sun. I saw the tears of the oppressed, and they had no one to comfort them. The power was on the side of their oppressors, and they had no one to comfort them" (Ecclesiastes 4:1).

Have you been feeling overpowered lately? Are the representatives for whom you voted *not* functioning? "I considered the dead happier, because they were already dead, than the living, who must still live their lives; but happier than either of them is the one who has not yet been born, because he has not yet seen the evil things that are done under the sun" (Ecclesiastes 4:2-3). King Solomon—the wise one—experiences a bout of depression as he writes his autobiography. What might *your* autobiography say?

Look up, now. Jesus is our ultimate ruler. "If it has been proclaimed that the Messiah has been raised from the dead, how is it that some of you are saying there is no such thing as a resurrection of the dead? ... Messiah *has* been raised from the dead, the first fruits of those who have died. Death came through a man, also the resurrection of the dead has come through a man. For just as in connection with Adam all die, so in connection with the Messiah all will be made alive" (1 Corinthians 15:12-22). After death, there is eternity with Him. Earthly rulers can't stop that.

Praise you Jesus for giving us eternal life with you. Amen.

JUNE 22
SHARK ATTACK

Now that it's summer time, there's an exercise I do daily. To keep the yellow algae from congealing on the pool walls, I wade around in the water, running the balls of my feet along the rough sides of the pool. It's definitely exercise since I hold onto the pool's edge and bob up and down. I "foot-sweep" the circumference—shallow end to deep end. I feel as if I'm in a dunk tank at a carnival. Yellow algae is a Fun Killer—pool-darkening slimy filth.

So can be my anger. Since we live around and with people, we're gonna get angry. Have you ever been so angry that your heart might explode outta your chest? Our anger can be like that yellow slime forming on the sides of my pool—a joy killer in need of eradication. "Be angry, but don't sin—don't let the sun go down before you have dealt with the cause of your anger" (Ephesians 4:6).

"Well, thanks Paul." Now I'm angry at Paul who's dead and with Jesus. Drats. What to do when you get *so* mad?

Remember Jacob and Esau? They were Isaac's sons, the Isaac for whom Abraham waited so long. What happened? Before Isaac dies, he gives his blessing to the wrong son. "Your brother came deceitfully and took your blessing" (Genesis 27:35). Wow is Esau ticked off! His father then tells him, "I have made him lord over you and have made all his relatives his servants, and I have sustained him with grain and new wine" (27:37). Anger turns into ... well, murder, the kind that engulfed Cain who killed Abel. "I will kill my brother Jacob" (27:41). Later, deceit returns to Jacob when he falls in love with his heart's desire. He works for Rachel's hand in marriage for *seven* years, but then he doesn't receive what Rachel's father promised him. "Laban brought together all the people of the place and gave a feast. But when evening came, he took his daughter Leah and brought her to Jacob, and Jacob made love to her. ... When morning came, there was Leah! So Jacob said to Laban, 'What is this you have done to me? I served you for Rachel, didn't I? Why have you deceived me" (Genesis 29:22-25)? What does this story have to do with acquiring relief from our anger? Hey, God will one day judge us: "The wicked God will judge" (Ecclesiastes 3:17). And the saying is true: *What goes around comes around.* Pray. We may not *see* people get justice for the wrongs done to us; yet God sees all injustice.

God, give us a calm spirit as we wait through our hurts. Amen.

JUNE 23
SUFFERING A BLOW

"Please help me put the flour mixture into this large baggie," my son said with raw chicken ready to coat with flour.

"Joy, while you're up, can you get me my finasteride so I can fill my pill box?" my husband asked.

I looked from my needy son to my pleading husband. All the while, I have sausage frying, toast about to pop, and the microwave beeping. What to do when you're in the middle of crosswinds? Reba McEntire once said: "Being a strong woman is very important to me. But doing it all on my own is not."

Can we "have it all?" Work, be moms and wives?

Some days, I feel at the brink of collapse because there's so much to do and so many family members, acquaintances, and people in ministry who need me. Are you feeling stretched at the limbs? Are the demands in your live leaving you windswept? There's help.

I tell my son, "One day I'm not going to be around to help you with the simple things 'cause I'll be with God."

David the psalmist once said, "Even though my father and mother have left me, *Adonai* will care for me." At some time, we're going to leave our loved ones. Isn't that what parenting is really about? Preparing our children for life after we're gone?

In times when we feel pulled in multiple directions by needy people, we can step back and take time for ourselves to replenish, recover, and fill ourselves with God's care so we can return to helping others. "I keep myself calm and quiet, like a little child on its mother's lap—I keep myself like a little child" (Psalm 131:2). Let us sit on our Abba Father Adonai's lap, with the Holy Spirit breathing peace into us. "My covenant ... is one of life and peace" (Malachi 2:5). God is Jehovah-shalom, God of Peace. God first mentions his comforting name in Judges 6:22-24: "Peace to you, do not fear." What will we receive in return? "The Lord is near! Don't worry about anything ... but make your requests known to God by prayer and petition, with thanksgiving. Then God's *shalom*, passing all understanding, will keep your hearts and minds safe" (Philippians 4:4-7). Shalom keeps us alive until, "You will join your ancestors in peace and be buried at a good old age" (Genesis 15:15). We can work, and be spouses, and be parents. Just not all at the same time.

Jesus, we need your peace and presence every second. Amen.

GOD DESIGNED

JUNE 24
LOVE?

Remember the oak trees I wrote about last fall? They're gone. I had them removed. Yippee! No more Squirrel Highway on my roof. Now-and-then comes relief from life's struggles and difficulties. Are you experiencing that sort of reprieve today? Is *everything* going fine, good, or smooth as silk? Even the finest strings fray....

Remember the trouble I was having with my 87-year-old dad and his, well, "female friend?" Last night I received word, she died. Wow, I prayed long and hard for God to take care of this complicated situation, but I *never* thought God would call my dad's woman friend "Home." For the past three years, I've struggled daily with my aging dad and their relationship that felt like a raging thunderstorm. I've sought relief from God, and sometimes turning to old habits, then repenting in prayer. I even wrote a short story about a teenage Martian girl who lives with her unemotional dad who's a miner. She has a self-seeking step-mom Rona who married him for his money. No matter how hard we work to handle a difficult situation, try to change people, manipulate situations to our liking, we can't because we haven't let God into our private worlds.

Have you ever heard the song, "I Surrender All" by Judson W. Van Deventer? "All to thee my blessed Savior, I surrender all."

Have you surrendered *everything* to our Lord? Every area of your life? The bad and good? The secret passages of your heart? The "inner you" you just *can't* and *won't* show anyone?

Lately, I've been getting quotes from contractors about repairing my pool enclosure. It's a massive undertaking. Many of the screens are rat-bitten, possum punched, and raccoon thrusted. Most times, I see life as through a screen. My "filter screen" is in need of serious repair ... by God. "Throw all your anxieties upon him, because he cares about you" (1 Peter 5:7). Not toss, not hand over, not give-and-pull back like an Indian giver, but "throw."

Brothers and Sisters, let Jehovah-sabaoth, the Lord of Hosts, have and manage your *every* problem. "I will restore your health, I will heal you of your wounds" (Jeremiah 30:17). Those words "restore" and "heal" us so we can clasp hold of today. God has stamped us with His seal of Victory. He so loves us, and He holds us in his arms, and he can heal our deepest wounds, if we let Him.

Father, thank you for your mercies, new every morning. Amen.

JUNE 25
MISDIRECTION

In life, *change* means shifting directions, switching focus, and altering a routine. I think every day we change in some way; and many times, we have to change our routines, right?

Sometimes, a change in routine happens naturally, without life-altering complications, like changing your clothes (2 Samuel 12:20), a simple changing of your mind (Exodus 13:17), or experiencing a change "in heart" (Exodus 14:5). Sometimes a change in routine feels like an Indian burn, especially when you *pretend* to change your behavior, but you don't, as what happened to David who was on-the-run from King Saul. David made a fast flip in his routine when he sought refuge in the Kingdom of Gat [also Gath]. "David became very much afraid of Akhish king of Gat. So, as they were watching, he changed his behavior and acted like a madman ... scratching marks on the doors of the city gate and drooling down his beard" (1 Samuel 21:12-13). David had to leave family and country, wheedle his way into the good graces of pagan kings, and adapt to new cultures. Yet, those multi-changes in routine helped him. He was able to assess "the enemy" and win wars. "David and his men went to Ke'ilah and fought the P'lishtim. They defeated them in a great slaughter and led away their livestock" (1 Samuel 23:1-5). David had help—God! David *didn't* change his routine alone.

My father's "friend" recently died. He was attached to her like a droning bumblebee lapping pollen out of a drooping daisy. After his third wife (my stepmom) died a few years ago, Dad *quickly* began a new routine, which evolved into a daily ritual with his "friend." It gave him new goals and meaning. Now that she's dead, I hear loss of hope in his voice. He no longer wants to do the same things he did with her, which also includes volunteering. That decision could ring his death knell. Our routines need to involve God, or else we're just running on "we." I think of an example of true change. "He [Jesus] began to change form—his face shone like the sun, and his clothing became as white as light" (Matthew 17:2). Faster than a blink, we will all one day enter Heaven and have new routines. "Instantly I was in the Spirit, and there before me in heaven stood a throne, and on the throne, Someone was sitting" (Revelation 4:2). Let us bow before our King who will one day give us everything new in Heaven.

Jesus, we long for your brilliance in today's routine. Amen.

JUNE 26
POWER BALL

One of God's most powerful encouragements comes to us in the Old Testament through Joshua. He was a warrior who succeeded Moses. Imagine being the *first* generation to inherit Israel after forty years of desert wanderings. Imagine being the *first* ... of anything. You might not *think* you're a first, but are you?

In 1855, African American John Mercer Langston was the first African American to be elected town clerk of Brownhelm Township, Ohio. In 1910, Baroness Raymonde de la Roche of France was the first woman licensed pilot. The first Asian American in Congress was Dalip Singh Saund, elected in 1956 as a representative from California. Alan Shepard was the first to touch the moon in 1961. You might say, "Those are great firsts. But how am *I* a first?"

God has a command for you. He said this to Joshua eons ago; but because you accepted Jesus as Lord and Savior, His message is also for you. Just put your name here because right now, this moment, for you are *the first* to ripple a Godly legacy in your family, your home, and the lives you touch daily. You *will* be remembered. So let's start with what we can do something about—not the past, but now. Here God's message to you, for your life:

"Get up and cross into God's mission for your life, you and your family, to this present time with the spiritual gifts I'm giving you. I am giving you every place you will step on with the sole of your foot. All the places and lives you touch are *your* territories. No one will be able to withstand you as long as you live. Just as I was with Moshe, so I will be with you. I will neither fail you nor abandon you. Be strong, be bold; for you will cause other people to attain salvation [See Ephesians 1:18.). Only be strong and very bold in taking care to follow Jesus; do not turn from Him either to the right or to the left; then you will succeed wherever you go. Yes, keep Jesus' teachings on your lips, and meditate on Jesus and His ways day and night, so that you will take care to act according to everything He said while He walked on Earth. Then your undertakings will prosper, and you will succeed. Haven't I ordered you, 'Be strong, be bold'? So don't be afraid or downhearted, because *Adonai* your God is with you wherever you go" (Joshua 1:1-9). I know I took a few liberties with the Bible here, but to Him, you are a first, vital, and important.

Father, thank you for giving us true significance. Amen.

JUNE 27
CYCLE SHOP

When they were small, my children looked up to me, and wanted to be just like me. That's the way children are, and we grownups are their models. Thus, I'm always praying that I can be a walking Bible, and a model for them long after I'm gone from their daily lives or dead. "It is his doing that you are united with the Messiah Yeshua. He has become wisdom for us from God, and righteousness and holiness and redemption as well" (1 Corinthians 1:30)!

But like me, do you sometimes miss the mark as "an example?" Maybe your anger get just a little bit out of control. Or you're tired and didn't read that bedtime story, or you might have done as my parents used to say to me, "Just go out and play!" See your child's dejected expression? Or maybe you're a manager instead of a parent. What example for Christ are you modeling to children?

We need help, and wisdom that can only come from God. "Make me know your ways, *Adonai*, teach me your paths. Guide me in your truth, and teach me; for you are the God who saves me, my hope is in you all day long" (Psalm 25:4-5). How often?

"All day long," is the answer. We need teaching, and guidance, and truth. Most moments, we are in desperate need of being saved—from ourselves. Many seconds, we search for hope, and knowledge, and a good example. Where can we find a perfect example?

Jesus was perfection on Earth, and He called *you* for His own. "Those who have been called, who are loved by God the Father and kept for Yeshua the Messiah" (Jude 1:4).

Since we are "kept" for Him, we can "show" Him. "Yeshua ... sets people apart for God" (Hebrews 2:11). When we fail in some minor or significant way, what do we do? Is the situation hopeless? Irreparable? No. "We have confidence to use the way into the Holiest Place opened by the blood of Yeshua" (Hebrews 10:29). Go to Jesus for forgiveness and guidance after we fail someone, or as will happen, disappoint people, even those we love. He'll take charge of the situation and fixes failures for God's ultimate glory. When Jesus cured someone once, He said: "This sickness [Insert the mistake *you* made here.] will not end in death. No, it is for God's glory, so that the Son of God may receive glory through it" (John 11:14). People are resilient.

Father God, help us forgive and ask for forgiveness. Amen.

JUNE 28
DON'T LET HATE WIN

On Wednesday evening June 17, 2015 in Charleston, South Carolina, an angry white man pulled out his gun and killed nine people. They were all in Bible study at Morris Brown AME Church, and the disgruntled man was in attendance with them for an hour before deciding to shoot people. Obviously, his racist mindset had been festering for a while until he finally decided to take action. What do you think made him murder innocent strangers in cold blood?

After hearing news reports on this tragedy that killed 41-year-old Clementa Pinckney who was the pastor, a husband, and a father of two children; I believed I could hear crying that night in the wind—in waves mimicking an ocean of sadness that just wouldn't stop. The white supremacist's father had bought his son the gun as a birthday gift. Law enforcement learned the disturbed 21-year-old killer had been in trouble before as police also discovered the young man's anti-black manifesto. People around him couldn't predict his violent outburst? Again, we have to ask: *What made him wreck his entire life— 'cause surely he'll face the death penalty—and murder so many people in a sacred church where people gather for solace and worship?*

The Prophet Isaiah once said: "My soul desires you at night, my spirit in me seeks you at dawn; for when your judgments are here on earth, the people in the world learn what righteousness is" (Isaiah 26:9). See the word, "right," in "righteousness?" Righteousness means "being right with God." Desiring God with all our hearts and souls, seeking Him from "dawn" to "dusk," and knowing his laws; we "learn" right from wrong. Sadly, and with a grieving spirit, some people don't ever get that message. They remain lost. "We are the aroma of the Messiah, both among those being saved and among those being lost" (2 Corinthians 2:15). In that Bible study hour, could that young killer have heard the message of Jesus but failed to accept Him as his Lord and Savior? The enemy the Devil likes to abscond with souls. The Evil One works to make crooked, all of God's straight paths (Acts 13:10). What's the remedy? I'm teaching a third-grade Bible class for a week, and here's the first memory verse: "With your ears you will hear a word from behind you. 'This is the way; stay on it, whether you go to the right or the left'" (Isaiah 30:21). Our Lord speaks to us in the deepest recesses of our souls.

Father God, help us always listen and obey. Amen.

June 29
Workers Needed

A smiling little girl in my Vacation Bible School class looked up into my eyes and exclaimed, "Miss Joy, you look like my grandma!"

Memories flashed through my mind as lightning, moments when I'd *never* believe I could *ever* be a grandma. Now, I am. Do you too feel the seasons and generations changing? "For everything there is a season, a right time for every intention under heaven" (Ecclesiastes 3:1). In God's grand design of time-lapsed photography, generations come and go. There was the Industrial Revolution generation of the 1800s. Now, there are *six* generations. There's the GI generation, like my dad who served in WWII. The Korean and Vietnam generation, the Baby Boomers (me), Generation X (1965-1980), Generation Y (Millennium, 1981-2000), and Generation Z/Boomlets.

When I was in high school, I used to watch an old movie based on *The Time Machine* by H. G. Wells. There was a scene in which the main character, the Time Traveler, gets into his machine and catapults into the future. The sun, moon, and stars circle wildly above as if propelled on an invisible hula-hoop. We, the observers, see generations pass by in seconds. When does the machine stop? A.D. 802,701. I'm in 2015! A difference of 800,686 years into the future. Wow, what a vast expanse. Yet, in God's perspective, those years are so different. "With the Lord, one day is like a thousand years and a thousand years like one day" (2 Peter 3:8). Cycles are happening all around us. Have you ever thought, *Wow, today flew by so quickly*; only to ask the next day, *Wow, today slid by like slow molasses.* Life happens in the smallest of increments, yet people write history on the grandest scales. Cycles. I'm reminded of the Book of Judges, wherein debilitating sinful cycles cripple God's people, followed by God taking compassion on them to help them return to a path of rightness. "The Israelites lived among the Canaanites, Hittites, Amorites, Perizzites, Hivites and Jebusites. They took their daughters in marriage and gave their own daughters to their sons, and served their gods" (Judges 3:5-6). This is contrary to the covenant they made with God. "If you will pay careful attention to what I say and keep my covenant, then you will be my own treasure from among all the peoples" (Exodus 19:5-6). We need to listen, and obey. Our future generations depend on us.

Father, help us seek you always. Amen.

JUNE 30
MOTIVED BY

I have a pressure cooker. You know how one of those works? It's a giant crockpot of sorts in which you mix all your ingredients, set at a particular cycle, and push start. In a quarter-of-the-time, you're meal's done. Lately, I've been writing about cycles. Have you ever just wanted one of your bad cycles to stop?

"Take off the lid when it reads zero, Mom," my son Andrew shouts after I start the spaghetti sauce in the pressure cooker.

Taking off the lid that soon would mean the lid flying off and possibly slicing off his head! "No way!" I then explain how a pressure cooker works. To no avail. My son's stuck on how *he* believes the pressure cooker functions. The vicious cycles between mom, dad, and son continue. It's an argument that keeps stinging our family; and with each new argument, it just changes form. I'm reminded of Judges again, and the leaders who communicated with God to stop vicious sin cycles. What does it take to stop a bad cycle?

I pray: "Lord, I need you. I need help! We need help as a family. I believe in you, God, Jehovah-sabaoth, God of Hosts. With every help you can spare me, a sinner, who can never meet your holy perfect standards, I plead with you, with every atom of my soul ... help me, and help my family have peace."

I received an answer! I need a tent peg.

"What?" you're probably asking.

"Yep, a tent peg to hammer into the Devil's heart ... into sin.

"Ya'el the wife of Hever took a tent peg and a hammer in her hand, crept in to him quietly and drove the tent peg into his temple, right through to the ground; so that he died without waking up" (Judges 4:21). Or, I could use Ehud's double-edge sword to chop down the sin that keeps invading my home. "Ehud said: 'I have a message from God for you.' As the king arose from his seat, Ehud reached out with his left hand, took the sword from his right thigh, and thrust it into the king's belly. The hilt too went in after the blade, and the fat closed around the blade, for he did not draw the sword out of his belly, so that it came out behind" (Judges 3:20-22). Sin is like useless "fat." Sin is creates death, is heart debilitating, and needs to be slain—right into the belly of the Devil with prayer, our tent pegs. "God, please conquer sin!" He will, when Jesus returns.

God, we love you, worship you, and pray for final relief. Amen.

July 1
Atrocities

Evil takes various shapes and forms. In the Old Testament, Satan comes *always* to torment those who are destined for greatness. Saul turns nuts because of him. "But the Spirit of the Lord departed from Saul, and an evil spirit from the Lord troubled him" (1 Samuel 16:14). Then evil struck with the 8,728 enemies of Israel. God's people *always* cried out to Him for forgiveness of their sins, and God *always* had mercy on them and redeemed them. "The Lord your God hath delivered them [the enemy] into your hand" (Joshua 10:19). Also, there was the evil Abimelech (son of Judge Gideon in Judges 9). Abimelech uses idol money to hire "reckless adventurers" (9:4), and then they kill "seventy sons of Gideon" (9:18). In today's language, Abimelech would be considered a disillusioned sociopath.

Do we have still have evil around us today? ISIS, the Islamic State of Iraq and Syria, is the obvious. This brutal group has targeted Christians, beheading men, women and children. They claim religious authority over all Muslims, and they're compassionless. Their religion is the only religion. "The natural man does not receive the things from the Spirit of God. To him they are nonsense! Moreover, he is unable to grasp them, because they are evaluated through the Spirit" (1 Corinthians 2:14). We need Holy Spirit discernment and intervention in our minds and hearts every moment.

Do you ever wonder if God hears your suffering or the agony of people? He does. "It will be done to you; your dealings will come back on your own head" (Obadiah 1:15).

Justice always prevails. "Abimelech came unto the tower and fought against it, and went hard unto the door of the tower to burn it with fire. And a certain woman cast a piece of a millstone upon Abimelech's head and broke his skull. Then he called hastily unto the young man, his armor-bearer, and said, 'Draw thy sword and slay me, that men say not of me, *A woman slew him.*' And his young man thrust him through, and he died. And when the men of Israel saw that Abimelech was dead, they departed every man unto his place. Thus God repaid the wickedness of Abimelech, which he did unto his father in slaying his seventy brethren" (9:52-57). God hears your pain, cares about your grief, and will enact justice on your behalf one day. "*Adonai* avenges" (Nahum 1:2). He cares about your day.

Father, you hear our painful cries and intercede. Amen.

JULY 2
ARMADILLO DAMAGES

In a recent news article, I learned that armadillos *are* linked to the skin disease called leprosy, *mycobacterium leprae*. Some armadillos have it, and then people gardening contract it by touching the soil. Scary, huh? Leprosy starts as infected skin abrasions and then spreads in a rash across the body. In Jesus's time, such a diagnosis would render the leprosy-ridden banished to the mountains to seek refuge in a leprosy colony. The island of Molokai in Hawaii once had a leper colony that's been closed since 1969 after experts found a cure for it, called Hansen's disease. Still, stigmas can last long beyond a cure. Is there a label—a stigma from your sins—that you keep imposing on yourself, like a stamp on a letter, and you just can't shake it off?

When I visited Israel in 2009 and on the way to Masada, I saw dark foreboding caves in the mountains. The guide said, "That's where the lepers used to live in ancient times." I couldn't imagine such an existence. No water, scarce food, and people fending for themselves because they'd been ostracized by family and friends. Imagine transitioning *instantly* from rich to poor. Although the Temple used to collect funds for the vanquished, and their families passed them money, such abrupt changes in living conditions and physical changes in appearance probably caused many of those infected individuals to go insane, psychotic, or appear demon possessed. Even after a miraculous healing, however, a leper would *always* be known as, "The Diseased One," as was Simon in Mark 14:3 after Jesus healed him. Leviticus 14 describes in detail the signs of leprosy and what the priest and family of the suffering one must do. An entire chapter is devoted to leprosy and the steps an infected person needs to take for God to enact a cure. Moses said, "This is the law of leprosy" (verses 54-57). However, Jesus fulfilled The Law. He tells one suffering pleading leper, "'Be cleansed!'" At once, he's healed. Jesus then orders him, "Tell no one. But as a testimony to the people, go and let the *cohen* [priest] examine you, and offer the sacrifice that Moshe commanded" (Matthew 8:4). We've never been lepers, but we've sinned; and we're still sinning. "Be clean!" Jesus tells us, and we receive healing. The stigmas of our sins have been hammered into the fabric of His wooden cross *to be left there* for eternity. You are *clean* of your past. You are now free to do His will.

Father God, we worship you for your mercies. Amen.

July 3
A Church Divided

When we join an organization, we tend to gravitate to a group and begin *solely* planting ourselves there. We become a pack member, or part of the Inner Circle. The latter is special, huh? Then, we leave everyone else out. "I hear that when you gather together as a congregation you divide up into cliques," Paul preached.

Have you ever been, or felt, divided between friends, groups of people, companies, or institutions such as a church? You ever felt left out? The chasm of separation can be lonely and painful. How?

I've been a member of a church for over a year and volunteered for several projects. That's great, right? How do *you* feel people should treat you after you've volunteered for several of their projects? Do you expect a grand, "Thank You?" A simple acknowledgement? I'd like the people for whom I'm volunteering to at least know my name. Paul tells us, "There are many of us; and in union with the Messiah, we comprise one body, with each of us belonging to the others" (Romans 12:5). We can't have a whole without the parts.

What do we expect when we volunteer? I never expected a thank you or appreciation. Yet, I sincerely would like a connection to my church. I want to assimilate into the body of believers, becoming "one" in worshipping, loving, caring and sharing. We long "… to walk in the light [in fellowship with God] … causing us to have fellowship with one another," as prescribed in 1 John 1:7.

Do you remember the TV show, *Cheers*? Where "everyone knows your name" the regulars return for drinks, food, and conversation. We need human connection. We long to be "a part of."

Sadly, my church doesn't even "know my name." I've discussed this before, when someone in "power" suddenly replaced me. I was left in the dark with no explanation. That hurt. Are such actions "Christian" behavior? I kept returning, even though my soul's been screaming, *leave*. "Love your enemies, do good, and lend expecting nothing back" (Luke 6:35)! Jesus commands. Ouch—oops. Sorry, God. We can tell God we're sorry any time. He listens and forgives.

Have you ever cried from your soul, wondering: What should I do? "I passed by you, looked at you and saw that your time had come, the time for love. So I spread my cloak over you and you became mine," God tells Ezekiel. He heals hearts with love.

Father God, where your love resides lives true unity. Amen.

JULY 4
DEPENDENCE

Today is freedom day, the day in 1776 when representatives of the thirteen colonies of the United States of America told King George III, and I paraphrase, "We are parting ways with you and declaring ourselves free and sovereign from British rule."

Have you ever wanted freedom from someone or something? Being indecisive, but needing to decide urgently, can be overwhelming. Indecision can leave us preoccupied and sap our energy. Johann Wolfgang von Goethe, one my favorite German writers, once said about this human conundrum: "Indecision brings its own delays, and days are lost lamenting o'er lost days. ... Seize this very minute ... boldness has genius, power, and magic in it." Do I believe in magic? No. Yet I *do* believe God blesses us according to his plan. "The blessing of *Adonai* is what makes people rich, and he doesn't mix sorrow with it" (Proverbs 10:22). A *blessing* is: *approval that allows or helps you to do something; help and approval from God*; or, *something that helps you or brings happiness.* And what does "rich" mean? You're going to be surprised. *Rich* means: *having abundant possessions and especially material wealth; having high value or quality; well supplied or endowed; magnificently impressive; vivid and deep in color; full and mellow in tone and quality; having a strong fragrance; highly productive or remunerative; having abundant plant nutrients; highly seasoned, fatty, oily, or sweet; high in the combustible component; meaningful, significant; lush; pure or nearly pure.* This word provides intense fulfillment to our lives.

Rich does *not* mean God will grant us a lottery windfall. Maybe He blesses a few people that way, but not me. Still, according to the above definition, God keeps providing for my daily needs. Then I'm blessed, and I can be a blessing to others, *if* I choose. When we give, we receive a meaningful reward, a blessing. This past week, I've been a leader of a third-grade Bible class. I didn't know how I'd ever survive teaching seventeen 9-year-olds, but I did, thanks to the prayers I lifted up to God. And now, as I face several decisions about how to relegate a monetary blessing from my late Uncle Jim, I'll pray for His guidance. Are you in need of a blessing? Maybe you think you don't deserve one. You only have to ask our Provider God. "He may turn, change his mind, and leave a blessing behind him" (Joel 2:14). He loves us. We're His designs. Bless you, God.

Father Provider, thank you for *every* blessing. Amen.

July 5
Issues

Jesus always had *big* decisions to make. Are you up against a wall and needing to make a *big* decision that'll change everything? "*Adonai* will fulfill his purpose for me. Your grace, *Adonai*, continues forever. Don't abandon the work of your hands" (Psalm 138:8)!

You are "the work" of His hands. "He is your father, who made you his! It was he who formed and prepared you" (Deuteronomy 32:6)! Notice the exclamation points. God tells us He *forms* our atoms, and He is continually preparing us for wonderful purposes. Since He's come this far with you, isn't He now still involved in your lives? While cutting celery or changing car oil ... He is present.

"What you decide to do will succeed, and light will shine on your path" (Job 22:28). When we place the Lord in our decisions—big and small—He listens and involves Himself for our good and His purposes. At *many* points in life, you will be forced to make important decisions. "You decide ... what is the right course to follow" (Luke 12:57). The operative word is, "right." We need God's "right" arm around us—His holy commands and the perfect law He daily writes in our hearts. "His right arm around me" (Song of Solomon 2:6), He puts His *Torah* on our hearts and writes it on our minds" (Hebrews 10:16). He is always surrounding us (Psalm 76:12), and Jesus is always guiding us (Isaiah 30:21), and the Holy Spirit is present within us. "The Counselor, the *Ruach HaKodesh*, whom the Father will send in my name, will teach you everything. That is, he will remind you of everything I have said to you" (John 14:26). Let's allow Him inside our decision-making processes.

Other than dying for us, what big decision did Jesus have to make? He had to change His *entire* mission. He told his disciples: 'Do not go among the Gentiles or enter any town of the Samaritans. Go rather to the lost sheep of Israel" (Matthew 10:2-3). His focus didn't work out as planned. "Then Yeshua began to denounce the towns in which he had done most of his miracles, because the people had not turned from their sins to God" (Matthew 11:20). And so, Jesus changed direction, which proves God didn't tell Him everything. "Even though he had performed so many miracles in their presence [Jewish people], they still did not put their trust in him" (John 12:37-43). Thus, we non-Jews who believe are saved.

Father, help us keep our minds open to your will. Amen.

JULY 6
DOW DROP

Have you ever thought you knew someone so well—even family members—only to discover the person, or people, are *not* who you believed them to be?

In the middle of the night, I heard a one-way conversation my son was having with an on-line gaming companion, as follows:

"What the [@*!]! Why did you kill me, you [x*$%]!"

Two seconds of silence passed as the person at the other end of the game must have explained to my son why he shot, stabbed, or blew up his avatar. An avatar is a virtual character you pick in a computer game to represent yourself.

"You [*&@x%], I'm gonna shoot the [*~+#] outta ya!"

By now, I'm at his door. I can't believe what's coming out of his mouth. All the while, I'm thinking: This is not the son I've been raising. We don't cuss. Where does he think he's living? And as a Christian, he shouldn't be talking like this! After knocking once, I barge into his room. I tell him what's on my mind. I also tell him what God says about our minds, hearts, and mouths:

"Let no harmful language come from your mouth, only good words that are helpful in meeting the need, words that will benefit those who hear them" (Ephesians 4:29). Did you realize that doctors, dentists, counselors, teachers, and *anyone* involved in helping people must take an ethical oath of "Doing No Harm?" It's called Nonmaleficence. Similarly, the oath of Beneficence means to "Do Only Good and Be of Benefit." Those two ethics codes are in Ephesians 4:29. After all, if we don't do what's good and beneficial as a society, we'll have anarchy. God knew what He was doing when he doled out those commandments, right? There's a movie about people living in total chaos called *The Purge*. In such a relativistic world, we'd live according to how *each* person interprets the law. It's like the bouncing Stock Market lately. I don't know about you, but I don't want to "grieve God's heart" as in the days of Noah when the Lord regretted creating us (Genesis 6:6). "Blessed be God ... who has put a love for Him in our hearts, to restore us" (Ezra 7:27). And in Jesus our Savior, we can "set our hearts at rest in God's presence" (1 John 3:19). We can be true to ourselves and others. We can be kind. We can see and know people through Christ's loving eyes.

Father, help us demonstrate your love to others today. Amen.

July 7
God's Awesome Mercy

Yesterday in Bible study, we discussed John 10:1-17 and John 1:26-33. I kept pausing at verses 2 and 3: "But he who enters by the door is a shepherd of the sheep. To him [the shepherd of the sheep] the doorkeeper opens, and the sheep hear his voice, and he calls his own sheep by name, and leads them out."

I kept saying: In these verses, Jesus *must* be talking about his disciples and other Judeans (verse 19) around them since they'd be taking over His ministry after His resurrection. Those verses are not directed at us—you and me. Why might the difference be important? The video leader of our Bible study said that Jesus is talking about all Christians being "shepherd of the sheep." This is true *now*, because we *each* are on mission to bring people to Christ, disciple fellow Christians, and help them on their Christian walk. However, in these verses, Jesus *must* be *teaching* people *how* to lead God's Chosen People (*and* gentiles in verse 16) "through the door and into Heaven." Back then, this message was directed to teachers, and His church grew exponentially. Today, our mission is to keep up His work and lead people to Christ. There's only one way we can "get" to Heaven—through Jesus. He mentions the *exact* door, "I am the door of the sheep" (verse 7). Then comes, *the wolf....*

Jesus being "the only way to God" is *so* opposed to the alternatives: "a stranger" (John 10:5), "thieves and robbers" (verse 8), "the thief" (verse 10), "the wolf" (verse 12), and "the hireling" (verse 13). This parallels His talk in Matthew 7:15-16, wherein He warns us about wolves at work, purposely to lead *us* astray and off course from Christ. "Beware of the false prophets! They come to you wearing sheep's clothing, but underneath they are hungry wolves!" Jesus is emphatic and serious. In Mark 13:21-23, He expounds on the Last Days, concluding: "At that time, if anyone says to you, 'Look! Here's the Messiah!' or, 'See, there he is!' — don't believe him! There will appear false Messiahs and false prophets performing signs and wonders for the purpose, if possible, of misleading the chosen." What's your *wolf*? A TV show can be mine, or the beautiful dress I believe will make me feel better, or telling my feelings because "I have rights." I need always keep my hands *on* the doorkeeper's door, touching the wood of His cross (Matthew 7:7-8 and Luke 11:9).

God, we need your Holy Spirit's discerning guidance. Amen.

JULY 8
BOTTOM FALLING OUT

Have you ever encountered professional incompetence? I did today. An attorney's assistant said she sent me my inheritance check certified mail five days ago. Guess what? She can't track the letter. I wanted to stomp, because I had used pleasant language, complimented her, and expressed a calm demeanor only to have her tell me, "You're check's not here." Was she sticking her arm out the door with my check in hand or waving it out the window? *Uggggh*. A mind can go willy-wacky wondering why the person who's supposed to help you or serve you is instead ignoring you, lying, or brushing you off. *Ugggh!* A person could even become a bit paranoid, *Why doesn't he/she like me*, or, *Why are they hurting me this way?* "I am afflicted and hurting. God, let your saving power raise me up" (Psalm 69:30).

Our minds begin to change for the worse when we expect "something," a "service," "a particular treatment," or "a specific outcome," but receive nothing. We might have paid a tremendous amount of money, or expended an enormous amount of energy, as in a relationship that doesn't deliver what we *believed it should have delivered.* Then, we're left disillusioned, hurting, angry, and waiting.

An unknown person once said, "Never ascribe to malice that which is adequately explained by incompetence." In other words, I believe the individual who is "hurting" me is slighting me on purpose, doing evil to me, intentionally harming me, or maliciously wants to deprive me of the good that's supposed to enter my life. Ninety-nine percent of the time, when people who are supposed to be helping, or providing a service for us don't, they are just "incompetent." The word means, *not having or showing the necessary skills to do something successfully; inept, amateurish, substandard, inefficient,* and *lacking.* "Evildoers prosper; they put God to the test" (Malachi 3:15); and, "These people are grumblers and complainers, they follow their evil passions, their mouths speak grandiosities, and they flatter others to gain advantage" (Jude 1:16). What's to do? Jesus says, "If you forgive others their offenses, your heavenly Father will also forgive you" (Matthew 6:14). Anything else we do depletes us, wastes us, and kills spirit. "If you have anything against anyone, forgive him; so that your Father in heaven may also forgive your offenses" (Mark 11:25). We can't take $ to Heaven.

Jesus, heal our minds and hearts and fill us with love. Amen.

July 9
Prioritize

One of the most terrifying phrases speaking to us today out of the handwriting of Jeremiah is as follows: "The heart is more deceitful than anything else and mortally sick. Who can fathom it? I, *Adonai*, search the heart. I test inner motivations in order to give to everyone what his actions and conduct deserve" (Jeremiah 17:9-10). What does this mean for you and me today?

Taking apart the verse, I begin with the word, *deceitful*, which means, *dishonest, unprincipled, insecure, double-dealing, scheming, sneaky*, and *treacherous*, to name a few. We can agree, we don't want to aspire to being deceitful, right? Maybe some people are just naturally deceitful. So, let's admit, when we discover their deceitfulness, we need to run away fast, right? Yet, God is telling us that we *all* are capable of *deceit*. If not for the intervention of the Holy Spirit, we might trample down one another. Wait, there's help. God give us hope, inspiration, and encouragement in this sometimes deceit-filled world.

When left to our own tendencies, we are "mortally sick," or, "very intensely affected by physical or mental illness." Look on TV, read the papers, and notice what's streaming live. See the crimes here and abroad that God's talking about? We thought Roman crucifixions were bad … nope, only transformed into different modes of deaths and torture in our day-and-time. "Is there something of which it is said, 'See, this is new?' It existed already in the ages before us" (Ecclesiastes 1:10). The world appears pretty grim, bleak, and frightening at times, huh? Hold onto Jesus. "I am *Adonai* your healer" (Exodus 15:26). Hold onto his bright hand. "His brightness is like the sun, rays come forth from his hand—that is where his power is concealed" (Habakkuk 3:4). He changes us.

We want cures and answers for human trafficking, murderous dictators, home invasions, drunken driving, etc. If you're living a thousand years after today, and the Rapture hasn't occurred, there are evils and wickedness happening in your world as well, only in another form. Guess what? As we interact with people daily, you and I *are capable* of wickedness because of our "heart issues" that separate us from God. There's no telling what a person will do when pushed to the limits of his or her endurance or tolerance.

What's the cure we so desperately need *every second* as we subsist on air, food, water, shelter, and companionship? After Jesus gives a jaw-dropping description of the End Times in John 16, He says, "The time will come when anyone who kills you will think he is serving God" [verse 2: a prediction of ISIL perhaps?]. This occurs before Judas betrays Him. Jesus then prays to God, His Father, in John 17. In reality, His voice is rippling through the past, present, and future as He prays for you and me. Let's say this prayer right now as the desperate cure we need to make it through today. When you see the blank underline, insert *your* name. This letter is designed for you. I'd say it's the first interactive experience into which we can insert ourselves into the Bible and directly in front of Jesus to help us change. It's like the phone apps we use to alter our environments. In the following prayer, Jesus invites you to include yourself with your name into His holy spiritual world. He's present and can encourage and inspire you in your day.

"Yeshua looked up toward heaven and said, 'Father, the time has come. Glorify your Son, so that the Son may glorify you — just as you gave Him authority over ____, so that He might give eternal life to ____. And eternal life is this: to know you, the one true God, and him whom you sent, Yeshua the Messiah. I glorified you on earth by finishing the work you gave me to do. Now, Father, glorify me alongside yourself. Give me the same glory I had with you before the world existed. I made your name known to ____, who you gave me out of the world. ____ is yours, you gave ____ to me, and ____ has kept your word. Now ____ knows that everything you have given me is from you, because the words you gave me I have given to ____, and ____ has received them. ____ has really come to know that I came from you, and ____ has come to trust that you sent me. I am praying for ____. I am not praying for the world, but for ____ [who] you have given to me, because ____ is yours. Indeed, all I have is yours, and all you have is mine, and in ____ has been glorified. Now I am no longer in the world. ____ is in the world, but I am coming to you. Holy Father, guard ____ by the power of your name, which you have given to me, so that ____ and I may be one, just as we are. When I was with [my disciples], I guarded them by the power of your name, which you have given to me; yes, I kept watch over them; and not one of them was destroyed (except the one meant for destruction, so that the *Tanakh* might be fulfilled [Judas]). But now, I am coming to you; and I say these things while I am still in the world so that ____ may have my joy made complete in [herself/himself]. I have given ____ your word, and the world hates ____, because ____ does not belong to the world just as I myself do not belong to the world. I don't ask you to take ____ out of the world, but to protect ____ from the Evil One. ____ does not belong to the world, just as I do not belong to the world. Set ____ apart for holiness by means of the truth — your word is truth. Just as you sent me into the world, I have sent ____ into the world. On ____'s behalf I am setting myself apart for holiness, so that ____ too may be set apart for holiness by means of the truth. I pray not only for ____, but also for those who will trust in me because of their word, that they may all be one. Just as you, Father, are united with me and I with you, I pray that ____ may be united with us, so that the world may believe that you sent me. The glory which you have given to me, I have given to ____; so that ____and I may be one, just as we are one — I united ____ with them [Christians] and you with me, so that ____ may be completely one, and the world thus realize that you sent me, and that you have loved ____ just as you have loved me. Father, I want ____ whom you have given me to be with me where I am; so that ____ may see my glory, which you have given me because you loved me before the creation of the world. Righteous Father, the world has not known you, but I have known you, and ____ has known that you sent me. I made your name known to ____, and I will continue to make it known [through ____ and ____'s fellow Christians]; so that the love with which you have loved me may be in ____, and I myself may be united with ____.' "

Yes, I delved deeply into Jesus's words. But we need Him speaking to us so we can know His love and bring people who need encouragement to Him. With his love surrounding us and His words in our minds, we can walk with hope in this fallen world of lost and seeking souls. We will encounter the deceitful, and evil; but He walks with us as we trust Him in all His ways. "To you who fear my name, the sun of righteousness will rise with healing in its wings; and you will break out leaping" (Malachi 3:20). God is designing us through his power and for His glory *every* second of *every* day. Go forth today in the power of His holy name, Jesus. "Even if … even if … even if the sheep vanish from the sheep pen and there are no cows in the stalls; still, I will rejoice in Adonai, I will take joy in the God of my salvation. Elohim Adonai is my strength" (Habakkuk 3:17-19).

Abba Father, you are comfort. Amen.

JULY 10
SOUL MEDICINE

Sometimes, we gotta just laugh. Have you laughed lately? Or are you a sort of a serious person like me who has to analyze jokes to gauge if they're laugh worthy? Picking things a part too much is like being lactose intolerant. You're always reading labels and calculating percentages so as to *never* get sick. After years of living in analysis mode, we can become impervious to spontaneity and laughing.

Jesus probably laughed. He was always seeing the Big Picture in people and chaotic situations. When his disciples acted like cowering mice on the rocking boat on stormy Lake Galilee, He probably just remained on the water, chuckling at 'em all a bit. Wouldn't you? If you knew you could easily lift people out of the water, quiet storms, and drain lakes, wouldn't *you* be like a smiling parent sitting back in the shadows and watching your children playfully explore?

Yes, Jesus was happy at times, and He made people happy. "Yeshua put to shame the people who opposed him; but the rest of the crowd were happy about all the wonderful things that were taking place through him" (Luke 13:17). What are they happy about? Attentive caring Jesus is an engaging Lord who listens to their problems, their sufferings and grief, and then He heals them—even on the Sabbath which is a Jewish holy day like our Sunday, a day of *no* healing. "Yeshua was teaching in one of the synagogues on *Shabbat*. A woman came up who had a spirit that had crippled her for eighteen years. She was bent double, and unable to stand erect at all. On seeing her, Yeshua called her and said to her, 'Lady, you have been set free from your weakness!' He put his hands on her, and at once she stood upright and began to glorify God" (Luke 13:10-13). Now, Jesus is teaching in a synagogue where women aren't allowed. This woman is "bent double." She must have had two contortions occurring on her body at once. How utterly painful, right? Everyone must have parted to let her pass through the crowd to Jesus. This must have been one of the highlights of His ministry—to cure her and extract a torturous demon out of her. First he "sees" her. He looks *right* into her soul. Then he "puts His hands on her." Imagine our powerful God moving directly through us with healing lightning. Everyone must have gasped in awestruck happiness at her instant recovery. Even our Jesus was happy for her. He's happy with us.

Father, give us always a spirit of your healing laughter. Amen.

July 11
New Horizons—Pluto

For just a moment near dawn and dusk each day, the illumination on Earth matches that of noon on Pluto, yielding what cosmologists call Pluto time. My next Pluto time will be 8:26 p.m. tonight. Yes, we're approaching Pluto, at least New Horizons is three million miles away. "*Adonai*, God! You made heaven and earth by your great power and outstretched arm; nothing is too hard for you" (Jeremiah 32:17).

What will the Last World that used to be categorized a planet look like? NASA scientists have spotted a "whale" image on the surface and "the heart." *Pareidola* is our tendency to give names to unexplainable images and events in our cosmos. Pareidolia is well alive on Pluto. And who knows what brilliant phenomena or discoveries the New Horizons satellite-explorer will transmit to us.

Might God be preparing us for a future into the cosmos? Space/time travel? Could we one day glide to an exoplanet because the Sun is expanding and heating up Earth to intolerable conditions in the year 1,999,2015? Little steps mount into giant leaps, as Neil Armstrong once said. "One small step for a man ... one giant leap for mankind." One little act can multiply in ways we might not see.

I don't know about you, but I'd like reassurance that my offspring will have a nice future, that I'll live on in them through my DNA, and that everything about me won't fizzle out like a smoldering cinder after I die. But that might not happen. *Anything* can happen to our offspring that will stop our lineage, that's if we even *choose* to have children. "An unmarried man concerns himself with the Lord's affairs, with how to please the Lord. ... Likewise the woman who is no longer married or the girl who has never been married concerns herself with the Lord's affairs" (1 Corinthians 7:32-34). Some Christians will not have descendants. Yet our actions ripple in positive directions as New Horizons is inspiring us now.

Brazilian author Paulo Coelho said: "Never. We never lose our loved ones. They accompany us; they don't disappear from our lives. We are merely in different rooms." Jesus said a similar thing about rooms. "Don't let yourselves be disturbed. Trust in God and trust in me. In my Father's house are many places to live. ... I am going there to prepare a place for you. ... I will return to take you with me" (John 14:1-4). His Kingdom surrounds you now.

Jesus, instill within us always your divine assurance. Amen.

JULY 12
HOW SAFE IS YOUR....

While looking for jeans for my son who's preparing for summer camp, Andrew suddenly stopped and exclaimed in pain, "Ouch!"

I thought he'd stepped on a nail. "What's wrong?"

Lifting up his right foot, he picked out one of those clothing security tags—the pin an inch long. I saw blood. "Oh my gosh!"

Hopping in pain, he pulled out the security pin. "This went all the way into my foot!"

After making sure he was okay, and taking pictures of the pin and his bloody puncture, I sought out a sales rep. Another customer intervened and whispered, "Make sure you get a manager to take a report." I thought of two things: paying for a doctor's bill if an infection should occur and money from a lawsuit. A voice deep down in my gut spoke to me: "Look, he's probably going to be okay. And he's had booster shots." Thanks, Holy Spirit—*whew*!

My husband texted our son, saying, "Tell the manager you're in pain." I see where this is going. He's seeing dollar signs, *ka-ching*! Easy lawsuit money.

Andrew told the manager: "Yeah, it's hurting. It's painful."

Peering at him sideways, I said: "Of course he feels pain now, but we'll wipe the spot with peroxide when we get home and then apply an antibiotic to it. I'm sure he'll be okay."

Accidents happen, right? However, people sue businesses because the entryways don't have handicap thresholds. Or, someone purposely puts a roach in a salad. That's what "the world" does to milk "the system." Politician Jack Kingston says about this sinful tendency to acquire money: "Frivolous lawsuits are booming in this county. The U.S. has more costs of litigation per person than any other industrialized nation in the world, and it is crippling our economy." What does God say? We need to do the right thing, be the right person, and stab our Pole of Rightness into the earth. Take the right stand. "Be a doer of the work ... then you will be bless in what you do" (James 1:25). Robert Perry discovered the North Pole and drove his flag into the ice, and Neil Armstrong jabbed the moon's meteorite-stricken regolith with the American flag. You are God's unique child stamped with His special gifts. Plant yourself firmly today, and wave your banner reflecting the glory of Jesus.

Jesus, then they will see us and know we are of you. Amen.

JULY 13
LIVE IT OUT

Our son Andrew has been gone for one day to Bible camp. Yippee—six more days to go! The peaceful non-argumentative atmosphere has been like floating on an inner tube over a sparkling calm lake. In those instances where there's peace and quiet in the middle of storms, we can feel God's blessing of shalom relaxing our muscle aches and relieving our stresses. Can you grab hold of some calm and quiet today? Shalom in melting spiritual butter can be yours in the relaxing moments we make with God while enduring the struggles, difficulties, and hardships in life. God already has the solutions to our problems planned out anyway, so why not sit back, ride the up-n-down, back-n-forth mechanical horse of life, and let Him have the reins? Why not let Him guide your steps?

Because we've got problems and issues. *"Adonai,* I know that the way of humans is not in their control, humans are not able to direct their steps as they walk" (Jeremiah 10:23). Riding the bobbing, and, often, tidal waves of life's trials are hard. We cannot "direct our steps." We need God and Jesus. "Having one's mind controlled by the old nature is death, but having one's mind controlled by the Spirit is life and *shalom.*" (Romans 8:6). We can let *Him.*

Jesus encountered all sorts of forces on a daily basis. He met wickedness head on. "When Yeshua arrived at the other side of the Sea of Galilee, in the Gadarenes' territory [near modern Kersa], there came out of the burial caves two men controlled by demons, so violent that no one dared travel on that road" (Matthew 8:28). This scene must look like a horror flick as demons assault people. The rugged Gadarenes' territory is about 31 miles southeast of the Sea of Galilee. People who died at the hands of their enemies were simply dumped there, their bodies lost to posterity. That's where two demon-controlled men violently attack Jesus. "Go!" Jesus commands, expelling the demons from their two hosts. "So they came out and went into the pigs, and the entire herd rushed down the hillside into the lake and drowned" (Matthew 8:32). Just as He fixed their spiritual lives, Jesus repairs us and our situations. Can you see Him working for you beyond what you believe material possessions can do for you? Peace, or chaos? Calm, or Jesus? Let us allow Jesus to quell our stressors with shalom today.

Father God, draw us always closer to you. Amen.

JULY 14
JARRING GLOBAL MARKETS

"The experiences we've gone through help shape the person we are today," I'm sure you've often heard.

What would we be like if our "old natures" never existed? That's a good question. What if, you *never* sinned? What do you think you'd look like and be like right now?

I imagine a world where there's honesty, no anger, no hunger, no selfishness, no self-seeking, no vengeance, no gossip, and no evil. I guess we'd all be walking around happy and living out the Ten Commandments perfectly. We'd be helping one another in all our needy conditions, and giving up our possessions freely to those who might lose them to natural disasters. Don't worry about giving everything away, because we'll also be receiving plenty from others.

Do you buy my world? Think this heavenly utopia is possible? That's what my imaginary world would be like, Heaven. In it, I wouldn't be the person I am today, with all my weaknesses. Analyzing myself objectively, I think I'd be boring, not courageous, and not a strong-survivor type. Why? It's my dark past—my sinful nature—and my progress in fighting my sinful nature that's fashioned me—and continues to mold me—into the person I am today. And your past as well has ironically gifted *you* today. Learning does that.

Paul tells us: "What the *Torah* [religion] could not do by itself, because it lacked the power to make the old nature cooperate, God did by sending his own Son as a human being with a nature like our own sinful one [but without sin]. God did this in order to deal with sin, and in so doing he executed the punishment against sin in human nature" (Romans 8:3). Jesus—God in the flesh—became human because He wanted to know us intimately. Then, He became *every* sin while He suffered on the cross. For the first time since God existed, God turned His back on Jesus, His own flesh-and-blood, when Jesus absorbed our sin and died. God is love and holy. Sin repels Him.

When we believe those truths, we are saved and made—stamped and sealed—holy by God. "Trust in the Lord Yeshua, and you will be saved" (Acts 16:31). After death, we will inherit eternity with Jesus, and receive a glorified body as did Jesus when He rose from the dead. He will return in a Second Coming, and so will we. We will *never* perish. He has defeated Death.

God, we gain salvation through Jesus the doorkeeper. Amen.

J.P. Osterman

July 15
Tragic Ending

I first learned of ballet dancer Tanaquil Le Clercq from a PBS show chronicling her life and career. I'd never seen such grace, eloquence, dexterity, and art converging on a human body put to music. As a principle dancer in the New York City Ballet in the 1950s, Tanaquil caught polio while touring Europe. It ended her burgeoning ballet career. What loss to the world. Complicating her life, she loved George Balanchine, the master dancer who discovered her. Their relationship appeared always tumultuous—a bandying ball on a ping-pong table. They eventually married, but their marriage ended when he left her for another muse. It's a story of unrealized beauty and giftedness, a gardener accidentally pruning a budding American Beauty rose. Watching one of Tanaquil's performances, I couldn't help but cry as I said to God, "What I wouldn't do to have such a talent in this world." Do you ever feel that way, asking God, "What talents do I have that I could use to make a difference, because I don't feel like I'm doing anything by being who I am?"

Brothers and Sisters in Christ: throughout time, *no one* has existed with your exact "prints." You have Holy Spirit talents.

No one will ever exist in the universe as you are living right now. Here's proof. "I thank you because I am awesomely made, wonderfully" (Psalm 139:14). "I made you" (Genesis 6:7). "I am guiding you through human means with reins made of love" (Hosea 11:4). "I made the Pleiades and Orion, and bring deathlike shadows over the morning, and darken the day into night, and calls for the water in the sea and with it floods the earth—*Adonai* is my name" (Amos 5:8). And, "He makes [man and woman] one flesh in order to have spiritual blood-relatives. For what the one [flesh/union] seeks is a seed from God [You]" (Malachi 2:15). You are "seed" from God, a planned and planted human being He foresaw since the beginning of time. "You made me trust when I was on my mother's breasts" (Psalm 22:10). "It was you who fixed all the limits of the earth, you made summer and winter" (Psalm 74:17). And, "*Adonai* made me as the beginning of his way, the first of his ancient works" (Proverbs 8:22). You are special, unique to His purpose, and gifted … just as you are. *As you are,* you are wonderful to Him. Doesn't that make you wanna cry tears of joy? His boundless love.

Father, we worship you with humility and gratitude. Amen.

JULY 16
CLIMATE FORECAST

After creating devastation in Japan, Typhoon Chan-hom is speeding toward China with 125 mph winds. People are evacuating. Meanwhile, across the world, we in the U.S.A. are accosted with hurricanes, just another name for typhoons and cyclones. Have you ever had people or situations strike your life in the same way? And you're struck trying to define what the event means and what to do?

For me, the hurricane came as an unexpected imposition from an acquaintance when I'm already pressured for time. "Can you drive me to the doctor and wait?" The blood pumping through my heart felt like a whopping 75 mph hurricane deluge. Then came the rush of thoughts in typhoon intensity, *Do I say yes and just smile, or how can I say no without getting bashed behind my back?* Wait now for the swirling cyclone in my mind: *Yes, but I really don't want to* [inhale and hold breath]; *I can't* [!]; *well maybe; how do I get out of this and still look good and save face* [??]; *what's the time involved* [yikes!]; *what's the commitment* [urgh!]; *how do I help while doing the least amount of work*; and, *just say yes and stop complaining* [now, exhale]. Wow, can our thoughts become like a debris field in a hurricane, huh?

Conducting some research on "chaotic thoughts," I found a quote by Australian-born pastor and theologian James Sidlow Baxter. "Every opportunity has a difficulty, and every difficulty has an opportunity." *Hm*, opportunity in a hurricane?

Before He died on the cross for our sins, Jesus knew this truth well. He so longed for His Chosen People to accept Him and His new way of living—The Way. They didn't, and He couldn't force them, and He couldn't manifest in the lightning-striking clouds and proclaim, *I Am God*. "You did not recognize your opportunity when God offered it" (Luke 19:44)! In the process of forming us, God sowed within our brains seeds of faith and free will. Now, He sends opportunities to mature us and to make a difference in the world, even if His influence might be picking someone up for an appointment or showing up for someone in need. "It will prove an opportunity for you to bear witness" (Luke 21:13). Opportunities come in cyclones. "I am sure of this: that the One who began a good work among you will keep it growing until it is completed on the Day of the Messiah Yeshua" (Philippians 1:6). We can do a little thing.

God, give us opportunities that inch us closer to you. Amen.

JULY 17
DESPONDENCY TO HOPE

At times in our Christian walk, we'll encounter events that are impossible to locate and resolve in the Bible. Have you ever had a problem for which the Bible has *no* practical help? I have.

Nine-year-old "Rileigh" is her name. Last week, I had her as one of my third-grade, Vacation Bible School students. I encountered a problem for which I believed my background in graduate psychology should have prepared me. It didn't. "You who teach others, don't you teach yourself" (Romans 2:20)?

It all started on Friday, the last day of VBS when the children were lining up and I was taking attendance. Blond-haired, white-skinned Rileigh was hugging a black woman. "Who are you?" I approached her. "Rileigh's Bible school teacher?"

"Oh no," she chuckled. "We have different skin color, but I'm her mom," she lovingly answered, stroking Rileigh's blond hair.

I introduced myself, telling her how special Rileigh was to our VBS class and what a delightful helper she was to me. She was always at the front of the line and eager to assist. Her mother then shared that they were in the process of moving. To where? She wasn't sure, but all week long she'd been working to make her home presentable to buyers. I know that feeling. So for a minute, we walked through a "to do" list. Later, Rileigh had a bit of an angry expression on her face as she looked up into my eyes. "That woman ... that black woman is my mom," she exclaimed through forked eyebrows with her arms folded across her chest.

"And your mom is so nice!" I replied, shame stricken. Rileigh was obviously disturbed that I hadn't recognized her mother as "her mother." Have I done damage? I've been feeling downright horrible and searching for an answer. Jesus has a special place in His heart and Kingdom for children. "Whoever ensnares one of these little ones who trust me, it would be better for him to have a millstone hung around his neck and be drowned in the open sea" (Matthew 18:6)! I've been wrong in blaming myself, especially since I've looked up this particular verse. My heart and mind were focused on *helping* all those children, not "ensnaring them." Wow, can Satan twist God's words. We must always be *in* God's word so that mischievous creature and deceiver can't wrongly convict us.

Father, point us toward your word and comfort. Amen.

JULY 18
HEART ISSUES

"If I regard iniquity in my heart, the Lord will not hear me" (Psalm 66:18). Yet, the Bible also says, "Whosoever shall call on the name of the Lord shall be saved." Have you ever come across conflicting verses and scratch your head to make sense of them?

In Bible study, I had a question: I'm a sinner and always sin, so how can God hear me, and forgive me? Do you ever sit back, in shock, after hearing some verses and wonder: Am I *really* saved? Am I *really* in his Kingdom since I *did* accept Jesus? I'm not feeling "saved" now though, 'cause I sinned, and I've even committed some sins without knowing it because I'm part of this culture.

I stewed over these questions while enjoying God's beauty in my backyard. "Do you hear me, God? I sin so many times. Do you have me in your arms? Do ya still love Sinner Me?" I break down and cry because I want to see Him one day in all His glory and sing out my soul to Him with all the other choruses of Christians and angels. Yes—let's sing. "Oh, how He loves us so ... oh how He loves us ... how He loves you and me." On our knees and with outstretched arms, we can sing to Him, and glorifying Him—our Creator, Master, Shepherd, Soul Filler. That's who He is, always filling our souls with Him. How? Because of Jesus's sacrifice on the cross for us. So insert your name right here ____. You are Jesus designed, loved by Him, precious to Him, and heard by Him.

Do you know, even the angels know you *and* your name? "Whosoever shall confess Me before men, him shall the Son of Man also confess before the angels of God" (Luke 12:8). You have an angel, dispensed to you from God. "It is his angel" (Acts 12:15); and when we sin, confess our sins, and return to Jesus, "There is joy among God's angels when one sinner repents" (Luke 15:10). Do you mean, angels sing *every* time we sin and repent of our sins?

Yes. Heaven must sounds like billions of souls and angels, all cheering us on as we journey through life ... every step we take ... they're rooting for you and me. All of us sin and fall short of God's glory. But "regard" means, "esteem," "care," and, "love." There are people who love *iniquity* and relate sinfully to people in this world. It's not too late for them. Believe on Him. He hears and saves souls from the chasm. He who is pure holiness and love empowers us.

Jesus, we love you, cling to you, and desire to share you. Amen.

JULY 19
LOST ... PLEASE FIND

While driving, we heard *squeeeak-creeek* under the front of the car. Feeling unsafe, I grabbed the door brace. "What was that?!"

My husband had a grim face. "Probably the front suspension."

"Will the wheels fall off? Should we pull over?!" I was almost hyperventilating. But since taking on this daily project, I prayed, and breathed. Have you ever felt your safety suddenly threatened?

Needing a fast-acting Bible-boosting remedy, I returned home, only to receive a call from my daughter. The company for which my son-in-law works will soon be laying people off. With their new baby, they feel frightened, even though they have a financial cushion for such disastrous events. Okay, now the burdensome bricks are stacking into a precarious unsafe tower of troubles. Right after her phone call, I walked outside and spotted a jagged hole in the top of my swimming pool screen. "That's gonna cost a couple hundred bucks to fix! Had a squirrel had gnawed into *my* territory?"

Before you know it, surprising uncontrollable events can stack up into a swaying unsafe tower of troubles, unsettling us and threatening our safety and security. What does your "tower of power" look like? Mine feels high and bright red as if it might topple onto me if one more thing happens today. It will, without God. It'll leave me defeated and weak, without God. We need God's safety to know without a doubt that He has control over everything. In the building of the tower, He's alongside us. "God controls the clouds and makes his lightning flash" (Job 37:15); and, "You control the raging of the sea. When its waves rear up, you calm them" (Psalm 89:10). Gideon trusted God who helped him defeat the enemy. "When I return safe and sound," Gideon tells the men in the city of Peniel who are supposed to be his allies but who turn him away when he needs safety and provision. "When I return safe and sound, I will break down this tower" (Judges 8:9)! God is the only one capable of sledge hammering the heavy threatening bricks that stack up and separate us from Him. Job layoffs, car breakdowns, fear of being robbed.... The list extends. "Go in this strength of yours. ... Because I will be with you," God tells Gideon. He builds us up with His power and strength through the Holy Spirit so we like Gideon can stand firm against the towering troubles in our lives.

Jesus, with you, our bricks of burden become soft cotton. Amen.

JULY 20
NO MATTER WHERE YOU GO, THERE YOU ARE

Did you ever notice that people can do the dumbest things?

In today's paper, I read about a police officer who stopped a woman, but then she tried running him over with her car. Then a burglar broke into a house to rob it, and wound up falling asleep on the sofa.

Sometimes, *we* can do dumb things. We might write a vindictive letter in the heat of anger and then regret *sending* our Unleashed message into the ether of the internet. Or, we might come home after an exhausting day's work and taking out our frustration on our spouse, roommate, or child. Now-and-then, we just don't manage ourselves the way Christ would have us conduct our lives. Jacob realized this after he manipulated his father Isaac and stole his brother Esau's birthright. He had to go on the run and live in fear because he cheated Esau on the spur of the moment to get what he wanted. What does he do thereafter? God commands him and those who go into hiding with him, "Purify yourselves, and put on fresh clothes" (Genesis 35:2). Then Jacob tells everyone who decides to remain with him, "We're going to move on and go up to Beit-El. There I will build an altar to God, who answered me when I was in such distress and stayed with me wherever I went" (Genesis 35:3). There is "an oak of weeping" in the vicinity where Jacob inhabited that land with his community. There are times we weep and pray.

Do you have an "oak of weeping" somewhere? Is there a place of retreat where you can kneel and talk to God, number your sins before Him, and ask Him for forgiveness? "After Jacob arrived from Paddan-Aram, God appeared to him again and blessed him. God said to him, 'Your name is Jacob, but you will be called Jacob no longer; your name will be Isra'el.' God further said to him, "I am *El Shaddai*. Be fruitful and multiply." When the Lord forgives our sins through Jesus His son, our precious loving Savior, God remembers our sins no more. Our weeping is over. Our spur-of-the-moment idiosyncratic behaviors—or just plain weirdness—He forgives and forgets. Still, don't *ever* get rid of your weeping tree. You'll need it the next time you....

Jesus, we praise you for all your wonders. Amen.

JULY 21
THROWING IN THE TOWEL

Is there an area in your life that's not going as planned?

Do you feel like giving up on a task or project? You've heard of the expression: "I'm throwing in the towel!" What's its origin?

When boxers used to fight, they'd have a sideman, like a manager who would wipe sweat and blood off the boxer's face. If the sideman believed the boxer had taken enough of a pounding, he'd throw the gory sponge into the ring as a signal that they were conceding the match, giving up, losing. How do *we* know which road to take in tough circumstances? How do when know to throw in the towel, or go the distance, which might lead to failure, loss of money, a dead-end relationship, or a project ending? The experience can be like lying down under a pendulum and watching it swing.

Persistence means sticking firm and not throwing in the towel until God decides what's next for us.

Do you recall when Jesus visits His hometown and heals the paralyzed man? This sick man is lying on a mattress, and those who "trust" Jesus believe He can make the incapacitated, helpless, and powerless man well. "Trust" means, "confidence," "belief," "faith," "conviction," and "reliance." Who are these people from Jesus's hometown? They had to have known Him. One thing is certain: their trust is so firm in Jesus that Jesus "sees" it. "Courage, son! Your sins are forgiven. ... Get up, pick up your mattress, and go home! And the man got up and went home. When the crowds saw this, they were awestruck and said a *b'rakhah* to God the Giver of such authority to human beings" (Matthew 9:1-8). Mark and Luke also document this event (Mark 2:1-12; Luke 5:18-26). What is a "b'rakhah?" Blessings and hope. In Jewish culture, the root word is a verb, meaning to kneel and worship in a blessing. This slice-of-life is important in Jesus's ministry. It shows the perseverance of those who trust Jesus; however, doubts ensue from the Rabbis. Jesus pushes through them to call Matthew to be his disciple. What encouragement Jesus must have experienced, a soul-boost from His Father and the Holy Spirit. He never threw in the towel then, and He doesn't throw in the towel where we're concerned. He's involved every second in our lives, enmeshed in our projects, and kneading our relationships. We just need to ask Him, and let Him.

Father, we need your encouragement today. Amen.

JULY 22
SIGNAL

There are people and events we can handle. And people and situations we *believe* we can't handle. And then, there are things we just *can't* handle. Are there people, places, events and things that are leaving you feeling disgruntled, agitated, and awake fretting at night?

We need our Savior Jesus to handle those hard-to-deal-with people and situations for us. "For in him, bodily, lives the fullness of all that God is. And it is in union with him that you have been made full—he is the head of every rule and authority." (Colossians 2:9-10). What is "the fullness of all that God is"? "Consecrate yourselves in preparation for tomorrow" (Joshua 7:12). We have a consecrated position with Him and our roots grow deep, in Him. He is our Author who wrote our DNA. "The righteous will flourish like a palm tree, they will grow like a cedar in the L'vanon. Planted in the house of *Adonai*, they will flourish in the courtyards of our God. Even in old age they will be vigorous, still full of sap, still bearing fruit" (Psalm 92:12-16). A palm tree's roots descend deep in the ground.

Last week, I transplanted a beautiful white hibiscus in front of my tall Florida palm. Wow did I have to dig deep to situate that white hibiscus into the soil! For the next few days, I checked on the shrub. Today I noticed a beautiful big red flower in front of the palm tree. I couldn't believe my eyes. I had been working hard to make it grow. I had been watering the shriveling shrub and fertilizing it for *two* summers. I had almost given up, until, a beautiful red bloom. "There's no longer any seed in the barn, is there? And the vine, fig tree, pomegranate tree and olive tree have produced nothing yet, right? However, from this day on, I will bless you" (Haggai 2:19). What do we need to handle what we believe we *can't* handle? We need to know Jesus in a deep and spiritual way—His way. He's communicating with you now, deeply rooted *in* you, now. In the Holy Spirit and His word, He dwells in you. That's not all. God is *growing* you, and deeply rooting in all your situations. Why? His glory is in resolving our difficulties so that in time we'll know He's in control and can handle our lives. "Can a fig tree yield olives ... or a grapevine, figs? Neither does salt water produce fresh [water]" (James 3:12). We can't be everything to everyone. Be yourself, in Jesus Christ our Lord. He loves you. He designed, *you*.

Father God, thank you for life and spiritual watering. Amen.

JULY 23
CASCADING EFFECTS

"But in my mind I keep returning to something, something that gives me hope—that the grace of *Adonai* is not exhausted, that his compassion has not ended. [On the contrary,] they are new every morning! How great your faithfulness! *'Adonai* is all I have,' I say; 'therefore I will put my hope in him' (Lamentations 3:21-24). Jeremiah wrote these verses in the form of a poem. Mapping the rhythm, we can hear Jeremiah singing his heart-felt soul song right into the lap of God. Perhaps he had been complaining to God? He does acknowledge he's depressed. "Remember my utter misery ... . They are always on my mind. This is why I am so depressed" (verses 19 and 20). Do you ever have those kind o' days where you just feel depressed, like a smelly sack is on your back because people are giving you a hard or difficult time? Misery can build up like hard-water spots in a toilet, making it difficult to scrape off our sadness or anger. "God—why?!" Have you ever asked, "God, why me?"

Have you fallen into the Complaining Bowl again? Are ya swishin' around in there? Sometimes, I fall in, I have to admit.

Moses did, too. "Who am I, that I should go to Pharaoh and lead the people of Isra'el out of Egypt" (Exodus 3:11)? And then: "But I'm certain they won't believe me. They won't listen to what I say, because they'll say, *'Adonai* did not appear to you' " (Exodus 4:1). You know what "yes, but" means? When you say those two words in the same sentence, you're really saying *no*. "Yeah, I like what you did, but I woulda done things different." We can easily lose hope when situations don't go our way, an illness takes us off guard, we're hit with an unexpected expense, a family member lets us down, or others fail us in some way. Our hope can drain right out of us like vital sap in a withering plant. What's that look like? "The wormwood and the gall" in Jeremiah's Lamentations (3:19). Wormwood is bitter, and bile tastes bitter when we burp up acid. When events in our lives leave us in complaining or in bitter spirits, let us pray for hope. We need God's Hope which is refreshing water when troubling events bubble up in our lives, or people treat us meanly, or disrespect us. "Endurance produces character, and character produces hope" (Romans 5:4). Today, we can return to God's hope, which is His grace and compassion. They are new every morning.

Father, we trust in you. Help us endure. Amen.

JULY 24
COLLAPSE

I've been quickly depleting my dead Uncle Jim's inheritance on home improvements. The money is like water in a sieve. No sooner had it hit my bank account than it flowed into a tree removal project, palm planting, screen enclosure improvements, a water treatment system, and roof repair. Ouch. We believed we'd planned out the money to an exact science, until we encountered a problem with the special Florida glass sections on our screened-in pool enclosure. We were hoping to have the installer fit the special screen perfectly as quoted, but then came a problem....

"Ma'am," the installer began, "I just can't fit these measurements of the screen to your triangular aluminum." He stood sweating and perplexed at the center of my patio. He began pacing the area and time-and-again discerning the spaces and available material. He had already wasted yards of Florida glass, which is actually a special and expensive sun-protective screen.

I began to cry in disappointment. I saw his fatigued-frustrated face. He wanted to finish the job today. He might not at all.

Do you as well have situations in your life that turn sideways? You believe an event might turn out a certain way, but then the opposite happens.

Paul the Apostle knew what it was like to pursue one task with skill and fervor only to encounter obstacles and a brick wall. He felt disappointment and encountered sinful Christians (1 Corinthians 5), but he never gave up. He had a heart for Jesus. "When he arrived in Jerusalem, he attempted to associate with the disciples, and they were all afraid of him, because they did not believe that he was a disciple. But Barnabas took Saul, brought him to the apostles, and related to them how he had seen the Lord on the road, that the Lord had spoken to him, and how in Damascus he had spoken out boldly in the name of Jesus" (Acts 9:26-27). Paul could have quit. Jesus's eleven disciples didn't believe he had converted to "the Way." Yet Jesus chose Paul. "I myself am an emissary sent to the Gentiles. I make known the importance of my work" (Romans 11:13). What do you believe is your most important work today? "Think carefully about Yeshua, whom we acknowledge publicly as God's emissary (Hebrews 3:1). We are examples who show Jesus. You are, today.

Father, help us love, persevere, and show your example. Amen.

July 25
Service

Today was our turn—those of us in Tuesday's Bible study class—to prepare dinner for the homeless, transport the dinner, and serve about one hundred people in our community. There are desperate people out there ... whether you're living in 2016 or 20016. What's the need in your community? Are you helping? Here's a bit of what happened with a few cooks stirring "the broth."

Potato peeling Cindy was hunched over a running sink. "I've never in my life bought forty-pounds of potatoes!" She kept peelin' away. Meg had dishwashing duty. Peggy had onion cutting duty.

Anne and Shelly were meat-loaf mixing. "Should we add garlic?" Anne called. Someone found garlic powder. "Yes," she said excitedly while sitting on a stool and smash-mixing oatmeal, egg, salt, pepper, and ground beef. She has diabetes but was determined her "sugar levels" wouldn't stop her. We were all working for God—*yes*.

Shelly asked if she could help me butter the giant aluminum pans for the brownie mix. Let me tell you, I've never seen such giant packages that could feed a hundred people. "No, I can do this," I answered as Mary, the woman in charge, said I had twenty minutes to prepare the brownies and insert the aluminum sheets into the oven. We were running on fast time—a ticking clock by which we were counting down to 3 o'clock. We were the cookers, and others were scheduled to transport the meal to the shelter, where the servers—those reaping the results of our hard work—were scheduled to dish out our prepared meals to the homeless. Do we get any credit? Do we get acknowledgement? Nope. "See ya'll later," we waved bye.

What's your circumstance today? Are *you* being acknowledged for what you've done? What if the project or task you're doing goes unnoticed? Breathe and *know* ... God sees everything. "I am with you. Don't be distressed, for I am your God. I give you strength. I give you help. I support you with my victorious right hand" (Isaiah 41:10). Who gives you strength to keep going when people might not recognize your hard work and commitment? "The purpose is that you should enter into the covenant of *Adonai* your God and into his oath which *Adonai* your God is making with you today" (Deuteronomy 29:11). With you. The Holy Spirit is in you and directing your life. God *is* rewarding you ... and oh what a reward.

Father, help us know your ways and be humble. Amen.

JULY 26
GATHERING READINGS

Have you ever heard of climate proxies? They are ways we read global climate change over the centuries. We have cave records, sediment cores, coral skeletons, tree rings, glacial layers, ice samples, ancient pollen skeletons, detailed sailors' logs, explorers' sketches, and artwork on cave walls. In each of these specialty fields, we need experts to gather data, compare results, and draw conclusions. Studying any one of these climates proxies involves years of research, with older people teaching the younger generations and contriving new ways to preserve data for posterity. We all need proof, right? Have you noticed how "experts" in a field constantly question their colleagues' results? Being on the receiver's end of blowback and reviews can be heart wrenching. Throughout our lives, we'll train for various jobs and have several roles. Are you a student in a particular field, but feeling uncertain about which direction to take? Are you trying to discipline your child and not quite sure what method to use?

How do we make a decision God's way, and know our decisions are the right ones? Just as climate proxies read time-lapsed changes, we can look back on our behavior patterns and do a "self-reading." Jesus said, "If anyone wants to come after me, let him say 'No' to himself, take up his execution-stake [cross], and keep following me" (Matthew 16:24). When are the times you've said no to the things you want and sacrificed for someone else? That's important because those changes from self to others show your growth toward Christ. "A wise man is strong; yes, a man of knowledge grows in strength" (Proverbs 24:5). Someone once told me, "Be humble, teachable, and listen to criticism because you can learn." List the times where you've learned and changed because education (knowledge) and wisdom go hand-in-hand. "Keep growing in grace and knowledge of our Lord and Deliverer, Jesus the Messiah" (2 Peter 3:18). Just as Jesus extends us grace, have there been times when you've extended grace to others? That's compassion, mercy and forgiveness—vital qualities that show we're on a road to conforming to Christ. After all, "The whole Body, receiving supply and being held together by its joints and ligaments, grows as God makes it grow" (Colossians 2:19). Jesus is talking about the church, but He also knows you and me. He has a purpose for you; so pray, and ask Him for His will in your life today.

Father, have mercy on us and direct our lives. Amen.

JULY 27
HEAVEN VS. HELL

There are times in life when we're confronted with life-and-death challenges ... times when we're kneeling in deep prayer at the cross ... times when we feel like we're drowning....

I belong to two groups. One group, I'm secretary. The other, I'm a just a member. I had an idea: What if both groups could hold a selling event? My simple idea to help people turned into a line of complicated knots. What's to do when you do your best to help people but others feel frightened or anxious for some reason?

Everyone suffers at some time. That's part of life. "Let not all this suffering seem little to you that has come on us (Nehemiah 9:32). [Also, 1 Peter 3:17]. What are *you* suffering through today? Now let's counter the negative with the positive. What are your blessings?

Jesus talks to us all the time. "Let the children come to me, don't stop them, for the Kingdom of Heaven belongs to such as these" (Matthew 19:14). We are His children and can talk to Him at any moment. No one can keep us from communing with him. What a blessing on which to cling.

"*Adonai* is my Rock, my fortress and deliverer, my God, my Rock, in whom I find shelter, my shield, the power that saves me, my stronghold" (Psalm 18:3). Is a person, thing, or event overwhelming you? Hold onto our Rock, God. Once at a church service in Texas, ushers handed out stones. I remember thinking: "A rock? Really? What's going on?" I still have that smooth black rock because it represents God's ability to calm and shelter me when I'm in the middle of chaos. It's a symbol of God's protection when I'm experiencing disorienting events. God has the ability to alter any situation for His purpose, and God could send armies of angels if He so desires. "Samuel took a stone, placed it between Mitzpah and Shen, and gave it the name Even-'Ezer [Stone of Help], explaining, '*Adonai* has helped us until now' "(1 Samuel 7:12). What's an Ebenezer stone? Help. The little shiny rock from church is a tangible reminder that God is present with me and in my relationships daily. When I hear the name Ebenezer, I think of Scrooge. Ebenezer is the "stone of help." In Dickens' *A Christmas Carol*, Ebenezer needs divine help to change. God gives us help in many forms—the Holy Spirit inside of us, people, and angels.

Father, we are grateful for spiritual relief from turmoil. Amen.

JULY 28
ROAD TRIP

This is summer when families go on road trips. An acquaintance has just returned from an RV trip along the Appalachian Mountains. She and her family trekked all the way to Maine. Are you thinking about taking a trip, going away to school, or leaving for a conference?

God, King David, Esau, and Apostle Paul can give you some advice. "Things go well with the person who is merciful and lends, who conducts his affairs with fairness" (Psalm 112:5). We can become irritated when TSA agents, checkers, restaurant servers, hotel personnel, flight attendants, coffee servers, etc., don't give us the time, service, or attention we deserve. Yet *every* person deserves mercy and to be treated fairly. Yesterday, a server didn't charge us for my husband's meal, only my meal. We could have paid the flimsy check and then slid out the door ... taken advantage of her mistake. But that would have been wrong because she might have been fired, or forced to pay out of pocket for her slight. In good conscience, we couldn't let that happen. We all make mistakes, right? God is *writing* mercy, fairness and rightness on our hearts. (He 8:10). We need to listen to Him, and treat others right.

Before we travel, we need to know how to pack "right." Jacob's brother Esau has so much stuff, he can't move to where he wants to live. He has to remain close to Jacob who stole his inheritance. Pack light and only what you need. Things can hold us back.

Paul tells us that traveling can leave us vulnerable. "In my many travels I have been exposed to danger from rivers, danger from robbers, danger from my own people, danger from Gentiles, danger in the city, danger in the desert, danger at sea, danger from false brothers. I have toiled and endured hardship, often not had enough sleep, been hungry and thirsty, frequently gone without food, been cold and naked. And besides these external matters, there is the daily pressure of my anxious concern for all the congregations" (2 Corinthians 11:26-28). Wow, did he go to the extreme to spread the Saving News about Jesus, plant churches and turn people to Christ and save their souls. "It is not his purpose that anyone should be destroyed, but that everyone should turn from his sins" (2 Peter 3:9). No matter the place or time, what can we do today? One *little* act or testimonial word can save someone, or bring us closer to God.

Jesus, give us words to touch peoples' lives. Amen.

JULY 29
FAMILY TIME

I remember taking summer vacations with my dad and stepmom. The first year I lived with them at thirteen, we drove in the blue Chevy to the East Coast. We saw such wonders. We rode the elevator to the top of the Empire State Building. We saw the Liberty Bell and Independence Hall where the Founding Fathers debated the Constitution. We came within a few inches of Plymouth Rock, and I took the boat ride under Niagara Falls. I felt so excited. But my stepmom liked to shop, everywhere. I mean stop-and-shop at over-the-freeway rest areas and just about every souvenir store. Maybe that's where I got shop-till-ya-drop, in early adulthood. Then, my brother and I always fought over space in the back seat. We'd argue over an inch of space. "Dad—he pushed the cooler into me!"

"No, Dad, she shoved it into *me!*" Then we'd fight over who could sit in the center of the back seat and talk to Dad and Mom.

"I got here first," I'd holler, squished by the cooler.

Tom elbowed my left arm. "No—I got here first!"

Through anger lines, Dad snapped, "Sit back or I'll crack ya!"

Now let me tell you, you'd *never* want a spanking—or a cracking—from Dad. You couldn't sit. We both sneered at each other and then stared out our windows at the changing landscapes.

Have you ever been embroiled in fights or arguments to make yourself known or present your ideas? People might not be all that enthused, except you. You believe in "the cause." I'm reminded of Paul and his commitment to succeed on his missionary journeys. The word, *missionary*, means, *sent.* Who sends Paul? God. "Compelled by the Spirit, I am going to Jerusalem" (Acts 20:22). He makes four missionary journeys, possibly going north to Spain. That's how committed, motivated, and inspired Paul was by Jesus, who personally appeared to Paul for the job. Jesus could, if he wanted, appear to you and me right now. "The sign of the Son of Man will appear in the sky, all the tribes of the Land will mourn, and they will see the Son of Man coming on the clouds of heaven with tremendous power and glory" (Matthew 24:30). Why doesn't He? "When the Messiah, who is our life, appears, then you too will appear with him in glory" (Colossians 3:4). We're not raptured yet. So make today and every moment a special road trip for God.

Father, help us utilize our talents to love others. Amen.

JULY 30
DANGEROUS!

Sometimes, we need a lifeguard. We *need* God, Jesus, and the Holy Spirit. We need them *every* moment, because in our controlling moments, we could interfere in God's business.

Today in Bible study, an old man named Jack stood up and told the class bad news. "I have stage-4 lung cancer. I'm going to die soon." He stuttered and held back tears. Except on TV, I don't think I've ever seen an elderly person cry. I cried. Wouldn't *you* cry?

Jack continued giving us words of wisdom from our Lord. "Let God be the Driver in everything you do, everywhere you go—even in the bathroom! And let Him be in every word you speak."

After class, I listened to more of what Jack said and compassionately touched his shoulder. I might not ever see Jack again, so I wanted to look straight into his blue eyes and absorb every wise word emanating from the Holy Spirit speaking through him. I wanted to remember so I could pass his words onto posterity, for *you*, who are God Designed. Being created by God is what he preached. We came from God. We'll return to God. "Trusting is being confident of what we hope for, convinced about things we do not see" (Hebrews 11:1). We're going to Heaven! "*Adonai*, haven't you existed forever? My God, my holy one, we will not die" (Habakkuk 1:12). Do you want to live fully? Trusting God was Jack's message, and backing off from doing things *our* way because we might hurt people in whose lives God is working to change.

Where I live, rain is pouring down. "He gives rain to the earth, pours water down on the fields" (Job 5:10). Yet I can't stop hurting for Jack's diagnosis, and wanting to help him while he transitions to hospice. Can prayer be sufficient? "Pray for each other, so that you may be healed. The prayer of a righteous person is powerful and effective" (James 5:16). Right now, I'm praying for Jack. But you know what? I never intended to attend that particular Bible class. Interesting how God put me there to learn, from Jack. Trust in God. In what happens today—good and bad—we cannot discern His giant perspective for our lives. Habakkuk says: "I will stand at my watch post; I will station myself on the rampart. I will look to see what [God] will say through me and what I will answer when I am reproved" (2:1). God is with us even in the bathtub.

Father, help us stay out of *your* will for others' lives. Amen.

July 31
Scary Critters

Florida's Everglades has invaders that are threatening our ecology and population as they expand their invasion into our food chain. At the latest Everglades Invasive Species Summit, researches showed a picture of people who snagged a fifteen-foot Burmese python. Turns out pythons are breeding by the hundreds and eating deer, possums, dogs, and our endangered bobcats. Oh, and don't forget the giant, creepy, sneaky Nile monitor lizards, and Giant African Snails that grow 3 inches high and 8 inches long. They harbor a parasite, rat lungworm, that if eaten can cause meningitis. Then we have the lionfish and Argentine tegu lizard, not to remind you of my thick nemesis growing on hormones behind my fence: Brazilian pepper trees with Stretch Armstrong branches.

Do you have irritants in your life today? Little—or big!—irritating pesky critters that just won't leave you alone? They could invade your life in the form of noises, someone "harping," a pushy colleague, a complainer, a whining relative, or a child who won't stop squealing, "I'm so bored." Did you know, people can get so bored they can become stressed out? Stressors and irritants can all go away if we get moving. It's called "self-agency," which is really, "sense of agency." We have self-agency because we're *aware* that we're initiating, executing, and controlling our own actions. *I'm* doing my own moving and thinking. *I* am responsible. *I* have control of how *I* respond to people and events around me. Are you, self-controlled?

Paul tells us, "Let us, too, put aside every impediment—that is, the sin which easily hampers our forward movement—and keep running with endurance in the contest set before us" (Hebrews 12:1). The word, "hamper," means: "to restrict the movement of by bonds or obstacles; to interfere with the operation of; disrupt; restrain; to interfere with." Impediments block us. They're barriers, obstructions, and limitations. Impediments are sins. If we allow every-little-thing to get under our skin and irritate us to nonstop complaining, we become ineffective in what we do today, a hindrance to our growth, a "hamper" to showing God to others, and a restraint for God who's offering us so many gifts from the Holy Spirit. With God's intercession, we can fend off these sins the Enemy uses *to try* to hamper us, and to keep us from falling prey to sin.

Holy Spirit, deliver us from debilitating stressors now. Amen.

AUGUST 1
EARTH TO PLANET 452B

Yesterday, Matthew was working on our screen enclosure while Jésus and Joshua from the water treatment company installed our whole-house system. I don't believe in coincidences. I told Drew, "Is God telling us something?" He uses things and people for His glory all the time. Later, while driving our 2006 Magnum with 140,000 miles, we heard *screeeech-creeak* from the front end. "What was that?"

Drew then visited and returned from the repair shop with bad news. "We need a set of struts, shocks and some other parts."

Feeling dejected, I said: "Gosh, why is everything hitting us like a hurricane? How much will it all cost?" You ever notice how things seem to break down all at once? Thanks to God, we still had a thousand dollars left of Uncle Jim's inheritance money. I had planned to stock that away into a retirement fund.

"The mechanic quoted $1,100.00."

"Darn!" I thundered. No putting money away. What do we do when we're planning for our future and our plans sink like fishing pole lead in a lake? God's plans are permanent. He never changes.

Two great prophets give us some advice for today. "*Adonai*, you are my God. I exalt you. I praise your name. For you have accomplished marvels, fulfilled ancient plans faithfully and truly" (Isaiah 25:1). Whose God is He? *Our* God, and He knows you personally. You can claim Him any time for help. What has He done? Accomplished marvels. What's a marvel? A "wonder," "miracle," "spectacle," "phenomenon," and "splendor." Go to a mirror and look at your reflection. He created you. You're God designed and a miracle, wonder, and splendor to Him. Furthermore, He has a plan for you and your life. "I know what plans I have in mind for you, plans for well-being, not for bad things; so that you can have hope and a future" (Jeremiah 29:11). God has our lives "in mind." What does He want for you? "Well-being," "hope," and "a future." Sometimes, God speaks to us in the little occurrences in our lives. How many coincidental encouragements will it take for us to acknowledge that He's working *personally* with us? "God is not human, that he should lie, not a human being, that he should change his mind. Does he speak and then not act? Does he promise and not fulfill" (Numbers 23:19)? Our promises can be lines of sand.

Lord, people will fail us, but never you. Amen.

AUGUST 2
FIRSTS

"Don't you know that you are God's temple, and God's Spirit lives in you? So if anyone destroys God's temple, God will destroy him. God's temple is holy, and you are that temple" (1 Corinthians 3:16-17). Paul is talking to a Christian church in Corinth, but he's also instructing us as to our identity. Are you taking care of yourself today? Have you stood back at some point, trying to figure out how to make your mind, body, and soul more fit and healthy?

A man named "Doug" has just finished doing some repairs for us. For the past several days as Doug's been coming and going, Drew and I have been striking up conversations with him. I've also been giving him cold water and leaving our restroom door open for him to use. Doug finally confided in us a problem he's been having. "I can't stop drinking water. I'm thirsty all the time. And lately, I've lost so much weight—30 pounds. I hope I don't have diabetes."

"I can test your blood sugar," Drew offered, and then he told Doug about *his* diabetic condition. This morning, he tested Doug, whose fasting blood sugar level was 368! "You need to see a doctor, right away," Drew instructed him firmly but gently. "With the right medication and diet, you can manage diabetes. But if you don't get control over it, you'll hurt your organs and damage your body." Wow, did we scare Doug who said working at our house had to be divine intervention. Sometimes, God will allow a scary event or sudden illness to happen so that we'll turn to Him and take better care of ourselves. "You belong to the Messiah, and the Messiah belongs to God," Paul tells the Corinthians (1 Cor. 3:23). Aren't his words comforting? We "belong" to God—*belong* to Him. In life, when confronting our troubles; and in death and after death, He is *attached, affiliated, integrated* and in deep spiritual *fellowship* with you and me. Jesus tells Pontius Pilate, "The reason I have been born, the reason I have come into the world, is to bear witness to the truth. Everyone who belongs to the truth listens to me" (John 18:36). What is truth? Pilate asks Jesus, *"Quid est veritas?"* Jesus doesn't answer, we don't know His answer, or Pilate doesn't wait for Jesus to answer. Yet, we know "the truth." Jesus! You are His precious temple, belonging to the God of the Universe who designed—and is—designing you. Care for yourself because He loves you.

Father, help us listen to your directions for our health. Amen.

AUGUST 3
POOR TESTING

Today I'm continuing yesterday's Pontius Pilate topic. Pilate appears to be a testy person. He's all Roman, all warrior, and the epitome of Roman stoicism. "Stoicism" is the "endurance of pain or hardship without a display of feelings and without complaint." Pilate was expert at inflicting punishment, enforcing Roman rule ["All hail, god Caesar!"], and motivating people to submit or die. That was Governor Pontius Pilate.

Do you have a streak of bullheadedness that pops up in your life now and then? Poet Maya Angelou once said about stubbornness: "There is a difference from being convinced and being stubborn. I'm certain what the difference is, but I do know that if you butt yourself against a stone wall long enough, at some point you realize the wall is stone and that your head is flesh and blood" (http://izquotes.com/quote/337312).

Pilate's story may help you overcome stubbornness.

"Some people came to tell Yeshua about the men from the Galil whom Pilate had slaughtered even while they were slaughtering animals for sacrifice" (Luke 13:1). What was this about? Here's a recap of Luke Chapters 12 and 13:

At the beginning of Luke 13, Pilate kills "sinners" at the temple who are sacrificing animals to God for forgiveness of their sins. They were preparing for a special "qorbanot" [draw near] ceremony that could only be performed at the Temple, which is no more.

Why would Pilate kill them?

In the previous chapter, Jesus rebukes the Pharisees, and then he says, "Don't fear those who kill the body but then have nothing more they can do." He's trying to get us to focus us on eternity. We're more than flesh and blood. We're His—*forever*. He is *pure* Truth.

Then He tells us, "Whoever acknowledges me in the presence of others, the Son of Man [I] will also acknowledge in the presence of God's angels." After you die, Jesus will proclaim *your* name in Heaven. That's how special and loved you are to Him. Remember this promise as you go throughout your day today.

Then Jesus introduces us to the future presence of the Holy Spirit. Thereafter, He gives us a lesson on sharing. And then He discusses the brevity of our lives on Earth; and then, our problem with trust. The instructions come as fast hard balls for us to attend to and absorb into our lives. Have enough "then"? Here's more.

Then Jesus gives us a lesson about "where our wealth is so is our heart;" and then, when He'll come back in the Second Coming; then, "I have an immersion to undergo" [His immersion into death for us]; and, lastly: "You know how to interpret the appearance of the earth and the sky—how is it that you don't know how to interpret this present time?" He is God among us—the only interpretation.

That's when "some people" tell Jesus about Pilate "slaughtering" those who are "slaughtering" animals as sacrifices for sins. Jesus answers: "Do you think that just because they died so horribly, these folks from the Galil were worse sinners than all the others from the Galil? No, I tell you. Rather, unless you turn to God from your sins, you will all die as they did!"

To think that we can just "slaughter" an animal and believe God will forgive us by its shedding blood is faulty. Pilate kills people because they are sacrificing to God and not worshipping Caesar. After all, as a stoic Roman, he must prove to Caesar his loyalty and devotion. The Roman emperor of the time was considered a god under the direct influence of the gods and goddesses of the time, like Zeus, Venus, Dionysus, Apollo, and Hades, to name just a few.

Jesus tells us the true one-and-only way for forgiveness of our sins. We need the True God—Adonai—His Father. Turn to God. He's knocking. Let Him help. We don't need eclipses and psychics to interpret events around us. We need Jesus. "We no longer trust because of what you said, because we have heard for ourselves. We know indeed that this man really is the Savior of the world" (John 4:42). Let Him inside the details of your life, and let Him heal the shadows in your mind and crevices in your heart to work His marvelous wonders. "I will show them wonders" (Micah 7:15). What's a wonder? "A feeling of surprise mingled with admiration, caused by something beautiful, unexpected, unfamiliar, or inexplicable." God has wonders in store ... for you. Thus touched by Him, imagine the people you will encounter and possibly change for God today? You are, His wonder. Perhaps that's why, at Jesus's trial, Pilate asks Jesus if he's from Galilee. Galilee has special significance to Pilate, perhaps a reminder of his own sins, which he's too bullheaded to acknowledge. We only need to admit our sins, "I did ___." Then, ask Jesus, "Please forgive me." He is Restorer.

Father, give us humility to see our sins. Amen.

AUGUST 4
TREKKING

Being propelled by evolving computing and Smart-tech homes and offices, we have to ask: How does God feel about robots? On July 27, 2014, HitchBot, the wonderful robotic social experiment in human nature and behavior began a long journey.

Canadians David Harris Smith and Frauke Zeller of Reyerson University created HitchBot, the light-and-friendly hitchhiking robot that [who?] successfully hailed rides from strangers across Canada and Europe. Google for Hitchbot images, and you'll encounter a short, solar-driven, buckets-n-bolts robot with a cute, pixelated-smiling square face that stands at the roadside, arms outstretched like an approval-seeking baby waiting for someone to pick it [him/her?] up along the roadside. Completely dependent on humans for travel, HitchBot had basic machine vision and a microphone to detect motion and speech, could speak, carry on multiple conversations, and had some face-to-face capability so it could communicate with people who could then relay messages via social media about HitchBot's welfare and location. Where did HitchBot get all this knowledge? Wikipedia, the collaborative database that replaced *Encyclopedia Britannica*, is still available in 18 volumes if you prefer a hands-on experience. Was it hands-on desire that made someone in the City of Brotherly Love beat the pulp out of Hitchbot *who* had visited Boston and was on *her* way back to *her* inventors in Canada? Yes, Hitchbot's short life ended at night on August 2, 2015 with its blue-spongy left arm pointing north over its smashed-in body and severed head.

How does God look at *us*? We could ask Him, as we ask Hitchbot's creators, "Why did you make Hitchbot that someone destroyed? On TV interviews, they're not angry or seeking revenge. Anywhere along Hitchbot's long and delicate journey, anything could have happened to her—oops, I mean *it*. "Thus says *Adonai* the maker, *Adonai* who formed the universe so as to keep directing it—*Adonai* is his name: 'Call out to me, and I will answer you—I will tell you great things, hidden things of which you are unaware' " (Jeremiah 32:2-3). You are wonderfully made, simply by His "calling out" for you. "Let us make humankind ... and let them rule over ... every creature that crawls on the earth" (Genesis 1:26). How will *you* rule over even the little things you bring into existence and do today?

Lord, give us hearts to treat *all* creatures tenderly. Amen.

AUGUST 5
VIEWPOINTS

Garbage has a way of piling up, for some of us more than others. Have you ever heard of a hoarder? A person afflicted with this disorder is obsessed with "something" and thus compelled to collect things, permanently. They experience intolerable anxiety even discarding garbage. On a smaller scale, we collect things, right? There are car collectors, coin collectors ... doll, diamond, soap, seashell, china, art, handbag collectors. You get the picture.

What's your collection? What would happen if you were forced to sell it? Lose it in a disaster? Someone steals it? Or maybe you're carrying around—in a tight collection—garbage from your past.

David once told God, "I will keep on trusting even when I say, 'I am utterly miserable,' even when, in my panic, I declare, 'Everything human is deceptive' " (Psalm 116:10-11). There are days when we're "utterly miserable." *Everything* around us appears "deceptive," "misleading," "distorted," or, "fake." The prophet Elijah became so depressed once that he wanted to die because things weren't going right. "He sat down under a broom tree. ... 'Enough! *Adonai*, take my life. I'm no better than my ancestors' " (1 Kings 19:4). He's saying, *I'm gonna die anyway, so now's a good time.* All the little inconveniences we have to endure, the slights, the plans that don't work out, our irritations, insomniac nights, over-indulgences, sacrifices we make that go unnoticed, and the times when we try but fail can stack up piece-by-bit into a garbage pile. Some people have several piles of "smelly personal garbage." What the cure?

Fresh Holy Spirit air. "We have all kinds of troubles, but we are not crushed," Paul begins. "We are perplexed, yet not in despair; persecuted, yet not abandoned; knocked down, yet not destroyed. We always carry in our bodies the dying of Jesus, so that the life of Jesus may be manifested in our bodies, too" (2 Corinthians 4:8-10).

Because we have the Holy Spirit within us constantly communicating with God and Jesus, we can pray, and allow *them* to discard the things we can't throw away on our own. Jesus tells us, "Let your light shine before people, so that they may see the good things you do and praise your Father in heaven" (Matthew 5:16). We can exercise our spiritual gifts and unique God-given talents to generate freshness in the world. He eradicates all our garbage.

God, you don't make garbage, so heal our hurts. Amen.

AUGUST 6
THE POLES

Today is one hot and humid day, so my thoughts are on keeping cool. Remember nippy-autumn days and crisp nights? White winters and snow-dusted steps? You'd give *anything* to have *something* warm. I've heard of "it's so cold outside" jokes. Here are a few.

It's so cold outside you could pour water on the sidewalk and start skating. It's so cold outside, if you'd blow bubbles they'd freeze. It's so cold outside I wish I could provide housing for the homeless. Well, the last one isn't a joke, is it?

There are times when we find ourselves at the outskirts of possibilities. We believed everything was possible, but found ourselves at the end of our endurance or at opposites with people—like summer and winter. When we need help, who can we count on?

Jesus calls for us to help one another, no matter the inconvenience and no matter the size of our problems. *Help* in some way, the best way you can today. "When the Son of Man comes in his glory, accompanied by all the angels, he will sit on his glorious throne. All the nations will be assembled before him, and he will separate people one from another as a shepherd separates sheep from goats. The 'sheep' he will place at his right hand and the 'goats' at his left. Then the King will say to those on his right, 'Come, you whom my Father has blessed, take your inheritance, the Kingdom prepared for you from the founding of the world. For I was hungry and you gave me food, I was thirsty and you gave me something to drink, I was a stranger and you made me your guest, I needed clothes and you provided them, I was sick and you took care of me, I was in prison and you visited me.' Then the people who have done what God wants will reply, 'Lord, when did we see you hungry and feed you, or thirsty and give you something to drink? When did we see you a stranger and make you our guest, or needing clothes and provide them? When did we see you sick or in prison, and visit you?' The King will say to them, 'Yes! I tell you that whenever you did these things for one of the least important of these brothers of mine, you did them for me'" (Matthew 25:31-40)! Jesus is calling for a Christian *family* of believers who could depend on one another. This was in a world of Roman dominance and self-preservation. Can we, today, help someone in some way with our strengths, gifts and talents?

Father, help us love and help in all we do. Amen.

AUGUST 7
LOST, NOW FOUND

Big news in the papers today. People cleaning a Reunion Island beach discovered a 6-foot-long, *flaperon* wing part believed to belong to the missing Malaysia Airlines Flight 370. The plane disappeared on March 8, 2014, killing 239 people. A piece of chopped-up luggage also washed up on the shore. Can you imagine knowing a loved one, friend, or colleague is dead but not having a body to bury?

Most days, we go through life with every day giving us a "first." We meet someone for the first time, notice shape-shifting clouds, bask in our Sun's photonic light, or marvel at one of God's unique rainbows. I've only *pinched* a swath of your important day.

What are your "firsts" like so far? Most likely, they've been fun and happy, right? Are you noticing them in the moment? Perhaps, your firsts might be traumatic or physically hurtful—like a car wreck, illness, reaction to something you ate, or an unexpected chewing out by someone. Years ago, as I drove down the freeway in Hawaii, two racing trucks struck me. One launched me into the Zipper lane. The other drove right over the roof of my Volvo. If I would have been driving the Sebring, I would have died. Two years later, *to the date*, I was driving the Sebring in Thousand Oaks when a car smacked my front end, totaling it. Both were car accidents, firsts in different ways. God used saved my life. Did I get it? He loves me.

Yet, how can God exist and allow *bad* things to happen?

Jesus gave the Sermon on the Mount, with His "blessed are those who," statements. You can image the persecuted, the needy, the desperately hurting, the victims, the angry, and the impoverished listening to Him and yearning for answers from Messiah. They were His firsts, and He saw *every* face just as He sees *your* face and is involved in *your* firsts today. Jesus concludes that historic day with: "You have heard that our fathers were told, 'Love your neighbor— and hate your enemy.' But I tell you, love your enemies! Pray for those who persecute you! Then you will become children of your Father in heaven. For he makes his sun shine on good and bad people alike, and he sends rain to the righteous and the unrighteous alike" (Matthew 5:43-45). Why? Rewards (Matthew 5:46; Revelation 22:12). In Heaven, He will present each of us with rewards. We are not God's puppets. He gives us free will *to choose* good or evil.

Father, keep us from evil so we can show love and you. Amen.

AUGUST 8
BOMBSHELL

We have a tendency to chase things. In the news, a dentist who likes to hunt wild game killed a famous lion, Cecil. Outraged, people are hunting *him*, chasing leads on his location, and signing petitions to have him extradited to Zimbabwe. Officials there imprisoned the two guides who lured Cecil out of his protected habitat. You're not a hunter though, right? I've heard of women being called "man eaters" or womanizing men nicknamed lady killers. People can chase cars, dreams, fireflies, and rainbows. When I was a kid, I'd run to find the end of a rainbow because Grandma said that's where leprechauns stash their pots of gold. Wait—the chasing hasn't ended yet. I also remember playing a game called statues. I'd swing my opponents around; and when they'd stop, they'd pose like statues. Then I'd touch someone, and they'd chase me. A chase though always has to end in being caught. Are you chasing after something or someone? Or, have you caught the thing or person you've been chasing? Maybe *you're* the one who's been caught.

Whatever the case, you can now rest. God has you. He chased *you*, and *He* won. David knew what it was like to be on the run. For years King Saul and his minions chased after him. How exhausting for David. "The wicked in their arrogance hunt down the poor ... the wicked boasts about his lusts. He blesses greed and despises *Adonai*. Every scheme of the wicked in his arrogance [says], 'There is no God, [so] it won't be held against me'" (Psalm 10:1-4). David begs God to intervene—to show everyone in every nation—His majesty and divinity. "The helpless commits himself to you. You help the fatherless. ... As for the evil man, search out his wickedness until there is none left. *Adonai* is king forever and ever! The nations have vanished from his land. *Adonai*, you have heard what the humble want. You encourage them and listen to them, to give justice to the fatherless and oppressed, so that no one on earth will strike terror again" (Psalm 10:14-18). There's one thing about *being* chased and chasing: you're never standing still long enough to *be*. You're always moving, never relaxing, searching, and not enjoying what you have in the moment. David stops and says, "You [God] are my hiding-place and shield. I put my hope in your word" (Psalm 119:114). Jesus is our shelter. We can stop all other useless pursuits.

Father, help us live "in the now" which you've given us. Amen.

August 9
Burning Fires

We all have quirks. Here are a few of mine. I tend to think that when relationships go wrong, it's my fault. I can't forget the strands of my hair that over time stick in the shower drain, drivin' my husband nuts. I also like borderless flowerbeds, waking up to a clean kitchen sink, and locating objects when I need them, organizational perfectionistic me. I'm also quick to target the Sloppy Joes in my family who've left their plates on the ant-lined TV trays, shoes in the middle of the floor, and lights on everywhere. Aren't there quirks about others that just make you appreciate the times when you lived alone without the Oscar Madisons and Gregory Houses of the world?

Wait a minute, we all make mistakes. Not *one* person is 100% normal and perfect. Jesus, but no one else. Everyone has irksome quirks. King David began his career with a few oddities. "The youngest … tends the sheep … . With ruddy cheeks, red hair and bright eyes, he was a good-looking fellow" (1 Samuel 16:10-12). God anoints a "good-looking fellow" as king? No, there must be more. "*Adonai* doesn't see the way humans see. Humans look at the outward appearance, but *Adonai* looks at the heart" (1 Samuel 16:7). Author Flavia Weedn said about people, "Some people come into our lives and leave footprints on our hearts and we are never ever the same." Isn't it because of our "quirks" as well that we are who we are? After all, we have to dodge around quirks, accommodate them, overlook them most times, and learn to live with quirks that over time really become endearing. They change us, and mold us as fingers and hands shape beautiful clay pots. Are peoples' oddities, peculiarities, foibles, or hang-ups bothering you in some way today?

God once told Isaiah to strip and walked around naked, yet his visions of the Messiah were fulfilled in Jesus Christ (Isaiah 20:1-2). God orders Jeremiah to take off his underwear ("loincloth") and bury it under a rock. Later, God asks him to return, dig up the filthy clothes, and put them on, a symbol for God's patience (Jeremiah 13:1-11). God instructs Hosea to marry Gomer, a prostitute. They have a daughter, Lo-Ruchamah, her name meaning "not pitied." God uses quirks as special stamps He imprints on our lives. In all our quirks, He loves us for *His* glory. In peoples' quirky behaviors, He displays His undying affection. He helps us grow and shine, for Him.

Jesus, help us have compassion on others and not judge. Amen.

AUGUST 10
TRUE FULFILLMENT

The Psalmist David once sang to our Lord, "I will never forget your precepts, for with them you have made me alive" (Psalm 119:93). A "precept" is, *a general rule intended to regulate behavior or thought, principle, doctrine, commandment,* or, *order.* So we have to ask: How do God's precepts make us alive? Are *you* really *living* today?

An authority on death and dying, Elisabeth Kubler-Ross once said, "Our concern must be to live while we're alive—to release our inner selves from the spiritual death that comes with living behind a facade designed to conform to external definitions of who and what we are." So according to her, we are *alive*, but we might not *be living* because we are hiding behind a mask. Are you living according to how people expect you to live? For me, I don't mind wrinkles and four-year-old wardrobe. I feel truly alive, because I'm God's child, and enjoy writing for Him. I feel driven, for Him.

Author Mary Manin Morrissey once shared about being alive: "Start living now. Stop saving the good china for that special occasion. Stop withholding your love until that special person materializes. Every day you are alive is a special occasion. Every minute, every breath, is a gift from God." Elisabeth and Mary are repeating a similar chorus King David once sang while strumming his lute. "Your precepts, God, have made me alive." God fashioned us from the beginning of time to exist (Isaiah 44:2), but there's more to life than walking and breathing. There's truly living. For David, God's precepts *in* his life *make* him truly *alive.* Again you might ask, How can God's commandments, principles, and order help me live to the fullest? "It is through His Son [Jesus] that we have redemption—that is, our sins have been forgiven. He is the visible image of the invisible God. He is supreme over all creation, because in connection with him were created *all* things—in heaven and on earth, visible and invisible, whether thrones, lordships, rulers or authorities. They have all been created through him and for him. He existed before all things, and he holds everything together" (Colossians 1:14-17). At God's will, He formed your first atoms. You are part of His order. With His supremacy, He is guiding you to be everything you can be. Jesus has you securely in His sight *every* second. You are thus lovingly designed, and today fully alive.

Father, thank you for calling us into *being.* Amen.

August 11
Outlining in Ink

At times, have you ever noticed how nations can be thoughtless?

In 2007, Chinese scientists tested a ground-based anti-satellite weapon on one of their outdated weather satellites 530 miles above Earth. The experiment shattered the satellite into 3,000 ricocheting pieces. Now the International Space Station and other satellites need to maneuver around the field like a car swerving around potholes in the pouring rain. You'd think the Chinese would have considered the consequences. King David said, "Your [God's] words are a doorway that lets in light, giving understanding to the thoughtless" (Psalm 119:130). Thoughtlessness *isn't* predictable. We could stop it.

Do you ever find yourself acting or speaking without thinking? Remember when Abraham and Sarah laughed at God's knowledge of the future when God told them they'd be parents (Genesis 17:17-19)? God had to send them angels to reinforce what He'd told them (Genesis 18). Habakkuk the Prophet also questioned God. "Why don't you hear my call for help and why is evil enduring?" Have you ever noticed that "evil" becomes "evil" only when people die or are hurt? A hurricane, tornado, earthquake, and avalanche are Natural Evils though, leaving death and destruction in their wake. *Is* God around? "God, ya listenin'? Ya hear me? Yoo-hoo ... why?"

Have you been asking God "why" lately?

God answers these important questions for us so we can go about our day in relief, apologize if we've said something or done something wrong, and feel connected to Him when people thoughtlessly hurt us. "Look around ... . What you see will completely astound you! For what is going to be done ... you will not believe, even when you are told" (Habakkuk 1:5). God acts inside the seconds of our day, but He never tells us what He's going to do. He just does it, and the results you will "not believe." Before Isaiah foretells of Jesus the Messiah in Chapter 53, he says about God revealing His ways and plans, "To whom is the arm of Adonai revealed" (53:1)? We might have thoughtless moments, and we'll be in the wake of people who are experiencing thoughtless moments. However, God is the Thoughtful One, the Vigilant One, ever-present with us. "God thunders wonderfully with his voice, He does great things beyond our understanding" (Job 37:5). Let's let Him.

Father, in thoughtless moments, give us compassion. Amen.

AUGUST 12
GARDENS

I've often wondered where the word, "saved," as in, "I was saved [born again]," originated. In Luke 18:18, a "good," rich town leader asks Jesus, "What should I do to obtain eternal life?" "Eternal" means, "everlasting," "endless," and, "immortal." We live Eternal, in a state/condition of Eternal after *our bodies* die. Have you noticed how Death is hard to accept for people? Approaching Death usually causes extreme anxiety. Especially for those who don't *know* God, Jesus, and the Holy Spirit. They believe we expel energy when our hearts stop. On the contrary, Jesus focused on Eternity, instructing us what to take-and-not-take seriously while in our temporary bodies. People then, and now, find it hard to believe that each person has a soul *who*, at death, transitions to "the Kingdom of God." The Gospels have this phrase and "the Kingdom of Heaven" 51 times. "I will overturn the thrones of kingdoms" (Haggai 2:22). What power.

Have you ever stopped to marvel at any one of the 250,000 magnificent species of butterflies and moths? In my community, Tim Harrison, Deborah Jeffries, and Anna Hutson are planting butterfly gardens like little kingdoms at schools for children to study. There's something about beholding majestic butterflies in their colorful splendor flittering toward the sky for migration. We want children to be experience their elegance, nurture them, and realize their importance as pollinators and prey in the ecosystem. We want to make sure their species is "saved" for posterity. Safe and saved.

You are saved, for Eternity. Jesus answers the "good" city leader who like us is hungering for an answer to Death, "What is impossible humanly is possible with God" (Luke 18:27). In verses 15 through 17, Jesus had been instructing people about the Kingdom of God. Some people find it impossible to imagine life after death—to believe there's more that will happen to us after we leave this tangible world in which we rely on our five senses. Some TV shows attempt to tackle life after death: *Proof, Touched by an Angel,* and *Dead Like Me.* What must we *do* to *have* the Kingdom of God? "Who can be saved" (Luke 18:26)? Jesus answers in verse 17, "I tell you that whoever does not receive the Kingdom of God like a little child will not enter it at all!" Wow, exclamation point. I'll talk more on August 14 about receiving "the Kingdom of God like a little child."

God, help us have children's hearts. Amen.

AUGUST 13
20/20

Out of Revelation, here are seven special blessings from God for you today. I hope you cling to these blessings, and absorb them into your DNA. They will fill you with inspiration and a vital boost by our Holy Spirit. We're God designed, and He's still designing you, now, in this very second....

From Jesus Christ our Lord, John tells us today and every day: "Blessed are the reader and hearers of the words of this prophecy, provided they obey the things written in it! For the time is near (1:3)! Notice the exclamation points. John is serious. God is serious. Are you living as if today was your last day?

If an angel were to appear and tell me I had twelve hours left of life on Earth, I'd kneel, cry, and thank God for giving me the warning. Then I'd be present with my family and tell them, and others as well later on, the heartfelt words I've always thought but forgot to say to them in our conversations. Thereafter, I would tell as many people as possible about Jesus, so that after I die, as God had predicted, they'd believe in Him and change. I'd say, "Hey, I'm dying tomorrow, so believe Jesus died for your sins, too!" I'd have nothing to lose, right? Even if they arrest me, or cart me off to a hospital, I'll shout that out in the mall, Walmart, and street corners.

What one thing can we do to make a lasting difference for God today? Like the Butterfly Effect, where the fluttering of a butterfly's wings may set off currents that will grow into a large storm, we can change. We can inspire change in others.

Another blessing from Revelation comes to those who have made the most profound change—accepting Jesus as their Savior. "'How blessed are the dead who die united with the Lord, from now on! Yes,' says the Spirit, 'now they may rest from their efforts, for the things they have accomplished follow along with them' " (14:13). This is the Holy Spirit talking, the Holy One in Genesis 1 who hovers over the waters to enact God's Word and create Earth (1:2). When you die, you go *right* to God. However, in the future, there will one day be "the War of the Great Day." So when the battle between good and evil begins, "How blessed are those who stay alert and keep their clothes clean, so that they won't be walking naked and be publicly put to shame" (16:15). As Jesus says in Matthew 24:36, "When that day and hour will come, no one knows—not the angels in heaven, not the Son, only the Father." Therefore, we can't let ourselves be fooled by false teachers, astrologers, and psychics who try to steer us in the wrong direction and lead us down a false path. Our rewards will slip away from us.

A Revelation blessing number 4 invites you to a huge buffet. "How blessed are those who have been invited to the wedding feast of the Lamb" (19:9)! You are saved, so I'll see you at that glorious table one day. Have you ever noticed how God's feasts and festivals all involve eating together? We're called to keep his feasts and festivals as worship opportunities and community gatherings, to serve one another and communion with our Great God Adonai (Exodus 34; Leviticus 23, and Numbers 28).

Here's another job we'll have together. "Blessed and holy is anyone who has a part in the first resurrection [the rising of all believers]; over him the second death [White Throne Judgement of the wicked] has no power. On the contrary, they will be *cohanim* [priests] of God and of the Messiah. They will rule with him for the thousand years" (20:6). For 1,000 years, *you* will be one of God's priests and rule "with Him." Wow—what jobs we'll have. We'll learn from Him, hear His words, sit around Him, fellowship about Him with one another, and eat with Him daily. Are you preparing for it now? He's preparing you for Him and that Day now.

In everything you do today and *every* day, Jesus is holding your hand, guiding you, and telling you: "Look! I am coming very soon. Blessed is the person who obeys the words of the prophecy written in this book (22:7)!" He is coming soon, and we can do the best we can as His church and children to be in His word and let Him guide the moments of our days.

As our Bright Morning Star (22:16), He gives us this same blessing one last time: "How blessed are those who wash their robes, so that they have the right to eat from the Tree of Life and go through the gates into the city" (22:14)!

When we meet God, Jesus, and the Holy Spirit for the first time—face-to-face—I want to be clean.

I want to walk guilt free, head high, and with my shoulders straight into Heaven.

I'll see *you* there and along the way.

Father God, we say: "I want and need to know you." Amen.

AUGUST 14
GOLD AND SILVER

A few times, I've acted childishly. I stomped my foot, unleashed a snarling comeback, or grumbled a cross word under my breath. Have you ever acted childishly? Paul says about being a child, "When I was a child, I spoke like a child, thought like a child, argued like a child" (1 Corinthians 13:11). You've heard children talk. They have a short vocabulary; and based on their age, they stumble for words to express themselves. And can children throw tantrums.

Yet, as Jesus noticed them, He saw something spectacularly magnificent in children. "Unless you change and become like little children, you won't even enter the Kingdom of Heaven" (Matthew 18:3; Mark 10:15; and, Luke 18:16)! What does He mean?

There are things your parents did that you probably can't remember: rocking you to sleep; fretting at your bedside when you were running a fever; pacing you around when you were teething; crying when you stepped into preschool; waiting for you on your first date; and calling everyone when you didn't show up on time. There are more. Just as God watches our actions, aches with us, and is joyous along with us, your parents will always see you as their child. We are God's children. "In him we live and move and exist. Indeed, as some of the poets among you have said, 'We are actually his children.'" (Acts 17:26). The child developmental psychologist, Jean Piaget, once said: "Children have real understanding only of that which they invent themselves, and each time that we try to teach them something too quickly, we keep them from reinventing it themselves" ("The Century's Greatest Minds," *Time*, 1999). Children are inventive, spontaneous, and creative. They speak their minds. They don't always believe what they're told, and they can argue back. They are innocent, receptive to all sorts of possibilities, powerless, dependent, trustful, and naturally naïve and gullible. Jesus values these qualities. Imagine the love His Father, our God, feels for Jesus. They are in constant communion as we experience communion with them. His disciples once asked Jesus, "Who is the greatest in the Kingdom of Heaven?" Jesus called a child to him, stood him among them, and said, "Yes! I tell you that unless you change and become like little children, you won't even enter the Kingdom of Heaven" (Matthew 18:1-3). We need hearts of love, like teachable children.

God, relieve us of our masks so we can show our souls. Amen.

AUGUST 15
WRITTEN NOTICE

I don't know about you, but on rare occasions, I experience doubts about God's love for me. Do you ever find yourself asking the questions: "God, do you really love me? God, where do I stand with you?" Doubt comes in levels.

When I was a kid, carnivals used to have a game called a High Striker. It's a strength tester lined with levels inside a tower. A player takes a mallet, and wallops the base of the tower in the hope of sounding the top bell. "Step right up and test your strength!" Even if you can't "ring the top bell" with your best-'n-hardest strike, along the puck's journey upward, the tower will light up with a yellow indicator of how strong you are. I'd probably light up the first row. What level on the Doubt Tower might you illuminate today?

No matter how intense my doubt, fear also accompanies it. I could say "the puck" is my doubt and "the yellow indicator light" is my fear. What can we do to quench our doubts and fears?

The *nanosecond* we accepted Jesus as our Messiah, God began a good work in us. "The One who began a good work among you will keep it growing until it is completed on the Day of the Messiah Yeshua" (Philippians 1:6). When is the Day of the Lord? The first day of total peace on Earth. "The earth shall be filled with the knowledge of God, as the waters cover the sea" (Habakkuk 2:14). Our Lord sees us as special. He has Paradise in the form of His Kingdom for you. Furthermore, He has this profound truth indelibly written by the Holy Spirit on your heart. "This is the covenant which I will make with them after those days. I will put my Torah [law] on their hearts, and write it on their minds. ... . And their sins and their wickedness I will remember no more" (Jeremiah 31:32-34). We are secure with Him now *and* forever. How comforting to know His love for you, and His unchanging promises to which we can cling in our doubts and fears. Jesus reaffirms His Father's special treatment of you. "Aren't sparrows sold for next to nothing, five for two assarions [half-a-penny of our money]? And not one of them has been forgotten by God. Why, every hair on your head has been counted! Don't be afraid, you are worth more than many sparrows" (Luke 12:6-7; Matthew 10:29-31). The last sentence sounds like it could be a Commandment. "Don't be afraid." Feel His peace today.

Father, eliminate our doubts and fears so we can live. Amen.

August 16
Today's Must Read

Have you ever noticed a leak over time? It grows. Like a small sin we don't catch that grows, a leak gradually gets larger until … burst.

For the third time in three weeks, a leak has sprung in our solar panels on the roof. The last two times, technicians fixed them. I *believed* they had plugged the leaks. Problem resolved, *whew*. Not so. As I walked to the side of the house this morning, I spotted drips from the gutter. In a bit of a panic—'cause I'm scared the roof might leak—I ran into the house. "Call the solar company! Now!" We feel powerless when we encounter problems we can't fix. I'm no solar tech. I've *no* idea what special plugs to use let alone the self-assurance to climb a ladder and stand on the roof. Middle age is a time to realize you're not as limber and balanced as you were at forty.

Yet, God gives us plenty of encouragement so we don't have to live in discouragement. With his presence and power, He equips us to accomplish tasks for His glory. Remember Gideon? In today's culture, he'd be an ordinary person, yet the angel of the Lord appears to him under a pistachio tree. This is really Jesus, and I bet He grabs a few of those nuts, shells 'em, and pops 'em into his mouth. Gideon is threshing wheat in a wine press to hide food from Israel's enormous powerful enemy. Here's their conversation from Judges 6:

"You valiant hero! *Adonai* is with you!" the angel tells him.

Gideon stops. "If God's with us, then why is everything bad happening to us?"

"Go in this strength of yours," the angel begins, "and save Isra'el from the hands of Midyan. Haven't I sent you?"

Gideon is shocked. "My family is poor, and I'm all they have because I'm the youngest." In other words, where can I raise the money to defeat an army, who will believe I can accomplish that, and how will I get people to follow me?

I imagine the angel getting up into Gideon's face. "Because I will be with you, you will strike down Midyan as easily as if they were just one man." If God's Messenger isn't good enough, God gives Gideon three signs—really encouragements—so he'll believe Him without a shadow of a doubt. Sometimes, we need someone to have faith in us and point out capabilities we can't see in ourselves. Then we can accomplish the task. With God's power, today, you can.

God, give us encouragement, and help us obey and act. Amen.

AUGUST 17
LIGHT AND LIFE

Have you taken the time to see light glitter on the water, light flame along pine needles, and light magnify through brilliant colorful rainbows? Light was God's first display of His power and glory in our world, and He's fueling *us* with life on Earth. "Let there be light,' He commanded, and there was light" (Genesis 1:3). Light is vital to our sustenance. "God made the two great lights—the larger light to rule the day and the smaller light to rule the night—and the stars" (Genesis 1:16). These are the Sun, moon, and stars … all light. Lately, we're busy wondering what all those lights in the Deep Field mean for the Beginning of Time. Hubble and earthly telescopes are working to locate the exact time our universe came into existence.

What will they find? Theoretical physicist, Laurence Krauss, said about our connection to the universe: "Every atom in your body came from a star that exploded. And the atoms in your left hand probably came from a star than the atoms in your right hand. It really is about the most poetic thing I know about the universe. You are all stardust" (www.bigfishink.com). God leads us in the light. "*Adonai* went ahead of them in a column of cloud during the daytime to lead them on their way, and at night in a column of fire to give them light. Thus they could travel both by day and by night" (Exodus 13:21). He leads us, when we listen. Jesus told us we are light. "Let your light shine before people, so they may see the good things you do and praise your Father in heaven" (Matthew 5:16). *You* are light.

We can shine, for Him. "No one who has lit a lamp covers it with a bowl or puts it under a bed; no, he [she] puts it on a stand; so that those coming in may see the light" (Luke 8:16). What is your lamp? It is your God-given gifts, strengths, talents, and abilities. You can make a difference in this world—yes, you. "Then, your whole body is filled with light, with no part dark, it will be wholly lighted, as when a brightly lit lamp shines on you" (Luke 11:36). These are words to you from our Lord Jesus. He's giving you suggestions on how you can shine and sparkle in this world because He designed you. He is continuing to guide you in this often-distressing tumultuous world. "This was the true light, which gives light to everyone entering the world" (John 1:9). You are here by His design. The Holy Spirit illuminates you from within. Today, shine.

God, give us confidence to fulfill your designs. Amen.

AUGUST 18
THE BIG PICTURE

I can be so regimented with my daily routines that I don't see the days rippling past me like rustling leaves tumbling across a street. Does that ever happen to you? You don't or can't see the big picture?

I decided to do what I did for my children. I sifted through family photos, picked out pictures of me through the years, and then compiled a select few into a 57-year timeline. Wow—I can't recognize *any* of my present-day facial features from those bygone days. Our faces and bodies change, but the biggest change we'll notice is how we've grown in faith, love, and trust in God who always knows the big picture and what's best for us. "*Adonai* will give every person a reward suited to his uprightness and faithfulness" (1 Samuel 26:23). Looking back on how your faith has matured over the years, would you consider yourself a sturdy oak tree or a spindly Charlie Brown Christmas tree? Even if you're a faithful persevering person when an unpredictable trial strikes your life, have you realized that tree boughs straighten back up after a storm. God's there.

As for your ability to love, have you changed any since adolescence? "Here is how love has been brought to maturity with us: as the Messiah is, so are we in the world. This gives us confidence for the Day of Judgment" (1 John 4:17). Jesus is our encourager. He always loved, and He's building us with love through His word. He even gave love to his enemies, the people who crucified Him. "Father, forgive them. They don't understand what they are doing" (Luke 22-32). Matured over time, love yields faster forgiveness, prolonged tolerance, and offers help to others when we don't feel like loving. "'You man [Daniel] so greatly loved, don't be afraid. *Shalom* to you; and be strong, yes, truly strong.' His speaking to me [the angel] strengthened me, and I said, 'My lord, keep speaking, because you've given me strength' " (Daniel 10:19). When we're in communion with our Lord Jesus, He strengthens us and squashes our fears. Then we can serve Him by serving others and showing them our love. "Your love has given me much joy and encouragement," Paul tells Philemon. "Brother, you have refreshed the hearts of God's people" (Philemon 1:7). We—*you*—can be a refreshment to others. And our joy and Christ-given confidence will reflect outwardly to the needy and desperate we meet today.

Father God, help us reflect you to others. Amen.

AUGUST 19
SIGNS AND MIRACLES

Paul tells us, "We are of God's making, created in union with Jesus for a life of good actions already prepared by God for us to do" (Ephesians 2:10). I read the preceding verses and then the verses thereafter. The structure of Chapter 10 is as follows: Our standing with God and our behavior prior to Jesus; how God's mercy, grace, and intense love "brought us to life along with the Messiah" (4-6); and, how we're now God's possessions and in His family.

Where did all of God's newness for our lives begin?

John's Gospel is famous for bombarding us with the Good News. Jesus is the Messiah, the Savior of the world. John proves this by telling us the experiences of the people Jesus healed and profoundly changed. "The Word became a human being and lived with us, and we saw his Sh'khinah [glory]" (1:14). John and the people of his time saw Jesus and His glory. They *experienced* Jesus reflecting God and glory through our world like sunshine. He is our Creator who has "good actions already prepared for you today," Paul states. Why? "So that through [Jesus], everyone might put his trust in God and be faithful to Him" (John 1:7). That's Jesus's saving message. John gives us eight undisputable signs that the Old Testament Law has passed away, replaced by a New Law, Jesus, now living among us through the Holy Spirit. At a wedding, Jesus changes water in "six stone water-jars" into wine (Chapter 2). Also in Canaan, "at one o'clock in the afternoon," He resuscitates an officer's dead son over thirty-fives miles away in Capernaum (4:46- 54). The third sign occurs in Jerusalem. Jesus heals a 38-year-old ill man who keeps getting shoved away from Beit-Zata's healing waters (Chapter 5). Then, Jesus feeds thousands of people with "five loaves of barley bread and two fish" (6:1-15). Sign five occurs when He "walks on the Lake" (6:16-24). Jesus heals "a man blind from birth" with His mud and spit: sign six (9:1-41). I bet you can guess signs seven and eight. Jesus resuscitating Lazarus (11:1-45) and His Resurrection into His glorified *new* body (Chapter 20), an example of the bodies He'll give us at the Rapture. "The Lord himself will come down from heaven with a rousing cry, with a call from one of the ruling angels, and with God's *shofar*. Those who died united with the Messiah will be the first to rise" (1 Thessalonians 4:16). Spread the Good News.

God, your glory is Jesus and the Holy Spirit, Counselor. Amen.

AUGUST 20
BEST APPROACH

Do you ever have days when you find yourself going nonstop? Today is one of those days for me. I wish I had a reset button. I'd start my day over, but only if I could travel back with all my accumulated knowledge. Then I'd know which events to prioritize and postpone. However, that ability would require omniscience, being all knowing, a super-cerebral power we don't have but sure would like to add to the human species, right?

God is omniscient. "He reveals deep and secret things. He knows what lies in the darkness. Light dwells with him" (Daniel 2:22). Have you ever wanted to know the truth about yourself, someone else, or a situation? After all, we have this tendency to wear distorted glasses out of which we view people, events, and ourselves. It's called perspective, but perspective isn't always truth. God *is* truth and knowledge. He even knows our minds. "I know how your minds work" (Ezekiel 11:5). Have you ever felt your Awareness Lightbulb turn on? Perhaps Daniel 2:22 is where the expression comes from. At moments when we realize a truth, it's like a brilliant flash of light illuminates in our thoughts, changing us forever. "Someone on earth who blesses himself will bless himself by the God of truth, and someone on earth who swears an oath will swear by the God of truth; for past troubles will be forgotten, hidden from my eyes" (Isaiah 65:16). There's more. Jesus had the same omniscience as his Father. When He picks Nathanael to be one of His discipline, He calls to him, "Here's a true son of Isra'el—nothing false in him" (John 1:47-51). Jesus knows Nathaneal, inside and out.

Nathanael stops in his tracks. "How do you know me?"

Jesus answers, "Before Philip called you, when you were under the fig tree, I saw you."

Truth in lightning-fast awareness floods Nathanael in saving grace. "Rabbi, you are the Son of God! You are the King of Isra'el!"

As Jesus reset our lives the moment we embraced Him, He welcomes Nathanael into His Kingdom. "You believe all this just because I told you I saw you under the fig tree? You will see greater things than that! Yes indeed! I tell you that you will see heaven opened and the angels of God going up and coming down on the Son of Man" (1:49-51)! *Three* exclamations for your day.

Father, we are yours, *eternally*. Amen and thank you.

AUGUST 21
VOW

I remember times in my life when I turned away from God to my own devices—shopping, smoking, self-indulging, and just plain doing what I wanted. I got "Me-zeal." Have you ever experienced such a time? Guess what made me repent fast? The pain. "What one earns from sin is death. But eternal life is what one receives as a free gift from God in union with Jesus, our Lord" (Romans 6:23). Some people read this verse and say, "That sin didn't *kill* me." However, something died a little, right? Maybe a painful bill arrived from the shopping spree, or there's the next morning's pounding hangover that killed a few too many brain cells, or loss of opportunity because you chose your way. "Be careful to guard against all forms of greed" Jesus begins, "because even if someone is rich, his life does not consist in what he owns" (Luke 12:15). Greed *sees*, then *wants*, then *has* to have. It swallows us up. When we feel we're going beyond a point of no return, we aren't. He's there for us, even *in* the sin.

Do you need forgiveness today? "It is for *Adonai* our God to show compassion and forgiveness, because we rebelled against him" (Daniel 9:9). Where does forgiveness come from so we can forget our diversions and move forward? God. He shows mercy and forgives us, even though "we rebelled against him." Sin—doing life our way—is plain rebellion. Feel like a rebel lately? Wanna go out, splurge a little, have some fun? I saw a YouTube video of a teenager who rode his bike off a roof into a swimming pool. He broke his leg in three places. There's a video of the angry teacher who smashes a student's phone. Career end. Then there's a video on "the Dangerous Girl," which I've no inclination to watch but I'm sure it ends with her doing something horrible to some unsuspecting "sinning" guy. Death comes in many forms; however, "the Lord is worthy of trust. He will make you firm and guard you from the Evil One" (2 Thessalonians 3:3). However, He can't guard us if we turn from Him *to* sin. "Since you know this in advance, guard yourselves; so that you will not be led away by the errors of the wicked and fall from your own secure position," Paul instructs. How do we *stay* united with Jesus so sin can't kill us in some way? Like Jesus, we need to be "united with the Father" in His word, in prayer, and in fellowship with Christians (John 10:38). Today, you are free.

Lord, help us remain fixed on you today and not stray. Amen.

AUGUST 22
BLINK OF AN EYE

My husband took our car in for repair, again. This time, the ball joints, control arms, and torsion bars needed replacing. Surfing the internet, he found a parts company that appeared reputable. The mechanic gave my husband the okay to order the parts, and he'd use them to fix our car. Did this bomb *big* time. A drive test revealed a squeaking problem with those faulty ball joints. The mechanic had to charge my husband double labor for repairs. I bit my tongue at another $1,000.00 bill—*ergh*. "Maybe you can call that bad company and return those faulty ball joints," I suggested to my husband.

"You just have to rub it in, don't you," he returned angrily.

"Well, you could try to get our money back." You can guess what happened next—an argument. Have you noticed how arguing and blaming are a waste of time? They're lost moments we'd give *anything* to have back with a loved one. We need God repairing.

Later that afternoon, a cardiologist read my husband's wild EKG. "You have a loud heart murmur. I know there's plaque in your arteries ... and most likely you'll need a stent. I'm scheduling an echo cardiogram and heart catheterization procedure."

Our lips opened in shock. We asked question after question. We knew the blame—my husband. Blaming, like arguing, *never* helps, right? That night I had a nightmare. We were at a university with the configuration of a maze, and walking around aimlessly, trying to locate a lecture hall. We split up to cover more ground. After I couldn't find the building, I phoned my husband. No answer, time-and-again. I asked people right-and-left, "Do you know where this room is?" I kept getting various answers. Then I dropped my phone. It broke. Then my glasses broke on a tram. Then I almost lost my purse. Still, no Drew! I felt lost, disoriented, and alone. Are we, alone? How can we steady ourselves and re-orient ourselves?

Paul tells us: "We live in relation to the Lord; and if we die, we die in relation to the Lord. So whether we live or die, we belong to the Lord" (Romans 14:8). People fear death. And when we're alive, we're so alone in our bodies. After all, no one *ever* completely 100% understands our reality. Except Jesus. We are "in relation" to Him, and "belong to the Lord." He is with us *every* second, orienting us, repairing us, and fixing our relationships.

God, one day our connection will be complete with you. Amen.

AUGUST 23
INSIDE JOB

After I saw a marquee, *Inside Job*, I remembered a phrase I heard. "Life is an inside job." What's *that* mean? Is life all about me? You? Getting rich and keeping your riches? Being smart? Famous? Successful? Being liked and approved of? Is life about belonging to a religion? "What's life all about?" Wow—a philosophical twister.

The Holy Spirit is the One who most likely asked you those questions, and The Holy Spirit is answering them. Yes, the Holy Spirit is a real person and part of the Trinity. He's inside you, now. In Greek, He's παράκλητος, "paraclete," the one who consoles, comforts, encourages, uplifts, refreshes, and intercedes on our behalf as an advocate would represent you in a court of law.

An advocate in court? Paraclete is another word for lawyer. When will we need the Holy Spirit as a lawyer? On Judgement Day. You'll be there. Are you ready? "The dead, small and great, stand before God. And the books [are] opened. And another book [is] opened, which is the book of life. And the dead [are] judged out of those things which were written in the books, according to their works" (Revelation 20:12). On that day, the Holy Spirit will stand up for you—represent you. At the Great Trial, He'll announce: "[Your name], is covered by the blood of Jesus, saved, and grafted into God's family." Wow—we're in. Jesus says about The Holy Spirit: "It is to your advantage that I go away; for if I don't go away, the comforting Counselor will not come to you. However, if I do go, I will send him to you. When he comes, he will show that the world is wrong about sin, about righteousness and about judgment—about sin, in that people don't put their trust in me; about righteousness, in that I am going to the Father and you will no longer see me; about judgment, in that the ruler of this world has been judged" (John 16:7-11). To help Him do His work, we can tell people, "I'm a sinner and believe Jesus died for me." It's that simple. The Holy Spirit's job is to save them for eternity. If you have the opportunity today, can you say those words? Yes, life *is* "an inside job." The Holy Spirit guides us to growth. We only have to yield to Him, like that yellow signs by the roads. God says, "I live in the high and holy place but also with the broken and humble, in order to revive the spirit of the humble and revive the hearts of the broken ones" (Isaiah 57:53). We're saved.

Father, oh, how great your love is for us. Amen.

August 24
Stack It On

Childhood "tapes" like to replay in our minds at times, huh? You know them, the deeply ingrained thoughts that can mess up your day. Here are a few samples: After a serious beating, you're told, "Come on, that didn't hurt." The message is, *don't believe your senses.* "You never think before you act!" Message: *You're stupid!* "Why can't you be like your brother, or sister? Message: *You're a disappointment.* For me, I never felt satisfied about *anything* I have done. Then there were the "messages" from my peers. "You stink!" Everything else rhyming with my last name Pink. What are your messages? There's help. Thank you, God. God writes over hurtful tapes with His love.

Psychologist and writer, Dr. Howard Halpern, said about the lingering effects of our childhood, "Frequently we are so limited by habitual ways of acting and thinking, so needful of the approval of others, and so afraid of their disapproval that we don't own ourselves at all." Those childhood tapes are ghosts that have morphed into automatic thoughts. They confuse the neurons in our heads, interfere with reality, deplete our energy, and defeat our purpose.

So, what's the tape we need to replace with *old* childhood tapes? Ephesians 1:11 is part of the answer. God's word and *new* actions.

Paul tells us to put our importance on God, and then everything else will fall into place. "Let anyone who wants to boast, boast about *Adonai*; because it is not the one who recommends himself who is worthy of approval, but the one whom the Lord recommends" (2 Corinthians 10:17-18). You want something to be happy about? News that's going to make such a big difference so as to save peoples' eternal lives? Talk about Jesus, God and the Holy Spirit. Those are "the tapes" we need to set our minds on so our words and actions can make a difference in this world. I remember riding the New York subway seventeen years ago when a preacher entered the car and began handing out a saving message to people. Most people turned away. Wow though, did the guy have guts. I knew our Lord at the time, but still I took his handout. He needed encouragement. I remember the man's enthusiasm for Christ and his persistence. He was called by God, and confident in God's approval of him. That was his mindset, his *new* Christian tape. What an impact *you* can make in your day to bless someone you meet.

Father, erase our bad tapes and give us true life. Amen.

AUGUST 25
DOORS AND WINDOWS

You matter to God. Are you ready to do what *really* matters?

Before his death, King David turns Israel over to his son Solomon in a beautiful blessing ceremony (1 Kings 2). In his speech, we can discern what keeps us linked to God through the Holy Spirit and how our actions can make an eternal difference for God. Paul says, "To me, life is the Messiah [Jesus], and death is gain" (Philippians 1:21). You might not be called to missionary work in a dangerous country as God singled out Paul, but little spoken words and planting Jesus seeds in peoples' lives can change a heart, make someone stop and consider vital spiritual matters today. John wrote, "When the Spirit of Truth [the Holy Spirit] comes, he will guide you into all the truth; for he will ... say only what he hears. He will also announce to you the events of the future" (John 16:13). What future event might you be able to effect in someone's life? An eternity altering event. You can have that much of an impact by asking; "Do you know for certain you're going to Heaven if you die today?"

Sometimes, blessing someone will make him or her think about God existence. Some days, I say, "God bless you," fifty times. Hey, praying for someone changes people and events. Peter said, "The Spirit of the *Sh'khinah*, that is, the Spirit of God, is resting on you" (1 Peter 4:14)! "Sh'khinah" (in Hebrew, שכינה) means, "the dwelling or settling of the divine presence of God." We have the Holy Spirit on us and in us day-and-night, and standing with us when we proclaim Jesus Christ. Where is His temple? Before David gives Solomon the designs for the First Temple, he tells him: "Know the God of your father. Serve him wholeheartedly and with desire in your being; for Adonai searches all hearts and understands all the inclinations of people's thoughts. If you seek him, he will let himself be found by you. ... See now that *Adonai* has chosen you to build a house for the sanctuary; so be strong, and do it" (1 Chronicles 28:9-10). We're sanctuary builders. When people accept Jesus as Savior, they'll have a *real* sanctuary inside of them, the indwelling of the Holy Spirit. "Be strong, be bold, and do it! Don't be afraid or become discouraged! For *Adonai*, God, my God, is with you. He will not fail you or abandon you until all the work for the service in the house of *Adonai* has been finished" (28:20). You can. You're called.

Father, we will fill with joy when we give for you. Amen.

AUGUST 26
PRESERVATION

What are the questions you're going to ask Jesus when you stand before Him? He'll call your name, and give you His undivided attention. What you will say will be *so* important to Him.

I'll have a few questions. "What did you mean when you said *three* times, 'I am the living bread ... the bread that I will give is my own flesh. ... Whoever eats my flesh and drinks my blood has eternal life' " (John 6)? I'd also ask: "After you had said those words, people left you in droves until only your twelve disciples remained. You even said to them, "Don't you want to leave too" (6:67)? It's as if you were purposely pushing them away. Or were you testing them?

Doesn't Simon Peter tickle your heart when he answers: "Lord, to whom would we go? You have the word of eternal life. We have trusted, and we know you are the Holy One of God" (6:68-69).

Where would we be without Jesus? Before you knew Him, how did you live your life? *I* wasn't a happy camper. I remember feeling lost, empty, and confused. I searched *everywhere* for happiness, purpose, friends, truth, and a soul connection. Today, I don't know how I'd go through the day without crying out to God in hard times, "Abba, Daddy, I need you and love you." How does he answer? In stillness when I pray, in the soft air around me, and in the encouragement of Christ-centered friends. Isn't it wonderful to have Him? He is our real soul mate, grafted in our very souls, a temple.

In the days of the Second Temple, only priests could eat from the Table of Showbread, wash from the cleansing basin, sacrifice the blemish-free animals, and enter the Holy of Holies. Where was God? "The glory of *Adonai* appeared to all the people! Fire came forth from the presence of *Adonai*, consuming the burnt offering and the fat on the altar" (Leviticus 9:23-24). When Jesus says, "Eat my flesh and drink my blood to have eternal life and be raised up on the Last Day" (John 6:44-51), He is fulfilling the Law. He's actually saying: "I am the one who has received the Temple offerings since its inception. Now everyone can have access to me if you'll only trust in me and my Father who sent me." Jesus opens Heaven to *everyone*. He is the gate, the bread, the blood, living water, and fertile soil. He is the fulfillment of the Old Testament, to stamp out evil and Death, and to procure for us eternal life with Him.

Father, thank you for true spiritual nourishment. Amen.

AUGUST 27
RETURNS

There are times when we get lost and need to find our way back to the "high tower," God. It's those times when we're breathless and exhausted from working to control people, places, and things. We feel sick and fed up. We're at step zero, forced to decide which way to walk next. We kneel from the heavy weight, maybe crying. "Lord, help me come back to you. I need *you* to find me 'cause I can't change without *your* help." He rebuilds us in the right direction, multiple times. Do you eagerly need new blocks with which to build a high tower today? They are His word; the mortar, his strength.

David once said, "I always set God before me; with him at my right hand, I can never be moved" (Psalm 16:8). However, at times we move, right? Whether by accident, enticement, or choice; we move *from* Him *to* someone or something we believe will make our lives easy, fun, right, and fulfilled. What's your high tower like today? If it's tall and strong—maybe with a few cracks—great. "King Asa did what was good and right in the eyes of the Lord his God. ... He built up the fortified cities of Judah, since the land was at peace. No one was at war with him during those years, for the Lord gave him rest" (2 Chronicles 14:-6). God is the Great Builder. We can let Him begin His reconstruction on our thoughts and actions any time. Rebuilding is better than abandoning Him for good.

When I was young, I accidentally slipped away from my family at a Chicago car show. I became flooded with strangers. How disoriented I felt ... and confused, unconfident, and nearly squashed. I cried for my mom. Nowhere! Suddenly, a smiling person bent down into my face, took my hand, and guided me to a security guard who escorted me to Lost and Found. Let me tell you, this is not the time you want to be famous with your name echoing through a loud speaker in a convention center. After drinking a soda pop, my angry mom appeared and we returned to the show. "Most High, when I am afraid, I put my trust in you. ... You have kept count of my wanderings; store my tears in your water-skin—aren't they already recorded in your book" (Psalm 56:3-9)? Even when we move away from Him and are lost, He's there. With Jesus offering His hand to us, He's watching our steps. When He finds us, we return to Him. Our sins get "crushed before the Lord" (2 Chronicles 14:13).

Abba Father, we need your Word *not* to stray. Amen.

August 28
Distinct

I remember my Grandma Theresa cooking blackberry jam. My brother Tom and I would pick blackberries off the vine, set them delicately in our baskets—after eating a few—and hand them off to Grandma. She knew the ingredients and measurements by heart. But the pièce de résistance was her homemade bread—a delectable spongy delight we'd eat and then suck the best-tasting jam *ever* off our fingertips. Those were her legacies still trickling down through our family. Eighteenth-century author, John Allston, once said, "The only thing you take with you when you're gone is what you leave behind." Grandma died Monday, May 2, 1983 in St. Petersburg, Florida, but she's still so alive in my mind today. She once said, "I pray for you and your brother daily." I still think her prayers are helping me today. "Listen to the prayer your servant will pray toward this place" (1 Kings 8:29). Prayer works.

Who are the people who have influenced you, and how are they alive in you today? Have you noticed how we tend to replay old TV shows and nostalgic movies? The actors, who once inspired us, like William Shatner's Captain Kirk of the *U.S.S. Enterprise*, are old now. Many of his *Enterprise* crewmembers are dead. Yet, no matter how many *Star Trek* remakes Hollywood produces, they can't recapture the 1960's collective experiences the original *Star Trek* crew brought to life on the screen. It's the same with our lives. Our actions affect the people we encounter daily and our families. What "jam" are you "preparing" and "leaving" for your family and others today?

Our five senses are feelers in this world. God acts with the Holy Spirit and Jesus to affect lives for generations. "Deep is calling to deep at the thunder of your waterfalls. All your surging rapids and waves are sweeping over me" (Psalm 42:8). He sweeps His love over us. "From this you can know that *Adonai* your God is indeed God, the faithful God, who keeps his covenant and extends grace to those who love him and observe his law, to a thousand generations" (Deuteronomy 7:9). His waterfall of grace "thunders" over us into the depths of our souls. "I will betroth you to me forever; yes, I will betroth you to me in righteousness, in justice, in grace and in compassion" (Hosea 2:21). He "surges." His Holy Spirit is "rapid" in "waves" in our lives. What magnificent things you can accomplish.

Father, help us affect the world in beautiful ways. Amen.

AUGUST 29
BULWARK

While reading the Old Testament, phrases might puzzle us or skip unnoticed like a rock skimming over a pond. Here's an example: "Where there are no oxen, the stalls are clean; but much is produced by the strength of an ox" (Proverbs 14:4). I don't even know where I can see an ox except at a zoo. What's the significance? Not long ago, farmers used oxen as powerful machinery, stone grinders for wheat and olives, transporters of goods, pulley lifters, and bulwarks during construction. There's a metaphor coming your way, serving people as Jesus desires us to serve. Have you thought about service lately? We actually serve and are not aware of it. There are also good and bad things to serving. As oxen leave a messy smell, Christian serving might also cause a mess in our lives because of people and their personalities. So much so, that at times, we might want to quit or run away. Why? We have an Adversary—the Devil—who "roams through the earth, wandering here and there" (Job 1:7). For what purpose? "Your enemy, the Adversary, stalks about like a roaring lion looking for someone to devour" (1 Peter 5:8). Devour? Yes, meaning, "to eat hungrily and quickly." However, we *can* escape the Enemy's deceptive practices by reading God's Word and casting that Enemy far away like fast-skipping pebbles over water. "Go!"

Today, you can study His word by picking out something you perceive is irrelevant and researching the scripture. How might the above Proverb apply to us? Jesus served, and He instructs us to serve people throughout our day. In the Parable of the Faithful and Sensible Servant, Jesus is the Master who puts an obedient servant "in charge of the household staff to give them their food at the proper time" (Matthew 24:45-51). The servant who does his or her job well when Jesus comes will be blessed. However, the servant who brutally mistreats the staff, falls into gluttony. He becomes an alcoholic at the bar because he believes Jesus won't return. He becomes, wicked. Jesus has a punishment waiting for the Wicked Servant. What are our obstacles to service? Life happens, and the lurking, interfering Adversary doesn't help us. Yet, there's justice for you if you serve and somehow get hurt in service for our Lord. I know. I've been there when service has gotten messy. Jesus knows our pain. "It will go well for you" (Matthew 24:46). Yes, you.

Father, help us do the jobs you give us. Amen.

AUGUST 30
EGGS-ACT *EGGS*-ITEMENT

Puns and Onomatopoeia are literary devices writers use to create a figure, picture or image. These devices are meant to grab a reader's attention and help shape their perception about the author's theme. I saw an advertisement selling soup spoons. Buying them and using them would be a "soup-*erior*" way to eat soup. Catchy, huh? You won't find this one so attractive if you're an investor: "Dow Jones Downer." In the last two weeks, the Stock Market has dropped 1,000 points, thanks to the China Syndrome. The Chinese government has been devaluing their currency, dive-bombing markets worldwide. In politics, we have Biden-buzz. The Vice President is contemplating, "President Joe Biden?" Can Bulldozer Biden plow down Hillary who's been in Clinton Crash since the detonation of her email-*nukes*? See how a person can acquire a brand? A brand is a way people remember you. Donald Trump has several brands he's using on his campaign. The media are twisting-and-turning words and modifying phrases to reel us into their written worlds. Here are a few more I'm paraphrasing: "The Donald is Trump-*acious* at the poles." "Trump-palooza!" "We're experiencing a Trump-pendium." "It's panda-monium for panda bear Mei Xiang that had twins." Can you conjure your branding expression? God has one for you.

Let's look at a few Bible characters and how we might brand them. Adam-*Anarchy* lost us Heaven when *ecto*-Eve strode toward Satan-*dom*. Paul-*active* pounded the pavement for Jesus. *Metric*-Martha loved kitchen cooking while *meta*-Mary mingled with Rabbi Jesus and His *multi*-crowds. Timothy-*terrific*, Paul favored. Just James always knelt for prayer. Branding is vital when we're making a name and living. To develop my brand, I looked for the best in me. I pursue important goals as if they're life-or-death. I'd brand myself, *Joy-pacious*.

James said something like that about faith and works. "Suppose a brother or sister is without clothes and daily food, and someone says to him, '*Shalom*! Keep warm and eat hearty!' without giving him what he needs. What good does it do? Faith by itself, unaccompanied by actions, is dead" (James 2:14-17). You are God's display of His glory. He has branded you and me, "Christ's Child [your name]." How do you brand yourself to work for Him today?

Holy Spirit, we need your guidance to affect change. Amen.

AUGUST 31
JANUS FACED

When you were in school, did you ever study the Roman god Janus? People prayed to this "god of beginnings and transitions" when they were threatened by war nationally and felt personally threatened. Any transition or life passage also warranted a visit to Janus's temple in ancient Veii or outside Rome in ancient Janiculum. See Janus's two-faced duplicity emerging? He's depicted on statues and coins with *two* faces. Do you see big problems with being two-faced?

On a small scale, we can be Janus faced. We make promises we don't keep, make phony first impressions, or tell a white lie to save face. However, in Matthew 23, Jesus warns religious leaders and teachers *not* to deceive people into believing in false teachings and gods. They are His eight, "Woe to You" doctrinal points. What do Janus-faced hypocrites do? "Whatever they tell you, take care to do it," Jesus begins, "but don't do what they do, because they talk but don't act" (23:3). Church leaders, teachers, pastors, and elders are to be examples for us. If they're not doing what they're preaching but self-promoting, "Woe to you!" Jesus warns. We are to be humble and serve. What else were the Pharisees and Sadducees doing? "Shutting the Kingdom of Heaven in people's faces, neither entering nor allowing those who wish to enter to do so" (23:13). How were they "shutting the Kingdom of Heaven?" Jesus answers, "How often I wanted to gather your children, just as a hen gathers her chickens under her wings, but you refused" (23:37)! Jesus is the "Strait Gate" in Matthew 17, the *only* way into Heaven for those who do God's will, which is to accept Jesus as Messiah. Those "teachers" were putting obstacles in Jesus's path so He couldn't win souls for God.

A Janus-faced person also appears spic-n-span. He/she *needs* confused and searching people to cling to their every word. They also have a tight-knit following with gatekeepers, and they disappear with the money when the truth comes out. They are "blind guides" (23:16), "robbers and self-indulgent" (23:25). They're "whitewashed" tombs, which look pure, but on the inside are full of bones and rottenness (23:27). Pee-yew. Jesus implores us to investigate what people tell us. At a church, the pastor once said, "Help others, because when *you* need help, you want people to be there for you." That shocked me. Help others to be helped? *Hm*, no.

Father, lead us to do what is *right*, always. Amen.

J.P. Osterman

September 1
Power Aid

An operating room technician has just begun wheeling my husband on a squeaky gurney toward the cardiac catheterization room. Watching his body roll by, I remember this past week's ordeal.

What's routine for some people isn't routine for everyone. Have you ever experienced a situation, where you're *not* in someone's routine? Last week after my husband's EKG, the doctor quickly explained the problem and then immediately scheduled a cardiac catheterization. We felt swept away. We had so many questions, even the next day when my husband had an echocardiogram. After *four* days of waiting for the results, the day prior to the surgery, a nurse finally calls my husband. "Your results are moderate to worse than expected." Then she hung up without telling us where to check in. The next morning while racing around to prep him for surgery, the hospital nurse asked for a list of his meds. Frantically writing them down, we figured the doctor would have sent them. *Uhhh.* We're terrified, and they're like an assembly crew. *Uhhh!* What do you do when busy people don't understand how vulnerable or uncertain you are feeling? Your weak position? We can glean … God's power.

In Mark's Gospel, Jesus's cousin John is the prophesied messenger. "Look! I am sending my messenger to clear the way before me. And the Lord, whom you seek, will suddenly come to his temple" (Malachi 3:1). God designed John to be "the voice," calling people, "Prepare the way for the Lord. Make straight paths for him" (Mark 1:3). John preaches a baptism of "repentance for the forgiveness of sins" (1:4). We had better look to the only expert who can forgive sins by the covering of His blood, Jesus. John points *everyone*—the vulnerable, the needy, the sinful, the seeking—to Jesus. The next thing you know, we meet "The Man" himself. "As Jesus was coming up out of the water, he saw heaven being torn open and the Spirit descending on him like a dove. And a voice came from heaven: "You are my Son, whom I love. With you I am well pleased." Could this be the moment Jesus recognizes His *exact* calling? God is addressing Jesus *directly.* "You're *my* Son. I love *you.* I'm *proud* of you." Wham. After that, Jesus begins His quest to bring souls to God. In our vulnerable moments, when we don't know what's going on, and feel tossed about and ignored, God has us.

Father, we cry to you in our distresses and we need you. Amen.

SEPTEMBER 2
DEBT FREE

After my husband's cardiologist had cleared him to go home, I picked him up at the hospital this morning. He only had to have *one* stent inserted in his heart when we believed he might need open heart bypass and valve replacement surgery. "The God of your father, who will help you, by *El Shaddai*, who will bless you with blessings from heaven above, blessings from the deep, lying below, blessings from the breasts and the womb" (Genesis 49:25). Sometimes, blessings from God rain down in our lives. We can have only one response: "Thank you, God, and praise you, Holy Most High. Amen."

I found my keys in my purse. "I can't drive," my husband said.

My heart skipped. *Yes—I can go shopping!* I dropped him off safely at home and then went to Walmart to pick up his new drugs. In the garden center, I saw a large, white rocking chair. *I want that!* Have you ever had one of those deep conversations with yourself like the debating angel and devil? *I gotta have it. No, ya can't. Just buy it. No. Just charge it.* My little voice of reason I call the Holy Spirit intervened. "*Call and ask him. He knows our financial situation.* I picked the best white rocking chair and asked Doug to set it aside for me. Then I went to pick up Drew's meds, and then a few groceries, and then I received a phone call. "What are you buying, Sweetie?" I could have lied, purchased the chair, and said it was a surprise. I didn't. I told Drew the truth, and he gave me our financial facts.

"All the following blessings will be yours in abundance if you will do what *Adonai* your God says" (Deuteronomy 28:2). Eyeing the chair, I quickly recalled the parable of the Unfruitful Fig Tree. "A man had a fig tree planted in his vineyard, and he came looking for fruit but didn't find any. So he said to the man who took care of the vineyard, 'Here, I've come looking for fruit on this fig tree for three years now without finding any. Cut it down—why let it go on using up the soil?' The caretaker answered: 'Sir, leave it alone one more year. I'll dig around it and put manure on it. If it bears fruit next year, well and good; if not, you will have it cut down then' " (Luke 13:6-9). You can apply this story to any area of your life. I couldn't buy the rocking chair. It wasn't in God's will for me, today. What's the fig tree in your life in need of care and nurturing so it can grow?

God, help us discern what is crucial. Amen.

September 3
Iconic

Whatever year we're in, God has placed us where we are at this moment for a reason. Knowing this, and trusting that He's working everything out for His glory and our best interest, we can have peace today.

Do you believe this? "A person whose desire rests on You, You preserve in perfect peace because he trusts in You" (Isaiah 26:3). The hard question is: What is your desire? Maybe you have more than one? Isaiah is personifying, *desire*. Our *desires* are *resting* on God.

These past few days have been exhausting. The cardiologist plugged my husband's artery. Naturally, my husband has been riding the Anxiety rollercoaster. Since arriving home, he's been a sunken body reclining in his couch seat with his legs draped over the ottoman. "Can you get me more water?" "Can you hand me the TV changer?" "What's for dinner?" The list is the Yellow Brick Road.

Naturally, my son has been a basket case because of the surgery. "Mom, I'm hungry. I found this recipe on YouTube for steak. I need to buy a steak and the ingredients to make a rub."

My desire has been to have some time for myself, sleep, and make my son take more responsibility. I don't want to serve! Still, in the few moments I do have, I gaze into the blue sky and wispy clouds. I see two white egrets pecking for food at the shore of a retention pond and three tall lean sand cranes lumbering lazily through a neighbor's yard. Their squawking reverberates as echoes in a canyon. Beautiful! In these moments of serenity, I feel God connected. I am resting with Him, and receive a boost of energy and relief. If you are experiencing chaos, stress, problems, or troubles today, or if you're at a crossroad and don't know which decision to make, set your concern at His feet. All solutions rest with Him. I believe it's our responses to life's events that become the catalysts of our desires. Paul says, "The fruit of the Spirit is love, joy, peace, patience, kindness, goodness, faithfulness, humility, and self-control" (Galatians 5:22). I'm not perfect, but since I've been a believer in Jesus, I see improvements. Hey, I didn't complain out loud this time about serving my husband and son. "It is through the Spirit that we have Life. Let it also be through the Spirit that we order our lives day by day" (Galatians 5:25). Resting in Him takes practice.

God, give us self-control so our desires can rest in you. Amen.

SEPTEMBER 4
TRAILS

As this week's Dow roars back from a downward spin, someone shot a TV journalist and her photographer on live TV, and Dust Lady from 9/11 died. All I can do is sit back helplessly, watch, and pray. I've also been waiting for the eagle to return. Every morning, I glance out my backyard's double doors, praying for him to perch once more on the towering electric pool yards behind my fence and reclaim his terrain. As in previous years once he's re-established, he'll fly high and interlock with a mate. Then they'll nest as expectant parents at the center of our preserve. It's majestic watching them fly behind my backyard. When I lived in Texas, traveled west, and drove north, never once did I spot one eagle.

Have you ever prayed hard to God for Him to answer a prayer?

I've heard an expression about prayer. God says yes, no, or wait, which means, maybe.

What's your prayer today? He's listening. "*Adonai* has heard my pleading, *Adonai* will accept my prayer" (Psalm 6:10). What will His answer be? Many times, people tend to pray when they are in trouble. "When they were troubled, they sought you," says Isaiah (26:16). We also pray when we make mistakes. "This is a prayer of Habakkuk the prophet about mistakes: "*Adonai*, I have heard the report about you. *Adonai*, I am awed by your deeds. Bring your work to life in our own age. Make it known in our own time; but in anger, remember compassion" (Habakkuk 3:1-2). After our mistakes and return to God, He might be angry, and He might discipline us with consequences, but He's compassionate.

Will we get what we want when we pray? Jesus says, "When you pray, go into your room, close the door, and pray to your Father in secret. Your Father, who sees what is done in secret, will reward you" (Matthew 6:6). Oops, He does not say we're going to get what we want. Yet in another place, Jesus tells a crowd, "You will receive everything you ask for in prayer, no matter what it is, provided you have trust" (Matthew 21:22). This occurs after Palm Sunday and after He curses the fig tree that immediately dries up. It's a lesson on trusting and not doubting. We can approach God in prayer to give us our "daily bread" and "to keep me from evil." Prayers worked for me today, and they will sustain you, too. God is love.

Jesus, forgive our sins as we forgive others. Amen.

SEPTEMBER 5
FRESH SCENTS!

Every day we need to make praise time for God, right?

Late yesterday evening, I was swinging on my back patio swing when I looked up south and saw large flapping bird wings. "The eagle is back!" I exclaimed. Come on and see!" I pointed at the tall electric pole behind our fence. Perched on top and peering at his terrain was our living mascot of Eagle Lake Two. "He's majestic!"

"And big," My husband added, putting his hand on my shoulder. *He's doing well after surgery now, thank you, God*, I thought.

We can all use a bit of praise time throughout our day, even when circumstances turn for the worse or uncontrollable situations arise. "Halleluiah! Praise God in his holy place" (Psalm 150:1).

Jesus experienced bad times. People mocked him and laughed at him. He then died for us. Yet after He died, people began praising Him. "Crying out with a loud voice, Jesus said, 'Father! Into your hands, I commit my spirit' (Luke 23:46). He fulfilled David's verse: "Into your hand I commit my spirit. You will redeem me, *Adonai*, God of truth" (Psalm 31:5). Praises for Jesus began then and have never stopped. "With these words He gave up his spirit. When the Roman officer saw what had happened, he began to praise God and said, 'Surely this man was innocent' " (Luke 23:47)! Why did one of the soldiers begin praising Jesus? He saw Jesus's spirit lift out of His body and ascend to Heaven. What an unexplainable profound sight, akin to the moment when God said to Jesus after John baptized him, "This is my Son." Everyone saw and heard God. How else could a murderer like the Roman officer and Paul realize their sins and accept Jesus as Lord and Savior? We need to praise Him often. Praise lifts us up, and infuses our tired minds and weary hearts with God's love. Isaiah said about thanking God: "*Adonai* will comfort Zion, will comfort all her ruined places, and will make her desert like Eden, her Arabah like the garden of *Adonai*. Joy and gladness will be there, thanksgiving and the sound of music" (51:3). I flew over "Arabah" in July of 2008. It's a dry, hot area with little shrub and water. But God can change the desolate areas in our lives. As He brought the eagle back and gave my husband more years through the skill of expert surgeons, He is also working in your life. See His blessings, acknowledge them, and praise Him for His gifts.

God, thank you for the little things and great events. Amen.

SEPTEMBER 6
CONFLICT RESOLUTION

You've had arguments with people. I recall a saying: "I'm not arguing. I'm just explaining why I'm right." Synonyms can be: *quarreling, contending, nitpicking, debating,* and *disputing.* Whatever the word, an argument leaves us disjointed, guarding our hearts against further hurt, and consciously and unconsciously preparing for the *next* argument.

We want to win, don't we? What's easy, is arguing with God. He doesn't appear and argue back. Arguing with Him, however, troubles our minds and lives. "Woe to anyone who argues with his maker, like potsherds lying on the ground (Isaiah 45:9)!" The "woe" in an argument with God comes when our lives turn to pieces "on the ground." We fall apart emotionally, a job falls apart, or a relationship ends. What's the answer?

In his Sermon on the Mount, Jesus gives us one of His eight-great Beatitudes, blessings. "Blessed are those who make peace! They will be called sons of God" (Matthew 5:9). He calls us, His believers, to be peacemakers. "You are fellow-citizens with God's people and members of God's family" (Ephesians 2:19). As God's sons and daughters, we can create peace in our relationships and in the lives of people we encounter today. You can be a peacemaker.

You might ask, "How? That person hurt me!" or, "I have to keep fighting to get what I want on my job." or, "My spouse doesn't understand me." When we find ourselves embroiled in a conflict, fight, or argument, there are steps we can take to practice peacemaking. First, listen carefully to the other person. Second, define the problems. "You want me to do the dishes but I want to rest." Third, outline the areas of agreement and disagreement. "I agree that the dishes need to be washed, and you disagree that I need more rest." Fourth, each person needs to identify his or her contribution to the problem. Here's where we take responsibility for where things are going wrong, what we've done, or the tasks we haven't done. "I haven't been listening to what you need." Fifth, each person must be willing to state the changes they can make to resolve the argument, create peace, and make up. "How about if you give me another half-an-hour to rest and then I'll help you?" My son did, so I'm going to help him make a smoothie now. This works.

Father, help us place others first in our peacemaking. Amen.

SEPTEMBER 7
RAZZLE DAZZLE

Since my husband has been recuperating, he's been taking his blood pressure every fifteen minutes. "It's up five points!" he called.

"Great," I said, emptying trash cans. The work in front of me is like a long road in need of asphalt. Has his life's work evolved into monitoring body readings? He's anxious about his health—rightly so. I'm stuck with monitoring the rising rain level at the side of our house and moving patio furniture. A hurricane disintegrated into a tropical storm.

We all find ourselves monitoring something, wouldn't you say?

I recall Jesus observing the crowds, keeping an eye on their levels of anger, hate, and irritation. When he heals the man with the shriveled hand on the Sabbath, some religious leaders leave and begin "plotting with some members of Herod's party how to do away with him" (Mark 3:6). There's even a time when Jesus's mother and "family" come to get him. "He's out of his mind" (Mark 3:21)! Why do they believe He's out of his mind? He cures Peter's feverish mother-in-law who would have most likely died (Mark 1:29-31). He heals the paralyzed man (Mark 2:1-12). He heals the man with the shriveled hand (Mark 3:1-5). He drives out spirits from the demon possessed (Mark 1:23). He keeps company with "tax-collectors and sinners," many of whom are his followers (Mark 2:15). With God's authority, He forgives sins (Mark 2:5). Jesus must be the best teach ever because He instructs religious leaders as one who has "authority himself" (Mark 1:22). The religious leaders accuse him of violating the Sabbath, blaspheming, and coming from the Devil (Mark 3:22-23). What does Jesus tell His mother Mary and relatives? He has someone relay a message. "Whoever does what God wants is my brother, sister and mother" (Mark 3:34)! Three exclamation points send anyone apprehending Jesus in another direction. Like a pressure gauge, He knew when to stay and when to leave (Mark 1:45). He had a specific mission that is still working in the world today through the Holy Spirit. "The ones who need a doctor aren't the healthy but the sick. I did not come to call the 'righteous' but sinners" (Mark 2:17). Remaining in God's word and practicing what we learn, we can become better at monitoring the times when we need to get back to God's guidance and chuck sin behind us.

Holy Spirit, move our minds to holiness. Amen.

SEPTEMBER 8
SOUNDING OFF

I don't know about you, but I'm not good at confronting people. Confrontation is interwoven with hurt and anger. Who wants that?

If you need a little encouragement in the confrontation department today, let's examine some people who have confronted others artfully.

Duane Charles "Bill" Parcells coached several football teams. He's had quite a bit of experience with *confrontation*, which is, *a hostile or argumentative meeting or situation between opposing parties.* "I think confrontation is healthy because it clears the air very quickly." Confrontation can be pulse pounding. The level of emotion hinges on what's at stake. If someone steps in line in front of me, my emotions won't be as charged as if I've been standing two hours in a long hot line. Bill adds another element about confrontation in today's corporate world. "If you are afraid of confrontation, you are not going to do very well" ("Bill Parcells." BrainyQuote.com. Xplore Inc, 2015. 1 September 2015.). How do we "do" confrontation?

Apostle Mark portrays Jesus's teachings in ways we can transfer to our lives. Jesus lived free of sin and fulfilled the Old Testament prophesies. However, He didn't do that without confronting people, and people accosting Him. In Mark 1:23-28, a volatile one occurs between Jesus and a demon-possessed man *in* the synagogue. This man is different looking because of his voice. He probably went there in a sane moment in search of a priest to help him. Then, the demon sees Jesus. "What do you want with us, Yeshua from Natzeret? Have you come to destroy us? I know who you are—the Holy One of God!" "Us" means more than one walking the Earth.

Jesus scolds it. "Be quiet and come out of him!" The "unclean spirit" throws the man into a convulsion as it leaves his body. The aftermath has a ripple effect. "The news about him spread quickly through the whole region of Galilee." What's to learn? Jesus has a calm self-assurance that leaves a lasting impression. If you need to confront someone, know your facts and what you want as a result. Also, know the policies of your school or job. Can there be a compromise? A mediator might help if you're up against a group. In the end, the confrontation will pale compared to how people will remember you and how you handled the situation.

Father, let us pray first for you to handle our situations. Amen.

J.P. OSTERMAN

SEPTEMBER 9
BACK TOGETHER

As the saying goes, many times throughout our lives, things will fall to pieces.

Is there an area in your life in jeopardy of falling apart? Earlier today, I shuffled through images on the internet and found a few depicting puzzle pieces. Some were colorful segments scattered on a white floor, and some were suspended in air as if waiting for someone with a vision to assemble them into a coherent picture. We don't like chaos, right? We want closure to problems, stability in our lives, fix-it ingenuity, and our plans to work out without falling *to pieces*. Did you ever notice though, that puzzle pieces have lines and curves? In our scattered confused moments when we can't see the whole picture, and fix our situations, there's an outline, or shadows, of calmness and stability. Majestic God has the answers. "I keep myself calm and quiet, like a little child on its mother's lap. I keep myself as a little child" (Psalm 131:2). David waited for Daddy God to gather the pieces of his life and create a beautiful reality—King David. What do your pieces look like today? Small, or in a pile?

Today has been a mix for me. My son's world appeared to scatter when he couldn't wake up for school. "Leave me alone!" Morning puzzle crash. Scatterbrained, I raced around the house, aligning everything like Constellation Scorpio to connect his clothes, food, and school supplies. Dizzy, I plopped down in front of the newspaper with a picture of war-ravaged immigrants digging under razor fences to run to new lives. They *live* in pieces. They *exist* tired, hungry, on-the-run, and fearful of being apprehended at gunpoint or directed to a dirty refugee camp. "Lately my people behave like an enemy, stripping both cloaks and tunics from travelers who thought they were secure, so that they become like war refugees" (Micah 2:8). To keep their countries disruption free, governments are redirecting refugees. "Don't gather the grapes left on the vine or fallen on the ground after harvest; leave them for the poor and the foreigner. I am *Adonai* your God" (Leviticus 19:10). Compared to displaced people living piecemeal, we have everything. "Give to the poor, and you will have riches in heaven. Then come, follow me" (Matthew 19:21)! Our leftovers can be satisfaction to someone. Even giving to Goodwill can help others, a simple act in someone's shattered day.

Father, help us see where we can fix brokenness. Amen.

SEPTEMBER 10
MOTHERHOOD

My granddaughter is almost nine months old, and her dad needs to leave home for five days to help his parents.

"Do I take Rachel?" my daughter asks. "Or do I stay home?"

Rrrg, I can't give my opinion. The decision is between her, her husband and God. Still, fear of loneliness can take many forms.

"Yes, He [Jesus] will rebuild the temple of God. He will take up royal splendor, sitting and ruling from his throne. There will be a cohen [priest] before his throne. They will accept each other's advice in complete harmony" (Zachariah 6:13). But we're not in the New Heaven and New Earth right now.

How do we help our loved ones when their situations are none of our business?

In the Epistle to Philemon, Paul counsels Onesimus, a runaway slave. "I have sent him with Onesimus, the dear and faithful brother, who is one of you. They will tell you everything that has happened here" (Colossians 4:9). With a letter Paul co-writes with Timothy (Book of Philemon), Paul sends Onesimus back to face his aggrieved master Philemon. The entire theme is "to do the thing you ought to do" (Philemon 1:8). What *are* we supposed to do?

My granddaughter has been taking her first steps. Jennifer texted, "She's taking a step when I hold her hand!"

I wrote back, "I knew she'd be walking any day."

Jennifer called later. "What if Keith misses her first steps?"

"Keep a camera handy," I replied. God gives us modern tools in this fast-paced world so that, really, we don't need to miss a thing. Still, Jennifer has been changing her mind about flying on a plane with Rachel. We checked the prices on flights. Exorbitant! I offered suggestions on what she could do for those five days, from staying with my dad, Rachel's great-grandfather, to taking Rachel to the places I took Jennifer when she was a baby. We can always suggest.

Paul says in the letter to Philemon: "Onesimus" means 'useful;' and although Onesimus was once useless to you, he has now become most useful—not only to you, but also to me. In returning him to you, I am sending a part of my very heart" (1:10-12). When we talk as parents to our children and help them contrive their *own* solutions, we are giving them our hearts. At any age, we can parent effectively.

God, help us parents be guides and encouragers. Amen.

J.P. Osterman

September 11
Recurrence

If you cut an ocean sponge into pieces and put them in a tank of water overnight, they'll re-unite. No one can explain deep down in the genetic code the morphogenetic process, *beginning of shape*. No one can explain how a sponge can re-assemble, amphibians can re-grow tails, and flatworms can remodel their tissues. Wouldn't it be great if a doctor could inject us with a solution that could re-grow body parts?

That day might not be as far off as you think. However, what can we do about our hurts and fears that wear us down?

God re-directs many of the Old Testament prophets toward difficult tasks. "*Adonai*, your Redeemer, the Holy One of Israel says: 'I am *Adonai*, your God, who teaches you for your own good, who guides you on the path you should take'" (Isaiah 48:17). With what special trait—a morphogenetic brain call?—did God equip these men and women so they could receive communications from Him and relay His messages to nations? "In the old days, when someone went to consult God, he would say, 'Come, let's go to the seer;' because a person now called a prophet used to be called a seer" (1 Samuel 9:9). A *seer* (Hebrew, *ro'eh*) is one who *sees* beyond the realm of our natural senses. People also hailed them as *nabhi* (callers and announcers). Prophets announce messages given to them by God. They have insight into God's will, foresight into God's plans, exhort people to do as God commands, and predict God's punishments. John the Baptist prophesied Jesus as Messiah. He announced Jesus' coming *and* introduced Jesus to the world. People called prophets: Preachers, Predictors, and Watchmen. Those were their God-given jobs. In the cases of Miriam (Aaron's sister in Exodus 15:20-21), Judge Deborah (Judges 4:4-5), Isaiah's wife (Isaiah 8:3), and Huldah Keeper of the Wardrobe (2 Kings 22:14); these women were God's Ministers and Administrators. All prophets pointed toward Jesus who fulfilled God's plan for humanity. It's in our DNA to believe in God through faith, a morphogenesis of our souls. "'If someone from the dead goes to them, they'll repent!' But Abraham replied, 'If they won't listen to Moshe and the Prophets, they won't be convinced even if someone rises from the dead'" (Luke 16:30-31). Can we convince someone in some small way today of Jesus' love and sacrifice?

Father, give us gentle spirits and kind words for others. Amen.

GOD DESIGNED

SEPTEMBER 12
FEASTS AND FESTIVALS

We have a *great* treasure. Are you aware of your "treasure" every day? What are you doing to care for it? "Follow the pattern of the sound teachings you have heard from me, with trust and the love which is yours in the Messiah Jesus," Paul tells his protégé Timothy. In prison, Paul writes his last letter, giving Timothy command of the Christian church in Ephesus. He continues, "Keep safe the great treasure that has been entrusted to you, with the help of the Holy Spirit, who lives in us" (2 Timothy 1:13-14). Notice how the Holy Spirit is a "who" and not a power, force, or spirit. We can see the Holy Spirit (*Ruach HaKodesh* in Hebrew) present in many passages when Jesus walked on Earth (John 14:15-17).

Did you know there is a Jewish festival and holiday celebrating the Holy Spirit? The day is called Shavuot and commemorates the day when God gave the Torah to the nation of Israel at Mount Sinai (Exodus 34:22 and Deuteronomy 16:10). It took seven weeks for the Israelites to travel from Egypt to Mount Sinai. *Shavuot* means "weeks" and refers to this seven-week journey. Shavuot, Passover, and Sukkot were the three Biblical pilgrimage festivals requiring Jews to travel to the temple to worship with the high priests.

Besides observing the Sabbath, we see Jesus participating in Passover with His parents (Luke 2:41-42). Passover was the last feast he celebrated with his followers before His death (Luke 22:11). Yet because of His death, we have the Holy Spirit active in us now. He is our treasure! When we accepted Jesus, the Holy Spirit immersed us in God's grace and forgiveness. "John used to immerse people in water; but in a few days, you will be immersed in the Holy Spirit," Jesus proclaimed before he ascended into Heaven (Acts 1:8). What do we receive when we're immersed in the Holy Spirit? "You will receive power when the *Holy Spirit* comes upon you. You will be my witnesses ... to the ends of the earth" (Acts 1). The Holy Spirit changes our minds and hearts (Acts 10:42). "All the prophets bear witness to him [Jesus], that everyone who puts his trust in *Jesus* receives forgiveness of sins through his name" (Acts 10:43). When we remain open to God's direction, He hears us through our treasure, and changes us for His glory. Let us hear and obey our great treasure today.

Father, help us always cling to your words for life. Amen.

September 13
Tashlich Prayers

Do you ever find yourself in need of a smidgeon more of belief? In John's Gospel, the word "believe" appears 22 times. John wants to knock your socks off with faith in Jesus.

Remember when God appeared to Moses in the burning bush and introduced Himself? "I am the God of your father ... *Ehyeh Asher Ehyeh* [I am/will be what I am/will be] ... *Yud-Heh-Vav-Heh* [*Adonai*] ... This is my name forever. This is how I am to be remembered generation after generation" (Exodus 3:4-15). Do you see the many "I am" words? They are God's names, *forever.* As the earth warms, as cultures change, as leaders step down, God won't change one bit. Most importantly and amazingly, He is *your* Father, *always* holding your hand.

Jesus says to Martha, Lazarus's sister: "I AM the Resurrection and the Life! Whoever puts his trust in me will live, even if he dies. And everyone living and trusting in me will never die. Do you believe this?" He asked *you* that question before you accepted Him as your Savior (John 11:26-27), when you approached His throne of repentance, grace, and mercy. As Martha replied, you also said, "Yes, Lord, I believe you are the Messiah, the Son of God, the one coming into the world" (John 11:25-27). Remember? You acknowledged He died for you at a time when you had the Stone of Lazarus over your heart. You *had* the Sin of Adam covering you. I understand. I was there and doing the same things to find anything and anyone to make myself feel better and self-fix. The Apostle Paul was once under the deadly weight of the Lazarus Stone. "They have lost all feeling, so they have abandoned themselves to sensuality, practicing any kind of impurity and always greedy for more." (Ephesians 4:19).

Is your day hard today? Are you under a heavy weight or burden? Are you on the fringe of diverging from Jesus and needing faith? Our unchanging loving God is the answer. He gave Jesus "all authority in heaven and on earth (Matthew 28:18)." The second you believed, the Holy Spirit immersed you into the reality of the Father and His Son Jesus (28:19). "And remember! I will be with you always, yes, even until the end of the age" (28:20). He has rolled away your Lazarus Stone, freed you, and is standing *right* at your side, lifting your burdens, confusions, and doubts. Cling to faith.

Father, now help us obey and love others, for you. Amen.

SEPTEMBER 14
LOYALTY

When Ruth's husband dies, her widowed mother-in-law, Naomi, tells her: "Go back to your mother's house. ... May God grant you security in the home of a new husband" (Ruth 1:8). Naomi's other daughter-in-law obeys her and leaves. Ruth doesn't. She is loyal to Naomi. Even though Ruth would be better off without her elderly ex-mother-in-law, who would be like a rag doll, old and useless, Ruth experiences a higher order of responsibility and commitment to Naomi. "Don't press me to leave you and stop following you; for wherever you go, I will go; and wherever you stay, I will stay. Your people will be my people and your God will be my God. Where you die, I will die, and there I will be buried. May *Adonai* bring terrible curses on me, and worse ones as well, if anything but death separates you and me" (Ruth 1:16-17). Now, that's determination, wouldn't you say?

Sometimes, however, our level of commitment sinks, and we need help, a sounding board for our feelings, or encouragement.

While at our jobs, swinging a child on the playground, waiting for a doctor, standing in line, or selecting produce; God puts people in our lives to give us what we need. And in turn, we will feed them in some way. It's the same principle as when Jesus feeds the crowd in Luke 9:16. We're always feeding people; and, in turn, they help us. All sorts of hungry people touch our lives daily. Some are hungry for answers, and some need help because they've argued with somebody. Some people are dejected because a relationship ended, and some are like Naomi and might have had their driving privileges revoked or are facing an end-of-life illness. In their hunger for answers, we can be loyal to the commitment we made to Jesus to reach out to people who might need us to be a sounding board or a large help.

Two weeks ago before a predicted hurricane, I was filling the propane tank at the store. A man was in front of me, and I said, "God bless you and your family." He introduced himself as a pastor, handed me his card, and invited us to his church. We had been scouting for another church for a while. For two weeks, we have been attending his church. "They threw in their net, and there were so many fish in it that they couldn't haul it aboard" (John 21:6). We *receive* answers and blessings when we *become* answers and blessings.

Holy Spirit, we *know* God because Jesus anointed us. Amen.

SEPTEMBER 15
JOBS AND WORK

I had to rush to the store because the milk curdled. While in line, I overheard the cashier and a customer talking about work.

"In two hours I'll be happy because I'll be off," the cashier said.

The customer snarled. "I've got an entire *day* of work ahead o' *me*." They both seemed to dislike their jobs, a lot.

So I wondered: how does the rest of the U.S. population feel about their jobs? According to the Conference Board, 52.3% of people are dissatisfied with their jobs. "What makes employees happiest at work? Fifty-nine percent said 'Interest in work," (Forbes Magazine/susanadams/2014/06/20/most-americans-are-unhappy-at-work). We need to ensure we're happy with our field of employment, right? Are you satisfied with your job and the field you've chosen?

After God had created Adam, He created work. "Adonai God took the person and put him in the Garden of Eden to cultivate and care for it" (Genesis 2:15). *Cultivate* means "to grow or raise (something) under conditions that you can control." Plows weren't there, so God must have given Adam special equipment or creatures to plant and harvest His heavenly garden. God knows we need to work to eat. Paul reiterates this. "We gave you this command: if someone won't work, he shouldn't eat (2 Thessalonians 3:10)! Work is meant to pay for our daily needs and wants. Those dissatisfied 52.3% of the workforce might say that's the *only* reason they're working—for the money. No wonder they're dissatisfied.

Did you know that work is a blessing with purpose? "How happy is everyone who fears God, who lives by his ways. You will eat what your hands have produced. You will be happy and prosperous" (Psalm 128:1-2). Fearing God and living by His ways will make you happy and prosperous. What does it mean "to fear God?" Respecting Him and not wanting to offend Him. *Prosperous* means *flourishing, successful, profitable,* and *strong*. Fearing God, we won't necessarily become rich. However, we will, "enjoy the good that results from all our work ... for all the days of our lives that God has given us" (Ecclesiastes 5:17-19). We can reach unsaved people in our work (Galatians 6:10), and minister to others (John 15:16). We are fruit bearers with a purpose in *everything* we do, as John says.

Father, use us in your way to reach others for Heaven. Amen.

SEPTEMBER 16
SCREENINGS URGED

"Please tell me the movie is half over!" I shouted to my son and husband on the edge of their seats and watching *Mad Max: Fury Road*. I didn't have to see but hear a violent sand storm spraying bodies into the sky. I recalled another movie we had watched last weekend.

Tomato-meter "Tomato Critics" gave *Birdman* a 92% rating. According to my son, the website Rotten Tomatoes is the place to visit if you're contemplating going to a movie. During *Birdman*, I told my son: "This is just another wherein people value others according to their jobs and fame. None of these films mentions God."

"I know that, Mom," he returned.

"Okay, then give me a scripture that shows your value in God's eyes." Waiting, I'm tolerating *Birdman*, but I don't approve. Have you ever been forced to tolerate what you *can't* tolerate? It's nerve grinding. Maybe you might be like me a bit, and allow certain movies or behaviors because you're picking your winning battles. "Teach me to do your will, because you are my God. Let your good Spirit guide me on ground that is level" (Psalm 143:10). You've heard of the Little Engine That Could? He tugs and chugs uphill, mustering every bit of energy to make it to the top.

There's always a final goal to keep in mind as a parent. We need to prepare our children (or students or employees) for what they will have to face when they don't have us in their lives. The prophet and spiritual leader Joel knew this absolute truth. "Hear this, you leaders! Listen, all who live in the land! Has anything like this ever happened in your days, or in your ancestors' days? Tell your children about it, and have them tell it to theirs, and have them tell the next generation" (Joel 1:1-3). Joel lived during a time when the Jewish people believed God would only judge pagan nations. Really? How do you act when you think you can get away with anything? Joel, whose name means "the Lord is God," delivers a message of intolerance from God. "Oh no! The Day! The Day of *Adonai* [Judgement] is upon us" (1:15). What a wasteland our lives become for the generations when we divert from God to sin. But it's never too late to repent. "I will restore to you the years that the locusts ate" (2:25). God restores us to Him and makes our lives straight when we turn back to Him. We have a tolerant, loving God.

Father, guide us in your truth and inspire us. Amen.

September 17
Generation after Generation

My granddaughter Rachel is in the process of learning to walk. She wants my daughter to guide her by the fingertips *everywhere*. "She walks around the coffee table. She won't do what I want her to do," my daughter Jennifer said, appearing worn and a bit bored.

"Facetiming" with them, I see Rachel's head bobbing up-and-down. "You might consider putting soft items around the edges so she won't fall and bang her chin." I remember those days when my children were active, excited to learn, misjudge distances, and *bam*, hit their chins on tables. Jennifer wants to make sure Rachel doesn't have to take those same knocks. I understand, but can we shield people from the dings and pings they're going to experience in life? How do we prepare them for inevitable hurts?

Titus was Paul's interpreter and secretary. In a special letter, Paul appoints him Bishop over the church in Crete (Titus 1:5). He outlines instructions for godliness to the men and women in that Christian community. He instructs the men to be "serious, sensible, self-controlled and sound in their trust, love and perseverance" (2:2). He then tells the older women: "Behave the way people leading a holy life should. They shouldn't be slanderers or slaves to excessive drinking. They should teach what is good; thus training the younger women to love their husbands and children, to be self-controlled and pure, take good care of their homes and submit to their husbands" (2:3-4). These are community-sustaining qualities. Christian needs.

Wouldn't Paul's instructions work well for our families as well? Shouldn't we parents, "be self-controlled; and, in everything we do, set an example by doing what is good" (2:6)? We want our offspring to thrive, survive, and "demonstrate complete faithfulness always so that in every way they will make the teaching about God our Deliverer more attractive" (2:10). Our children live on after us. Sometimes, I wonder: hundreds of years ago, did my ancestors ever throw out some prayers for me? Am I living *their* dreams for a better life? Perhaps, eons ago, one of your ancestors gazed into the sky and proclaimed, "God, whatever my future generations have to endure, please keep them from evil and close to you." In our perceived mundane tasks, we are imprinting moments into our children's minds. They'll carry on after us. What will *they* whisper up to God?

Father, give us Holy Spirit vision to energize our day. Amen.

SEPTEMBER 18
SELF-LIMITING

"Listen to me," begins God, "I have borne you from birth, carried you since the womb. Until your old age, I will be the same. I will carry you until your hair is white. I have made you, and I will bear you. Yes, I will carry and save you" (Isaiah 46:3-4). We tend to set our own limitations. *We* impose labels and limitation on ourselves. No one else does. Are you *limiting* yourself spiritually? In other ways?

Above, God is talking to His people as a nation. However, He's also addressing us on an intensely personal level. He loves you. So much does He love you that he *knew* you in your mother's womb. The Perfect Weaver, He created the color of your skin, texture of your hair, bones, and blood type. Your DNA, fingerprints, eye scan, brain configuration, etc., make you one-of-a-kind. The Chinese might have manufactured your dishes, but you're God-Made. Although life is hard at times, God sustains us in our circumstances. We become God polished-and-shiny for His glory.

When I recall the hardships I've endured, I must admit, I'm better because of them. "He who goes out weeping as he carries his sack of seed will come home with cries of joy as he carries his sheaves of grain" (Psalm 126:6). How do we know God is here with us? "Don't throw away that courage of yours, which carries with it such a great reward" (Hebrews 10:35). Look to Jesus and receive faith. He suffers *with* us. "I have eagerly desired to eat this Passover with you before I suffer" (Luke 22:15). You *never* cry, or fear, alone.

In everything, God reveals Himself. Paul tells us, "The person who is righteous will live his life by trust" (Romans 1:17). How do we trust? One day, everyone will see Him. "The earth will be as full of the knowledge of *Adonai*'s glory as water covering the sea" (Habakkuk 2:14). He imprints Himself on us, so we can daily behold limits and see His mighty works. "What is known about God is plain to [you], since God has made it plain to [you]. For ever since the creation of the universe, His invisible qualities—both His eternal power and His divine nature—have been clearly seen. They can be understood from what He has made" (Romans 1:19-20). We have no excuse but to trust and know we belong to Jesus. "Righteousness comes from God, through the faithfulness of Jesus the Messiah" (Romans 3:22). We are right with Him today.

Jesus, help us do what brings us joy (Ecclesiastes 5:20). Amen.

SEPTEMBER 19
EVERY DAY PEOPLE

"If I raise my eyes to the hills, where will my help come? My help comes from *Adonai*, the maker of heaven and earth" (Psalm 121:1-2). You've seen God rays, called Crepuscular rays or sunbeams. They're atmospheric optics generated from the point where the Sun is located. Facts help us, right? Yet, when we are in need of sound advice and turn to His word, we receive a special infusion of help.

Is His voice loud and clear for you today? He is your pure genuine help, your Shepherd and Maker. He's *always* in the process of creating.

Jesus said, "I came out from God, and now I have arrived here. I did not come on my own. He sent me" (John 8:42). Do you see His rays showering you with love, energy for His purposes, strength, and spiritual sustenance? In Old Testament days, God would descend from a cloud and manifest in the Temple. People *knew* He was there and worshipped Him. Then Jesus came to Earth as God in human form. Many believed Him to be the sacrificial lamb for our sins. Some did not. We've never seen Jesus, yet we know Him through His word. He tells you today, "Blessed are those who do not see but trust anyway (John 20:29)! He means this blessing for *you* because you trust Him even though you've never seen Him.

What does trust of that magnitude take? "Blessed are the pure in heart! They will see God (Matthew 5:8). The word, *pure*, (Greek, *katharos*) means, *that which is purified by fire or by pruning*. We are pure because we have been declared innocent through the work of Jesus's death on the cross. We are continually being sanctified by His refining fire and spiritual pruning (Matthew 3:11; Malachi 3:2; John 15:1-17). "How blessed are the eyes that see what you are seeing" (Luke 10:23)! See His beauty today. Know He has created, you.

Then we can conclude what Paul pronounced. "Since we are surrounded by such a great cloud of witnesses, let us, too, put aside every impediment ... which easily hampers our forward movement. Let us keep running with endurance in the contest set before us, looking always to the Initiator and Completer of that trusting, Jesus. He ... endured execution on a stake as a criminal, scorning the shame, and has sat down at the right hand of the throne of God" (Hebrews 12:1-2). He's with us, forging us, and pruning us today.

Father God, we humble ourselves before your majesty. Amen.

SEPTEMBER 20
BEAUTIFUL FEATURES

When I was a teenager, I used to hate the space between my front teeth. Ugly. Furthermore, my self-confidence dwindled on the sideline of some bullies rhyming my last name with everything pink. Have you ever noticed how past hurts only destroy you? How does God see us when we have trouble seeing beauty in ourselves?

Jesus commands us to love and pray. "Love your enemies! Pray for those who persecute you! Then you will become children of your Father in heaven" (Matthew 5:43-48). So many times back then, I wondered: why am I alive because I *hate* being here, God? "As the Father raises the dead and makes them alive, so too the Son makes alive anyone he wants" (John 5:21).

Sometimes, we hurt down deep from what others do to us. What a recurring wound memories can be, as David knew. "I am worn out with groaning; all night I drench my bed with tears, flooding my couch till it swims" (Psalm 6:7). We take our pains to our Father. In John's Gospel, he calls God, Father, over eighty times. God *is* our Father. "Those who have been called ... are loved by God the Father and kept for Jesus the Messiah" (Jude 1:1). When we hurt, He loves us because He called us. When you ache, He hears you. He's with you. He knows you. "You have kept count of my wanderings; store my tears in your water-skin. Aren't they already recorded in your book" (Psalm 56:9)? Those were David's words after he sinned. He lusted after a woman, had her husband killed, and then he committed adultery with her (2 Samuel 11). God forgave him, but David never forgot. In the nadirs of our lives, we can cling to our Father. "You have rescued me from death, my eyes from tears and my feet from falling" (Psalm 116:8). God saves us, and then we can let go of hurts to live. "He rescued me because he took pleasure in me" (Psalm 18:20); and, "I sought *Adonai*, and he answered me. He rescued me from everything I feared" (Psalm 34:5); and, "You rescued me from death. You kept my feet from stumbling so that I can walk in God's presence, in the light of life" (Psalm 56:14). God said about a cedar tree, "I made it so beautiful" (Ezekiel 31:9). How more beautiful you are to Him. "Do not be afraid, you are worth more than many sparrows" (Matthew 10:31). Know he loves you, values you, and treasures you.

Father, we praise you and glorify you as our Maker. Amen.

September 21
The Caring Center

I may feel alone. I may think I am all alone. I may perceive I am lonely....

However, God says in Hebrews 13:5, "I will never leave you nor forsake you." We are *never* alone when we are united with Jesus.

Jesus is God's Caring Station. You've entered His caring station when you pick up his Word, the Bible, and open it. Open His Word now, and experience His caring center. He cares and loves you. "God so loved the world that he gave his only and unique Son, so that everyone who trusts in him may have eternal life, instead of being utterly destroyed" (John 3:16). He loves you. He is, pure love.

Any place and at all times, we have God's Caring Station within us, painted by and decorated by the Holy Spirit. We are saved by Christ, right with God, and wreathed in the Holy Spirit.

In addition, a home with Him is His promise, although at times I can forget it. Sometimes, my feelings dominate me. I can feel lonely, unimportant, ineffective, helpless, directionless, longing, searching, angry, or agitated. Still, no matter my feelings, I am not forsaken. I am always in, The Father's Caring Center.

I once had an argument with my own father. My stepmother died, and almost immediately he found another woman. I heard so many opinions: at least he won't be alone; at least he can spend his last years in companionship with someone; at least he has someone; at least he can pal around with someone; and, he's socially connected.

Hah. I wanted to spit. How dare he not even spend six months mourning for the death of his third wife? I was puzzled beyond belief, remembering so many times in the past when he had forgotten my little brother and me to pursue his *new* lady. What a negligent, thoughtless, selfish, father. He was. And we was hurt at the hands of future abusive stepmoms and stepdads. Until I found God's Caring Center. He forgave me, and I could then forgive my unequipped parents.

I need to respect Dad, and know he is in God's Caring Center as well. God says, "I will repay" (Romans 12:19). God is dealing with those who have hurt us. Their relationship with Him is not our business. I need to remain in His Word and watch *my* life, so that my children and grandchildren cannot say: "I am alone. Where is she?

Lord Jesus Christ, help us love when loving is hard. Amen.

September 22
Diaper Genie Elite Sold Here

Today I experienced a recurring memory from my childhood. Do you have recurring memories you feel powerless to control? God has the power to intervene as He's been helping me. Join me....

I was eight, in second grade, and couldn't change my baby sister's diaper. My mom ordered me to, but I didn't have the skills. When I reported back to her, "I can't, Mom," she punched me with her fists, slapped me, and bit me. Shaking, I raced back to my half-sister and wrapped that cloth diaper 'round her tush and pinned it. I was terrified I might stick her with those gigantic pins. I can't remember her face, only large pins. I did stick myself a few times, but I didn't feel the pricks, only the bite mark my mom left on my cheek.

Later, I went to school to Miss Black's second-grade class. She asked, "What happened to your cheek?"

"My mom bit me," I replied casually. I walked into class, sat down in my little chair, and began working on the morning's reading assignment. But I was so hungry—my stomach a growling. I had to tell Miss Black: "My mom didn't feed me. I'm sick."

She sent me to the cafeteria where the kind worker gave me cinnamon toast and milk. *Mmm....*

Angels. They minister to us and intervene for us. Jacob saw one, actually Jesus prior to God sending Him to Earth. "The angel of God said to me, 'Jacob!' I replied, 'Here I am.' " (Genesis 31:11). We can insert our names at any time because God is calling us to His Word and is with us. "Here I am. I am here. I will do your will," I say.

Are you struggling with putting the past behind you and moving forward with your day? Ya need help? Thank goodness, for angels who help us in our dire circumstances. They are God's blessings when the Enemy, or the world, attempt to render us unproductive for God. "He shall give His angels charge over thee to keep thee in all thy ways" (Psalm 91:11). In John 3:8, the Holy Spirit is a constant wind of divine communication into our souls. The wind undulates like ocean waves, and affects everything—from the largest animal on Earth to atoms. Jesus said that God cares for the birds. We are greater than they, so is His presence in our lives. "More holy than the holies holiness is Adonai-Tzva'ot! The whole earth is filled with his glory" (Isaiah 6:3)

God, help us be in awe of all your works and blessings. Amen.

September 23
Kids Zone

It's a childcare facility and day school, a safe place for trusting parents to drop off their children while they're at work. It's an invitingly decorated barnyard house that kids can't wait to enter to learn and play. It's, the Kid's Zone. We're all kids in a way, and we need a spiritual zone. "You've put a protective hedge around [us], our house and everything we have" (Job 1:10). He is God, our Protector, Shepherd, and Provider we can count on, no matter what. Are you depending on Him and trusting Him with *everything* today?

When I lived with my Aunt Arlene and Uncle Joe for two years, I attended preschool. All seemed well with my little Play Dough creations, until I contracted the chicken pox. Not fun. The administrator, a stout woman with black hair, secluded me on a closed-in porch where I sat for days until I was well. *Not* fun.

Thankfully, God doesn't work that way. God's with us, always.

In John 15:29, people bring the lame, the blind, the crippled, the mute, and the distressed to Jesus. "They laid them at his feet, and he healed them." Jesus has a special kids' zone for you, me, and *everyone* who seeks him and accepts him as their savior. Three verses later, Jesus says, "I feel sorry for these people." Our savior knows our illness, weaknesses, and frailties. He feels for us and hears us in his Kids' Zone. The place is giant—and never fills up—God's arms. In John 20:34, Jesus is filled with tenderness for pleading people who are begging him for healing. They enter, God's Kids' Zone.

Daily we encounter trials and temptations. We can choose to pass into God's Kids' Zone or fend for ourselves. You name it, the World has an answer: drugs, nefarious internet sites, TV gluttony, shopping, and the list goes on in Replay mode. When life stalls on you, or difficulties arise, or a crisis begins, do you go to Your Zone or God's Kids' Zone? Edgar Allen Poe said: "I have absolutely no pleasure in the stimulants in which I sometimes so madly indulge. It has been the desperate attempt to escape from torturing memories, from a sense of insupportable loneliness and a dread of some strange impending doom." How enslaving dependency on *things* must be. Poe indulged in them, yet received no pleasure. He died on a curb. We, however, have our Savior's love. In Him, we live.

Lord, please deliver us from any dependency other than on you (John 21:9). Amen.

SEPTEMBER 24
DEMPSEY'S FOOD SERVICE

They deliver all types of food and supplies to restaurants and fast food eateries. If not for those giant roaring food service trucks, I might not have my McMuffin at MacDonald's or favored French toast sticks at Burger King. Restaurants make life easier and softer, and make time fly by faster. They're like well-oiled machines, with hard-working people processing our food in factories in other states. Somewhere, people on an expansive assembly line in some massive warehouse fix the food, and package it. Then a food services company, like Dempsey's, rolls out the product via a matrix of intercontinental roads. No need to *bake to the bone*, shop, or work when I can count on a fast food machine to do the work for me. Thanks also to transport companies like Dempsey's.

What's making your life easier and softer?

Guess what? Fast food, like fast fixes, get old.

That microwaved sausage or ham can leave a tangy taste of sour on our tongues. Reheated pancakes are sometimes stiff, and restaurant syrup is artificial. Just yesterday, I tossed in the trash a fast-food fish burger that had been in the fridge for over a month and hadn't turned stale. Makes me wonder what that fish, cheese, and bread were *really* made of. I think I'm getting tired of it all, how about you? I've had enough window service and delivery service. Besides, how many people are in the pipeline and handling those foods, and their sowing and harvesting, or ingredient mixing. "Here! Throughout the whole earth I am giving you as food every seed-bearing plant and every tree with seed-bearing fruit" (Genesis 1:29). I wonder, what are we giving away when we take the easy-soft ways?

God has a unique delivery system, and I know the exact location of his wisdom, will, and saving grace: His Word, the *Bible*. What are some of Our Father's delivery services? The cradle of Jesus Christ, the Holy Spirit, the *Our Father*, and even a little stone David tucked into his meager slingshot to kill Goliath. We have "the full armor of God" (Ephesians 6:13). When we seek, we will find; when we knock, Christ opens the door for us. He is our perfect deliverer, Savior, and provider of daily grace so we can feed on real food—not fast food.

Lord, deliver us your perfect wisdom so we can do your will. "Look closely into the perfect *Torah*, becoming a doer of the work it requires. Then [you] will be blessed in what [you] do" (James 1:25).

SEPTEMBER 25
TARGET

Sometimes, I get way off target. A habit twists its way into my life like a wild grape vine, and I miss God's mark of perfection and holiness. I'm human; I let it happen. Do you have any weeds germinating in your heart today? Or, are weed seeds sprouting?

Jesus knows us. He *knows* we battle three powerful forces: the flesh, the World, and the Devil (Ephesians 2: 1-3). What a daily struggle, huh? I don't know about you, but sometimes I get tired. My strength melts out of my muscles. My spiritual defenses take a pounding. How can I ever live up to God's expectations and holiness? I can't. I think of the Target logo, a large red bull's eyes with a white circle around it. David probably had something like that red dot in sight when he aimed and focused on Goliath. Sometimes, my sins appears gigantic, and me, a meager ant with a little pebble in my whirling slingshot. Where do we even begin to aim?

We need Jesus, God, *and* the Holy Spirit because we get distracted, wander, and lose interest in His Word. But when we stop, and return to Jesus, The Holy Spirit helps us re-focus on God. We can then get back on track with our walk with our Lord. "We concentrate not on what is seen but on what is not seen, since things seen are temporary, but things not seen are eternal" (2 Corinthians 4:18). We need to concentrate on the bull's eye, the sin, and let God's powerful Biblical words fight those three atrocious forces.

Target *appears* to have it all: groceries, clothes, gardening supplies, holiday decorations, and the newest wrinkle creams. They even have a Starbuck's and Pizza Hut. I can end up with a stuffed cart if I don't have a list and targeted goal. David instructs us: "Commit your way to Adonai, trust in him, and he will act. He will make your vindication shine forth like light, the justice of your cause like the noonday sun" (Psalm 37: 5-6). We can *always* open God's word where His ink comes to brilliant life and light. Sin leaves me pained, hurting, and alone. The people I love suffer. However, when God convicts me, and I recognize I need help, I often turn to David's contrite Psalms. "I cry aloud to God, aloud to God; and he hears me. One the day of my distress I am seeking Adonai; my hands are lifted up" (Psalm 77: 1-2). We can get rid ourselves of weeds by stamping them out on our knees in prayer.

Lord, help us today to focus on your holy Word. Amen.

SEPTEMBER 26
SPEED BUMP AHEAD

Have there been any speed bumps in your life lately? A few times, I accidentally hit a speed bump going too fast. Hey, a sign wasn't there to warn me of my impending clash with lumpy asphalt. Then—

Bong, thump.

My front end jerked down and the rear tires plopped on the pavement.

"You coulda damaged the frame," my husband exclaimed.

Now, I'm always attentive to signs warning me of those lumps of car torture. However, there aren't any warnings of impending spiritual speed bumps. When one of those occurs, like an unanswered prayer or a situation not going my way, my plans stall or go sideways. I can become anxious or depressed. "Why is God telling me no?"

Have you ever asked, "Why are you doing this to me, God?"

Jesus experienced all sorts of speed bumps on his walk with us on Earth. One time, a "woman from Canaan," a foreigner *not* of the house of Israel, begs Jesus: "Son of David! My daughter is cruelly held under the power of demons!" (Matthew 15:22-28). The disciples want her gone. The needy crying lady is pestering them and keeping them off-mission. She's worse than a speed bump. Jesus, however, uses their rejection of the woman as a teaching moment. He knows what he's doing. He tells the woman, "I was sent only to the lost sheep of Israel." He also knows she believes in him, and he wants everyone around him to know the truth. *Anyone* who acknowledges his divine Lordship and accepts him as savior he welcomes into His kingdom, God's family. How does he answer the desperate woman now on her knees, begging, "Sir, help me!" Jesus compares the Canaanite people to dogs. What an insult. What's he doing? She says, "But even the dogs eat leftovers." Wow, she *accepts* what he calls her: subhuman. I am reminded of the words in Matthew 8:8, "Lord, I am not worthy for you to come under my roof, but just say the word, and my servant will be healed." He tells her, "Lady, you are a person of great trust." He heals her daughter right then. We can be like one of those metaphorical speed bumps, now-and-then clashing with God's desire for us and our lives. We can take his crumbs because He's molding us for his kingdom.

Lord, we beg you for mercy and help with speed bumps when we encounter them. Amen.

September 27
Caution, Storm Drain

When I see a storm drain sign, I know there's trouble when it rains, especially if the giant drains are clogged. "The sun and moon stand still in the sky at the light of your arrows speeding by, at the gleam of your glittering spear" (Habakkuk 3:11). God can handle our storms when troubling storms come in all forms and in all directions on us. Lately, we've had rain every day, and my neighbor told me a story about her experience of "high waters" that occurred a few years ago. "The drains clogged, and water rose almost to our garage doors!"

The deluge reminds me of an old saying: *When it rains, it pours.* Sitting and watching drops plunk into my pool, I recall the story of Job. There are forty-two chapters of metaphorical rain that plops down upon poor Job. In my Bible, the deluge—no hurricane—of troubles rumble from pages 993 to 1046. Now, I'll add the verses in all those chapters: 1,090 verses (in my Bible). This has to be the longest book. Why, I wonder? I think, storms.

There isn't another story filled with such distress, languishing illnesses, and dire consequences, almost to the point of death, other than Job and his turmoil. Are you experiencing turmoil, storms, today? If so, read a few verses from Job. If you're not, say a little prayer of thanksgiving. What I find amazing is God's perfect confidence in Job. God calls Job, "his servant" (Job 2:3). He tells the Devil, "There's no one like Job on Earth." Job fears God, shuns evil, and holds onto his integrity. What does, *integrity*, mean? In Chapter 27, Job tells a friend [Friend? Yeah, right!]: "I swear by the living God ... that as long as my life remains in me and God's breath is in my nostrils, my lips will not speak unrighteousness. ... I will keep my integrity till the day I die" (verses 2-5). *Integrity* is: "the state of being whole and undivided;" and, "the quality of being honest and having strong moral principles." In Latin, the origin of *integrity* is *integer*, meaning *intact*. Though Satan flings almost every illness and detestable infection at Job, Job remains fixed—glued, cemented, interwoven, tight, connected—with God. The storms keep pummeling Job, but Job's confidence in God and God's promises to Job are ever-flowing. Job's example provides us with lessons of endurance and encouragement. They leave us with God's calmness.

Lord, help our integrity grow, so we can show you to the world. Jesus, let us see you as the calm center in our storms. Amen.

SEPTEMBER 28
CHEAP CHEAP GLASS

I like cheap. Or, should I say, inexpensive. I like shopping at places like Dollar Tree and Dollar General. I also like buying decorations, tableware, and cute ornamentals for holidays. However, those finer things in life can be expensive. So, I'm a bargain hound. Have you noticed that cheap comes at a price? When my family and I lived in Hawaii, I *decided* to buy a cheap shovel. When the rain morphed into one of God's tropical downpours, I had to trench the backyard—rain pummeling my face and the mud like claws yanking at my boots. The cheap shovel broke, and I was left staring at a splinter against a long line of red mud slowly inching toward the house like the Angel of Death. I was struck with "the shoulda couldas," again.

However, there is one decision I have never regretted: accepting Jesus Christ as my savior. The price He paid for my sins was not cheap. The point of no return to the cross Jesus endured for you as well is certain. Paul says, "He was humiliated and denied justice" (Acts 8:33). John also tells us about the sacrifice Jesus willingly gave for us. "This is how we know what love is: Jesus Christ laid down his life for us" (1 John 3:16). Jesus himself tells us: "I am the good shepherd. The good shepherd lays down his life for the sheep" (John 10: 11). The imagery in Jesus's words illuminates his purpose. He "lays down his life." Willingly, He allowed soldiers to apprehend him. Willingly, He accepted a crown of thorns. Willingly, he stretched out his arms and lay down on the execution stick—the cross. When he *permitted* those acts, He knew your name and my name. "The Son of Man did not come to be served, but to serve, and to give his life as a ransom for many" (Matthew 20:28).

That's the Good News. He had you and me—all humanity—foremost in his mind and heart when he died for us, *to secure us to* God. What makes His sacrifice glorified is His resurrection three days later. He shows us our future. Our bodies will die, but our souls will live out eternity with Christ.

Jesus says this in his prayer to his Father. "Father glorify your Son ... so that he might give eternal life to all those whom you have given him" (John 17: 1-3); and, "I give unto them eternal life, and they shall never perish, neither shall any man pluck them out of My hand" (John 10:28). His expensive price was his life, for *us*.

We pray, help us testify to someone of your glory, Lord. Amen.

SEPTEMBER 29
EMERGENCY WALK-IN DENTAL CARE

I've had teeth pulled. It's no fun. Looking in the mirror and seeing three front teeth missing is like confronting a different person. The change is disorienting. Adding to the awkwardness, I experienced anxious dissonance. "Dissonance" is: "a tension or clash resulting from the combination of two disharmonious or unsuitable elements." There's nothing like smiling at your toothless reflection that can cause deep psychological tension. Yet, God has us in those anxious moments when we feel as if we're losing ourselves, and changing. "I brought you up from the land of Egypt. I redeemed you from a life of slavery. I sent Moshe, Aharon and Miryam to lead you" (Micah 6:4). He rescues us, redeems us from the world's expectations, and gives us an identity with Jesus. Our looks aren't important to Jesus. What changes in your life might be causing you dissonance? Here's what happened to me during one tooth-pulling session.

In January of 2012, I was numbed up and sitting in the dentist's office when I received a call from my dad. My stepmom had a heart attack. Her prognosis was grim. Paramedics worked to resuscitate her, but her brain was deprived of oxygen, thus rendering her brain dead. With cotton stuck on my gums, I mumbled, "I'll be there are soon as I can, Dad." Then, I cried. Now, it's no fun having your dentist's face two inches from your nose when you're experiencing a flood of tears. I also felt numb throughout my body. What do we do in those times when we go numb in life? When trials hit hard?

I prayed. Then, dissonance flowed into my very bones. *I'm going to die at some time.* Maybe not a heart attack, but death *will come* in one form or another. Now, I could take that truth and let it trample me under. Or I can hold onto the words of Jesus Christ: "Very truly I tell you, whoever hears my word and believes him who sent me has eternal life and will not be judged but has crossed over from death to life" (John 5:27, NIV). I see two powerful words in the above quote: "very" and "truly." In other Bible version, the same substitutions for those words are: "I tell you the truth," and "truly truly," and "I assure you," and "timeless truth," and "I can guarantee this truth," and lastly, "In most solemn truth." So hear His "word," "believe God," and spend eternity with Jesus. Jesus saved us, and accepts even our toothless selves as precious. He has special eyes.

Jesus, today help us focus on you and show your light. Amen.

GOD DESIGNED

SEPTEMBER 30
ENERGY DRINKS SOLD HERE

Zap.

I feel suddenly drained. I get a depleted feeling almost daily after I eat lunch. It's like what happened to the Wicked Witch who kept melting in *The Wizard of Oz*. "I'm melting ... melting ... oh no!" I want to take a siesta, one of those long naps. Maybe it's because I'm in my fifties, or I don't get enough vitamins. I don't know ... I just feel fatigue, and I wanna plop right down and sleep.

How can we get back energy? Especially spiritual energy that's revival energy?

Experts say the B vitamins particularly help stave off bouts of fatigue and increase energy. Researchers conducted studies on this. There are two groups: one getting a particular vitamin and one not taking the vitamin. After controlled conditions, researchers tally the results and announce them. People believe those results. According to an online CNN article written by Madison Park, dated April 13, 2011, she reports that more than half of U.S. adults are popping vitamins and supplements. Then she asks, "Has it [vitamin popping] made Americans healthier?"

Most people hop right onboard this popular *energy* bandwagon, but those vitamins certainly haven't worked miracles for me. I might take them for a while, but as they begin to wear off, I'm reminded of the truth. No matter what I do, I will have weaknesses. And I will experience illnesses. I'm riding on the Death train. It doesn't have an arrival time for Heaven yet, but my body is constantly on wind down. No matter the vitamin, the supplement, the cure—you get the picture—our lives will one day expire. Destination, Heaven.

However, until that great arrival time, we can count on *one* energy and power for reviving us: the Holy Spirit. The Holy Spirit is an eternal Niagara whose fabric intertwines with Jesus and God. In Isaiah 28, verses 28-31, we know for certain: "The Everlasting God, Adonai, the Creator of the ends of the earth, does not grow tired or weary. He gives strength to the powerless." We will grow tired and "weary," meaning, "worn out," "exhausted," or "spent." Life does that to us. However, "those who put their hope in Adonai will renew their strength; they will soar aloft as with eagles' wings." Right now, I received a dash of energy ... a revival rushing into my blood.

Thanks you God for your countless blessings. Amen.

J.P. Osterman

October 1
Identity Theft Protection

Identity theft. Scary words! Here are a few scenarios. You try to cash a check at a bank, or open an account, or apply for a loan; but instead you're rejected because some lawbreaker has stolen *you.* Have you ever been stolen? It's like your metabolism going haywire as you wait for experts to straighten out the problem. "The problem is that they haven't all paid attention to the Good News and obeyed it," Paul says about the lost people in this world.

We live in times of cyber hacking, debit/credit card manipulation, and password duplicating. We shop with cards most times, and the majority of stores no longer accept checks. Just the other day, I heard of another cyber-attack. Cyber criminals gleaned "card" information from customers who bought products and services at Home Depot. I shopped there last week—*yikes.* With enough information, identity thieves can hunt down our social security numbers, birthdays, and address, and then steal our identities. "Identity snatching" is like invasion of the body snatchers, and it happens every minute. Companies like Identity Guard, LifeLock, and ID Freeze, to name a few, sell identity-theft protection. However, I've seen their ads, and they cannot guarantee 100% protection against someone stealing your identity. Fear ... are we going to live by it? Be a slave to fear?

No, but what's a person to do when someone *steals,* "you?"

Countering fear is one of the greatest passages inscribed on bookmarks and church banners. "The Lord is my shepherd ... I will fear no disaster" (Psalm 23:1-4). I may have things stolen, lifted, pilfered, burned, or lost; but no one can abscond with my identity in Christ. God's firm salvation through Jesus is stamped with the words, The Lord knows his own" (2 Tim 2:19). My saving faith in Jesus Christ has sealed me to God. I have Jesus's stamp on my soul. The Lord knows me. You, too, are indelibly written into His Book. I'm reminded of what Joseph's brothers did to him, basically, try to kill him in order to wipe his identity off the face of the earth. It didn't work. "You meant to do me harm, but God meant it for good," Joseph said (Genesis 50:19). He could have wiped them off the earth, but he reflected God's mercy instead. What love, huh?

Jesus, help us look with eyes of continuous gratitude for your stamp of salvation. Amen.

OCTOBER 2
YIELD

Have you ever driven a bumper car? You squish your body into a tiny car covered in rubber pads, and then drive *smack bang* around in aimless circles. There's no beginning, no end. No one yields. The ride is supposed to be fun. But it left me with a crick in my neck.

Don't ya just wanna get even sometimes with people who don't yield and who are just downright mean? "This is my prayer," Paul beings, "that your love may more and more overflow in fullness of knowledge and depth of discernment, so that you will be able to determine what is best and thus be pure and without blame for the Day of the Messiah" (Philippians 1:9-10). Love vs. meanness....

Not yielding ends in pain. The word, "yield" means: "give way," "submit," and "surrender." Yielding to someone while driving is the courteous thing to do. And you'd better yield when you see the yellow sign, 'cause if you don't and cause an accident, *you're* at fault.

In the world of agriculture, "yield" means to "produce." But we're in the car-driving world—a street called, "Outta My Way." People don't like yielding. We like to be first, be right, have our own way, and take up as much space on the road as Arizona. We self-full ... full of ourselves. "Warn a divisive person once, then a second time; and after that, have nothing more to do with him" (Titus 3:10).

Yesterday, I experienced a yield problem. I didn't want to admit I was wrong. I was speaking angrily, like a steaming tea kettle. I needed to calm down, and yield *not* to people but to Jesus.

His orders are explicit in times of anger, impatience, and selfishness. Paul instructs us: "Do not offer [yield] any part of yourselves to sin as an instrument for wickedness. On the contrary, offer yourselves to God as people alive from the dead" (Romans 6:13). As not yielding to motorists could land me a huge ticket, result in an accident, or culminate in hurting others; not yielding "offers" up myself to sin. I become susceptible to wickedness and possibly a hindrance to God who is working to save others. How cannot *yielding* make me wicked? "I'm not wicked. I'm just asserting my rights!" I'll answer the question: When my target is retaliation or revenge, I'm really hurting God when I hurt others. Hurting or being a road block not His perfect will for us and his purpose: "Whatever you do ... do it all so as to bring glory to God" (1 Corinthians 10:31). Love.

Lord, help us see your face in the faces of strangers. Amen.

October 3
Outliers Welcome

I saw the above title on a flier on a college billboard. But no one likes, or wants, to be an outlier. An "outlier" is: "A person or thing situated away or detached from the main body or system; a person or thing different from all other members." My experience with being an outlier was not good. My maiden name was Pink, and you can imagine the rhyming names kids called me. Even the teachers laughed at times. Being an outlier hurt. Often I cried. And because teens band together, I didn't have many friends. Instead, I progressed through school as a "fence kid" who stood alone along the aluminum fence, rocking, feeling left out, lonely, and watching people. Can you relate? Did you ever get bullied, and for minutes, become an outlier? Jesus was an outlier. "He wants all humanity to be delivered and come to full knowledge of the truth" (1 Timothy 2:4).

There was an upside to being on the fringe. I had time to look into the sky, ponder God, imagine angels in the cloud shapes, talk to Jesus about my sadness, and beg the Holy Spirit to make me popular. Sometimes, or for a period of time, bad things happen. Sorrowful times strike; and even when we pray, our prayers go unanswered. God is replying "yes," "no," or, "wait." We know God's "Yes" when our prayers are answered. Halleluiah! Sometimes, however, God doesn't answer. What to do? For me, I couldn't change my name.

I'm reminded of the prophets—those brave men like Noah, Job, Isaiah, Jonah, and Jeremiah. When people mocked them, they prayed in their times of severe ostracism. Jonah had to have appeared like a speckled ghost after the whale spit him out with all those gastric juices blanching his skin. One of Isaiah's prayers offers consolation in times of emotional pain. "We wish you would tear open heaven and come down, so the mountains would shake at your presence" (Isaiah 64:1)! That's what I wished for when kids were shouting "Pink stink" and "Pink purple." Every time, I remember what happened to our Savior Jesus. Name calling could have been much worse … what He got. Jesus was "jeered at," beaten, and crucified (Matthew 20:19). Throughout his three-year ministry, people ask Jesus to leave their towns (Matthew 8:34). Relief comes when we recognize another type of blessing in life: what *hasn't* happened that could be *worse* than our current situations. That's an answer, right?

Lord, help us keep a heart of gratitude and forgiveness. Amen.

OCTOBER 4
NO RIGHT TURN ON RED

Have you ever accidentally made a right turn at a red light when the sign says not to? The cops could be anywhere—to the right, left, or two cars behind, watching. Or, have you ever wanted to slip through a situation as you've inched through a red light before stopping?

Just recently, the city put a new, *no right on red* light—not a sign— high up where the stop light is situated. The light is a right-turn arrow that flashes either red for *no right turn*, or green for *go*. It's the first of its kind I've ever encountered, and so confusing, because I'm used to seeing a sign. And if I hadn't noticed the new light and turned right-on-red, I could have received a ticket or caused an accident. Laws abound everywhere; but accidents happen, and sometimes signs aren't perfect because *people* create and erect the signs. People ... we're flawed. As hard as I try, I always find myself either not seeing a sign, or well, disobeying the sign because I'm in a hurry. *Ops*, but no one *saw* me sneak through that right on red, right?

Wrong. We get hungry for speedy endings. We don't stop and consider that time *doesn't* speed up, but is methodic and steady. In God's holy omnipresent realm, He sees everything. One of God's names is *El Ro'i*, The God Who Sees (Genesis 16:13). He created time. From birth, He's seen you and me and knows we've missed His perfect mark because of Adam's sin. You and I need help and Jesus's forgiveness so that God can see us in holy light. For Jewish people, today is Yom Kippur, the holiest days of the year. Observing this "holy-day" (holiday) is spent in prayer and fasting, and asking God and others, "Will you forgive me?" They're humbling words. Jesus said a prayer of forgiveness himself: "Father, forgive them. They don't understand what they are doing" (Luke 23:34). The people who caused our Lord pain and suffering were oblivious to what they were doing: killing the *divine* person who could have secured them eternity. Yet His sacrificial death and resurrection gives you and me eternal life when we acknowledge that Jesus lay down on the cross and died in our place. He didn't speed through the cross, He embraced it. "We have come to be considered righteous [right] with God because of our trust" (Romans 5:1). We are new. "You open your hand and satisfy the desire of every living thing" (Psalm 145:16).

Lord, help us repeat your promise throughout the day: that we are new, and for you. Amen.

OCTOBER 5
BLINDS OF ALL KINDS

I drew dots on paper to count the times I've moved. About thirty-one times. In my younger years, many places I lived in were apartments. They came with blinds, although not the nicest window coverings. Some of the places I lived in were rental homes and didn't have blinds in every room. I had to buy them, or patch them. Six homes we owned we had to purchase blinds, or curtains, and install them. What a job. After installing sixty or so all together, now my trusty drill and I can surmount just about any task concerning blinds and curtains. Oh, and don't forget, you need a ladder or at least a good stepping stool. Seems like the hard work is never done....

Including God's work with us. What's God working hard on changing in you? "For indeed when we came into Macedonia, our bodies had no rest. On the contrary, we faced all kinds of troubles—altercations without, apprehensions within" (2 Corinthians 7:5). We're like blinds that are bent a bit by our anger and bitterness. or Our emotional hurts and past scars are as curtains with holes. Often, I like to believe I've *finally* arrived at the point where I'm satisfied with myself. "I'm just fine right now," or, "I don't want to experience any more growing pains." Then, a crisis ensues, demanding a change in me. Sometimes, we need to inject something new into our personalities, God's touch. Guess what? I need Him and his power *all* the time. Paul tells us: "And I am sure of this: that the One who began a good work among you will keep it growing until it is completed on the Day of the Messiah Yeshua" (Philippians 1:6). I may be tired of change, and I most likely will fight change, but the truth is: I must constantly change. God says it's going to happen, so we might as well welcome it, and let Him do some needed repairs to our personalities and souls. Like a home in need of improvements, I need the Holy Spirit to infuse me with wisdom and knowledge so I can in turn show Jesus at work in the world. Aren't we supposed to be His emissaries? How can others come to Jesus unless *we* show Jesus to them? If I'm acting out *my* damage, I can't. Peter gave us this instruction: "If someone speaks, let him speak God's words; if someone serves, let him do so out of strength that God supplies; so that in everything God may be glorified" (1 Peter 4:11).

Father God, help us "open our blinds," and heal us, so we can be on display for your glory. Amen.

OCTOBER 6
THANK YOU

I saw a *Thank You* sign after leaving the drive through window at Hardy's.

"You're welcome," I thought, smiling.

Then I remembered seeing this sign so many other places: after exiting a Disneyland ride; when leaving Grand Canyon National Park; and, driving away from my local beach, to name a few. "In everything give thanks, for this is what God wants from you who are united with the Messiah Yeshua" (1 Thessalonians 5:18). When was the last time someone thanked you? It feels good to be thanked, huh? The gesture is one of appreciation and thoughtfulness after we've done something nice or accommodating.

Usually parks tourists' sites follow their thank you with, *come visit us again*. I say *thank you* several times throughout the day. One day, I decided to count them—tried—and I tallied twenty times. I thanked the greeter at church for opening the door for me, I thanked a man at the grocery store for politely taking my shopping cart, and I thanked my husband for putting my medicine in my hand at 6:30 a.m. But the most important thank you is the one I pray to God who allowed his son, Jesus, to die on the cross for me. We can thank God: "I give you thanks with all my heart. Not to idols, but to you I sing praise" (Psalm 138:1).

We probably don't say thanks to Him as often as we should. The gravity of Jesus's sacrifice warrants thanks *every* second, if we could. After all, if not for His sacrifice for our sins, we wouldn't have an eternity sharing in his glory. "God demonstrates his own love for us in that the Messiah died on our behalf while we were still sinners" (Romans 8: 8). I remember my days prior to being saved. They weren't good. I had a hole in me the size of a state. No one could fill it, and nothing I fed that hole satisfied me. I felt empty, and entrenched in a culture that champions "feeling good." My problems at that time were: I need a wonderful face cream; where's the new beautiful dress; who's the new boyfriend; I need a happy med, or which guru's New Age advice can fix me? Only Jesus's sacrifice on the cross filled my voids. I must continue *daily* to remember who I was before Jesus and who I am now. "It is his doing that you are united with the Messiah Yeshua" (1 Corinthians 1:30). Thanks, God.

God, throughout today, help us thank you (1 Peter 5:8). Amen.

October 7
Use Both Lanes

Most times, I like taking the comfortable ways—the easier decision, or the quickest way to the end. I consider those choices, *the fast lanes in life*. Usually, when I'm in the fast lane, I've rushed into something without contemplating all options or thinking about consequences. When act on impulse or take on a project without doing some sort of planning, I experience pain. Can you relate? It's like diving in a pool. The blue water appears deep, but it's really shallower than what I'd anticipated. Diving in those waters, you end up hitting your belly on the pool bottom.

I remember a time when I was young and took too much time getting out of my car in a parking lot. A man jumped me. I became a victim of a crime. Has something terribly ever happened to you, and you became a victim? God had the right thing in mind when he gave the following rule: "If the man comes upon [a girl] out in the countryside, and the man grabs her and has sexual relations with her, then only the man who had intercourse with her is to die" (Deuteronomy 22:25). I'm sure you've asked God, *why* do people have to unleash their pains, hurts, and anger onto innocent people? I want sin eliminated. God does as well, but we all have to go through Jesus. I remember the day after the assault when I had my arm in a sling and my neck in a brace. Whimpering and despondent, I called my dad and stepmom, "Can I *please* come back home?" I didn't know how I was going to make it through the day. The answer? No. This should be the story of the Prodigal Son, but I'd prefer to talk about surveying surroundings, and noticing signs and problems.

On that dreadful night, I didn't consider my dark environment. I'm not blaming myself, but I wonder: if I would have been more aware, perhaps the sinner might not have targeted me. Most likely he would have hunted someone else. I wouldn't have wanted that either!

Jesus tells us the Parable of Signs. He uses the weather to demonstrate a truth. We're not good at reading signs and just as bad as denying our sin sickness. "When you see a cloud-bank rising ... you say a rainstorm is coming ... when the wind is from the south, you say there will be a heat wave" (Luke 12: 59). He asks the most important question a person can answer in a lifetime: "Why don't you decide for yourselves what is the right course to follow?" Jesus.

Lord, help us be aware of our spiritual condition. Amen.

OCTOBER 8
MINI STORAGE

Waking up in the middle of the night and not being able to fall back to sleep is hair pulling. Everything magnifies: the mosquito bite; the neighbor's droning air conditioner; my heart beating; and, the Engine of the Past speeding memories through my mind like a runaway train without a caboose. Ever have a night like that when even the pillow over your ears won't stop all the noise—outside and inside yourself?

My mind's seems to pick the worst time to sift through bad experiences and then whip me with the guilty stick. "Pharaoh saw that the rain, hail and thunder had ended; he sinned still more by making himself hardhearted" (Exodus 9:34). I wish sins could become solid, like furniture. Then I could pick them up, box 'em up, seal 'em with duct tape, shove 'em in a storage container, and lock the place up tight. Maybe I'd even consider not paying the bill so someone else could claim and burn the dreadful items. Too bad memories can't morph into tangible objects. However, God made us so we *can't* forget—the happy and the sad, the good and the bad. I guess, we need to think before we do, 'cause there's no forget button.

What if we *could* forget our sins and how they hurt others? What would you forget?

Memories are like rubber stoppers that keep the fizz inside a bottle. Let out the fizz, and vital parts of us leave as well. In his parable of the Weeds in the Grain, Jesus talks about the good mixing with the bad. A parable teaches a moral or spiritual lesson. In this one, He's teaching the Kingdom of Heaven. But we I can apply the "good seed and bad weeds" to ourselves. In Matthew 13, we learn an important truth: No matter how hard we try, we cannot extract, escape, forget, or erase what we've done. Those weeds of the past are there, but now forgiven by God when we accepted Jesus Christ. "Where do the weeds come from" (verse 27)? "An enemy has done this" (verse 28). Our enemies Word, we have the power to resist sin; and when we sin, to return to his good and excellent graces. I am reminded of his forgiveness: "In union with him, through the shedding of his blood, we are set free, our sins are forgiven; this accords with the wealth of the grace" (Ephesians 1:7). Now, we can sleep. He has forgiven what we *need* to forgive, and forget.

Lord, when our sins resurface, help us remember your promise and cling to it as a comforting pillow. Amen.

October 9
Deadline for Medicare Coverage

It's that time of year again. Flu shot time. Enterovirus D68 is spreading. Recommendation? GET your flu shot, now. By the way, seniors have a shot specifically formulated for them.

I'm not a senior yet, at least according to most establishments, except AARP, but I'm off for my shot. After striking out at *two* pharmacies because sick people were invading them like D-Day, we found what appeared to be an empty parking lot. Empty store then, right? Yes! So we got stuck and injected … *ah*, whew. Now, no flu. What a minute…. Later, I came down with the chills, felt queasy, and the injection site stung. Four hours later, I'm fine. I feel relieved that I've taken a precaution and sought out preventative care because newscasters have been reiterating what doctors are vehemently instructing: Get your shot before October 31. Then, I've just learned that this year's flu vaccine will only be 30% effective. You ever gone to extreme lengths to acquire care, believed you're impervious thereafter, and then discovered you're vulnerable?

Deadlines have a tendency to scare us and make us act before it's too late. The prophets announced deadlines all the time: Repent and change your sinful ways. God told Jonah to go to Nineveh. "Proclaim to it that their wickedness has come to my attention" (verse 1). Well, that sure strikes a fear in me to repent. What about you? I can think of a few things I'm sorry for doing, and not doing.

God told Ezekiel to make his city "realize how disgusting all her practices are" (Ezekiel 22:2). When we get caught up in sin, we don't "see" our disgusting behaviors, nor feel shame. Master God wants our attention. "Listen to me … I am he who is first; I am also the last. My hand laid the foundation of the earth, my right hand spread out the heavens" (Isaiah 48:12-13). He calls us to repent of our sins and change. He offers a solution. "I am Adonai, your God, who teaches you for your own good, who guides you on the path you should take" (Isaiah 48:17-18). He is Lord, and Holy. He has the answer to those stressful times when deadlines approach that leave us vulnerable: Jesus. "God demonstrates his own love for us in that the Messiah died on our behalf while we were still sinners" (Romans 5:8). Listening *and* heeding God's instructions, we can accomplish his will. They are His deadlines. And, He gave us doctors and shots.

God, help us *hear* the lines of behavior you draw for us. Amen.

GOD DESIGNED

OCTOBER 10
RETURN HERE

Every morning I go through a cycle. You probably have one too. What's yours?

Mine goes like this: make coffee; sausage; toast; clear the dishwasher; wake up son [actually peel son out of bed!]; and, sweep the leaves and acorn shells in the driveway into a bucket. Now, mind you, there are mini-steps in between the above duties, but sweeping the driveway is like a never-ending song. And the days are getting shorter, the nights longer. Tomorrow, we set back the clocks. Cycles, seasons, routines, and schedules are predictable.

Is there ever an end? "He has given human beings an awareness of eternity; but in such a way that they can't fully comprehend, from beginning to end, the things God does" (Ecclesiastes 3:11). No end, until He decides when it all ends, right?

I don't hear much about the two books of Chronicles at the end of the Old Testament before Matthew. 2 Chronicles concludes with the King of Persia ordering his workers to rebuild "God's house," the Temple in Jerusalem. Then King Koresh says: "Whoever there is among you of all [God's] people, may Adonai be with him! He may go up...." That's the end. These two books are supposed to be an ending, but their long ancestral and historic accounts of the Nation of Israel leads us right into the genealogy of Jesus.

1 Chronicles 1:34 talks about Abraham, and Matthew 1:1 begins with Abraham. The family lineages in Chronicles are mired in detail. However, imagine *one* person cut off from his or her family branch or lost land. The break would have rippled down to Jesus. In 1 Chronicles 4:10, Jabez (Ya'betz) might have been one of those severed offspring. He lived somewhere after Moses' time and into the time of the Judges. He prays to God: "Please bless me by enlarging my territory. May your hand be with me! Keep me from harm, so that it will not cause me pain." God grants Jabez his request to drive out pagans and take possession of God's Promised Land. Maybe this was the place Jesus was born, died, or rose on the third day. No endings of cycles here ... only creations and beginnings. All of the Bible is Jesus directed, from Genesis to Revelation. Jesus will returns to claim Earth and proclaim victory.

Lord, today help us see your divine purpose for our lives and cherish every moment. Amen.

OCTOBER 11
FRITO LAY, GOOD FUN

My favorite junk food is French fries, Baby Ruth bars, and Frito Lay corn chips. When I was young and active, I could eat a small serving and fat wouldn't drift to my waist. But every now and then, I get a craving for a little grease, salt or sugar. They're not good for me, but they beckon me like Homer's Sirens. Before you know it, the candy bar is drizzling chocolate on my blouse because will power flew out with the wind.

"The tongue has power over life and death; those who indulge it must eat its fruit" (Proverbs 18:21). Blurting out words *and* blowing our diets have consequences, right?

What's your delectable snack you just *can't* deny as it harkens you from the pantry, triggering your gustatory cortex to generate saliva?

How to resist an overwhelming craving or desire? Perhaps if we recall a few Bible verses when we're in the middle of battling a craving or desire, we could win over it. Let's try....

The word "craving" means, "a powerful desire for something;" and the word, "desire" means, "a strong feeling of wanting to have something." A craving and a desire are synonymous. They're powerful emotions. The key is the word *power*, and we can see the consequences of this power in our lives. "The love of money is a root of all the evils; because of this craving, some people have wandered away from the faith and pierced themselves to the heart with many pains" (1 Timothy 6:10). "Craving" has its roots in Old English, *crafain*, meaning, "claim, right, demand." When I'm experiencing a craving, my mind is directing: I want [fill in the blank] because it's my right." How to stop the *craving*? Paul says: "put to death the earthly parts of your nature ... now, put them all away" (Colossians 3:5-11). Good, but *I* might fail. Now what? "Be renewed in the spirit of your mind and put on the likeness of God" (Ephesians 4:22-24). How do I renew "the spirit in my mind?" The word of God *is* God, infusing us with the Holy Spirit via the Bible. So let's trace this back. Reading God's word renews our minds and puts to death the earthly parts of our nature. The craving then loses its powerful hold on us. Yes! So we need to flee the temptation, read a verse or two in the Bible, and pray. The process worked for Joseph.

Lord, help us recall *your* words of truth so *you* can claim victory over our cravings, desires, and tendencies. Amen.

290

OCTOBER 12
FRESHLY MADE FOR YOU!

Notice how ads are geared to *you* so they can reel you in?

Most of them are food items, like Sara Lee, Dunkin Donuts, Coke, catering trucks, and specialty mini-restaurants on wheels. There's a product, a fee, and a cashier you pay. Very rarely does anyone say, "How are you?" or "How's your day going?" or "Merry Christmas" [You can insert another holiday as well.]. When I was a kid growing up in Hammond, Indiana, I remember clerks at Goldblatt's department store wishing my mom happy birthday and offering to gift wrap anything other than food. No more. Long gone are the days when a cashier knows your name, 'cause he or she is just there until the better job comes their way. Lately I've noticed another tendency we have. We call, *How are you?* to people like we sip water or scratch an itch. Do we really expect an honest answer? We usually receive the answer that has cemented itself in our American collective conscious: "Fine."

Really?

I never read once of Jesus asking anyone: "How are you?" He had an inviting way of speaking and bonding with hurting people. "What do you want me to do for you" (Matthew 20: 32)? "What do you want" (Matthew 20: 21)? He's direct. You can almost see his inviting eyes as He greets people right where they're at, sick or healthy, poor or rich, smelly or high class.

When a man asks him a question, "Rabbi, what good thing should I do in order to have eternal life?"

Jesus answers: "Why are you asking me about good? There is One who is good! ... Come follow me" (Matthew 19: 16:22).

What can we do today to meet people the way The Master touched peoples' lives? Jesus acts with a mission in mind. He has little time to point people to God. He is all about action.

"How are you" and "What do you need" are probing invitations. They are meant to reach hearts through peoples' senses. Using those probing questions wisely and waiting for an answer, we can show Jesus to others. We can see Him *in* our fellow Christians. There are other greetings I could offer people I meet today, such as "What's new with you?" or "Tell me about your [day, week, plans for the week]." Jesus wants us to touch lives to help people know Him.

Jesus, help us today to greet people your way. Amen.

October 13
Let's Go Places

People can travel in luxury almost anywhere in the world and enjoy the most exquisite accommodations. Viking cruise packages and round-the-world excursions offer jet-setting tourists the experiences of their dreams. For the rest of us, we have cars, SUVs, and pick-up trucks. Then there's bike riding, taking the bus, and plain old walking. Driving to our destinations, we see people walking places and waiting for buses *all* the time. They might not have cars.

How do we view them? The people less fortunate, the homeless? "Share your food with the hungry, take the homeless poor into your house, clothe the naked when you see them, fulfilling your duty to your kinsmen" (Isaiah 58:7). Is *everyone* our kinsmen, though?

We tend to be prideful and arrogant and at times, even downright condescending. But let's look at some *real* traveling heroes—the prophets—and the mode and duration it took them to travel to accomplish God's orders. See if you can guess this first one:

He didn't wanna go. You can almost see him shake his head at God and escape. Ultimately, a whale swallows him. Three days later, it drops him on dry land. Yes, it's Jonah. Jaffa to Nineveh is about 565 miles. On foot, and walking about 25 miles a day, the journey probably takes about twenty days if Jonah is fit. Most likely, someone helped him though, perhaps a man hauling animals or textiles from the busy port of Jaffa. He and several other tradesmen probably picked up Jonah the hitch hiker, thumbing his way across country. Can you imagine Jonah's appearance? Skin parched white, clothed in rags, and his hair half missing and bleached? Yet, people help him. "It is good to wait patiently for the saving help of *Adonai*" (Lamentations 3:26). Here are two more traveling-prophet heroes....

Ezekiel was with the Israelite exiles when God called him from Heaven (v. 1). And God called Jeremiah, saying: "Before I formed you in the womb, I knew you; before you were born, I separated you for myself" (Jeremiah 1:5). Let us be reminded, every minute of every day, and every path we take, we are called through Christ to be messengers of Christ to everyone, whether they're waiting or walking. It's our wonderful purpose. At least we're not living in the days of old when we had to ride over bumpy roads in horse-drawn carriages or on a donkey as Mary endured while expecting Jesus.

Jesus, help us show kindness at all times. Amen.

OCTOBER 14
GENERIC AVAILABLE

You know it when you taste generic. There's a slight difference in fizz in Mr. Pibb, blandness in the Great Value peanut butter, less "barbeque-ness" in the Kroger potato chips, and a wilting quality in the off-brand French Fried Onions I use in my green bean casserole. Yuck. Buying generic, we saved money, but many times at the cost of our taste buds, quality. It's a balancing act. Quality vs. savings … when do we sacrifice and how do we decide when to spend extra?

The debate happened in my house yesterday after we bought an off-brand inexpensive butter. The saltiness was profound. My son exclaimed, "What's this? Hard yellow oil?" Oh-oh. We forced it down our throats, but vowed, "Never again, even if butter costs $4.15 cents a pound today when last year it was $2.75 a pound."

The "real things" are accelerating in price—called inflation—like rockets flaring on the 4th. But they're food for our bodies, not our souls. "How blessed are those who hunger and thirst for righteousness! They will be filled" (Matthew 5:6).

What might be generic to us Christians that we need to run from fast in order to produce quality in our lives?

Jesus talks about "The fake" quite often. He warns us about their flashing and dazzling colors offering us pleasures but at the cost of our souls. "Beware of the false prophets! They come to you wearing sheep's clothing, but underneath they are hungry wolves" (Matthew 7:15)! False prophets appear like the real thing, but they're "hungry wolves." What's that mean?

I remember a TV evangelist I used to watch before I trusted Christ. She talked about harmonizing with God, God's love for everyone, and how our attitudes needed modifying. If we could do specific things—adjust our attitudes; think positively; and, change our perceptions of people, events, and circumstances—we'll be happy, content, and experience Heaven right now. Is she right? Is that all we need to do? Well, I made those changes several times but continued to spiral down into misery—Hell on Earth—and still feel empty, disgusting, and miserable. She was false, *fake*. "After I leave, savage wolves will come in among you" (Acts 20:29). We need Jesus, and to read His words. They are our shield from all the fakes and faulty messages in this world.

Jesus, help us discern the wolves, and flee. Amen.

October 15
Dance Studio

Remember the art, music, or dance lessons you used to take, or the sports you played as a child? Those were the times when you experimented with what might fit into your life that you'd liked.

When I was four I took ballet lessons. I remember crossing my arms and *plié*, a dance movement. But I could never *plié* and *demi-plié*. I didn't have the right hip-and-joint configuration, and my feet wouldn't align as the instructor directed. *Topple tumble.* Embarrassing. What was one of your embarrassing moments? "Even in laughter the heart can be sad, and joy may end in sorrow" (Proverbs 14:13).

I remember feeling devastated. I wanted to be a ballerina. Every little girl gets pajamas or bedspreads with ballerinas, right? My disproportionate body type turned out to be hard lesson and realization number one. Many more came thereafter: my try at the swim team; my goal to be an exchange student in Germany [The deciding team for some reason didn't chose me.]; understanding atoms in high school chemistry; and, my anxiety while singing onstage that crushed my dream of being a singer. So, I gave up. I went in a bad direction and killed more chances at accomplishing *other* dreams. "You are to tell them that *Adonai* says: 'If a person falls, doesn't he get up again? If someone goes astray, doesn't he turn back?' "(Jeremiah 8:4). I was seventeen, and lost. Who is capable of making choices of a lifetime at 17? Today, we'd say no one.

The *best* choice in my life was accepting that Jesus Christ died for me. I have eternity. *We* have eternity. Paul offers advice my parents and church leaders should have told me. "Do not let yourselves be conformed to the standards of the 'olam hazeh [this world]. Instead, keep letting yourselves be transformed by the renewing of your minds; so that you will know what God wants and will agree that what he wants is good, satisfying and able to succeed" (Romans 12:2). Now here's a different view of success. Having perfect feet position, singing onstage, discerning atomic structures, peer acceptance, or winning at competitive sports are peoples' standards. What does God want for us? Everything good and satisfying. *His* will is for us to succeed, by *His* standards. That's a promise we can cling to when we stay in His perfect word and trust Him.

Lord Jesus Christ, direct the Holy Spirit in us so we can use the gifts you've given us to advance your kingdom. Amen.

OCTOBER 16
SPEED PASS

SpeedPass is a little thumb-sized sensor I can use when I buy gas. I simply pump the fuel, wave the little whistle-sized device under a scanner, and voila, easy transaction. More has happened in capability since SpeedPass appeared that's supposed to make our lives easier: iPhone payment apps; scan coupons; hashtag ads, etc.

Do you use any of these? There could be problems with 'em!

I recently downloaded a Starbuck's app into my iPhone 5C. Now, I can load the app with money and buy coffee by scanning my phone app with the Starbuck's store's app. The capability is spreading in popularity like TV did in the 1950s.

Until a store's firewall gets hacked, and our identities become compromised. Oh no! "You, *Adonai*, are a shield for me. You are my glory. You lift my head high" (Psalm 3:4). God is our rock and shield, our fortress, watch tower, and perfect source of comfort.

Hackers can suck computer codes out of *anything* with their special devices. The criminals can morph a picture into code, upload it to their devices, and then snatch our accounts and misuse them. We're *all* targets, and money-making opportunities to them. It's scary, and can leave us feeling quite vulnerable.

When Paul was preaching the Gospel, he encountered these same problems. He didn't have a portable device, of course, but con artists lived two thousand years ago. What did he do?

Early Christians living in the port city of Thessalonica were used to charlatans and swindlers. "The appeal we make does not flow from error or from impure motives. ... Never did we employ flattering talk, nor put on a false front to mask greed" (1 Thessalonians 2:3-6). As a sales rep at the mall can perform disappearing tricks to sell a magic kit, and an astrologer can interpret the future in the stars, and a psychic can commune with to dead, or a false teacher can spread false Christian doctrine information; the Christians in Thessalonica were tired of being lied to, conned, and victimized. So much so that, "When you heard the Word of God from us, you received it not merely as a human word, but as it truly is, God's Word" (1 Thessalonians 2:13). They were so fed up with frauds, they hungrily embraced God's truth passionately. I think Paul missed these people the most, and he teaches *us* to be on guard.

Holy Spirit, help us see everything fake and false. Amen.

OCTOBER 17
UTILIZE EASEMENT

Behind my house there's a small natural habitat or preserve. Beyond it, electric poles and utility wires. Eagles like to nest back there, and turtles make the place their home, and snakes and squirrels. Lately, the oak tree in my front yard has been blossoming with acorns—a squirrel's delight. My roof has become Squirrel Highway for the critters to transport their treats. I hear them—*pit pat tap tat tat*—across my roof. After a while, the noise and mess become tiresome.

Is there anything annoying around your yard? How about an irritation or lingering problem that just refuses to resolve? To me, the squirrel aggravation is a back itch I can't reach to scratch.

I went to my driveway this morning to clean up their "acorn garbage." Sweeping under the tree, I got kerplunked on top o' my head. Acorn kernels are hard, inside and out. The squirrels like the green skin more than the yellow inside. Either that or they're like fat picky kings, so satisfied with the overabundance that they're taking one bite and then tossing them to the ground. I wish the pesky squirrels would just disappear. I keep contriving ways ... to get rid of 'em. While standing under the tree, wishing I had an ax and dodging shells, I asked God: Did anyone ever disappear from the Earth without dying?

I found my answers. One person was Enoch. In the Complete Jewish Bible, his name is Hanokh which means, *initiated*. "Hanokh walked with God, and then he wasn't there, because God took him" (Genesis 5: 24 and Hebrews 11:5). Tell me more about this guy, will ya God? What did he do that was so special? Let's look at another person God took. "Suddenly, there appeared a fiery chariot and ... Elijah went up into heaven in a whirlwind" (2 Kings 2:11). These two people obviously had such special relationships with God that God did *not* want them experiencing death. A *walk* with God means eternal life. God has that much power. He commands Life. He communes with souls. Our Lord's power and dominion over life, death *and* eternity is unfathomable, but so very real. Elijah and Enoch are still in Heaven. As believers in Christ, we will also share in their glory. One day, maybe we'll talk with these Biblical giants (Romans 5:2). Glory to God in the highest.

Lord, you are all powerful over the forces in the universe. Amen.

OCTOBER 18
ADOPT A ROAD

Years ago I read a book called *The Road Less Traveled*. M. Scott Peck opens his book with the phrase, "Life is difficult."

Yesterday, someone gave me a string of criticism about one of my books. She was reading it with editing eyes and not from the perspective of a reader, for enjoyment. If I make *her* changes, I'll cripple my "voice" *and* characters. I'll have to scrap the entire book. In her hands, my book is a land mine, and she's a mine detective combing it with her bomb detector. Everything needs to be exploded, for a price. My anxiety increased threefold. I tried self-talk to deal with the pummeling. I've re-written the book ten times already. Even the newspaper contains errors. This lady just writes children's books, so what does she know about my genre? I cried, and then after a long, hard agitated day, my husband said, "Turn it over to God." I could be re-writing the book a hundred times. "With his mouth the hypocrite can ruin his neighbor, but by knowledge the righteous are delivered" (Proverbs 11:9).

What do you do when you feel attacked?

How do you defend yourself?

"My God, my Lord! Defend me and my cause" (Psalm 35:23)!

The Israelites were attacked physically, psychologically, and spiritually from all sides. They faced powerful armies with false beckoning gods. According to *Bible Gateway*, an on-line Bible resource, the Israelites had a total of 8,728 enemies. Today, the Jewish people continue to fear for their lives and Israel. However, in the Old Testament, God saved them time-after-time. "Adonai is around his people henceforth and forever" (Psalm 125:2); "That we should be delivered from our enemies and from the power of all who hate us" (Luke 1:71).

How can we claim God's strength and power to fight against fear, uncertainty, and doubt? As Christians, we can cling to a promise. "You did not receive a spirit of slavery to bring you back again into fear ... you received the Spirit who makes us sons, and by whose power we cry out, *Abba*" (Romans 8:15)! Abba means Father, Daddy. I can go to God as a child and ask for his help in all my troubling times. Criticisms will *never* pass until I leave this world.

Jesus, we let you have all our worries and anxieties. Please help us show *your* face to people today. Amen.

OCTOBER 19
TRUNK OR TREAT

Yesterday, I attended a *huge* church function, a community gathering for Halloween. While walking toward decorated cars and trucks with candy stuffed in their trunks, my husband noticed an earring on the sidewalk. The earring wasn't expensive, but someone was missing its dangling amber presence.

"Let's walk around and see if we can find the match," I told him.

You really get to notice people when you try to match them with their missing property. Meantime, I kept wondering, Does the woman know her earring is missing yet?

Have you ever lost something while out in a public and began searching wildly to find it? So many things can be lost. "These days would be remembered and observed throughout every generation, every family, every province and every city, that these days of *Purim* would never cease among the Jews or their memory be lost by their descendants" (Esther 9:28).

I put myself in the woman's shoes. I, too, have lost things. *We might be passing by each other,* I kept thinking. I wished the wind were a person, or the trees endowed with consciousness because I could ask *them* to search for her from *their* high perspectives. Giving up, I turned the earring into Lost and Found. But even when indoors, while facilitating a ring-toss game, I looked for her. I told my husband, "Praise God that he always knows *our* whereabouts.

I'm reminded of the Old Testament woman, Hannah. She couldn't have children, but desperately wanted a boy. It's like she and God were passing in the night. She never gave up hope though and continued praying: "If you will give your servant a male child, I will give him to [You] for as long as he lives" (1 Samuel 1:1-20). Her prayer to God strikes at the core of worship to our God whom we can't see but who surrounds us and speaks to us through his Holy Spirit. "The earth's pillars belong to Adonai; on them he has placed the world" (1 Samuel 1:8). God sees everything and has no boundaries. Later in the story, God calls Samuel to choose Saul as King of Israel. Thereafter, He anoints David as King. When God spoke to Samuel, he always responded with, "Here I am" (1 Samuel 3: 1-21). As a prophet, he had steadfast faith, belief, and confidence in God. He always *knew* God and where to find Him.

Lord, give us more faith so we can know your presence. Amen.

OCTOBER 20
MASSAGE

Are you stressed? Now and then, I get stressed. There's an option for relief. "'You looked for much, but it came to little. And when you brought it home, I blew it away. Why?' asks *Adonai-Tzva'ot*. 'Because my house lies in ruins, while every one of you runs to take care of his own house'" (Haggai 1:9). God wants us focused on Him.

In every ten-mile radius, there must be at *least* one business offering massages. They used to be called "parlors;" but today that has a sour ring, so now they're massage therapies, wellness centers, and spas. And the more degrees and experience in these therapies you have, the more clients you'll attract and money you'll make. To *de*-stress is the rage: check into a hotel that has a spa and let all your stressful troubles slough off your back and trickle out of your mind.

I once did such a thing when I attended a writers' conference in Maui. I stayed at the Grand Wailea and paid $50.00 to enjoy their Spa Grande that had five bathes (mineral, mud) and waterfall showers. A day to remember. Then I had to return to the Real World, trials and tribulations. There's a saying: no matter where ya go, there ya are. Jesus tells us: "United with me, you may have shalom [peace]. In the world, you have *tsuris*. But be brave! I have conquered the world" (John 16:33)! Jesus exclaims these two vital sentences.

The word, *tsuris*, originates in the Hebrew word, *tsarah*, which means *trouble*. Its synonym, *litzrot*, means, *to become narrow*, or, *to be in a tight place*. I think of walls closing in around me, a squishing, confining, terrifying feeling, real anxiety. In the book, *The Joys of Yiddish* by Leo Rosten, the word *tsuris* is plural. It can transcend the realm of the individual to include a nation. "The word is used liberally in connection with illness, money woes, relationships and especially children." Author Eileen Lavine wrote an article for the online magazine momentmag.com, entitled "Nobody Knows the Tsuris I've Seen." In Jewish circles the word is used liberally to describe areas where real hurts can generate life-threatening stresses. Jesus prays to his Father: "I made your name known to them ... so that the love with which you have loved me may be in them" (John 17:24-26). Jesus conquers the world and all its *tsuris* with his love for you and me. When we unite with him and the power of his words, our stresses change. Jesus truly is the only therapist.

Lord, we aim to stay in your word and be a stress-free. Amen.

OCTOBER 21
SUNSHINE STATE

The sun's shining right now, so stop what you're doing for a second and take a little peek outside into the fresh air. Today is a day of gratitude. We're alive, thanks to our Creator, Elohim. *El* means *mighty/strong*; and, *ohim*, means, *Creator* (Genesis 1:1). Yes, we are alive and breathing, thank you, Elohim, Creator God. "Haven't you known, haven't you heard that the everlasting God, *Adonai*, the Creator of the ends of the earth, does not grow tired or weary? His understanding cannot be fathomed" (Isaiah 40:28).

We slept through another night and awoke this morning, and breathed. No matter what our troubles are, we are alive, this second.

Maybe it's fall where you're at with a crisp breeze blowing. Where I'm at, the sun's rays are shimmering over my neighbor's rooftop. Through the pine trees in my backyard, beams of God rays are firing awake the green pine needles. Where ever you are, breathe deeply, and know this moment is God given. The Lord of the Universe is infusing every living thing and atom with life and energy. You have this second, right now. And most likely, you'll have the entire day. Some people won't. They'll die. Yet our Father continues to remind who is in charge of every pine cone, bee, and light.

The first thing God creates is light. "Let there be light; and there was light" (Genesis 1:3). Do you know it takes over 100,000 years for a photon to travel from the core of the Sun to the surface? But from there, light takes a little over eight minutes to touch your skin. I wonder how God felt that day when he held sunlight in his glorious hands. "God saw that the light was good, and God divided the light from the darkness" (verse 4). A entire eighteen verses in the first chapter of Genesis have to do with light. The sun is that important to our survival as a species. Everything else stems from light energy, like flowers need roots and animals need plants. "God put them in the dome of the sky to give light to the earth" (verse 17). Even at night, God realizes we need moon light and star light. *Night* and *light* rhyme. But we don't live outdoors, so God provides us with indoor light. "People couldn't see each other, and no one went anywhere for three days. But all the people of Israel had light in their homes" (Exodus 10:23). All of his creation ... He pronounced "very good" (1: 31). We are his created works, His designs.

Lord, let us acknowledge your creation wonders. Amen.

OCTOBER 22
WORKERS AHEAD

When we first moved to Florida, while we were house hunting, we lived in an apartment complex around a tiny lake, actually a retention pond. Such waters are magnets for the beautiful bird. I began enjoying their splendor. One morning, I took our dog, Sparkle, for a walk. I heard a large *quaaawk*, and guttural rattling screams. "What's that?"

Sparkle stopped in her tracks. The sounds reverberated through the entire complex. Drivers on the freeway could hear them.

Have you ever been surprised by strange sounds or new surroundings that make you feel like you've landed on an alien world? There are so many exotic beautiful places to enjoy, if we open ourselves up to experiencing them. What haven't you notice today? "You have eyes—don't you see? You have ears—don't you hear (Mark 8:18)?

As Sparkle and I rounded a corner of the lake, I suddenly spotted the noise makers: two, three-foot-tall gray birds with long slender necks, and their baby bird. Sand Cranes have a small red crown on their heads. I had to wonder, Does God say anything about birds in the Bible other than in Genesis when He says, "Let the water swarm with swarms of living creatures, and let birds fly above the earth in the open dome of the sky" (Genesis 1:20)? Definitely, the Sand Crane is one majestic breed God saved during the Flood. And they're also vulnerable ... to people and car hits.

Last year, some of those cranes liked to walk across a busy intersection and peck cars. Conservationists tried relocating their nest, but the awful happened. Someone struck one of the cranes, and then his mate died. I was rooting for their safety, but death took them. I wonder how God views his bird creations. "And to every wild animal, bird in the air and creature crawling on the earth, in which there is a living soul, I am giving as food every kind of green plant" (Genesis 1:30). He gives birds souls. I never see a mention of animals going to Heaven; but I have to believe they must, or He must provide some type of special place for them after they die. Every living thing has a soul. Now, I don't want mosquitos, cockroaches or fire ants in Heaven, but I know we'll see Sand Cranes. Yes.

Lord, today help us see the wonder and awe of your mighty creation hand. Amen.

October 23
Buy Your Yearbook

I don't like looking at my high school pictures. Do you? It's like staring into the eyes of a stranger. You either wanna reach back in time and slap the person for making this-mistake-or-that-mistake, or hug the person for making the best choice ever. "Joshua wrote these words in the book of the Torah of God. Then he took a big stone and set it up there under the oak next to the sanctuary of Adonai. ... This stone will be a witness against you, in case you deny your God" (Joshua 24:25-28). God is our unchanging Rock.

As a teenager I didn't have a clue about the hard knocks of life. I had a bed, food, and time to sew, paint, and play the piano. I also went to ceramics class with my stepmom Tuesday nights for several years. We painted presents for relatives and cute pieces for the house. My dad still has the popcorn bowl I decorated in his kitchen cabinet. Still, a scroll of my pictures from seventh through twelfth grade is like hearing fingernails scratch across a blackboard. Recall Daniel the prophet? He is so different in the way he views his past.

In about 596 BCE, the King of Babylon conquers Jerusalem and picks the top Jewish gifted boys to train as his attendants. Daniel must be about 13 when he's kidnapped. He never sees Israel again. I can just imagine God's ultimate yearbook entry about Daniel while guiding him into his kingdom as follows:

"Daniel served four kings, and interpreted life-changing dreams for them which changed nations: Nebuchadnezzar (597 BCE), Belshazzar, Darius, and Cyrus (530 BCE). He served those kings well, from 597 BCE to 530 BCE. Sixty-seven years. He was captured at 13, and lived to the ripe age of 79. All the while, Daniel tugged at my heart strings. He had a great technique of disobeying famous people without exasperating them. He could weave words, and reframe perspectives to remain true to Me (Daniel 1:17). He delivered all my messages and dream interpretations to kings, and made me known to pagan nations. Daniel's prayerfulness always touched my heart. 'Blessed be the name of God from eternity past to eternity future. ... I give thank and praise you, God of my ancestors, for giving me wisdom and power ... and the answer' (2:20—23). Now, join me my good and faithful servant for always trusting me (1:17)." When we stand before God, what might God say about us?

Lord, help us stick to our convictions. Amen.

OCTOBER 24
SANDS OF TIME

The week *before* we turn back our clocks for Daylight Savings Time is my favorite time of the year. I've had fifty-six of these types of years, minus four, because I lived in Hawaii which doesn't observe DST. However, "on the mainland," I relish these early in-between-time mornings. The air is crisp, but not too cold. The sun peeks over the horizon at just the right time to go outside and inhale God's air. The nippy atmosphere undulating through rustling leaves ignites the birds into action. I pray at these times. My soul is filled with God's magnificence. His creation *sings*. Can you hear them? "*Adonai*, what you do makes me happy. I take joy in what your hands have made. How great are your deeds, Adonai! How very deep your thoughts (Psalm 92:4-5)! Today, do you feel his marvels? I'm remind me of the hymn, "All Things Bright and Beautiful," by Cecil F. Alexander. If you know the melody, you can sing it. It's also on YouTube: *All things bright and beautiful, All creatures great and small, All things wise and wonderful. The Lord God made them all.*

When I watched the YouTube video, a child was singing the song. How the Lord must be so overjoyed when we sing to Him. "He who trusts in *Adonai* will be raised high above danger" (Proverbs 29:25). We're *His* little children. Do you ever just sing to God spontaneously? When I'm feeling down, singing one of my favorite hymns improves my mood. Try it. You'll see. Singing works on our brain's limbic system, which is responsible for our emotions. "Spring up, oh well! Sing to the well" (Numbers 21:17)! The Holy Spirit is our spiritual well, lifting our needs and songs of praise to God.

One of the greatest singers must have been David. He wrote 150 songs, called *Tehillim* in Hebrew, meaning, *praises*. When we sing to God, we are praising him. "How good it is to sing praises to our God! How sweet, how fitting to praise him!" (Psalm 147:1.

I took these verses to heart last week. I was feeling a bit glum. I didn't want to get out of bed, and anxiety was churning in my stomach. I could not locate the epicenter of what in my life might be pinning me to my bed. Still, I crawled out of bed, walked into the perfect fall setting, looked into the sun's rays, illuminating His creations and proclaimed: "*All things bright and beautiful, the Lord God made them all.*" Repeat. Wow—it worked, and I could move on.

Jesus, let us sing spontaneous songs from our souls. Amen.

OCTOBER 25
LET'S GO PLACES

We live a little distance beyond the Indian River, a place where white sailboats skim the water, their tall sails outstretched like lifting arms embracing the powerful wind. Gliding pelicans and squawking seagulls snuggle belly close to the lapping water. As egrets dive beak-first into the ocean for food, a few flying fish launch out of the gray-blue water like ballet dancers through Fall's crisp air. Jesus *is* with us … and we can know Him. "They weren't thirsty when he led them through the deserts. He made water flow from the rock for them— He split the rock, and out gushed the water" (Isaiah 48:21).

Water. It's as important as light in sustaining us. Try cupping it in your hand, letting your fingers be a sieve. Water….

The Spirit of God hovered over it (Genesis 1: 2). Before God said, "Let there be light," there was darkness on "the face of the deep," and only water. In Hebrew, "darkness," in this context is, *choshech*. The second time choshech appears is when God wants his people free from Egyptian slavery. In Exodus 10:21-23, he spreads "darkness over the land." He institutes a state of existence prior to creation when the earth is, *tohu v'vohu*, unformed and a void. There was nothingness. God changed nothing … into water.

I'm reminded of a TV show called *The Universe*, and an episode, "Search for E.T." The narrator is certain, water is essential for life on *any* planet. According to Dr. Andrew Weil, our bodies are composed of 60% water. Water has unique chemical and physical properties: H_2O is comprised of two atoms of hydrogen and one atom of oxygen. Water is in the air, the ocean, and beneath us in aqueducts. Hawaii, for example, depends on abundant rainfall to infuse its aqueducts with drinking water. In a drought, people and animals die. All life extinguishes. That happening now, we'll need another place.

Jesus said: "Whoever drinks the water I will give him will never be thirsty again! On the contrary, the water I give him will become a spring of water inside him, welling up into eternal life" (John 4:14)! This water is Jesus's baptismal water. He said these words "near the field Jacob had given to his son Joseph" (John 4:5). You remember the story about Joseph. His brothers threw him into a well to die! But the well becomes life, through Jesus, our *living* spiritual water.

Jesus, as we drink water throughout today, remind us to give thanks to you for life. Amen.

OCTOBER 26
STAR GUIDE

In 2008, I traveled with my husband to Israel. Have you ever wanted desperately to visit to just *one* place? I did, and prayed hard to make a pilgrimage there that I said to God, "I'll *never* ask to go anywhere else if you just let me go to Israel." We flew to Israel. Thanks, God.

"God will be with me and will guard me on this road that I am traveling, giving me bread to eat and clothes to wear" (Genesis 28:20). Israel was that place for me. Maybe *your* dream voyage might be to travel to Mars and pray to God on its regolith surface ... or another outer space mission. God will be there (Psalm 91:11).

From our Israeli hotel balcony, we could see the Mediterranean Sea, boats in a little harbor, and people swimming and frolicking on the long shoreline from Tel Aviv to Joppa. But when I went down to put my feet in the water so I could say I touched the Mediterranean Sea, I saw trash bags, floating wood, and plastic bottles. Yuck. I was hoping the Dead Sea would be a better experience, as well as another stop on our *Footsteps of Our Lord* tour, the Sea of Galilee. The latter was the place I couldn't wait for the boat to launch.

Galilee is a transit zone, an area encompassing upper, lower, and western parts of the area. The word, *galil*, means *district* and *circle*. People must pass through Galilee to travel through Israel. Thus Jesus and his disciples must have visited this area often. What a view they had. We saw it too. Bordering Israel and Lebanon is a mountain range with Mount Hermon as its highest peak. The runoff is a vital drinking source. Mount Gilboa boarders the area of Galilee on the north. It's where King Saul charged the Philistines. Runoff from both mountains feed the Sea of Galilee. The name has changed because of past kings and Roman conquerors, but *they* didn't walk on water, command the wind, and alter the elements as Jesus did. At Galilee, he chose Peter and Andrew (Matthew 4:18). He rested there (Matthew 15:29), and our Lord demonstrated his power on that 33 mile-in-diameter Sea of Galilee (Matthew 14:2).

I saw that grand sea, originally called the Sea of Kinneret. Supposedly, it's in the shape of a harp or lyre, thus the root word *kinnor*. But when the captain launched his Jesus Boat from the dock, commencing our tour, I breathed in the air and felt the water spray on my face. We began singing, out of sheer joy and praise.

Jesus, we want to praise you every day. Amen.

October 27
Vote Early

Today I voted early. I could have waited, but I knew the candidates for whom I wanted to vote. Also, I wanted the process over and done with. You ever want something just over and done?

"*Adonai* said in his heart, 'I will never again curse the ground because of humankind, since the imaginings of a person's heart are evil from his youth. Nor will I ever again destroy all living things, as I have done' " (Genesis 8:21). We hear, from God's own heart, one thing he did at a time when he wanted *everyone*, over and done with. He vowed not to "destroy all living things" again.

We entered the library, voted, and then I stuck my completed form into the computer so it could tally my vote. There, done.

Nope. Have you ever had technology fail, rendering you stuck? The machine spit out my form! The clerk dashed over. "It doesn't like your card for some reason." She fed it back into the machine. The monitor cycled 'round-n-round, then spit my card into her hand. She then tried feeding my form into another machine. The machine sucked it in like a vacuum, wherein it stuck deep down inside. She knocked it, *twice*. By then, I had *two* polling reps at my side. The manager unleashed her special key, unlocked the machine, and tried grabbing my form. Oops, the machine guzzled it down, and the word *uncounted* flashed on the monitor. She assured me, however, my vote would be counted at the "center." I'll never know.

There were times Jesus had to appear in front of a court, magistrate, or Roman official (Luke 2:1). Before that, the Hebrews had to register with the High Priest and give God an offering (Exodus 30:12-13). In Numbers 26:2, a census is important because men had to register for the military. Even the clan or tribe you were in was important (numbers 26:2), and keeping track of ancestral land was vital (Numbers 26:62). However, it appears a person could not run for office as candidates do today. All leaders were appointed by "the king," prophet, or high priest. Numbers 17:17 indicates that a leadership position was inherited. In Judges, Chapters 4 and 5, we learn Deborah ruled over Israel for forty years. So, even though my voter card might slip through the cracks, God ultimately rules. "Just and true are your ways, king of the nations" (Revelation 15:5)!

Lord, help us remember your authority over all nations. Amen.

OCTOBER 28
INSTALLATION AVAILABLE

Have you ever had a God-centered dream?

"I will pour out my Spirit on all humanity. Your sons and daughters will prophesy, your old men will dream dreams, your young men will see visions" (Joel 3:1).

My husband woke up early this morning and told me he'd had a wild dream as follows:

He and I were with God prior to creation, and God sent us forward in time to interview people about their favorite animals. Then we'd return to God and tell him about our experiences so God could create animals. Fascinating, huh? Then my husband suggested we write a Christian science-fiction book about the story. I told him, "Bible-believing Christians might see your wild installment of God's story as kicking a hornet's nest."

We laughed, but our dabbling in fiction made me wonder about a few Bible characters who experienced visions that must have appeared far-fetched.

Ezekiel saw Nature in the raw: windy storms; a huge cloud with flashing fire; creatures with four faces and four wings; wheels inside wheels; and, a valley of bones re-forming into a massive living army (chapter 37). Today, anyone hearing Ezekiel might suggest he take meds. "Now we see in a mirror, dimly, but then face to face. Now I know in part, but then I shall know just as I also am known" (1 Corinthians 13:12).

People who have visions, wild dreams of God and Heaven, or claim to see angels are often ridiculed. But what about John's visions in Revelation? And Jacob wrestling with an angel? Mighty changes occurred because Jacob met God face-to-face and survived. The story ends with God renaming Jacob, *Israel*, meaning, *he who struggles with God* (Genesis 32:22-32). John's Revelation is a gradual unveiling of the future. He tells us what happened to him (Revelation 1:9-11). And then Jesus appears. His message to humanity is clear: "I know what you are doing—you have a reputation for being alive, but in fact you are dead! Wake up, and strengthen what remains, before it dies too." (Revelation 3:1-2). Our souls will be alive although we will one day die. What are your dreams? Write them down, and pray for revelation. The Lord is talking to you in those moments.

Father, help us know your will and how we can change. Amen.

October 29
Bargains (Part I)

Have you ever felt yourself spinning at-the-wheel with what you're doing in life, *with* your life?

Almost every day I get up believing my writing is a waste of time. I envision myself aging, inching up the scale to 100 years of life expectancy. Considering I abused my body with junk and smokes, I have about twenty-four years left, God willing. God, help! "You are to offer daily, for seven days, the food of the offering made by fire, making a fragrant aroma for Adonai" (Numbers 28:24). What can I offer you, God except for everything deep within me? Have you ever said that? He answers....

Recalling bits-and-pieces from childhood, I was *never* concerned about turning one day older. Actually, I couldn't wait for another birthday, could you? "Presents!"

Now, I feel Time pushing my face against a gray spongy wall. There's a yellow neon sign above my wrinkling skin with the words: *What should I be doing?* I ask the question: Are my daily actions—work—advancing His Kingdom? It's a soul question. What's your soul question you keep asking God? He answers....

This may take a few days, so let's go on a journey.

Time is a measure people scientifically contrived to keep track of the twenty-four hours Earth rotates on its axes and revolves around the Sun. Interpret these motions as hours, minutes, seconds, etc., and you have Time, ticking in strokes on your clock or flashes on your digital screen. Before Earth, there was no time. In space, no time. Beyond the Milky Way? If your space traveling, you better find a way to replicate our God-given circadian cycles or we can't survive, at least the way our technology stands. But I'm talking about time and His will for our lives, so I'll move on.

We have *seasons* on Earth. Immediately, I think of Ecclesiastes, Solomon's autobiography. Here must lie wisdom; after all, God gave Solomon wisdom as his heart's desire (1 Kings 4:29). "For everything there is a season," he writes (Ecclesiastes 3: 1), "and a right time for every intention under heaven." I read on to find *my* current season, "A time to search and a time to give up" (3:6). Actually, verses 1 through 8 are seasons *each* person experiences in a lifetime. I'll focus on this one, as it pertains to my question: "Am I wasting time, God?"

Lord, give us direction on the season of our lives. Amen.

God Designed

October 30
Bargains (Part II)

We are "called" by God to use our talents (1 Thessalonians 1:11-12), and He gives us tasks (Colossians 4:17). We each have a purpose. "We are made of God's making, created in union with the Messiah Yeshua for a life of good actions" (Ephesians 2:10). We each have a spiritual gift, too. "We have gifts that differ and which are meant to be used according to the grace that has been given to us" (Romans 12:6-8). These gifts come from the Holy Spirit who "manifests to each person for the common good" (1 Corinthians 12:4-7).

Have you ever asked the question: "What should I be doing?"

The first answer appears simple. God has *already* prepared a purpose for us. It began when He fashioned us. We are, God Designed. "He did this in order to make known the riches of his glory to those who are the objects of his mercy, whom he prepared in advance for glory" (Romans 9:23). One purpose is to glorify Him, in what we do and who we are. Give God glory.

Think of the odds of being conceived. Any other person with our father and mother's genes could be standing in our place. But God chose you and me. His divine hands are working in our lives. He "called us to a life of holiness as his people. It was not because of our deeds, but because of his own purpose ... which he gave to us who are united with the Messiah Yeshua. He did this before the beginning of time" (2 Timothy 1:9).

What about the purpose for *my* life? Looking at paragraph one, I have a calling. A "calling" is "a strong inner impulse toward a particular course of action." That strong inner impulse is the Holy Spirit, communicating to us (1 Corinthians 12:4-7). Where should I direct my purpose? The answer is, "the common good." "Tasks," "good actions," and "holiness" are purposes in life. Finally, the puzzle pieces are forming one nice picture. But there's one left to solve, and it's in Ecclesiastes. The book is a bit dismal. We live, we die, and the cycle goes on like the Earth keeps revolving and rotating. However, I find one verse helpful that answers my question. "There is nothing better for a [person] to do than eat, drink and let [yourself] enjoy the good that results from [your] work. I also realized that this [work] is from God's hand" (2:24). Are you enjoying your work or church ministry? What are the results? We have our answers then.

Lord, if we do not enjoy our work, show us another path. Amen.

J.P. Osterman

October 31
Everything Halloween

I remember my first trick-or-treat. Can you recall yours?

The first Halloween I remember experiencing occurred when I was six-years-old. *Lassie* had ended in black-and-white, and a capricious swirling of snow was stirring through the air. I had one of those flimsy plastic masks with holes for eyes and a mouth. To keep it in place on my face, the mask had a little rubber string fastened on both sides that I could stretch around my head. Playing with the mask earlier in the day, I broke the string. I cried, and my aunt fixed it with tape. *Whew*, problem solved. That night, I went out into the cold darkness with a little bag dangling in my hands. Running from house-to-house, I passed little Indians, cowboys, and white-sheeted Casper ghosts. Everyone was excited. Candy for a year! Still, no one knew who'd be behind all those closed doors we were knocking on and saying: "Trick or treat." We were all naïve compared to today's saw-and-sword wielding monsters and theatrically-contrived aliens.

Remember some of the creatures Jesus faced? They were Devil-spawned. "Many people held in the power of demons were brought to him. He expelled the spirits with a word" (Matthew 8:16).

Jesus saw hellish creatures and called them out for us. "I saw Sagan falling like lightning from heaven" (Luke 10:18). He tells us Satan's personality: "He [is] a murderer, and he tells lies, and he speaks in character because he's a liar—indeed, the inventor of the lie" (John 8:44). Scary, huh? There's a world all around us we can't see, something like the places behind closed doors. John tells us Satan's appearance: "The great dragon was thrown out ... known as the Devil and the Adversary, the deceiver of the world" (Revelation 12:9). Jesus calls Satan: the abomination that causes devastation" (Matthew 24:15; Mark 13:14). We battle the Devil. "Help us, God."

Jesus tells us: "I have given you authority; so you can trample down ... all the Enemy's forces; and you will remain completely unharmed" (Luke 10:19). We need to think from God's perspective through His word, not "human perspective" (Matthew 16:23). Paul says we struggle against "spiritual forces of evil" (Ephesians 6:12). We must stay alert and fight sin through reading and absorbing God's holy Word (1 Peter 5:8). He helps us, and with the Holy Spirit, we can see and fight the sinful luring around us (1 Corinthians 10:13).

Lord, help us see evil as a devouring lion. Amen.

NOVEMBER 1
HURRICANE SHELTER

"I'm not used to this wind," I told my husband this morning. After living with months of balmy weather, have you ever stepped outside to a surprising and startling 60°?

I wonder about the most extreme weather changes in the *Bible*. "'Prepare your chariot,'" Elijah orders Ahab, "'and get down the mountain before the rain stops you!' A little later, the sky grew black with clouds and wind; and heavy rain began falling" (1 Kings 18:45).

In the battle to gain the Promised Land, God makes the sun and moon stand still because He was fighting for Israel (Joshua 10:12-14). Imagine such a magnanimous day. The Earth is neither rotating on its axis, nor revolving around the sun. You might exclaim, "No way!" Let's look at some scientific facts that God had to alter in order to stop and hold still celestial bodies.

A spot on the Earth is actually moving 1,040 miles per hour, and the Earth is speeding around the sun at about 67,062 miles per hour. Gravity keeps us on solid ground and unable to feel this motion. For Joshua and the Israelites, God made all those movements of the sun, Earth, and moon synchronize perfectly so as to keep them in *one* spot and *one* continuous motion in deep space. Then, people believed the Earth was flat. That day 4,000 years ago, God proved it is *round*. Then there is another alteration of the Sun God instigates at another time in history. He makes a strange darkness spread across the land as one of the ten plagues against the Egyptians to make Pharaoh free the Israelites. No one could work. This was important. The Israelites were Pharaoh's slave labor. But for three days, Darkness "could be felt" (Exodus 10:21-23), darkness through which they couldn't see a thing but was touching them. They were groping around, bumping into one another. Imagine smack off "things" you can't see. *Darkness.* God had attacked their "sun god Ra. Ra lost. This darkness is the same in two places: Genesis 1:2, "The earth was unformed and void, darkness was on the face of the deep, and the Spirit of God hovered over the surface of the water;" and, "darkness so thick it can be felt" (Exodus 10:21). This darkness is suffocating. A total absence of light, as if bodies could almost lift off Earth and float into space ... if not for God. His hands ground us, always.

Lord, today we long to see the light of your awe-filled holy face. Amen.

November 2
Storm Shutters

The wind was so gusty this morning! Nature breathes in inhales and exhales … in rhythmic undulations. Where ever you are, just look outside for a bit, and notice the trees, flowers, and birds cascading through the air on the wind.

The Gaia theory postulates that we are intimately tied to Earth, which is a self-sustaining system and a living breathing entity. Think of each person as a cell functioning in a whole body. That's the Gaia theory of Earth; thus one bad cell has the potential to ripple negative effects on Earth. Conversely, one strong cell can positively change the world. I think of such awesome shining "lights" as the apostles, the martyrs, missionaries, and hard workers in the church who give up so much of their personal time to build the church body by dedicated service to others.

But I'm not any sort of the above "shining lights" group. Are you? What difference can *we* make on this planet that God the Father put us in charge of as Genesis 1:26 states: "God said, 'Let us make humankind in our image…and let them rule over the fish in the sea, the birds in the air, the animals, and over all the earth'." Do you see a positive "rule" happening in your life?

The word, "rule" means: "one of a set of explicit or understood regulations or principles governing conduct within a particular activity or sphere." We are to rule "over all the earth." The answer to my question must conclude with another question: What are you ruling over in your circle of friends and strangers with whom you come in contact on a daily basis? Yes, we go the store, or the post office, or a doctor's office. You can add what you do daily, most likely a hard job. Are you raising children? Caring and nurturing a baby? Have an elderly parent? Are you married? Yes, more questions! But in these Gaia realms of daily living, *you* make a wonderful difference in the lives of people you touch. Make your God-given difference in every moment of today.

Lord, lead us to sacrifice the trivial to show your glory to someone today. Amen.

GOD DESIGNED

NOVEMBER 3
HOT CHOCOLATE AVAILABLE

I have an easy special recipe for hot cocoa. I microwave a large cup of nonfat milk, stir in a small teaspoon of powdered cocoa, and then stir in a packet of sugar substitute. It's delicious and nutritious, as my stepmom used to say.

When I visited Israel, I drank teas, coffee lattes, and milk; however, there are several dietary restrictions concerning eating meat, "Take care not to eat the blood, for the blood is the life, and you are not to eat the life with the meat" (Deuteronomy 12:23); and, drinking milk at the same meal. "You are not to boil a young animal in its mother's milk (Exodus 23:19). However, Israel is most definitely is a food rich country. Have you ever visited a place where the cultural differences varied vastly from your own? What were you forced to give up, or add to your diet?

In Numbers, the land is "flowing with milk and honey" (13:27 and 14:8). There are fig trees, vast green grazing lands, underground springs, and even a sturdy supply of Dead Sea salt, an ancient commodity. But God brings up a problem with having "all you can eat" (Deuteronomy 31:20-22), and He gives a prediction, like a recipe, of how his people will fall because He knows "how they think" (v. 21). He lists the ingredients for Disobedient Soup: His people will eat their fill; grow fat; turn to "other gods;" and, then serve those false gods and idols. Then, they will "despise" the God who saved them from slavery and delivered them into His Promised Land. Only one *song* can turn their hearts: read the Torah before *everyone* so they can hear it; learn; fear God; and, obey His laws (verses 10-13). But there are a lot of laws. I can't do 'em all right! In less than a day, I'll definitely revert back to eating Disobedient Soup.

Blessed was I the day when I believed Jesus died on the cross for my sins, rose on the third day, and now sits with God the Father. Paul is clear about the new law which is to trust in Jesus. "We have been released from this aspect of the Torah, because we have died to that which had us in its clutches, so that we are serving in the new way provided by the Spirit and not in the old way of outwardly following the letter of the law" (Romans 7:6). The culture of being a Christian is worth any change because we have Jesus and are right with our Holy God.

Holy Spirit, remind us to be gentle and authentic. Amen.

NOVEMBER 4
BANK BRANCH

I have a barren tree branch in need of serious pruning. The bough is a part of a healthy pine tree, but this dead branch has no needles, just lifeless twigs. It's as if this one branch has a vicious bug sucking out the sap. However, the rest of the tree looks pine-fresh green.

Like our bodies, a tree is a holistic system. Plants need soil, light, water, dirt, and room to spread their roots.

Dead branches and slimy wilted flowers must be cut off from the healthy parts, or whatever is killing the greenery will spread, and someday render the entire tree or plant dead.

Where to strike? At the damaged area. "Right now, because of the word which I have spoken to you, you are pruned," Jesus tells us (John 15:3). Do you have any areas in your life that might need a bit of pruning? After pruning a plant, in several weeks I notice beautiful new growth.

I'm reminded of one bad "branch" in the *Bible*, King Ahab. He "did what was evil ... even outdoing all his predecessors in wickedness" (I Kings 16:29-34). Ahab also set up *asherah* for worshipping. The word comes from the Canaanite goddess Astarte whose masculine counterpart is the Assyrian, Ishtar god. Astarte's symbol is the stem of a tree deprived of its boughs, shaped into an image, and then planted in the ground ... in groves!

How God must have hurt to see *groves* of disgusting idols throughout His land that He intended for *His* sacred worship, and to watch his chosen people bowing and praying to false gods and idols. God announces, and then enacts, his plan through Elijah: to cut off the disease. Elijah tells Ahab, "There will be neither rain nor dew in the years ahead unless I say so" (I Kings 17:1). Elijah runs scared! There's no water, and you know people are going to be angry. But God provides for him; and three years later, God shows His presence when he consumes the offering of the false god. Elijah prays, "God, let it be known today that you are God, I am your servant, and I have done all things at your word" (1 Kings 18:36—37). God's people are thus healed at the demonstration of His use of the four forces in the universe. Serious pruning of sins in our lives works.

Lord God, cut off any false idols in our lives, right now, please. Amen.

NOVEMBER 5
SPY SOURCE PLUS

On top of a tall pole behind my backyard, an eagle likes to perch. In the winter, eagles from up north migrate south. "Harry" is back. Have you ever found something you thought was lost, or have someone visit you whom you haven't seen in ages?

"Esau ran to meet Jacob, hugged him, threw his arms around his neck and kissed him; and they wept" (Genesis 33:4). That's how the sad and complicated story of Jacob and Esau ends. Now, Harry....

"Harry's back!" I shouted to my husband as I took out my iPhone and snapped pictures of Harry. That's what *I* named the eagle. I can't tell you how I praised God when he appeared last month behind my backyard. Why is this a big deal?

I've always wished to see an eagle. A few years ago, we drove roundtrip from Texas to California, stopping at the Grand Canyon and Petrified Forest. I never saw *one* eagle. A week after moving into our Florida home, I walked outside and saw my wish come true. Coincidentally, my neighbor was in the front yard. He told me about the eagles who mate and have babies every year—behind our yards. "Wow!" I consider the sighting a blessing. It made me wonder about what God says about such grand majestic raptors.

One special verse I found is in Ezekiel 10:14. "Everyone [of the k'ruvim] had four faces: the first face was the face of a keruv, the second face was the face of a man, the third the face of a lion and the fourth the face of an eagle." Eagles are part Keruvim, two cherubic gold angels on top of the Ark of the Covenant. We're talking about eagle-like beings God placed on top of His tabernacle. "Their wings are upwards (between man and G-D) yet they face each other (between man and man)."

This, our physical world and the spiritual world are harmonizing in a realm between God and man, where eagles soar. Remember: back in those times, we didn't have airplanes. However, people saw the majestic flight of eagles. They can soar 10,000 to 15,000 feet. Have you ever seen their mating ritual? They fly high, entangle with their mate, and then pummel toward the ground and then unclasp. They're always together thereafter. No wonder God chose such an awesome bird to guard His law. He's with us, forever.

Lord, we need to keep contemplating your incomprehensible abilities that keep us humble. Amen.

November 6
Newly Empowered

When I was a child, I used to like breathing on the ice-cold window and sketch words and signs into the white crystals with my finger. I remember notching out hearts, my handprint, and circles. The words and symbols wouldn't last long but would drip like tears down the pane of frosty glass. Yet, long after winter, during hot summer days, whenever I'd squint closely at those places, I'd see their faint outlines, like hard-water residue. Do you ever wonder what impressions we leave behind? "Be strong, be bold, don't be afraid or frightened … for *Adonai* your God is going with you. He will neither fail you nor abandon you" (Deuteronomy 31:6). Everything we have done has molded us into who we are today.

I bet God views us in the same way as the day He created us in the womb, except we *never* disappear from his sight like washed out symbols. He holds us in his arms, like a child. Jesus tells us about God's special love for us when he prays: "I made your name known … so that the love with which you have loved me may be in them, and I myself may be united with them" (John 17:29—26). God breathed life into us. "Adonai, who made you, formed you in the womb, and will help you" (Isaiah 44:2). God doesn't stop there. He tells Isaiah seven times in all how He "formed" us (44:24; 46:3; 48:8; 49:1; 49:5; 49:15; and 66:9). In those verses, you'll find God *forming* you for a purpose in this life. "What is the purpose?" Let's dig deeper. God made people. "So God created humankind in his own image; in the image of God he created him: male and female he created them" (Genesis 1:27). Again he tells us in Jeremiah 1:5: "Before I formed you in the womb, I knew you." The word "know" means to be absolutely sure or certain about something. He breathed life into us, just as I breathed that puff of hot air onto the cold window. But God didn't stop there. He gave us a specific form to our bodies, a unique and modeled design. The word "formed" and "created" are action words. You can just picture God forming and creating *every* cell inside of you. What's your purpose? We reflect Him to the world through our gifts and strengths. We are His ambassadors. "In effect, God is making his appeal through us" so people can see us and our behavior, and come to Him (2 Corinthians 5:20).

Lord, as we breathe, let us work for you in thanksgiving. Amen.

NOVEMBER 7
GLUTEN FREE PRODUCTS

I remember watching my Grandma Pink make bread. She'd start with lukewarm water and add a packet of yeast. Then she'd slowly add flour and other ingredients like salt, sugar and eggs. Her arms were pumps, kneading the dough—pushing, pulling and stretching it. She'd punch it, mangle it some more, and then roll out the dough. After a ten minute rough-and-gruff workout, she'd put the dough in an oil-coated bowl and let it rise. After a few hours, she'd do her kneading exercise all over again. Those goodies baking in the oven gave off heavenly scents, making my mouth water. I can still *smell* them ... and my mouth is beginning to water as I write. No wonder she lived until eighty-six with all that kitchen work out. She would have lived longer if she had both of her kidneys I bet, because she and my grandpa owned a farm in Hannah, Indiana. Most of the food they ate, they cultivated, carved, froze, or canned. I was always a little overweight whenever I'd visit Grandma.

I notice God says a lot about working in the fields. "The angel who has rescued me from all harm. ... May they remember who I am and what I stand for, and likewise my fathers, Avraham and Yitz'chak, who they were and what they stood for. And may they grow into teeming multitudes on the earth" (Genesis 48?16). Have you ever consider starting a garden?

The first "field" study I discover comes in Genesis when God tells Adam: "the ground is cursed on your account; you will work hard to eat from it as long as you live" (3:18). I think about my grandparents working so hard since the early 1940s on their farm. They owned about 200 acres, and my grandpa owned three tractors. Most spring, summer and fall days, he'd be on the tractor. After working hours, he and my grandma would pick cucumbers, tomatoes, onions, peppers, corn, and green beans in their garden. Then we'd go on a search for wild mushrooms, asparagus, and all sorts of wild berries. Some nights, the house would fill with the scent of Grandma making jellies and jams. They worked the land, and I'm here to tell their story of how God rewarded them by leaving me wonderful memories. "See, my son smells like a field which Adonai has blessed" (Genesis 27:27). There is a wonderful and unforgettable fragrance, uplifting to God, as He beholds our deeds for Him.

Jesus, help us cultivate our spiritual gardens. Amen.

November 8
Freedom Press

Fear is so enslaving.

This morning, I joined a writing group and read one of my short stories. Was I scared. The better word might be *vulnerable*. I prayed in the car: "Lord, take away my fear." But I didn't pray before I stood up at the microphone. Fear consumed me, and I said to the audience, "I think I'm gonna be sick." Still, I read my story, "Homeless Man," to the end. Usually, I have trouble fitting in with people, but I really like this group, so I joined their fellowship

"Thus they are no longer two, but one. So then, no one should split apart what God has joined together" (Matthew 19:6). My husband tagged along with me.

Have you ever joined such a group, or were on a job, where you were afraid to put your skills and talents "out there" for people to experience, and judge?

Fear can be a powerful deterrent. The word, *deterrent*, is so close to the word, *detergent*. We know what a strong detergent can do: wash away the best *and* the worst.

I'm reminded to look at what God says about fear.

I do know we are to fear God. "Then he [Jacob] became afraid and said, 'This place is fearsome! This has to be the house of God! This is the gate of heaven'!'" Jacob was the grandson of Abraham whose father was Isaac, the son for whom Abraham longed to be a father. God tells Jacob that he is on Israeli ground destined for future offspring. I love the prayer Jacob lifts up to God: "If God will be with me and will guard me on this road that I am traveling, giving me bread to eat and clothes to wear, so that I return to my father's house in peace, then Adonai will be my God" (Genesis 28:16-22). Jacob resides *on* the house of God, the gate of heaven, His land. After acknowledging God's greatness and majesty, God tells Jacob that Israel will be the Heaven—the intermediary—between Him and Jacob's descendants. Isn't that what Heaven is at this point in the Bible? It's God's land He destines for the Jews. There is no fear in this relationship between God and Jacob. They are speaking and relating in harmony and unity. As followers of Jesus, God's divine son, we also share in Jacob's perfect wonderful inheritance.

Lord, we want to experience oneness with you daily and to show your love to everyone. Amen.

NOVEMBER 9
THREE CHURCH SERVICES

When I was a child living with my mom and stepdad, I would wake up with debilitating anxiety. I felt like something was sucking the breath out of me, followed by a crawling numbness. Growing up in that violent environment, sometimes I'd wet the bed until I left that nightmarish place to live with my dad and his new wife.

Do you ever experience, or suffer through, Unpleasant Memory Syndrome because of someone's treatment of you? "You, Lord, are a shield around me, my glory, the One who lifts my head high. I call out to the Lord, and he answers me from his holy mountain. I lie down and sleep. I wake again, because the Lord sustains me" (Psalm 3:3-5). God is our help in times when painful memories haunt us.

Over the years, that same anxiety has resurrected as a poison, preventing me from forming lasting relationships and staying in one place for very long. For most my life, I've lived a nomad. Fear at least has an object. You can say, "I'm afraid of _____, so now I can face the fear and eliminate it." Anxiety is different because the dread and hair-rising trembles are free-floating, unanticipated, and crippling. To battle this type of onslaught that has evolved into a structural processing pattern in my brain, I must concentrate on Christ's words, and allow his teaching to permeate my daily life—in the *seconds* throughout my day.

You know what? I've never met someone who doesn't struggle with "something." That's why the Bible is so vital, because Jesus ministers to us personally. "The Son of Man came not to be ministered unto, but to minister and to give His life as a ransom for many" (Mark 10:45). The word, *minister*, also is the word, *serve*, in many translations. These are healing words. "Jesus went about all the cities and villages, teaching and preaching the Gospel of the Kingdom, and healing every sickness and every disease" (Matthew 4:23 and 9:35). We also have a Comforter, the Holy Spirit, who is also called Counselor. We received Him into our souls when we accepted Jesus as our Savior. Comforter acts on our insides, ministering to us through God's word (John 14:25-26). Then we know for certain that we are never alone in whatever anxiety or fear we experience, or haunting memories we must confront.

Father, we need to stay *in* you as Jesus did when he faced anxiety before stepping toward The Cross. Amen.

November 10
Auto Works

Growing up, sometimes I would see my Grandma McCarten afraid. She had a habit of fidgeting with her fingers while exclaiming, "Oh no ... oh my." She'd repeat it, while pacing the floor, until someone solved "the problem." Life's difficulties have a tendency to unnerve us. So much that happens to us is *out* of our control like a baseball flyin' outta the park. Is something out of control in your day today? Jesus has answers.

Robert E. Lee once said: "I cannot trust a man to control others who cannot control himself." Self-control in the face of experiencing the uncontrollable seems to be the answer that stops anxiety and fear. How I react, respond, and fashion my attitude about uncontrollable events appears to be the only "thing" I can control.

Fear, anxiety, rage, and depression over the uncontrollable problems that can leave us feeling powerless and helpless are opposites of a prayerful response during trials and hardships. Not *one* person owns a Ticket of Avoidance to problems

What's your unnerving or rattling situation today?

Let's pray now ... and give our situation right into Jesus's hands.

He caught it. "Praised be God, Father of our Lord Yeshua the Messiah, who, in keeping with his great mercy, has caused us, through the resurrection of Yeshua the Messiah from the dead, to be born again to a living hope" (1 Peter 1:3).

I imagine the calmness of Jesus. He *could* have controlled events, but he didn't. Power and control were at his fingertips in the miracles and healings he performed to help people. He demonstrated God's ultimate authority over *all* events—the good and bad. He received His power from God. "My Father has handed over everything to me" (Luke 10:22). After this passage, we read his *Our Father* prayer, followed by Jesus directing us to pray for our every want and need. "Keep asking ... keep seeking ... keep knocking, the door will be opened" (Luke 9-10). God has ultimate control. "[He] thunders wonderfully with his voice, he does great things beyond our understanding. He says to the snow, 'Fall on the earth!' Likewise to the light rain, also to the downpour" (Job 37:5-6). Now that's control, no authority. When we lift up our uncontrollable circumstances to God, we can experience His calm presence.

Father, help us be aware of your authority. Amen.

NOVEMBER 11
HONORING OUR MILITARY

I grew up watching the first, the real-time media-coverage of the Vietnam War. I remember seeing reporters Walter Cronkite and Morley Safer in the trenches, reporting on the guerilla tactics of the Vietcong, our enemy. The enemy utilized hit-and-run strikes, ambushes, and booby-trapped tunnels to strike us. We weren't used to their gruesome killing and torture methods. They *liked* taking prisoners. I had a Missing in Action, stainless-steel bracelet. I lost it, but I'll never forget their popularity as I hoped for the MIA soldier, to return safely home. We were constantly bombarded with images of war machines and their devastation: Huey helicopters; trenches like deep winding rivers; sniper offensives; dive bombings; and, our automatic guns with their *pop-pop-popping* firepower. Our camouflaged service men had to be vigilant in Vietnam's dense forests and bonded to their comrades in a code of brotherhood. Daily we watched their struggles as valiant reporters brought the facts of war to the American people, in color. They endured and persevered.

What does it take for *us* to endure the battles and hardships we're fighting against the people, places, or things in our lives that try to make and hold us prisoners of habit?

One day, "He will swallow up death forever. *Adonai Eohim* will wipe away the tears from every face, and he will remove from all the earth the disgrace his people suffer" (Isaiah 25:8). God knows what's need to fight any war.

To go into battle, one must have qualifications. We read of the specific criteria in 1 Chronicles 5:18: "The descendants of Reuben, the Gadi, and the half-tribe of Manasseh included 44,760 brave men who were available for warfare, able to take up shield and sword, shoot with the bow, or make use of other war skills." Bravery is the first necessity. It means: *courage, nerve, daring, fearlessness,* and *boldness.* Remembering the Vietnam War, I recall draft dodgers who ran to Canada or Mexico to dodge the draft. Perhaps that was why they ran. As the verse states, people who fight have to be available, able, and have skills. There are all sorts of battles we confront, so let's start with exercising our capacity for bravery. "Be brave" Jesus says. "I have conquered the world" (John 16:33). We can progress.

God, we thank the soldiers who bravely fought for our freedoms, and those still fighting on our behalf. Amen.

NOVEMBER 12
NUTRITION FACTS

I was at Bible study last night; and as our leader ended our intensive studies, she asked that we sing a song. Have you ever been so deeply rooted in God's word that you want to burst out singing praises to Him? This was one of those irrepressible times.

A melody popped into my mind: "Lord, I need you, oh, I need you! Every hour I need you!" The song is by Matt Maher. I've sung it in choirs and in churches often. But when our leader began humming that *exact* refrain and we all began singing the lyrics, I felt shocked. No one can read minds, but wow. She and I had Matt's song in our minds. I recall another song, David's long wonderful hymn: "... I give thanks to you, *Adonai*, among the nations. I sing praises to your name" (2 Samuel 22; 2 Samuel 22:50).

The famous psychiatrist Carl Jung coined the term, *synchronicity*, which means, "the experience of two or more events that are meaningfully related." Some people just say "coincidence." But the Holy Spirit sees our hearts. Through Him, we receive encouragement and the building up of the Body of Christ. We're all thus connected. In the Book of Acts, early believers gather together as a church, and a great roaring wind fills the room. Then tongues of fire rest on each person. The Holy Spirit fills them, and they begin to talk in different languages (Acts 2:1-4). This Pentecostal occurs *after* Jesus ascends into Heaven. However, we experience Him as well, even though we are removed from that early church when the Holy Spirit first enabled those early believers to spread Christianity like wild fire (Acts 9:31). I'm also reading another interesting prediction found in Joel 3:1, repeating in Acts 2:17-21. "Adonai says: 'In the Last Days, I will pour out from my Spirit upon everyone. Your sons and daughters will prophesy, your young men will see visions'." I'm not going to delve into the End Times or Last Days. However, I can infer from the two above events that the Holy Spirit works in peoples' lives in ways we don't understand. Through Him, we're all connected, really.

We had been study the Lord's word, and spent time in deep prayer. Today, after that intense immersion, I feel so connected to everyone in our study. That incomprehensible edification can only emerge from our souls, the seat of God's Holy Spirit in our lives.

Father, we need to keep thanking you for your grace every day. Amen.

NOVEMBER 13
UNBEATABLE PRICES

I've heard of "unbeatable prices," until I find a store with cheaper prices. I had to buy an airplane ticket a few weeks ago and consulted several websites to find the best deal. As I was about to pay, I noticed a $50.00 charge for preferred seating (round trip), and a giant luggage fee. Shucks. It turns out that just about all the airlines have fixed rates, plus-or-minus those optional services and charges. To save money, should I skip taking luggage and arrive at my final destination with layers of clothes on my back? Optional? Yeah, right. Unbeatable? *Wrong.* Are there times when you feel taken by surprise by unjust charges, fees, or taxes? You're forced to sacrifice to acquire the convenience. Shucks. The world's not supposed to operate this way, right?

Sacrificing ones desires to save money is like paddling down a rapid river. But, I've always noticed a positive change in my character whenever I've persevered through a sacrifice. What about you?

Let's take a simple example as a measuring stick for change. When I was a teenager and didn't get my way or what I wanted, I'd get mad, sulk, or be embarrassed around others who had what I didn't have. Then I avoided those people. Now I respond differently. I spent years tiptoeing over the broken glass of unfulfilled wants and dreams that have yielded all sorts of calluses on my feet. Can you name a few things you wanted but never received, or goals you wanted to accomplish but didn't? Disappointments hurt, huh?

Over the years, our Lord has been a master sculptor to my changing character. As the Perfect Artist, He has accessorized me with some awesome qualities. In spite of the patches of rough sin-skin He has polished up with Jesus's healing Forgiveness Blend, I'm much improved. I'm reminded of what He says about us—His special renovation projects. "You, as living stones, are being built into a spiritual house to be *cohanim* set apart for God to offer spiritual sacrifices acceptable to him through Yeshua the Messiah" (1 Peter 2:5). A "cohanim" is "a member of the Jewish priestly class, having sacrificial, ministerial, and other sacred functions." We are "living" stones, the brick and mortar of His Church. *Everything* we do, He sees; our hearts, He knows. He molds and refines us as we endure our disappointments, sorrows, and sacrifices. Good changes, yes.

Lord, today help us see the little ways we can sacrifice. Amen.

November 14
Expert Advice

On several occasions, I've had to consult with expert tax preparers, scientists, and doctors. They have years of education and work experience, and are highly trained their field of expertise. You ever get audited? Believe me, you don't want to. Nevertheless, you'll need help if you do … a tax attorney.

An "expert" is "a person who has a comprehensive and authoritative knowledge of or skill in a particular area." I *expect* an *expert* to have a higher standard than the average person in his or her field of *expertise*. If someone is a teacher, for example, that instructor should adhere to a certain code of ethics or conduct. After all, we are paying them, learning from them, and giving him or her power. Counselors, for example, have a code of conduct they must adhere to under the American Counseling Association. "Helping" people requires "responding" to peoples' needs and caring for their welfare. Thus, we give experts a certain amount of power and control because we put our trust and confidence in them—sometimes, trust and confidence in saving our lives

What happens when experts victimize vulnerable people? Have you ever been a victim of a crime or "the system?"

Being a victim happened to me more than once. Looking back on those experiences, when I had to seek help for having "been taken" or "charged way too much," I might have been more studious in my research and prevented those specialists from taking advantage of me. However, other times, *no* research could have prevented my being victimized. The expert was a fraud. Is there justice?

God doesn't take fraud lightly. "Keep away from fraud, and do not cause the death of the innocent and righteous; for I will not justify the wicked" (Exodus 23:7). The word "justify," means, "declare or make righteous in the sight of God." If God will not justify the wicked person, He will not face the individual. That's eternity *not* facing God. Let me tremble in fear of such a horrible state. Committing fraud is not part of God's plan. "Do what is right and just; rescue the wronged from their oppressors; do nothing wrong or violent to the stranger, orphan or widow; don't shed innocent blood" (Jeremiah 22:3). Payback will come, in justice.

Father God, help us be a comforter to those experiencing sorrow and trials. Amen.

NOVEMBER 15
FALL CLOSINGS

I look outside to my back yard and see green leaves. A few are dabbled in yellow fringes and a few speckled with slight red tones. Florida doesn't experience fall like other states, yet each leaf has a special signature—intricate veins no other leaf possesses. God designed us with special signatures. Look at your finger prints and eyes signatures. There are security programs ready to implement eye signature technology and facial recognition technology into banks and ATMs so that machines can *read* special you.

I'm reminded of the Fibonacci sequence developed by Leonardo of Pisa, now known as Fibonacci. His theory postulates a pattern in nature that allows organisms and plants to grow without changing shape. Think of a rose bush. The leaves have a pattern on the bush. In the ocean, the chambered nautilus is spiraled in a pattern. This Fibonacci pattern can be used to model or describe an amazing variety of phenomena in mathematics, science, art, and nature. The ideas the Fibonacci sequence lead to "the golden ratio" of spirals, and similar curves, beauteous sights all around us.

God gives His divine order so we can think about His universe. Look around. Everything is marvelous, including you. Your thumbprint and DNA are unique to you. Is this coincidence? No.

God tells us we are His unique creation. "For you fashioned my inmost being, you knit me together in my mother's womb," David exclaims to God in praise and thanksgiving (Psalm 139:13).

He made us. You and I are important and special to Him. "Before I formed you in the womb, I knew you; before you were born, I separated you for myself" (Jeremiah 1:5). How long ago could that be? Eternity has no boundary, Sister and Brother. Years are humanity's time management, not God's divine time. Where will your soul end up?

That's how long He's known you, for eternity; and eternity is our ultimate home. Even Job the Sufferer embraced that fact when he proclaimed the following: "Naked I came from my mother's womb, and naked I will return there. Adonai gave; Adonai took; blessed be the name of Adonai" (Job 1:21). He owns our souls. Let us, in turn, reflect His glory and gentle love to others.

Father, help us show your love to people so they can see you and know you. Amen.

November 16
Experience Shopping

I had to *learn* to manage money, to change from a charge-it mentality to a save-for-a-rainy-day perspective. Have you ever had to revamp your savings and spending habits? It's hard, isn't it ... to make a big change in your life. Paul recognized how difficult it is to change, but he preached change nevertheless. "I am not writing you this to make you feel ashamed, but, as my dear children, to confront you and get you to change" (1 Corinthians 4:14).

Coming from a deprived background, when I did finally have the occasion to bask in a financial boon, I overindulged, overspent, and touched a black-bottom pool of debt. I felt ashamed for years about my bad spending habits. I had not been a good steward of what could have been a financial blessing. I had been proud, greedy, covetous, and vain. *Ouch*, but, admitting sin is a first step.

I'm reminded of several times when God disciplined people for having emotional flings with idols. They had heart issues. God wants us for himself because He created us and loves us dearly.

One Bible character who fell from God's high esteem is prideful Saul. God tells him to destroy Israel's enemy and everything they possess. The Amalekites were evil and committed abominable acts. Saul disobeys God. "Saul and his army spare Agag, the Amalekite king, and the best of the sheep, oxen, the fatlings, the lambs, and all that was good of the Amalekites" (1 Samuel 15:9). Later on, there is a punishing three-year famine. God explains why. "It is because of [Saul] and his bloodstained house" (2 Samuel 21:1). Later, God tells Samuel the prophet, "I am grieved that I have made Saul to be king because he has turned away from me, and has not carried out my instructions" (1 Samuel 15:1, NIV). Saul let God down.

We need to focus on our eternal prize in Christ Jesus. Peter prays: "Praised by God, Father of our Lord Jesus, the Messiah, who, in keeping with his great mercy, has caused us, through the resurrection of Jesus from the dead, to be born again to a living hope, to an inheritance that cannot decay, spoil, or fade, kept safe for you in heaven" (1 Peter 3-5). Jesus has sealed us to an eternity with Him. No amount of money or possessions can guarantee us a place and inheritance with Jesus our Savior. Materialism exacts from us a great price.

Lord, help us to see beyond this superficial world. Amen.

NOVEMBER 17
SELF-CHECKOUT

I walked outside into my backyard this morning, and the rain-fresh air invigorated me. The sun's rays appeared as golden kite tails drifting behind God's puffy white cumulus clouds. I prayed to God in his overwhelming show of majesty: "Direct my day, Lord, because everything I do for you in *every* moment I mean for your glory."

Our every breath, He gives us. Our lives, He sustains.

"Praised be, *Adonai*, Father of our Lord Yeshua the Messiah, who in the Messiah has blessed us with every spiritual blessing in heaven" (Ephesians 1:3).

His Holy Spirit speaks within us. "It will not be just you speaking, but the Spirit of your heavenly Father speaking through you," Jesus says (Matthew 10:20).

Before letting the dog back inside, I walked to my kitchen window to smell fragrant orange blossoms on a dwarf citrus tree. Among the white blooms were crawling ants heading into dark crevices in the bark. There are places insects can navigate where no person can see their perspective. Perspective is vital in nature and art, illuminating God's 3D-world. However, sometimes, my perspective topples, like falling Lincoln Logs. Have you ever come crashing down when your way of looking at people, places and things topples? Happening to me, I need a *fresh* perspective. I have trouble changing a perspective though. I get stuck on the round-about track as my brain fires answers. Until, *finally*, exhausted, I'm forced to give up looking at people, places, things and ideas my way. I need God and the Holy Spirit to infuse me with a *new* Jesus-oriented perspective.

Psalm 119 is packed full of ways to help us look at things from God's perspective. We will never know Him completely until we reach Heaven, but we can learn from Him in order to live out the rest of our lives for His glory. I see a prayer in the psalm. "May your grace come to me, Adonai … for I trust in your word … forever and ever" (41-44). Trust isn't always easy, "for not everyone has trust. But the Lord is worthy of trust" (2 Thessalonians 3:2-3). God made us and formed us (Psalm 119:73). He gives us understanding, if we just ask Him (v. 145-152). Sometimes, I've had to cry to God, as David did. Then, as I swing over the cliff of faulty perspective, I feel his hand clasp my hand. His new viewpoint is sunshine to my soul.

Jesus, infuse us with new perspectives and alleviate our pain.

NOVEMBER 18
TITAN CUSTOMER SERVICE

Have you ever had to complain about receiving bad service, being a victim of false advertising, or buying a bad product?

It's a rhetorical question, because this world is flawed. At some point, you will *not* receive the product you paid for, or the item might break prematurely, or you might encounter a cantankerous checker or a con artist. I remember a time when I was a child and shopped at Goldblatt's in Hammond, Indiana. I bought a wallet for my dad, and the clerk wrapped it for me and said kindly, "Merry Christmas." That was in 1967. Everyone appeared hardworking and considerate.

Times have changed, and those nice amenities no longer exist. Or if they do, you'll pay for them. Have you been, or felt, deprived? "I deserved that," you might exclaim. "I was here first!" "It's my turn." Or someone you *believed* was a friend passed you by as a fair-weather friend. "With friends like these as intercessors, my eyes pour out tears to God," Job says, the ultimate object of scorn, except for Jesus (Job16:20).

God will never let us down. He is our Titan Lord, Jehovah Jireh. Our Provider.

You can feel His loving arms wrap around you and comfort you in Psalm 23. David tells us right up front: "YHWH-raah, the Lord our Shepherd. YHWH-jireh: the Lord our Provider." Because of Him, "I lack nothing" (v. 1). This covenant God makes with us to provide for our needs originates in Genesis when He intervenes between Abraham's knife and Isaac's body. Abraham is faithful to what appears to be an outlandish command from God. Still, he obeys. In confusion, he obeys. He treks up that mountain to present his son to God. Decades rolled by for Abraham and Sarah before they conceived Isaac. Imagine God asking *you* to sacrifice the most cherished person in *your* life. God intervenes between a hand and a knife. He never had *any* intention of snuffing out Isaac's life. At the site of that mountain, God provides a ram as a perfect sacrifice instead of Isaac. "Abraham called the place Adonai Yir'eh [Adonai will see to it; Adonai provides]" (Genesis 22:14). What a test. Abraham's trust was strong, and God rewarded him as he rewards us when we trust, obey, and "do the right thing" in our daily lives.

Lord, help us keep the new commandment you continue to write on our hearts. Amen.

NOVEMBER 19
WELCOME WAGON

I've been going to church almost all my life, and I've never met *anyone* who has felt God's love and presence *all* the time twenty-four-seven. I myself included.

Do you always feel connected to God 24/7?

Yesterday at Bible study, several people discussed how they felt God's love as a father loves his child.

Hey! Rub some of that spiritual lotion on me! I kept thinking.

Then I wondered: What is wrong with me that I feel *so far* removed from God?

Where are you on the God Meter of intensity and feeling?

I remembered an event, wherein only after looking back did I realize God had His divine protection over my life. About twenty-four years ago, my doorbell rang at 10:30 at night. Something was terribly wrong. My daughter and son were sleeping in back bedrooms when I answered the door without opening the door. The man was someone I hired to move me a few months ago. I didn't *know* him! Why would he be returning at 10:30 p.m.? I succinctly ordered, "You're not allowed in here!" I believe the Holy Spirit pronounced those words. If I had opened the door, you would *not* be reading this. I called the police. Still, the man busted through my back door, severed my electricity and cut the phone line. The police arrived, broke through the door and killed the intruder. They saved us ... and the Holy Spirit saved us. Trust, faith, and hope ... from God.

The prophet Zephaniah tells us that God is our Savior: "Don't let your hands droop down. Adonai your God is right there with you, as a might savior. He will rejoice over you and be glad, he will be silent in his love, he will shout over you with joy" (Zephaniah 3:17). When we hold our hands high in prayer and praise to God, this verse proclaims a powerful truth. God is always holding our hands in desperate times. We don't *see* his mighty majestic fingers that molded the Earth. We don't *feel* his sure grip as we hang over the cliff of life's daily struggles, but He is with us. He rejoices over you and me because He made us, and He loves us. In Heaven, he shouts over us with joy. Remember what he said in Genesis? "God saw everything that he had made, and indeed it was very good" (1:31). Thank you Jesus for your caring saving presence in our lives.

Lord, help us show people how much you love them. Amen.

November 20
Preschool

My son gave me his Christmas list yesterday and it's not even Thanksgiving. Actually, he's been planning for Christmas for weeks, and his wish list is always changing.

Ya ever feel like you're jumping through loops, with someone always changing his or her mind?

Trying to figure them out is like watching the edge of a hurricane to see where it's going to strike, wouldn't you agree? You wanna shake the person a bit. "Make up your blasted mind already 'cause you're drivin' me *nuts*."

"I need a Smart TV," our son finally pronounced this morning.

"No, I want surround-sound speakers instead," he changed.

Then, "Naw, I really need a new game that costs $120.00."

His dad responds: "Just remember, your budget is $400.00. We already bought you a game." He dipped into his $500.00 budget.

We need to stay on budget. Our daughter is expecting a baby, and we want to buy our precious granddaughter something special. Which we did, yesterday, using PayPal. Charge it! We shouldn't use "the demon card" though because debt is a heavy weight and has a snowballing tendency. *Not* a peaceful way to live, right?

So, how can a person exist in peace, especially when a bit of life's chaos always surrounds us? And demands and expectations?

Ironic how the times when I'm feeling restless, I'm reminded of a peace I could have that could change my uncomfortable reality. "Don't worry about anything ... make your requests known to God by prayer and petition, with thanksgiving. Then God's *shalom* [peace] passing all understanding will keep your hearts and minds safe" (Philippians 4:6-7). This world and all "its advertised things" can leave us wringing our fingers and swooning with anxiety because there's always a better TV, cell phone, etc. Money *does* make the world go round. On the contrary, the word, *shalom*, means *peace of mind, peace between people, and peace between God and person.* In Greek, the word is, *Eirene*, meaning, quietness and rest. In Hebrew, *shalom*, stems from the word, *shalam*, meaning *to be safe* or *complete*. We cannot receive this peace from objects, possessions, or people. Only unchanging God, Jesus, and the Holy Spirit can imbibe us with peace.

Lord, we need quiet moments away from TV and social media to know your peace. Amen.

NOVEMBER 21
PROCESSING OFFERED

Today I had to create a sales banner for a book fair I'm attending tomorrow. I intend to Velcro my big ad to the front of my table to attract people to check out my novels. Creating the banner was hard. I asked myself several questions: Do I focus on only one genre? Do I include only *one* theme? Do I include a name of a great sci-fi writer?

Do you experience moments, wherein you don't know what to do, or it's not clear what to do? At these times, we need clarity, especially spiritual clarity, which first entails relegating our concerns to God and waiting for Him to guide us through the Holy Spirit. "In your love, you led the people you redeemed; in your strength, you guided them to your holy abode" (Exodus 15:13).

To sell a product, you need the take the best approach to attract customers. Look how famous people endorse products. My last idea felt too gutsy and arrogant, so I threw that option out. It just didn't "feel" right, "sit" right in my soul. "I am *Adonai*, your God, who teaches you for your own good, who guides you on the path you should take" (Isaiah 48:17). I focused on one genres, sci-fi. Still, the aspiring writer in me grappled, sweated, and brain froze over what I should call myself to promote myself. I felt so ashamed at any positive thing my husband wanted to include on the banner, even though I can substantiate, "Award Winning Author." I won two awards. Still, I am no braggart. "Who would *you* say I am, God?"

Did you know God has a banner? "Moshe built an altar, called it Adonai Nissi [Adonai is my banner/miracle]" (Exodus 17:15). The altar's name is, God is my Banner. Now why would someone call an altar that? At this point in history, God's people are in the Promised Land, but they face enemies, the Amalekites. Moses was old and worn out, but he could hold up God's divine staff to motivate and inspire people to defeat the enemy and claim their land. That staff was there when Moses met God in the burning bush. The same divinely infused staff he used to strike the Reed Sea, part it, and shepherd the Israelites to flee Egypt. When we experienced confusion over our identity, our position in this world, or our worth, what should we write on our minds for inspiration? God strengthens me (Romans 16:25). When we work for His purposes, He will guide us, and give us strength to accomplish our goals (Philippians 4:13).

Jesus, help us see your victorious hand in our lives. Amen.

NOVEMBER 22
GOVERNMENT OVER-REACH

Some people in my house have a bad habit of leaving the lights on. In the kitchen, my husband left the blaring ceiling light on.

After going to sleep, my son left his multi-bulb ceiling fan on. The electric bill last month was close to $200.00.

Do you have the same sort of habit, or another type of tendency, like not screwing back on the toothpaste cap after using it? Hey, every drop counts, right?

Light ... we need it but can abuse it and overuse the energy. However, God has a big function for light.

"Light," in powerful life-infusing rays, was one of God's first words. "Then God said, 'Let there be light,' and there was light" (Genesis 1:3).

Light is a powerful energy that makes people and our world function (Genesis 1:4; Genesis 1:5; Genesis 1:14; Genesis 1:15; Genesis 1:16; Genesis 1:17; and Genesis 1:18). Get the significance?

Without light, we have complete darkness, and *nothing* can survive. I'm reminded again of the "thick darkness" plague God sent into every Egyptian house and street ... a darkness so thick that could be felt (Exodus 10:21). Then, one day, there will be the darkness that will end our world and perhaps render Earth to outer space. "For the stars, the constellations in the sky, will no longer give their light; the sun will be dark when it rises; and the moon will no longer shine" (Isaiah 13:10). The end.

Now, breathe. God will never send that destructive "entity" into your life because that tangible darkness is hell. "And the angels that did not keep within their original authority, but abandoned their proper sphere, he has kept in darkness, bound with everlasting chains for the Judgment of the Great Day" (Jude 1:6).

We are of a different love and light, cradled in Jesus's caring arms. As a child of Jesus, you are light; and you shine. "If, then, your whole body is filled with light, with no part dark, it will be wholly lighted, as when a brightly lit lamp shines on you" (Luke 11:36). You are vital, born for a purpose. Are you living your purpose? Sisters and Brothers, show your brilliance. *Be* your creativity today, and change this world.

Jesus, tell us your will for our lives as we pray for what you desire for us. Amen.

NOVEMBER 23
BUY, TRADE, SELL

Friendships come in various sized packages, wrapped in all sorts of colors. As I shared a table with another author, I learned that lesson today at a book fair. We were working to glean attention to our books and sell our hard work.

Have you ever tried to make yourself, and what you do, appear important? To stand out among all the rest so people will notice you and the special things you create or do?

"Jesus answered, 'The most important is, Sh'ma Yisra'el, Adonai Eloheinu, Adonai Yisra'el, Adonai Eloheinu, Adonai echad' [Hear, O Isra'el, the Lord our God, the Lord is one.]," (Mark 12:29).

An author from another table walked over to my assortment of novels, picked one up, and opened it to the middle. I was in the middle of a conversation with a buyer when the scrutinizing snob said, "I see a few dangling participles, but this is a good story." Then he slammed my book shut, put it back, and returned with his nose up in the air to his table. I felt flabbergast. I'd *never* treat anyone so callously in front of other people. I pulled out my phone and Googled, *dangling participle*. I received a processing circle. I remained bewildered, until I arrived home and searched for the same thing via my internet connection. The blessing? God knows how to care for us even in disturbing situations. The author next to me had heard the man's insensitive remark. He wrote me a sweet poem; which after reading it, I wiped tears out of my eyes and give him a little hug. What a large beautiful present, *his* written supportive words.

I'm reminded of the presents God offers us in times when people can be cold, thoughtless, or combative. Sometimes, they can be downright cruel about what you've accomplished or worked so hard to create. "I call on Adonai, who is worthy of praise; and I am saved from my enemies" (Psalm 18:4). I cannot save *me* from people who might want to hurt me or gain attention at my expense. Only God can reach through that space of unwarranted hostility and sooth us with His Holy Spirit. I just have to pray to him at those confusing times. David did. "You [God] lift me high above my enemies, you rescue me from violent men" (Psalm 18:49). Violent men were chasing David. I wasn't in a battle with a violent person, but God did encourage me through my new poet friend.

Jesus, help us appreciate the angels you send us. Amen.

J.P. OSTERMAN

NOVEMBER 24
THE UNFINISHED MISSION

Last week we took our son Andrew to the optometrist again because Andrew has been experiencing severe vision problems. He gets a new pair of glasses; but then his eyesight is off kilter, and he strains to see at school. My stepmom Ceil would purchase hearing aids that never fixed her hearing. My dad often had to pay to have his partial repaired and thereafter couldn't partake of his usual diet.

Have you ever experienced a frustrating illness or disease?

We have irreplaceable parts on our bodies. When they fail, we're in trouble, at least until scientists find a way to grow, or replace, these vital organs and specifically tailor them to our bodies. Until then, if something fails, we're in trouble—from teeth to eyes. What to do?

After running tests, twice, the optometrist diagnosed Andrew with *keratoconus*, an eye disease affecting the structure of the cornea. What a shock! I'm sure at some point *you've* received shocking bad news as well. Now he needs specialized treatment. For days we've been Googling, Facebooking, calling other physicians, and consulting Andrew's insurance company. Treatments for keratoconus vary, and we've been on pins-and-needles because he only has one set of eyes.

We're trusting God and praying. Trust in God and prayer.

"Therefore, just as you received the Messiah Jesus as Lord, keep living your life united with him. Remain deeply rooted in him; continue being built up in him and confirmed in your trust" (Colossians 2:6-7). Trust—even in times of illness—is what Paul instructs. The word, "rooted," means, "establish deeply and firmly," and, "(of a plant or cutting) establish roots." A "root" is "the non-leaf, non-nodes bearing parts of a plant's body." A root has four major functions: the absorption of water and inorganic nutrients; anchoring of the plant body to the ground and supporting it; storage of food and nutrients; and, vegetative reproduction." Assembling the information, I conclude that being "deeply rooted" means we are to be established, absorbed in, anchored, grounded, fed by, and supported by the fabric of our Lord Jesus Christ. How do we do that? By reading his word and praying:

"Adonai my God, pay attention to your servant's prayer and plea, listen to the cry and prayer that your servant [Insert your name.] is praying before you today" (1 Kings 8:28). Thank you, Lord.

Jesus, we pray for your healing intervention. Amen.

334

NOVEMBER 25
THANKSGIVING CELEBRATED

"*Mm*, the turkey smells *so* good!" I remember saying to my Grandma Pink. My mouth watering, I'd run through the back porch, step into her farm kitchen, and give her a quick hug. An apple pie and pumpkin pie would be chilling on the porch as she poured her special apricot Jell-O into a round brass mold. I'd run pass her to the living room where Grandpa Pink and our football fanatic relatives would be watching the great game and cheering on the favorite team. I'd rush to Cousin Linda first and ask her a cascade of questions: "Where ya working? Ya bring any dresses for me?" Then I'd inhale the smell of homemade bread and strawberry jelly, my favorites. I'd dash back into the kitchen and wait patiently for grandma to finish stirring her homemade giblet-infused stuffing. She put so much concentration and care into everything she cooked, stirred, and backed. "Can I have just *one* little piece o' bread and jelly?"

"Naw, then I have to cut up the whole loaf," she replied.

"Drats," I pouted, stealthily dipping my finger in her Hungarian nut roll mix.

Have you ever noticed, memories can help us escape troubling or stressful times? What are your favorite Thanksgiving memories?

My past Norman Rockwellian Thanksgivings still filter into my mind like a lingering daydream. I readily and easily remember them, but now those scenes are lost to Time. Many of my relatives are dead, living on only in my mind ... or when I visit other family members and we reminisce. Unable to oust those memories this morning, I thought of a phrase: *Now will be the tomorrow I'll remember, but never have again, yet want more than ever.* I feel like a child standing under a plastic flowered umbrella with rain falling all around me— seconds in Time I can't touch. For some reason, the holidays remind me of how time is so fleeting.

In the New Testament, the word, *time*, appears 297 times in the Complete Jewish Bible and 675 in the Old Testament. "Stay alert! Be on your guard! For you do not know when the time will come" (Mark 13:33). Our future Day of Death is a wakeup call to the precious seconds we are living right now. Make *now* count. Make this moment, and all your seconds, matter.

Lord, give us the words to tell people how much we value them, and love them, while we have the chance, before it's too late. Amen.

November 26
Structural Integrity

Last night, a few of us discussed various fairy tales in which powerful entities grant characters their hearts' desires. I brought up the 1960s TV show, *I Dream of Jeannie*.

Someone said, "*Aladdin*."

What would *you* do with a *few* million dollars?

Money ... we need it to survive, but Jesus says amassing it—greedily—can lead a person down the path to hell.

Many wealthy people are doing wonderful work for the Lord and passing on their blessings. I'm not talking about them ...

I'm pointing at the greedy, thieving, lying swindlers who steal the life savings and financial cushions of hard-working people to support *their* extravagant life styles. I'm empathizing with their victims, unsuspecting trusting people who have worked so as to sustain themselves in their old age (golden years) and leave an inheritance for their families. Google, *con artists,* and you'll read about imposters and deceiving storytellers the likes of Charles Ponzi, Soapy Smith, and Bernard Madoff. I read an account in the newspaper last week of a woman who almost had a heart attack because two con men promised her a nice return on her investments but instead lost *all* her savings. She's 85, and can't start her life's work over again. That's Greed Street, and the junction tees at Hell Bound, ending, yep, at the Burning Gates. *Abandon All Hope Ye Who Enter Here.*

That's eternity ... there ... traded for a few dozen years of money *here*? What a waste, wouldn't ya say?

In the gospels of Matthew, Mark *and* Luke; Jesus talks to the rich man who asks him, "What good thing can I do to have eternal life?"

Jesus replies: "Go and sell your possessions, give to the poor, and you will have riches in heaven. Then come, follow me" (Matthew 19:16-22)! This doesn't end well. "When the young man heard this, he went away sad, because he was wealthy."

He's eternally lost.

My friend said that if she had a million bucks, she'd stick bills into the pockets of needy people.

Another friend said she'd give to various ministries and schools. There is *so much* need that money *can* solve. It's a blessing in the right hands, really.

Lord, strengthen your purpose in us so we can give. Amen.

NOVEMBER 27
GRATITUDE SERVED HERE

In a Thanksgiving prayer with friends before eating today, we focused on Psalm 103. So many times, I've thanked God for His blessings, but I forget to bless Him. That's how Psalm 103 begins.

"Bless Adonai, my soul! Everything in me, bless his holy name! Bless Adonai, my soul, and forget none of his benefits" [Verses 1-2]!

I began wondering: How can anything coming from little me blessing mighty God who owns everything? We say "bless" all the time, but so many meanings of the word give it impact and intensity. "God is so rich in mercy and loves us with such intense love" (Ephesians 2:4). His intense love *is* a blessing, right?

The root word of "blessing," is "bless," and it means: "God's favor and protection;" "sanction or support;" "call (God) holy;" "praise (God);" and, "a beneficial thing for which one is grateful." Are you grateful for someone or something in your today?

How are we to reply to God's blessing?

From the above definitions, when we say, "bless God," we are calling him holy, sanctioning him to ourselves, supporting his presence, praising him, and favoring him. That he made us and understands us in every waking moment merits our worship. "Just as a father has compassion on his children, Adonai has compassion on those who fear him. For he understands how we are made" (verses 13-14). One of God's personality traits is compassion; and relieving compassion because as human beings walking among flawed people in this object-obsessed world, we slip and stumble. We sin. In those moments, we need God's listening ear to absorb our hurts and prayers of contrition. God also has "everlasting grace" (Isaiah 54:8). "He is merciful and compassionate, slow to anger, rich in grace" (Joel 2:13). Through Jesus's words we well, God shows us his nature. "When Jesus came ashore, he saw a huge crowd. Filled with compassion for them … he began teaching them many things" (Mark 6:34). Let us tell others of God's desire to know them personally. "Praised be God, Father of our Lord Jesus the Messiah, compassionate Father, God of all encouragement and comfort" (2 Corinthians 1:3). When we keep our focus on Him, all is fine. We can discern purpose and importance in everything do.

Lord, help us be your messengers of love and encouragement to despairing people. Amen.

NOVEMBER 28
BLACK FRIDAY SPECIALS

We didn't wait long after Thanksgiving dinner to engage our car at full speed and do some early-bird Christmas shopping. I just had to buy bargains for gifts. I must have had ten ads crumpled in my hands. After gathering the basics for presents, I encountered an hour-long line. I kept calling my husband. "Can you find me a shorter line?" My back was hurting.

And customers behind me were complaining. "What's taking the cashier so long?" "How many things is that lady at the front buying, darn!"

After sighs and more groans, someone asked," Just what's holding up the front of the line, again?"

Are you like me, and hate waiting? You ever get impatient and squiggly 'cause the line isn't moving as fast as you want it to move? Waiting can be like eyebrow plucking. "If we continue hoping for something we don't see, then we still wait eagerly for it, with perseverance," Paul says about *waiting*. I prayed, "I wait for your deliverance [from this line], *Adonai*" (Genesis 49:18).

The traffic to the cashier was a snail's pace. What else could we eager-beaver wilting shoppers do but commiserate with one another regarding the long jagged line between two cashiers and us. By this time next year, the objects in our arms will most likely be worn out or broke. Looking back on the late night, I recall the people I talked to and our brief relationships. We were encouraging and comforting one another through our aches-and-pains. We also felt as if we were meandering toward a casket to pay our last respects. Our gifts felt like weights at times; but then again, we made a bit of a difference in one another's lives in that languishing hour we spent together.

I'm reminded of what pleases God in our daily lives. Is He pleased and honored by what we buy, or the lives we touch? Do we receive rewards in heaven for everything we accumulated, or the people we help? For certain, we *do* make a difference in life ... in the seconds we encounter people on the street, in lines, in waiting areas, in the produce section, in the pharmacy....

"Since we have received an unshakeable Kingdom, let us have grace, through which we may offer service that will please God" (Hebrews 12:28). In each moment, our lives *can* matter.

Lord, help us approach others as you would greet them. Amen.

NOVEMBER 29
NO FISHING, NO DOGS

After walking our dog, we stopped to talk to our neighbor when we spotted a strange bird. "That's an Osprey," he said.

Then we began discussing various beautiful places to live in Florida, except they're now overcrowded. I recalled Lazarus....

"A large crowd of Jews found out that Jesus was there and came, not only because of him but also to see Lazarus, whom he had raised from the dead" (John 12:9). A crowd can be a good thing, right? When flu season is over, being in a crowd allows us to spread a message. A saving message.

Have you ever found a beautiful place, but then everyone realizes it's beautiful? Your sanctuary becomes overridden.

Our neighbor agreed. "Yeah, this area *is* great. Just don't tell anybody." We laughed, but imagine having to contain your joy over experiencing Paradise or Jesus. Sadly, not once did I mention Jesus or Heaven to him. I should have, because as Christians we're supposed to let *everyone* in on the life-saving opportunity to accept Him as their savior and inherit eternal life in Heaven with Him.

Jesus *is* Savior. In John 4: 5-42, He encounters the Samaritan woman who offers him water from Jacob's well. He proceeds to minister to her soul, telling her things about herself that in *no way* could He or anyone from a distant land possibly know (v. 39). He tells her, "The water I give [you] will become a spring of water inside [you], welling up into eternal life!" From verses 5 through 18, at the beginning of their conversation, there are *five* exclamation points. Jesus is correcting her false beliefs about God and worship. "God is spirit: and worshippers must worship him spiritually and truly." Now, in the dissonant moments of change between her old beliefs and His truthful facts, he tells her in verse 26, "I, the person speaking to you, am he [the Messiah]." Now, she *really* changes, and she cannot contain her excitement. She runs and tells *everybody*. This "outcast" Samaritan woman becomes one of the first evangelists. After the townsfolk speak to Jesus, they accept him as the Messiah, too. "We no longer trust because of what you said," [they tell the woman] because we have heard for ourselves. We know ... this man really is the Savior of the world" (v. 42). They were saved, and now live with Him in Heaven.

Lord, we need to tell people about special you today. Amen.

November 30
Find the Good

At some point, who hasn't crossed the path of some "wise man" offering an opinion?

I did, at a book-signing event. Someone told me one of my books ended too smoothly. That's a personal preference, okay. Then someone else said, "You must have a violent mind." She stereotyped me, and flippantly gave a critique of my science-fiction books without reading even a line. I had to shake my head in abject confusion. She wasn't making sense because I write in other genres.

Has someone ever given you one of "their" opinions?

Do you need to *change* because of *their* opinion?

I'm reminded of so many phrases regarding opinions, such as: "Opinions are like body parts. Everyone has one;" and, "If you fuel your journey on the opinions of others, you are going to run out of gas" (Dr. Steve Maraboli). Another: "If one person offers an opinion, you could let it slide. If two or more people say the same thing, then that's a clue you should pay attention to the opinion."

So, whose opinions *really* matters?

I must admit: by this time in my writing career, I haven't been published or made money. I've written several books; yet, what's it all for? "Should I continue, God?"

After prayer and months contemplating God's will, I opened the Bible one morning to the following: "Stop relying on man, in whose nostrils is a mere breath. After all, he doesn't count for much, does he" (Isaiah 2:22)? I felt like God was sitting right next to me, whispering in my ear. I asked: "What do I want to accomplish with my writing?" You can ask the same for what *you're* currently doing.

If you are in the pursuit of money for money's sake, and that is your total focus, no matter how hard you work it, in the end, your pursuit will be for nothing. Here are God's hard facts. "On that day [the end of the world], Adonai will take away their finery—their anklets, medallions and crescents, their pendants, bracelets and veils; their headbands, armlets, sashes, perfume bottles, amulets, rings and nose jewels, their fine dresses, wraps, shawls, handbags, gauze scarves, linen underclothes, turbans and capes" (Isaiah 3:18-26). We die without $ and things. The sooner we de-focus off money and set our sights on attaining God's will, the sooner we'll realize a blessing.

God, help us see what is important for eternity. Amen.

DECEMBER 1
HEALING HAPPENING TOGETHER

I watched a TV evangelist pray over a crippled woman. "Lord God our Father, heal your suffering servant in the name of Jesus Christ. We believe you will cure our Sister, Marissa [a fictitious name for her anonymity] of her spinal injury. Amen."

Have you ever wanted to be healed of an illness, disease, or mental affliction so badly that you'd do or give *anything* to *anyone* claiming they have the ability and skill—or spiritual gift—to cure you or a loved one?

Jesus warns us to test churches and teachers. "There will appear false Messiahs and false prophets performing great miracles— amazing things!—so as to fool even the chosen, if possible.

I don't know if Marissa's was cured. We never do hear about the long-term results in these healing ceremonies, do we? However, I *do* know that in our painful and suffering moments, we'll give *anything* to get results.

Over the centuries, traveling salespeople have used drugs—or homeopathic or homegrown meds—to dull pain. Here's a couple of examples from history about pain. In 800 BC, Homer wrote an epic, *The Odyssey*, in which the character Telemachus uses opium to soothe his pain and forget his worries. In his 1664 *Treatise of Man*, René Descartes theorized that the body was similar to a machine, and pain a disturbance passed down along nerve fibers to the brain. This theory transformed the perception of aches and pains from a spiritual mystical experience to a physical mechanical sensation. Thus, curing pain could happen by locating fibers within the body. In 1858, Moritz Schiff formulated the specificity theory of pain when he demonstrated that touch and pain sensations travel to the brain along separate spinal cord pathways. Nowadays, is science the god of all cures? Is there room for a healing miracle from our Lord God?

James offers a solution. "Is someone among you ill? ... Call the elders. ... They will pray for him and rub olive oil on him in the name of the Lord. The prayer offered with trust will heal the one who is ill—the Lord will restore his health; and if he has committed sins, he will be forgiven" (5:14—15). Our Lord has ultimate control over healing. Even pillar Paul wasn't healed when he asked God for a cure (2 Corinthians 12:7-10). All things do work together for good.

Lord, help us discern *our* beliefs that make us vulnerable. Amen.

December 2
A Solution to Weight Loss Problems

People are always asking, "When is the end of the world?" "How will the Earth end?"

It's called the Apocalypse, which does not mean "ending." The word, *apocalypse*, comes from the Greek word, *apokálypsis*, which means, *revelation*, equivalent to *apokalýp(tein)*, meaning, "to uncover, reveal." Apocalypse actually appears to be a beginning.

God our Father tells us through the Apostle John that the End of Days is not a joke. He will reveal and uncover Himself to humanity, and everyone will believe. What do you believe?

Science says the fate of the universe is determined by density. Based on measurements of the rate of expansion and the mass density, Expansion theory favors a universe that will continue to expand indefinitely, resulting in a "big freeze" scenario, at time the universe will approach absolute zero temperature.

["Don't boast about tomorrow, for you don't know what the day may bring" (Proverbs 27:1).]

Have you heard of the Big Crunch theory? At some point, our universe will stop expanding and begin contracting. What about our galaxy colliding with Andromeda? By that time, the surface of the Earth will have already become far too hot for even water to exist. All terrestrial life will have ended. That date and time is estimated to occur in about 3.75 billion years due to the gradual increase of the luminosity of the Sun. If we survive, the product of the intergalactic collision has been nicknamed Milkomeda or Milkdromeda. The final product might look like a giant elliptical galaxy, with a center showing less stellar density than current elliptical galaxies.

I have bad news. We won't be here on Earth.

What is our Lord's design for this time, over 3.75 billion years in the future?

He created this universe and the space/time we occupy. "In days gone by, God spoke in many and varied ways to the Fathers through the prophets. But now, in the *acharit-hayamim* [the future of our universe; the end of days], he has spoken to us through his Son, to whom he has given ownership of everything and through whom he created the universe" (Hebrews 1:1-2). Every moment we live, and every breath we take is Christ given. He has us firmly, eternally.

Jesus, please help us walk in your likeness. Amen.

GOD DESIGNED

DECEMBER 3
VANISH WRINKLES

There's a saying: You never know how valuable something is until it's gone. Have you ever lost (or have someone *steal*) something special, valuable, or sentimental?

The loss can be heart wrenching, and leave metaphorical splashes of gunk on everything and everyone with whom we come in contact as we adapt to the loss.

I have lost things, but the theft of my coins I had been collecting since I was a child still haunts me. Do you think thieves care if what they're stealing is affecting their victims? I keep telling myself: "One day, you can just go to a coin store or antique shop and buy more coins." Not that simple. That's just self-talk I'm using as a coping mechanism.

Harder yet are the invaluable things we *can't* replace. I'm talking about our specialized organs such as a pancreas, eyes, and heart. At this moment in time, unless you have *great* insurance or are a multimillionaire, an organ replacement is impossible. As for the pancreas? Patrick Swayze deteriorated from buff and vibrant to a string bean while seeking treatment for pancreatic cancer. Right now, most organs are irreplaceable. However, what *can* we count on? God's promises. Follow me as we explore our wonderful God.

The Apostle Paul had a special connection to God. "I consider my own life of no importance to me whatsoever, as long as I can finish the course ahead of me, the task I received from the Lord Yeshua—to declare in depth the Good News of God's love and kindness" (Acts 20:24). Every person has a purpose, mission, and tasks to accomplish in his or her lifetime.

Ask yourself: What am I doing that will matter after I am gone? Brothers and Sisters, tomorrow is no guarantee. Today, through His Word, God is giving you a direction. "Consecrate yourselves, because tomorrow Adonai is going to work wonders among you" (Joshua 3:5). What does, *consecrate*, mean? The Hebrew word is, "Qadash," meaning, "to sanctify, prepare, dedicate, be His special creation. You are God's "Yatsar," his "divine activity of creation." Now, live life for His purpose. "I planted the seed, and Apollos watered it, but it was God who made it grow" (1 Corinthians 3:6-9)

Father God, help us see your purpose and will for us today. Amen.

343

December 4
Launch Schedule

Just when I need to stay healthy because I'm about to fly to California for my granddaughter's birth, I wake up with the sniffles. "Why now, Lord?" I ask in prayer. Seems like there might be some type of unconscious self-sabotaging going on. "A tranquil mind gives health to the body" (Proverbs 14:30).

Has that ever happened to you? You *believe* you're fine and illness free. And you know you *need* to *stay* fine, but then you wake up a tab-bit out of sorts? Maybe you even had a flu shot or took Zicam® at the first sign of your cold. Still, there's no guarantee any meds or preventative action on our part can keep us illness free, disease resistant, and completely healthy forever. One day, we're all gonna die. But wait. There's good news. We'll get new bodies!

When Jesus returns, He'll transform our souls into new bodies. We'll be back here, live here, and have bodies resembling His resurrection body. We'll be illness free.

"We are citizens of heaven, and it is from there that we expect a Deliverer, the Lord Yeshua [Jesus] the Messiah. He will change the bodies we have in this humble state and make them like his glorious body, using the power which enables him to bring everything under his control." (Philippians 3:20-21). That day will be a new beginning. So holy. So complete ... with God, Jesus, and the Holy Spirit.

We might be dead, buried or cremated, but our souls will be with Christ our Lord in heaven. "For in this tent, our earthly body, we groan with desire to have around us the home from heaven that will be ours" (2 Corinthians 5:2). We are growing ... to Heaven.

Looking back on my life, I recall so many relatives and friends who have died from old age or illnesses. My Uncle Charlie had a heart attack and died when I was eight. My mother died of a heart attack—the silent killer of diabetes—when she was 66. My stepmother died of complications from dementia in 2012. Death and illness are unwelcome and dreadful realities for us now. However, Heaven is our ultimate home. "He will wipe away every tear from their eyes. There will no longer be any death; and there will no longer be any mourning, crying or pain; because the old order has passed away" (Revelation 21:4). Look up. You are His, only on loan here.

Lord, we want to live out your purposes for our lives and set our sights on Heaven, with You. Amen.

DECEMBER 5
OPERATIONS AGENT

Opposites "operate" everywhere. For every positive, physicists say there's a negative. For every positive reaction, chemists say there's a negative. These laws rule existence, reality, and "things." You've heard the expression, there are two sides to every coin. Similarly, every decision has a consequence, good or bad. You give up chocolate, for example, and later you might have to fend off a craving. You decide on something, but have to make concessions.

At the CERN particle accelerator in Switzerland, scientists have produced negative matter. Problem is, if the negative isn't contained, that *tiny* bit could tear apart the fabric of our reality and destroy our universe. So much power, control and knowledge we now have at our fingertips. Just today, the Orion spacecraft jettisoned into space and landed safely in the Pacific Ocean. This craft ushered in a new era for future adventures into deep space—ultimately, unchartered places in the universe. Yet, also today, I discovered my son's eyes are deteriorating, and he will need to see a cornea specialist for treatment—anything from corrective contacts to surgical implants. In our daily ins-and-outs, we're constantly inhaling sweet positives while butting up against solid negatives.

The tiniest things can incite us to drop down on our knees in prayer. There's no easy fix, but God is in control. Has a sudden problem, decision, or affliction broadsided you in a terrifying way?

"Adonai [God] doesn't see the way humans see. Humans look at the outward appearance, but Adonai looks at the heart" (1 Samuel 16:7). Seeing is our major sense we use to encounter the world, navigate our environment, and relate to friends and family. Some people say the eyes are the windows to a person's soul; thus, being blind closes an experiential window. However, being physically blind needn't be a barrier. Animal scientists have discovered blind elephants that lead of their herds. When stricken blind, people claim their other senses become more pronounced. Still, there will be a day when our defects, weaknesses, and frailties will disappear. "On that day the deaf will hear the words of a book, and out of gloom and darkness the eyes of the blind will see" (Isaiah 29:18). We know that day is when we enter Heaven and touch Jesus. He will also give us new bodies when we return here with Him.

Lord, help us see beyond our pains to endure today. Amen.

DECEMBER 6
COLD AND HOT BEVERAGES

In new or unfamiliar situations, God is present. "I trust in God's unfailing love for ever and ever" (Psalm 52:8).

Sometimes, we need His love when we are struggling *to* love.

Today, I *had* to meet someone who, at the mere mention of her name, makes me shudder. I felt afraid of the situation—also anticipating a confrontation—so I built up a wall around me. I kept telling myself: *Just say hi, smile a lot, and don't say anything you wouldn't want her saying to you.* Have you ever been forced to like someone? When I don't like someone, which is rare, I can "let slip" an off-handed phrase or emit negative body language that might trigger an angry response. The situation would worsen. People know when other people rub them the wrong way, right? If I let lose one little comment, then she and I could get a bad cycle rollin' and make others feel uncomfortable. When we don't like someone and we're forced, because of work or family, to be pleasant, our human nature can be an automatic timer, making us appear, at times, mean. "Inside each of us, there is the seed of both good and evil. It's a constant struggle as to which one will win. And one cannot exist without the other" (Eric Burdon). How do we fight our nature and act contrary?

During family gatherings, awkward encounters can occur. A party *could* morph into an olive throwing spat, as what happened between one of my aunts and my mom.

The Holy Spirit within us *moves* us to evolve beyond being a puppet to our human nature and individual tendencies. Avoidance isn't the answer. In life, we meet and greet people all the time, even though we might be opposed to having them in our lives. Jesus has several answers. The first is a command. "I tell you, love your enemies and pray for those who persecute you" (Matthew 5:44). Love my enemies? The person I don't want to meet, however, isn't an enemy but an intruder, and untrustworthy. Can I *love*, in spite of my bad attitude? "This is how we know who the children of God are and who the children of the devil are: Anyone who does not do what is right is not God's child, nor is anyone who does not love their brother and sister" (1 John 3:10). Love is the outward display of my identity in Christ. I am reminded of the eternal souls at stake if I don't show strangers the face of Christ to this world. I'll change.

Lord, give us a heart for love and compassion. Amen.

DECEMBER 7
GEM STONE SALE

I saw my brother this weekend after not having seen him in three years. The last time we visited was when our stepmother died. Those were sad times, during which he had a birthday. I bought him a cake. Then we sang "Happy Birthday" and he blew out his candles.

"Oh, how good, how pleasant it is for brothers to live together in harmony" (Psalm 133:1). Whom would you like to see more than ever today? We can never know the moment we leave Earth. We *do not* have control over natural disasters and peoples' actions. Bad things happen. Unfair things happen. *Anything* can whisk us off to Heaven. However, we can't live in fear of something or someone killing us. We *can* call someone we've been longing to talk to today. We *can* reach out to someone we've been neglecting lately.

Before I said goodbye to my brother today, I told him about the message of salvation. I want to make sure I'll see him in Heaven.

Have you felt the urgency to talk about Jesus to someone? "Stand at the crossroads and look. ... 'Which one is the good way?' Take it, and you will find rest for your souls" (Jeremiah 6:16).

In the book of Hebrews, Paul makes his pronouncement clear. Jesus came as God on Earth to die for our sins. He's the one and only perfect sacrifice, and he shed his precious blood to eliminate the Old Testament need for a yearly Temple sacrifice for the forgiveness of sins. *Nothing* we do and *no person* can make us holy in the presence of God because we are under Adam's sin. We need a sacrifice so we can stand holy before God. And animal sacrifices do not suffice, for animals lack a will *to decide* their fate. Under the "old law," a high priest grabs the best of the herd and sheds its blood on God's holy alter of forgiveness. Animals cannot choose, so they become victims of someone else's choice. Yet, Jesus chose of his *own* free will to leave his holy Heavenly realm and to become human. To be born in a meager manger. To be a blood offering in human form. To eagerly obey God's will to die on the cross for the sins of humanity. "We have been separated for God and made holy, once and for all through the offering of Jesus the Messiah's body" (Hebrews 10:1-17). When I acknowledged Jesus's death on the cross for *my* sins, He no longer remembers them. I can then stand before him and exclaim, "God, I am yours. Now, who can I tell about you? Help me do so.

Lord, give us the words to help others know you. Amen.

J.P. Osterman

December 8
Produce and Bakery

I've just arrived in an unfamiliar city and need to slow down so I can navigate unfamiliar streets and locate stores.

"The people of Isra'el said to Moshe, 'Oh no! We're dead men! Lost! We're all lost' " (Numbers 17:27)! Okay, I'm exaggerating, but I felt lost, several times.

One problem is, the cars behind me are loaded with impatient drivers who don't know my lost and confusing circumstances. Another problem is, the speed I am forced to travel. I pass all the stores and street signs so quickly that I can't see addresses and markers. I end up long shooting my destination and making U-turns.

Have you found yourself lost lately?

There are such disorienting and confused feelings about being lost and isolated without a support system next to us to help us or direct us. During solar flares or satellite outages, even a GPS can fail, leaving us stranded. Can you think of one situation where you found yourself lost and searching for a specific location? Our emotions become intense at such times.

Similar to finding ourselves stuck in an unfamiliar city, we can become stuck, or go into hiding, because of a cycle of sin or bad habit. We can dissociation from our usual circles of friends and family, cut ties to church, or lie to continue sinning. Sin makes us shed our trust in God, and then we leave God out of our moments.

I might not think God doesn't notice my detachment and lack of dependence and trust in him, but He knows. "I remember your devotion ... how you followed me" (Jeremiah 2:2). He always wants us to admit our sin, repent, and return to Him. "'Return ... I will not frown on you, for I am merciful,' says Adonai. 'I will not bear a grudge forever.' Only acknowledge your guilt, that you have committed crimes against Adonai your God" (Jeremiah 3:12-13). When I isolate because I *want* to hide, or feel alone because a bad habit is separating me from my God and savior Jesus Christ, I need to tell someone what's *really* going on inside (become real) and ask them to pray with me. This humility helps us return to God's closeness. "'Do not be afraid ... for I am with you,' says Adonai, 'to rescue you'" (Jeremiah 1:8). He never gives up on us. He heals us.

Lord, help us understand what we have done, and return to you in complete trust. Amen.

DECEMBER 9
MEDICAL CENTER

When I was pregnant with my son and saw the first sonogram, I was ecstatic when the doctor said, "Your baby is growing normally and the heartbeat is just fine." Whew! I had taken that cautionary sonogram, doctor's orders, and gleaned relief from the results.

There are times when we might have a health concern, or experience something odd happening inside our bodies. However, we postpone preventative checkups or ignore the warning signs, for example, flaring heartburn, because we're afraid we might get bad news. Do you have an inclination to postpone a yearly checkup?

Today I saw the sonogram of my first grandchild—a little girl. "Grandchildren are the crown of the aged, while the glory of children is their ancestors" (Proverbs 17:6). My daughter's due date is December 10, but we don't think "little baby" will arrive at all tomorrow. No contractions. Yet, my daughter's doctor said the baby is "progressing normally and might not deliver for another week, or longer." Waiting ... who is good at waiting? How do you cope when there's a due date and you're looking forward to "the date" but the results don't arrive as anticipated? Waiting....

I remember four years ago when Drew and I waited for his post-op cancer results. We didn't postpone any treatments. We didn't know how extensively the bladder cancer had progressed and if the doctor had removed it all during surgery. I told my daughter that story, ending it with the following: "There is good waiting, as what you're going through with waiting for the arrival of your baby; and then here is hard waiting, such as what Drew and I endured as we waited on pins-and-needles for his blood test results. Things could be worse." She agreed. She's joyfully anticipating her daughter's arrival. Meanwhile, we'll just consider the waiting as an Endurance Test from God. "The crucible [tests] silver, and the furnace [tests] gold, but the one who tests hearts is Adonai" (Proverbs 17:3). Perhaps this is why wisdom comes with getting older. Since I've experienced *postponing* and *waiting*, I can encourage my daughter, and put her at ease with a bit of that "glory" in Proverbs 17:6. Still, the ultimate glory must go to God, who will determine when my precious granddaughter will arrive on this earth. "A person may plan his path [due dates the doctors predict], but Adonai directs his steps.

Lord Jesus, give us patient hearts and still minds. Amen.

December 10
Coffee Extravaganza

My daughter Jennifer asked me if I could alter a long-sleeve shirt into a short-sleeve shirt for her husband Keith. "Of course," I replied. Then I spent an hour contemplating how to do it. The shoulder seams are much longer than the underarm section, and I thought I could match up the long-sleeve shirt to one of Keith's t-shirts and use it as the pattern for the alteration. Everything went smoothly, until the old sewing machine needle broke ... twice.

My daughter said, "At least you tried ... but you must have done *something* wrong."

I took that as a criticism, but I bit my tongue. Have you ever felt like defending yourself, but realized the other person might be experiencing his or her own difficulties? "May the words of my mouth and the thoughts of my heart be acceptable in your presence, *Adonai*, my Rock and Redeemer" (Psalm 19:15). I was over halfway through with the alteration when the sewing needle broke. I felt so prideful at not being perfect, that I wanted to go to Walmart and buy a cheap sewing machine. Then I stopped, prayed, and realized I'm not perfect at all. I told her that; and besides, "My sewing machine from my high school days is at my dad's house, so I can finish making the alterations on Keith's shirt there." The point is, not everything we do turns out perfectly and works out just fine. God had to work on my pride and humility, and allow me to accept myself for not living up to my daughter's expectations. Still, I felt hurt because I wanted to make her happy and approve of me. Being prideful blinded me of God's approval.

"First comes pride, then disgrace; but with the humble is wisdom" (Proverbs 11:2). The word, *pride*, means, "a feeling or deep pleasure or satisfaction derived from one's own achievements, the achievements of those with whom one is closely associated, or from qualities or possessions that are widely admired." The word implies self-centeredness, not God centered. Thus, when I'm exuding pride, I am self-focused and concentrated on making others recognize *me*. A task not perfectly achieved then morphs into an abyss of self-denigration. I can't do *anything* in *that* state of mind. Days after the alteration, Keith put on the shirt. The short-sleeve hem was too high, making the shirt appear as a wetsuit top. We laughed.

Lord, *your* approval and *your* value matter. Amen.

DECEMBER 11
PIZZA AND PASTA

There's nothing more powerless than watching someone you love or care about suffer through pain.

Have you ever had to sit back, or pace the floor, as someone close to you was experiencing excruciating pain? It's soul shaking.

Today, my daughter is in labor. She's been trying every standing, sitting, and leaning position to alleviate her sudden and sharp contractions. They're like ocean waves in a storm that are continuously pounding the shore at an unrelenting tempo. I've been rubbing her back, and her husband is a life preserver onto which she's been clinging for dear life. In between difficult times throughout our day, I've been reading the Book of Jeremiah. I can't believe the pain that prophet endured as God's spokesperson. At dinner, as we tried to eat because I told her she might not be eating for a while, I told bits-and-pieces of his agonizing adventure.

Jeremiah heard God's words and accepted God's purpose. "Before I formed you in the womb, I knew you; before you were born, I separated you for myself. I have appointed you to be a prophet to the nations" (Jeremiah 1:5). Jeremiah had no opportunity to choose a career because God *appointed* him to deliver painful news to the Jewish people. "Today I have placed you over nations and kingdoms to uproot and tear down to destroy and to demolish, and build and to plant" (1:10). The people of Israel had reverted to worshipping idols and abandoning God's holy law (1:16). Jeremiah told them God's words. "'Your own wickedness will correct you, your own backslidings will convict you. You will know and see how bad and bitter it was to abandon *Adonai* your God, and how fear of me is not in you,' says *Adonai Elohim-Tzva'ot*" (2:19). For speaking God's decree, the king imprisoned Jeremiah and had him beaten several times. Still, God's edict through Jeremiah remained unchanged because people refused to repent. "People have done evil. … Therefore, the days are coming when [the Ben-Hinnom Valley] will be called the Valley of Slaughter" (7:32-34). All the tribes of Israel wound up killed or captives of Babylon. The king threw Jeremiah into a cistern to die (38:6). Yet, his faith and trust in God remained steadfast. There are pains, that when endured, produce life-changing results and new life.

Lord, help us endure life's painful moments. Amen.

December 12
Emergency

After spending eight *long* hours in labor, Jenny *finally* delivered her baby girl. I'm Grandma Joy. Wow—who woulda ever believed?

"See! This is our God! We waited for him to save us. This is *Adonai*. We put our hope in him. We are full of joy, so glad he saved us" (Isaiah 25:9).

I'm sure you know moments such as this: when a long wait, coupled with pain and hard work, bring someone or something special into our world. Maybe you've been working hard and putting in long hours into a creative project, or a task on your job.

I spent Jenny's time in labor waiting in a small TV room. I snuck back to the delivery room and stood behind a curtain to listen for a baby's cry, until the nurse caught me, drats. Oh well, I did have time to think about Bible characters who wanted children.

After the Fall of Adam and Eve, God promised He'd send a Redeemer. "When the appointed time arrived, God sent forth his Son. He was born from a woman, born into a culture in which legalistic perversion of the Torah was the norm, so that he might redeem those in subjection to this legalism and thus enable us to be made God's sons" (Galatians 4:4-5). How many years did God take to send our Savior Jesus? "There were fourteen generations from Avraham to David, fourteen generations from David to the Babylonian Exile, and fourteen generations from the Babylonian Exile to the Messiah" (Matthew 1:17). This doesn't include the generations prior to Abraham, but God made the first covenant with him and Sarah who wanted a son. "Sarah your wife will bear you a son, and you are to call him Yitz'chak [laughter]" (Genesis 17:19). Abraham laughed when God said He'd bless him with a son at the ripe old age of a hundred years—and Sarah ninety. Two more Bible characters wanted a child as well. Manoach and his wife (Judges 13:2) had Samson. "The child will be a *nazir* for God from the womb until the day he dies" (Judges 13:7). *Nazir*, means *consecrated* or *separated*. The nazirite is described as being "holy unto YHWH" (Numbers 6:2-7). Thus, he wasn't supposed to shave his head and had other restrictions, which we know Samson disobeyed. Still, he found redemption as God's divine purpose always occurs no matter how people deviate from his will. Every child is vital.

Lord, we want to bless you through our generations. Amen.

DECEMBER 13
LIVE IN LUXURY

I saw an old *Twilight Zone* show where the main character could read peoples' minds. Wow, did his world change. Think of *one* person whose mind you'd love to read and learn his or her thoughts. I'd consider knowing what my children were really thinking, or a friend, or the pastor of a church. Still, if we could know peoples' realities, what might change?

Again, however, God doesn't change. "God is not a human who lies or a mortal who changes his mind. When he says something, he will do it. When he makes a promise, he will fulfill it (Numbers 23:19). We have an awesome God. He is truth.

To *know* the truth is one of our many tendencies, or drives, even though we're repelled by the truth. It's like making lemonade and needing to add sweetener before drinking it. Here's a test. Think of a person whose thoughts you *don't* want to know. For me, it would be my dad, and my husband. If I'd learn something I *don't* want to know about me *or* them, I'd be crushed. However, couldn't I still be repaired? What an agonizing transition period though, right?

Perhaps this is what Jesus meant when he said, "Know the truth, and the truth will set you free" (John 8:32). Yet, how can *knowing* devastating information, like the knowledge mentioned above, set a person free? *Truth*, means, *an irrefutable principle or belief;* and, *sincerity, candor, honesty, accuracy.* The opposite of truth is *dishonesty, fiction, lie,* or *falsehood.* So, back to that character in the show. Peoples' thoughts were an open book to him, revealing each person's heart. He also learned each person's nature and character. I wonder, If I'd know that kind of reality inside every person, would I want to pass by people even while shopping?

When Jesus walked among people and looked them in the face, he knew each heart. He even knew peoples' evil intentions. "But look! The person who is betraying me is here at the table with me! The Son of Man is going to his death according to God's plan. ... They began asking each other which of them could be about to do such a thing" (Luke 22:21-23). That individual was Judas, a person Jesus walked with for three years and kept trying to save, I'm sure. What compassion, mercy, tolerance, patience and long-suffering *Jesus* must have had, and has. He knows *everyone* deeply and intimately.

Lord, give us a character of love and service today. Amen.

December 14
Fresh and Simple

There's nothing like a child's love for a parent, and it's only natural that children try so hard *to please* their parents and receive their approval. "Children too are a gift from *Adonai*" (Psalm 127:3). You've received and given gifts, so you know how eager you are when the Giver sets the wrapped package proudly in your hands. What a mystery is buried deep inside the wrapping! Cherishing each second, you want to unravel it slowly. Hopefully, you had parents who treated you with love, saying, "Thank you, God, for our child, who will unfold for your glory, and blossom for you in the world."

Some people don't, and haven't, lived in loving nurturing homes.

Yesterday, I visited my dad in California. I spent the day doing laundry while we intermittently watched a football game, talked about the weather, and discussed world affairs. We avoided—like dart throwing—conversations about *anything* else.

Sometimes, it's hard to know how to talk to broken people when they're experiencing troubles or have the Wall of China around 'em. "I am *Adonai* your God, who brought you out of the land of Egypt, so that you would not be their slaves. I have broken the bars of your yoke, so that you can walk upright" (Leviticus 26:13). Sin metastasizes in many forms....

The definition of *sin* is, *an immoral act considered to be a transgression against divine law, especially deliberately*; and, *act of evil/wickedness*. Our sinful state puts a chasm between us, God, and others. "It was through one individual that sin entered the world, and through sin, death" (Romans 5:12). The opposite of sin is favor with God, such as when Mary accepted God's divine plan for her life. "Don't be afraid, Miryam, for you have found favor with God" (Luke 1:30-33). What an unselfish act she agreed to when she replied to Angel Gabriel: "I am the servant of *Adonai*. May it happen to me as you have said" (1:38). The only way we can find favor with God so we can approach his holy throne with unstained hearts is through Jesus, God's son. His love is greater than the sins that blind people (2 Timothy 3:1-5). "God so loved the world that he gave his only and unique Son, so that everyone who trusts in him may have eternal life, instead of being utterly destroyed" (John 3:16). If our childhoods were hard, we now have an unfailing, unchanging, loving Father God.

Heavenly Father, we *cherish* and *receive* your perfect love. Amen.

DECEMBER 15
LIVING SPACE REALTORS

One of my favorite TV shows was *Parenthood*, a story about the ups-and-downs of being a mom and dad. The job of mom, dad, or caretaker can be as tumultuous as riding a rollercoaster. You might not be a parent, but you might own a pet, or are responsible for taking care of someone's pet while they're out of town. Who are you caring for today? What are the hardest moments and tasks for you?

The hardest part of parenting, as I've been observing these past few days since my granddaughter Rachel's birth, is successful nursing, followed by the baby pooping and peeing. We've been surrounding my daughter Jennifer like helicopters: "Can I get you some soothing cream? Water? Food? Motrin?"

At Rachel's every cry, everyone rushes to her and Jenny. Wow, can Rachel pound out a wallop of a scream! Already we've discerned her cries for attention, and she shrieks when mommy or daddy make a mistake in positioning her. Little, helpless, adorable Rachel is completely dependent on her parents ... mommy, especially. Do you notice, that when you're caretaking, *everything* you do is vital?

However, Jenny can't do *everything* right after giving birth. She's exhausted, so daddy Keith takes over, and then me when their bonding time is complete. God initiates a familial extension from the smallest to greatest: baby to mother and father; then grandparents; and, then outsiders.

In the Bible, God puts importance on the family, a family's land, and the necessity of keeping in contact with one's *entire* family. "You are to consecrate the fiftieth year, proclaiming freedom throughout the land to all its inhabitants. It will be a *yovel* for you; you will return everyone to the land he owns, and everyone is to return to his family" (Leviticus 25:10). The Jubilee (Hebrew *yovel*) year is the year at the end of seven cycles of Sabbatical years. The year had a special impact on the ownership and management of Israeli land. Slaves and prisoners were set free, and debts forgiven. The mercies of God would manifest throughout the entire nation. After watching my daughter and son-in-law scramble at the movements of their baby, and seeing them cry when they felt overwhelmed or in pain, I realized that simply being there, in the background, as a supporting pillar has made a difference. Your role is vital in your caretaking of everything.

Lord, we want to help, or simply be present in love. Amen.

DECEMBER 16
HOLIDAY HAPPY

Mother Teresa once said about smiling: "Every time you smile at someone, it is an action of love, a gift to that person, a beautiful thing." Have you smiled today? A smile can inspire someone to inspire those people to inspire ... you get the picture. Your smile can spread like a drive for fragrant cotton candy.

Research shows that smiling can alter our moods. It's just one way—even when we don't feel like it—to change. Smile ... even at yourself in the mirror. I did. I smiled. That's right! I forced these lips to curl up from a sleep-deprived pout I had been struttin' around with this morning. I had inspiration. My precious granddaughter.

Since Jenny brought Rachel home from the hospital, every now and then, between crying spells, Rachel smiles. I remember experts telling me that babies after birth *can't* smile. I disagree. Last night, when Jenny was burping Rachel, Rachel, with her blue eyes wide open, broke out in a very brief but beautiful smile. Let me tell you, her smile was like the best Swiss hot chocolate, melting our hearts and calming our tired souls. Here's what I think....

God made newborns to smile so unpredictably in order to give parents a rainbow in between those very first days of experimenting with the mother-father-baby bonding and trial-and-error feedings. So, Rachel's teensy-weensy smile felt overwhelmingly relieving and joyous. Of course, we unleashed our cameras trying to capture another, but nothing. Now, we at least know she's content, and Jenny and Keith are fulfilling Rachel's needs.

In those moments of knowing she is satisfying Rachel, Jenny appears so caring and blessed. I am reminded of another woman who must have felt the same overflowing joy after giving birth to Jesus: Mary. "My soul magnifies Adonai; and my spirit rejoices in God, my Savior. ... The Mighty One has done great things for me" (Luke 1:46-49)! In spite of giving birth in a stable and later having to escape for her life to save her child, Mary must have experienced an overwhelming trust, faith, and confidence in God. Another great truth about God, revealed through Mary and Angel Gabriel, harkens to us as well. "With God, nothing is impossible" (Luke 1:37). Rearing a child is hard work, but rewarding, with God's support.

God, give us hearts of faith, hope, love and trust in difficult times. Amen.

DECEMBER 17
FRUIT AND VEGETABLE FARM

Yesterday, I saw a friend I hadn't seen in years. I'm reminded of how Elizabeth, the mother of John the Baptist, felt when she finally saw her cousin Mary. Elizabeth was so excited, "the baby in my womb leaped for joy" (Luke 1:44)!

Have you ever felt that type of anticipation and excitement at the prospect of seeing an old friend?

"Perfume and incense make the heart glad, [also] friendship sweet with advice from the heart" (Proverbs 27:9).

There were times, however, when I believed our friendship had drifted into the Sea of Oblivion, but then "Donna" would email my husband, or call my dad, and find out my new phone number. Then Donna would call me, and we'd talk for a few hours. This would follow with months or years of another round of lost contact. So, I was surprised when we scheduled a meeting, and she showed up, early. I was late though because of rush-hour traffic. So *not* like punctual me. At the restaurant, we talked for a long time. On this visit with my daughter, I could have called other people as well, but I decided to focus on my family, and not contact old acquaintances whom I've hardly talked to since leaving California. When I have called or written them, they haven't replied, so I guess those "friends" are like gold rays at dusk ... fading beyond the horizon.

I can think of one occasion in the Bible when people have altered friendships. Isaac's son Jacob comes to my mind. Jacob is witty. He knows how to make money and prosper when Laban wants him to fail. "You know that I [Jacob] have served your father with all my strength, and that your father has belittled me and has changed my wages ten times. But God did not allow him to do me any damage" (Genesis 31:6-7). Jacob makes a special covenant with Laban and finally receives Rachel as his wife. Yet, years of hostility between Jacob and his brother Esau continue eating away at Jacob because he cheated Esau out of Isaac's blessing. You'd think Esau would want to kill him when Jacob wants to reunite with him. The opposite happens. "Esau ran to meet him, hugged him, threw his arms around his neck and kissed him; and they wept" (Genesis 33:4). There are bonds so strong such as family attachments that never fail. God wants unity, peace and reconciliation.

Jesus, we pray for peace and mercy in our families. Amen.

DECEMBER 18
COFFEE EXPRESS

Today would have been my grandmother's birthday, but she died in 1984. Today was also my granddaughter Rachael's initial due date when the doctor predicted she'd enter this world. And in three hours and one minute, I'm scheduled to fly home to Florida. At the airport, I'll probably grab a newspaper and read the "On This Day in History" column.

Do you like reading about significant world-changing events? It's in our blood to keep track of how far humanity has come, perhaps so we can predict how much faster we can accelerate ourselves? On this date in 1839, John Draper captured the first celestial photograph of Moon; and in 1957, the Shippingport Atomic Power Station in Pennsylvania becomes the world's first nuclear power plant to generate electricity. However, get ready, because today is also *your* day.

Time is constantly transitioning us into old age and memories. We live *in* transition. We can't hold onto sights, sounds, smells, and experiences, like the moment I first touched my granddaughter, or saw my own children, except now through photos and videos. That's why dementia is so distressing. One symptom is forgetfulness. It acts as a varnish remover in the brain, stripping memories that are vital adherents to our identities.

Moses knew all about life transitions and time—God's time and timing. He was always dispensing a deadline to Pharaoh while giving hope to his people. It's one of the rare times in history when a deadline's consequences yield disaster for one nation while reaping positive results for another population. Moses was 80 and Aaron 83 when they stood before Pharaoh (Exodus 7:7). Through God, Moses was constantly proclaiming time limits. "Adonai said to Moshe, 'Go to Pharaoh, and tell him: Here is what Adonai, the God of the Hebrews, says: Let my people go, so that they can worship me. If you refuse to let them go and persist in holding on to them, the hand of Adonai is on your livestock in the field—on the horses, donkeys, camels, cattle and flocks—and I will make them suffer a devastating illness' "(Exodus 9:1-3). In a moment, our circumstances can change, and life can proceed on a different path of transition.

Lord, help us keep hope and trust in you and your Word when situations in life appear bleak. Help us experience true joy. Amen.

December 19
Always on Time

Home. When you're away, you can't wait, to get back home, right? What's *your* favorite place you just can't wait to sink your body into when you finally arrive home? The place feels so good, doesn't it?

"Daniel went home. The windows of his upstairs room were open in the direction of Jerusalem; and there he kneeled down three times a day and prayed, giving thanks before his God, just as he had been doing before" (Daniel 6:11).

Last night, I arrived home from California. I've been missing Rachel, my daughter Jennifer, and my son-in-law Keith. After rolling my suitcase over the garage threshold and collapsing on my bed— after a delayed flight that landed me in Orlando after 1 a.m. and the drive home that took over an hour—I grabbed my favorite soft pillows and inhaled the fabric-softener scent of my sheets. Dorothy said in *The Wizard of Oz*, "There's no place like home." Several Bible characters came to mind as I likened their experiences to mine. Not all of them had ties to home though, nor felt as exuberant as I did to arrive at a point of safety.

The prophet John, Jesus' cousin, left his home for an important mission. "You, child, will be called a prophet of the Most High. You will go before the Lord to prepare his way by spreading the knowledge among his people that deliverance comes by having sins forgiven through our God's most tender mercy, which causes the Sunrise to visit us from Heaven" (Luke 1:76-78). This was Jesus' salvation message, and John was a Wilderness Man who proclaimed Jesus as the Messiah—Savior for humanity. John lost his life. Really, however, God exchanged his physical body for life in Heaven, *home*.

Paul, an apostle for Jesus, also realized our temporal state of existence on this Earth. "We know that when the tent which houses us here on earth is torn down, we have a permanent building from God, a building not made by human hands, to house us in heaven. For in this tent, our earthly body, we groan with desire to have around us the home from heaven that will be ours" (2 Corinthians 5:1-10). We amass meaningful things, collect significant objects, and work hard to provide a home and security for the people we love. However, we are also mission for Jesus, until, one day, we'll reach our final destination and real home. Heaven awaits.

Lord, one day, we will see you, and our ultimate home. Amen.

DECEMBER 20
PARTY PLUS CITY

Today I attended a Christmas party, a time set apart in the fabric of our busy lives to rejoice with people and celebrate. However, I want to write about "being alone." I'll return to the topic of parties tomorrow though; so wait until then and read tomorrow's story. Wow, that sounded like a real brain twister, but my merrymaking turned sorrowful when on the way home I saw more homeless people than I'd seen in a long while.

Do you ever wonder how some people can live off almost nothing, and in the most abandoned or desolate of locations? Like woods or a desert?

So many Bible characters experienced loneliness. John the Baptist, Jesus' cousin, was a solitary figure and contemplative, by choice. "In those days John the Baptist appeared in the wilderness of Judea, proclaiming, 'Repent, for the kingdom of heaven has come near.' "This is the one of whom the prophet Isaiah spoke when he said, 'The voice of one crying out in the wilderness: Prepare the way of the Lord, make his paths straight.' "Now John wore clothing of camel's hair with a leather belt around his waist, and his food was locusts and wild honey" (Matthew 3:1-4). I traveled through Israel once. From an airplane, I saw the desert as a gigantic spread of yellow-reticulating sand as far as my eyes could see. Then there's the Dead Sea, also called the Salt Sea. I floated in this oily-feeling water, actually like a tolerable slime. To think John liked living in those places, calling them home seems intolerable and lonely. Those hardship years molded him into boldness though (Matthew 3:1-17).

Diseases also left people alone and isolated. Naaman, a Syrian commander had a *tzara'at*, a mysterious skin disease believed to be a symbol for a sinful affliction. A diagnosis of leprosy, or tzara'at, left people instantly friendless, jobless, disconnected from family, and abandoned. Naaman asked God for healing, and after he dunked seven times in the Jordan, God healed him. Restoration for him was a bliss. As is life joyous for us after we repent of our sins. It isn't pleasant, standing at the fringe and observing people. "I've learned that there is no God in all the earth except in Israel" (2 Kings 5:1-19). We can be restored, and re-join God's graces at any time.

Lord, help us experience your comforting touch in our direst of moments when we feel separated from people and alone. Amen.

DECEMBER 21
BIRTHDAY

On this day in second grade, I remember a birthday party I had in school. I brought a box of twenty, ice cream cups preserved in dry ice; and after passing out the treats to my classmates, they sang "Happy Birthday" to me. Then I remember a subsequent birthday when I received checks, cards, and greetings of, "Happy Birthday, Joyce and Merry Christmas." This day, my birthday, is so close to Christ's birthday that it's easy for people to give me *two* presents in one. Then, I'd gawk in irritation, smile widely and saying a forced, "Thaaanks."

Have you ever felt gypped? Slighted?

Feeling slighted because of an unmet high expectation is part of the human condition. Aldous Huxley once said: "One third, more or less, of all the sorrow that the person I think I am must endure is unavoidable. It is the sorrow inherent in the human condition, the price we must pay for being sentient and self-conscious organisms ... subject to the laws of nature and under orders to keep on marching, through irreversible time, through a world wholly indifferent to our well-being, toward decrepitude and the certainty of death. The remaining two thirds of all sorrow is homemade and, so far as the universe is concerned, unnecessary" (from, *Island*). We are "sentient," meaning, "able to perceive or feel things." Furthermore, we are of a higher consciousness than animals, for we contemplate life, death, and are fully aware of "being slighted." However, we are not just "organisms" (Genesis 2:22). As a child who felt gypped, I'd say *thank you* but later on cry in private when donning the socks or PJs. The next month, in January, I saw what people gave my brother on his birthday. I seethed with envy at his toys and post-Christmas gifts. What do we do with our slights? When we believe we're not favored or treated the same as others?

Jesus once attended a marriage ceremony where celebration soured into vapid stares into empty wine vats. Then our Lord touched the emptiness. "The man in charge tasted the water; it had now turned into wine! He did not know where it had come from, but the servants who had drawn the water knew" (John 2:9). Let us remember the party we'll have in Heaven when we live forever with Jesus. Water to wine happened here. In Heaven? Mansions.

Lord, our birthdays will be celebrated with you. Amen.

DECEMBER 22
PARADE ROUTE

Have you ever focused on a task, only to be disturbed, interrupted, or diverted from your purpose? Maybe even several times? Getting back on the right track can be difficult, right?

That happened to me just now as I was doing dishes. I had plans to finish decorating the Christmas tree and then bake banana loaves for neighbors' presents. It seems that every time I stick myself to an important job that has a vital or special meaning for me; my son, or husband, divert my attention in another direction with their jobs. I'm left asking, "Isn't what I want necessary, too?"

Are you having difficulty with focus today?

I can think of a few Bible characters who experienced difficulties while embarking on or contemplating a course of action. One is the Rich Young Man in Matthew 19. He asks Jesus what he needs to do to have eternal life. He believes he's on the right path and going in an important direction because he's trying to obey the commandments. Jesus tells him differently. "'If you want to be perfect, go, sell what you have and give to the poor, and you will have treasure in heaven; and come, follow Me.' But when the young man heard that saying, he went away sorrowful, for he had great possessions" (21-22). This young rich man has lived a particular lifestyle, and is determined to live a sinless life. Right ... by being perfect? I don't know about you, but I'd fail at "being perfect" miserably. The man must also be a famous public figure or religious leader, like one of our movie stars or TV evangelists. Jesus tells him about a treasure in Heaven, and that he should consider taking another path in this temporary life as opposed to what he is trying to do perfectly *right now* in this tangible world.

I'm sure you can relate: at times, I'm a Doubting Thomas. Thomas was the disciple who never seems to be around when everyone else sees Jesus change. Yet, I can relate to Tom. I like seeing, hearing, and feeling; and then I believe. Jesus said to Tom: "Reach your finger here, and look at my hands; and reach your hand here, and put it into my side. Do not be unbelieving, but believing." Jesus was telling Tom to change direction and perspective. Only then could he discover something new about himself and re-focus.

Lord, we want to be able to see new opportunities in our lives. Help us see a direction *you* would have us implement. Amen.

DECEMBER 23
AFTER CHRISTMAS SALES NOW

I haven't baked in mass quantities in a few years. However, this year, I decided to give my neighbors gifts of homemade banana bread. I can't believe how, after I assembled all the ingredients, I felt like a stumbling child learning to walk. I had the flour and baking soda so spread out beyond the eggs that I needed Elasti-Girl fingers to reach them. I nearly tripped over the garbage can to hurry up and grab the measuring cups and measuring spoons. I almost spilled the entire bag of sugar while corralling the mashed bananas. Then, I needed to work fast to mix the butter, eggs, and vanilla; but the yogurt appeared curdled. Still, I blended them all together. The batch tasted just fine. My gosh, you'd think I'd just began cooking when in fact I've been using the oven since age nine.

Have you ever changed, so much so, that you're left wondering: What's happening to my body, or my mind?

Feeling scattered is what tends to happen when we're out of practice at doing something.

"Jesus made a practice of withdrawing to remote places in order to pray" (Luke 5:16). We can "make a practice of" talking to God.

Solomon knew the answers to everything. He's the only one in the Bible to whom God writes a blank check and says, "Whatever ya want, you can have." (1 Kings 3:5). Later, Solomon builds the Temple and establishes Jerusalem (1 Kings 5). He loves God, and offers God the finest sacrifices. Solomon could have asked for riches or immortality, but he asks for wisdom. "Give your servant an understanding heart able to administer justice to your people so that I can discern between good and bad" (1 Kings 3:9). He practices hard at exercising his wisdom in Ecclesiastes. He tries *everything*. Having such an understanding heart in the form of wisdom endows Solomon with a keen sense of discernment and instant adeptness at performing tasks—and an instant ability to decide between good and bad behavior. I suppose Solomon never had to wonder whether his mind was faltering, his actions were missing their targets, his decisiveness was slipping, or his physical abilities were deteriorating. Most likely, he simply prayed, trusted God, and performed his tasks. Yet, in Ecclesiastes, he questions everything. Even Solomon couldn't surmount the high standards of God's perfection.

Lord, we want the heart of patience to give to others. Amen.

December 24
Package Processing

While scurrying to catch a flight in Las Vegas, I sat down at the terminal and discovered I had left my nice sweater on my airplane seat. My heart sank. The sweater was cashmere. There was no time to return to retrieve it. When I arrived home, I filled out a form on the airline's internet site. For the past few days, I've been waiting for a reply. Between receiving a standard, "we're looking for your item," I keep metaphorically beating myself up. I've been sour, lately.

You might have a tendency to tell yourself these similar things: "How could you have overlooked it when you felt the sweater bulge right on your back?" or "I knew I should have packed it before I left because I might lose it."

"I'll forget my complaining. I'll put off my sad face and be cheerful" (Job 9:27). When am I going to *let this go?*

My husband said it was my fault because I had left it there—accident or not. This reminds me of the time when we moved, and I packed my coin collection deep inside a tub which I then taped between two plastic tubs. The movers still managed to dig through my things and stole my coins. I blamed myself for that, too! Has something akin to my situations happened to you? If so, does simply leaving something or having something stolen because of your trusting nature or confident packing skills mean you're at fault?

My parents and the people who raised me did one exemplary thing. They displayed strong examples of doing the right thing. My stepmom always turned items in when she found them, and my grandparents were always conscious of being considerate to neighbors and strangers. Throughout Exodus, God commands us to respect and value our neighbors and their property. "If someone borrows something from his neighbor, and it gets injured or dies with the owner not present, he must make restitution" (Exodus 22:13). Then there's this directive in Leviticus 6:1-7: "If someone sins and acts perversely … with his neighbor … by stealing from him, by extorting him, or by dealing falsely in regard to a lost object … he is to restore whatever it was he stole or obtained by extortion." Sin abounds in this world. Let's remember that everything's temporary. Let's give our wants, needs, and desires to Him.

Jesus, give us forgiving hearts so we can love, shrug off grudges, and *let go of* what is not important and wasteful of our time. Amen.

DECEMBER 25
AFTER CHRISTMAS DEALS

We don't know the exact date of Jesus birth, except one scholar, Joseph A. Fitzmyer, guesses He was born September 11, 3 BCE (Addison G. Wright, Roland E. Murphy, Joseph A. Fitzmyer, "A History of Israel," *The Jerome Biblical Commentary*; Prentice Hall: Englewood Cliffs, NJ, 1990, p. 1247). You ever wonder how his birth changed from the above to December 25?

In the early days of Christianity, church leaders chose a Roman festival as the perfect time to galvanize Jesus' birth in church doctrine. We don't know the exact date of His birth, but celebrating his birthday today reminds us of how vital he is in *each* of our lives— and how lost we'd be without him. "For a child will be born to us, a son will be given to us; And the government will rest on His shoulders; And His name will be called Wonderful Counselor, Mighty God, Eternal Father, Prince of Peace" (Isaiah 9:6, NASB). The world needed a Deliverer. I *need* a Deliverer. Before Jesus, I lived in unrest and inner turmoil. I couldn't fix myself, only Jesus could reach into my confused soul and questioning mind to save me, a sinner.

Actually, *we* need a *special* counselor and a *mighty* Jesus. No one else but Jesus could have removed the blinders off my eyes so I could see my wayward lifestyle, twisted ideals, and false perceptions of true, right, and good. "Aren't there twelve hours of daylight? If a person walks during daylight, he doesn't stumble; because he sees the light of this world" (John 11:9). Like the popular lyric goes, "Searching for love in all the wrong places," I set my heart on all the people, places, and things I believed would make me happy and whole. I was a drifting dandelion whose flighty tufts were always landing on parched cracked soil and incapable of rooting and producing *anything* good. Fueled by the childhood wounds, I kept connecting with other selfish and distressed individuals who were also walking blind and zombie-like in search of fulfilling their needs, wants and desires. However, I could spiral down only so far into shame and self-loathing before I heard and believed the saving message of Jesus. He shed his blood and died on a cross for me, and you. The proof of his divinity is his resurrection. When I accepted his blood sacrifice, He forgave my sins, and I repented and changed. What does *this* day mean? It's celebration saving day ... the best Xmas present I've ever received.

Lord Jesus, we thank for you your gift of salvation. Amen.

December 26
Gift Card Exchange

Have you ever given a gift only to have the receiver look at your gift as if they're staring down at a bowl of lima beans? You think you're giving something great, but not so. Then you feel your joy sink....

That scenario happened to us after we gave our son Andrew an expensive item for Christmas. We charged it, even though we vowed never to "charge it" again. We meant the card for "emergencies only," but it seems an emergency happens daily. Have you vowed you'd never use "plastic" again, only to find yourself desiring things? Convinced you *need* this-thing-or-that-*thing*? "He (Paul) speaks about these things in all his letters. They contain some things that are hard to understand, things which the uninstructed and unstable distort, to their own destruction, as they do the other Scriptures" (2 Peter 3:16).

I don't like charging even food, because having an unpaid balance builds up, like a resistant disease, and I become desensitized to paying the card off, a nightmarish cycle. Trying to please people with gifts at all cost never works. Both parties might be left disappointed, proving human nature's law of *having* "more" breeds *wanting* "more," an insatiable appetite. Then happiness and gratitude fly out the window because a person's Engine of Desire is on rev for the next best thing or newest model. I've wound up hurting more times because *I let* my wants and desires rule me. I became a slave to them, and not a good steward of the financial blessings from God. Spoiled is the word. Everything we have comes from God.

Ultimately, greed for money and possessions, materialism, hurts not only me, but also my family and merchants, the latter whom I couldn't pay back. Forget the disappointment I felt by not getting what I wanted. At my bottom, I began tackling the more destructive addiction: needing, and being driven by, possessions of others so I could "keep up." It's called coveting, which can lead to cheating, lying and stealing. Now, that's real trouble. I was there, unable to pay back merchants, and I felt miserable and lonely. "All who deal dishonestly are detestable to Adonai your God" (Deuteronomy 25:13-16). Micah in Judges 17 stole silver from his mother, but then returned it; and she blessed him when he repented. I repented of my sinful coveting, and I am finding *real* joy. Now to help my son....

Lord God, help us be content in all our circumstances (Philippians 4:11). Amen.

DECEMBER 27
GET OUT OF THE BOAT, INTO THE WATER

We've had a strange day of mishaps around the house, beginning with the following shocker out of the mouth of our son. "Mom! Dad! My computer broke! [#*&=!] We gotta get it fixed, now!"

You've experienced do-or-die situations that you *believe* are life-threatening, right? Have you ever over-reacted? "With this in view, we always pray for you that our God may make you worthy of his calling and may fulfill by his power every good purpose of yours and every action stemming from your trust" (2 Thessalonians 1:11). In a *big* crisis, there are usually two ways of responding: gushing at the mouth with words, or sucking back your thoughts. I go numb.

Assessing the situation, we saw Andrew had dismantled his computer's outer shell, internal circuitry, key board, and the monitor that appeared autopsied on our dining room table. He began jimmying cards in memory slots, poking the fan, jostling the motherboard, pulling-out-and-snapping-back colored toggles and pegs. Turning his "fixed project" on, he waited. There's nothing like waiting, right? "Have I enough strength to go on waiting? What end can I expect, that I should be patient (Job 6:11)? Waiting is hard.

Whir rev grind whir. Then nothing. Wow, did he cry and stomp. After trying to help him, we gave up, went out for a hamburger, and continued listening to his replaying solutions. "I haveta fix it! I *know* it's a bad hard drive. I need a new one. It'll work then."

We countered, "It'll have to be next year for a new system because we can't afford it."

You remember those camp songs when you'd sit under a Kaleidoscope of stars and tell scary stories? Sometimes, parenting is comprised of one, long, bad story, especially the times when you must helplessly watch your child endure emotional discomfort. Andrew has Asperger Syndrome. He sees his "technology" as an extension of himself as an astronaut orbiting Earth needs a space suit. Most times, we bite our tongues, and consider Jesus' words. "Be patient with me" (Matthew 18:29); and, "It will go well with that servant if he is found doing his job when his master comes" (Matt 24:46). We say, "No," for discipline, and take time outs when our son goes ballistic. Before immediately responding, it's said, a person has *three* seconds to pray for divine intervention and act holy.

Holy Spirit, fill us with patience, tolerance and love. Amen.

DECEMBER 28
TIME AND TEMPERATURE

I feel another lull after Christmas. The lull strikes the week between December 25 and New Year's Day. Are you feeling, "the lull?"

It seems every channel I turn to, and every newspaper or website is reflecting on the year. The writers, newscasters and bloggers focus on who's famous who died, the top fifty songs, the highest Nielson-rated TV shows, and the most popular movies up for an Oscar. Yet, all of those are so far removed from what's actually happened to you and me, our spheres of friends, and family. I'm forced to watch and read about who's-in-and-who's-out of fame and fortune that I miss assessing, or inventorying, my own weaknesses, and praying to God, Jesus, and the Holy Spirit for help to change. At this time, we can use time to search our consciences for failed or stressed relationships.

Did I hurt anyone, knowingly or unknowingly? We might not even realize that some of our behaviors or words offend others. For example, sometimes I'm a bit loud, especially when trying to voice my point of view. "The one who is evaluating me is the Lord" (1 Corinthians 4:4), Paul says. I need our Lord to bring to light what is hidden in darkness inside of me. He's the one who can expose my motives (verse 5), and fix me.

Need fixing? God is Master Fixer. "God has not abandoned us in our slavery, but has caused the kings of Persia to extend grace to us, reviving us, so that we can rebuild the house of our God, repair its ruins, and have a wall of defense in Judah and Jerusalem" (Ezra 9:9).

These lull days leave me questioning some of my motives and behaviors over the year. I might be in front of the bathroom mirror, glancing into a sink of dish-soapy water, or adjusting the car's side mirrors, but I'm seeing. Thank goodness, lull week is only a week. The process is like a dentist filling a cavity. However, if I want to improve because I'm tired of the consequences, I must be able to *see* my weaknesses so God can turn them into strengths. Then I can help others. Paul said, "If there is an ordinary human body, there is also a body controlled by the Spirit" (1 Corinthians 15:42-44). I only need to trust God and let his divine Holy Spirit change me. "I always set Adonai God before me … for you will not abandon me" (Psalm 16:7-11). Faith melts fear. Faith produces belief; then, we can change.

Lord, we pray for a heart for you and dependence on you.

GOD DESIGNED

DECEMBER 29
FINAL DAYS

Have you ever made a mistake? Come on … who hasn't?

I've made a few haunting—and rippling—mistakes for which I continue to wish I could blink myself back in time as Jeannie did in the 1960s TV and change what I did. Can you relate?

"Repent and turn to God, so that your sins may be erased," Paul tells us (Acts 3:19). Totally, erased.

I guess the intensity of our dream to redo the past directly correlates to the degree of our discomfort in the present. In other words, how did the *big* mistake impede our social, emotional, and financial lives? Venom comes in many concentrations and tastes….

I remember a *Twilight Zone* episode, wherein a poor old woman living in a dilapidated estate rides her horse over a hill and begins watching herself in the past. A time portal has activated, allowing her special access into the past. Her "younger self" is in love with a handsome man, and they're about. She yells at her younger naïve self: "Stop! Don't do it!" Through the portal, her counterpart hears her, but she thinks the old lady is deranged. The portal closes, space-time tricks stop, and the old lady realizes she wasn't successful because she's still living in squalid circumstances. Sad, huh?

There's a saying: When you're young, you see future possibilities; when you're old, you see memories. Is there a past event, to which you could magically return, and change? We can't. So, now what?

I'm reminded of a Bible character, Korah, who made an irreversible mistake and fought *against* Israel. That was like Benedict Arnold betraying George Washington. Korah was the great-grandson of Levi, the third son of Jacob born to Leah who became the progenitor of the tribe of Levi (Num.16:1; Gen. 29:31-35). The details surrounding the rebellion of Korah, Dathan, and Abiram appear in Numbers 16:1-40. Because they resisted Moses' leadership, the earth turned into a funnel, swallowing them up with their possessions. Those were the consequence of Korah's disobedience to God. However, as a long-term *positive* consequence, God spares Korah's children (Numbers 26:11) who later write Psalm 88. "Adonai, God of our salvation, when we cry, turn your ear to our pleas for help!" Crying humbles us to prayer, talking to Him.

Jesus, thank you for saving us from being "swallowed up" by our sins and mistakes. God, shepherd us toward your plans. Amen.

369

December 30
Wish List

I came across the Japanese word, *gaman*, which means, *enduring the seemingly unbearable with patience and dignity*. That's not usually our tendency, however, to persevere when the IRS audits us, when our car stalls on the hot freeway, when we lose a contest, or when *any* down-pour of hardship strikes us. Do you have *gaman*?

When the unexpected strikes your life in cracks of lightning and rumbles of thunder, what is *your* Gaman Level on a scale of 1 to ten?

This past year on social media, we've witnessed persecuted people in the Middle East being ripped and chased—displaced—from their homes and countries to live as refugees in Turkey, Lebanon, Jordan, or Iraq. In Niger, 5.4 million people are in danger of starving. Militias and government factions have forced families to abandon their homes to scavenge for what we take granted: food and water, even though some of us might *only* eat macaroni, beans-and-rice, or Cheerios tonight. On TV, we see the war-ravaged and sorrow-filled faces of the displaced and disoriented. They are refugees sitting motionless in small tents lined with sleeping bags. As many of them search for the necessities of life, their children play buoyantly around them, impervious to the uncompromising desert they've just crossed and their new homes, small tents with pot stoves. An aerial view of one of these refugee camps appears as a congestion of green-and-brown flapping forts, a "ten[t]ement" nation. I wonder, *What kind of a future can they possibly have after enduring such tragic loss?* We Americans are becoming sensitive to people who have a condition called Post Traumatic Stress Disorder. These refugees *will* have it.

The Israelites knew displacement. Several times, they had to move because of famine, war, or drought. "There was a famine in the land, so Abraham went down into Egypt to stay there" (Genesis 12:10). For over 2,000 years since Rome conquered Israel, the Jewish people have been longing for a peace-filled Israel. Let us not forget that Hitler's anti-Semitic propaganda is *still* rampant, even in America. Only God's peace can infuse us with incredible *gaman* so we endure hardships. Giving when I can is a healing trait for the displaced and suffering in the world. "How blessed are those who make peace! For they will be called sons of God" (Matthew 5:9). We can be peace to the displaced who are everywhere we go. We see them, daily.

Jesus, help us extend peace, mercy, and compassion. Amen.

DECEMBER 31
OUT WITH THE OLD; IN WITH THE NEW

"We'll start on the taxes first," I said to my husband this morning.

"After that, I'll pay the bills," he returned.

"Okay, but *after that* we need to install batteries in the smoke detectors." I pointed at the dusty package of batteries on an entertainment shelf. "We need to finish *last* year's New Year resolution."

Do you have any *failed* resolutions you want to fix *next* year?

He laughed, but that's the topic in several of today's newspapers, articles of well-intentioned but failed New Year's Day resolutions. Failed exercise schedules, cessation programs, diets, and looking-for-true-love behavioral changes. Sixty percent of the people who make resolutions break them (Sarah Kliff, "The Science of Actually Keeping Your New Year's Resolution," *Vox Media*). Motivation appears to dwindle because we run out of drive, determination, or caring. Old habits *are* hard to break.

What might be an old hard habit for *you* to quit? "If your brother is being upset by the food you eat, your life is no longer one of love. Do not, by your eating habits, destroy someone for whom the Messiah died" (Romans 14:15)! Our habits affect others.

In the Book of Exodus, God gives a stiff edict concerning bad habits. "If the ox was in the habit of goring in the past, and the owner was warned but did not confine it, so that it ended up killing a man or a woman; then the ox is to be stoned, and its owner too is to be put to death" (21:29). Wow, what a drastic consequence. Beware drunk drivers who kill people. In other words, if I *know* what I'm doing is *negatively* impacting someone, I need to amend my behavior and actions because they *affect* others; and those affects matter to God. You might counter with, "But my smoking, over eating, excessive drinking, bad dating experiences, etc., aren't hurting anyone." Really? "Here is what Adonai says, who made a way in the sea, a path through the raging waves; 'Stop dwelling on past events and brooding over times gone by; I am doing something new; it's springing up—can't you see it? I am making a road in the desert, rivers in the wasteland' " (Isaiah 43:16-19). Hurting others as a consequence of our actions is *not* in God's agenda, only love, care, mercy, self-care, consideration, and compassion, and selflessness.

Lord God, help us love you, and in turn, to love others. Amen.

Day 367
Surprise!

What if one day in the future, we'll need an extra day? A day 367? I'm giving that extra day to you. Whether humanity is colonizing a body in our solar system or space-folding to another planet, I am including a 367th day you can insert into the calendar.

What might you need to hear from God for encouragement and inspiration in the future? Firstly, I decided to analyze what people have experienced since God designed Adam and Eve. Secondly, for what might people in future eons pray? Thirdly, what issues will people encounter?

Psychologist Abraham Maslow postulated a five-tiered Hierarchy of Needs pyramid. Maslow considered himself a humanist. That is, through our feelings, emotions, and better understanding of ourselves; we can relate more effectively with others; enhance our relationships, and improve ourselves. However, God commands us to care for one another's basic needs. "Learn to do good! Seek justice, relieve the oppressed, defend orphans, and plead for the widow" (Isaiah 1:17; Jeremiah 7:8; Zachariah 7:10; Psalm 68:6; and James 1:27). As we provide for our basic needs and the basic needs of others, we become the best we can be for Him. We can "self-actualize" to our highest potential, as Maslow postulated, and make a difference for Him in this often chaotic world. After all, unless society invents and implements some type of worldwide, matrix control computer to monitor peoples' thoughts, interfere with their abnormal propensities, and inhibit their lawless actions, people are going to have free will and do as they please.

Our core needs are for food, water, clothing, shelter, and our psychological need for love. Studies show that if infants don't receive enough human contact, they'll die from Failure to Thrive. We need love—to *be* loved and to *give* love. Furthermore, people need their safety and security needs met. We can't study, learn, or work if we're constantly worried about where we're going to live the next minute or what we're going to eat. No one can think clearly or make meaningful decisions under threat of harm, intense stress, or deprivation.

Part of Maslow's paradigm for living outlines our need for freedom and not oppression. Have you heard of learned helplessness? In adverse, oppressive, and abusive situations, a person who has *learned* helplessness comes to believe that nothing he or she can do will prevent or eliminate their bad situation (Seligman & Maier, 1967). The individual becomes accustomed and anesthetized to the pain and abuse. They won't leave the situation even when someone opens the exit door. With PTSD, even *after* someone opens the exit door, the *trapped* individual keeps reliving the past. How can we counter "learned helplessness" to live productively? "Jesus loved Martha and her sister and Lazarus" (John 11:5). Jesus *is* love. He exists in love, thrives in His Father God's love, and dwells in the Holy Spirit. "As the Father has loved me, so have I loved you. Now remain in my love" (John 15:9). We must love. No matter the time in which we live, we must have compassion for the oppressed, abused, and tyrannized.

Then there will always be the quitters. They walk away from commitments. In whatever time you're living, maybe you want to leave today. Perhaps you long to quit "your love." Are you sure you want to stop loving? "Neither height nor depth, nor anything else in all creation, will be able to separate us from the love of God that is in Christ Jesus our Lord" (Romans 8:39). In our sorrows, pains, hurts, and desperate moments, God understands and is with us because Jesus *as God* suffered and experienced pain, suffering, and agony. "The Messiah had to suffer" (Acts 17:3). Our Messiah had to love.

"Father, forgive them; they don't understand what they are doing" (Luke 23:34)

You can love ... and forgive. As we need love, we need forgiveness, wouldn't you agree? *Not* being forgiven leaves a festering hole inside a soul. Everyone will have faults and make mistakes, I'm sure, even in the distant future, whether on Mars or an exoplanet. Forgiveness allows us to love and stay with our commitments. You can persevere and not quit because Christ loved you to the point of finishing His mission—dying for you. "As God's chosen people, holy and dearly loved, clothe yourselves with compassion, kindness, humility, gentleness and patience" (Colossians 3:12). No matter how God chooses to direct us His people, He will always manifest as love. "God so loved the world that he gave his one and only Son, that whoever believes in him shall not perish but have eternal life" (John 3:16). Love is what a child needs to thrive. If people do not receive love at any given age, people will fail to thrive.

I recall what my mother, Mary, once told me. She always talked in idiomatic phrases, like, "Where there's a will there's a way," her favorite. She also used to say, "You made your bed, now lie in it." Cold, yes, but there's a grain of truth in what she said. Every complaint—even an outrageous one—has a morsel of truth to it. What she was trying to say is: you cleaned the sheets, you put on fresh pillowcases, and you picked out the bedspread. The point? Every person *will be* flawed in some way or another, because no one, and no situation, is 100% perfect.

However, some people wave yellow warning flags in our faces that we ignore—or chose not—to see. It's there ... in their words or actions, but we tend to discount or excuse those warning signs that are shaking, *this won't work*, in front of our faces. The flags are waving wildly: *this is only going to cause you heartache, pain, and terrible consequences.* However, we see only pleasure in the person or situation. The Enemy likes to do that to us—show us "light" when there's only really "darkness" down a particular path on which we want to embark, or choice we want to make.

Perhaps the *excellent* monetary opportunity might be sending out a red flare. However, the job is really one wherein you'll be forced to compromise your values. Or, the partner you're considering marrying is not a Christian. Both scenarios will *try* to lure you across Denial Alley, to lumber through Pain Street. You'll end up aimlessly *banging* your noggin on poles around Disaster Square. *Disaster* is an ancient word. It'll be around in the future and taking people down.

Across the centuries everyone has, and will, experiences a loss. God discussed loss and bereavement in the form of theft. "A thief must make restitution; so if he has nothing, he himself is to be sold to make good the loss from the theft" (Exodus 22:2). *Loss* is "something that is lost," "dead," or "a failure to win." A loss hurts and leaves us bereft and grieving. At some point, everyone experiences losses—little and small. You'll "lose" something and can't find it, somebody'll die, someone'll leave you, or you'll lose a competition or promotion. *"Adonai* is slow to anger but great in power; and he does not leave the guilty unpunished" (Nahum 1:3). I remember a quote I once read by an anonymous writer, "the price of love is a loss, but we still pay."

God creates us with drives and needs. They're in our DNA. We'll always be subject to hurt as we intrinsically pursue what He's ordained us to be in life. People have free will and will hurt us, unintentionally *and* deliberately. "On the contrary, following the Holy One who called you, become holy yourselves in your entire way of life," Peter tells us (1 Peter 1:15). We'll hurt because of others' actions. However, *you*, as a believer, will not be hurt in the end. "He who wins the victory will not be hurt at all by the second death" (Revelation 2:11). We take consolation in His help. Paul had it and was able to accomplish wonders. "I have had God's help" (Acts 26:22). Even though we will not die but live with Him in a new Heaven and Earth, He commands us, "Let us pursue the things that make for *shalom* and mutual upbuilding" (Romans 14:19). Peace, encouraging others, and building others up is what God entreats us to do no matter how we feel and no matter how much our losses hurt. And when I'm tempted to do the opposite, I look the Devil square on. "Today's not your day, and Tomorrow isn't lookin' good for ya either! In Jesus name, flee." He'll leave you alone. The next move is up to you. "Flee the passions of youth. And along with those who call on the Lord from a pure heart, pursue righteousness, faithfulness, love and peace" (2 Timothy 2:22). Jesus is always pruning us to become more like Him.

Ultimately, He will reward you. "If someone gives just a cup of cold water to one of these little ones because he is my *talmid*—yes!—I tell you, he [she] will certainly not lose his [her] reward" (Matthew 10:42)! I once heard the expression, hurting people hurt people. In the future, unless scientists can map the human brain *perfectly* to eliminate emotional damage with neural implants or brain-computer interface, Hurt will always be around. However, He renews us in our aching. "Let me hear the sound of joy and gladness, so that the bones you crushed can rejoice" (Psalm 51:10). Injury to healing.

Yet, most people can't *see* their emotional injuries. Most people then can't *know* how they're hurting others. In his Hierarchy of Needs pyramid, Abraham Maslow has Self-Actualization at the top. Self-actualization occurs after we have all our basic needs met. Then we have time to look inward, discern our drives, analyze our motivations, contemplate our aspirations, examine our failings, innumerate our strengths, verbalize our desires, discuss our dreams, outline our occupations, delve into our psyches, and improve our spiritual conditions. Not everyone we meet will have self-actualized. Actually, no one *fully* self-actualizes while we're alive. Paul says it's a process. "The One who began a good work among you will keep it growing until it is completed on the Day of the Messiah Yeshua" (Philippians 1:6). Self-actualizing is God's goal, for us and for humanity. "Whatever work you do, put yourself into it, as those who are serving not merely other people, but the Lord" (Colossians 3:23). What do we do then as we encounter so many hurting people?

Jesus had the answer. "If you, even though you are bad, know how to give your children gifts that are good, how much more will your Father in heaven keep giving good things to those who keep asking him" (Matthew 7:11)! Jesus always looked at people through the eyes of a child. He *always* pitied diseased and ill people, those persecuted by the Romans, and those taken advantage of by the religious leaders. Jesus had compassion for the emotionally scarred and displaced, called children to Him, and had mercy on the most abject sinner. No matter the time or place, we need the Heart of Jesus—his sacred heart through which to view others.

Have you ever noticed, you can do all sorts of things when someone believes in you? "How blessed are the pure in heart! For they will see God" (Matthew 5:8). In the Beatitudes and Jesus's precious words, you'll receive answers to help *you* endure your losses and hurts. And He will show you how to respond to the people around you when they're hurting as well. Sociologist, historian, civil rights activist, and author. W.E.B. Du Bois once said, "The music of an unhappy people, of the children of disappointment; they tell of death and suffering and unvoiced longing toward a truer world, of misty wanderings and hidden ways." As adults, some people are still hurting children. Punching back will only reinforce their hurts more. "You are salt for the Land. ... You are light for the world. ... Let your light shine before people so that they may see the good things you do and praise your Father in heaven" (Matthew 5:13-16). Where you are right now ... are you shining? Never hide.

Another transcending absolute people in the future will experience is work. People will always have to work. "You will work hard to eat from it [the ground] as long as you live" (Genesis 3:17), God said. Work will be a constant, like the gravitational constant G. Furthermore, work gives us something to do and a purpose. "You have six days to labor and do all your work, but the seventh day is a *Shabbat* for *Adonai* our God. On it, you are not to do any kind of work" (Exodus 20:9-10). Did you know, after Jesus establishes His kingdom on Earth, we'll also work? "Don't you know that God's people are going to judge the universe? If you are going to judge the universe, are you incompetent to judge these minor matters? Don't you know that we will judge angels, not to mention affairs of everyday life (1 Corinthians 2-3)? No one knows our duties, but we'll have work to do, with Him. Today, let's do the jobs He'd like us to do. "So there is nothing better for a man [woman] to do than eat, drink and let himself [herself] enjoy the good that results from his [her] work. I also realized that this is from God's hand" (Ecclesiastes 2:24; 3:13; 5:17-18; 8:15; and 9:9-10). Jesus tells us to do what *He* calls us to do. "We have gifts that differ and which are meant to be used according to the grace that has been given to us" (Romans 12:6-8; 1 Corinthians 12:4-11; and, 1 Corinthians 12:28). We can choose our gifts from among those God provides us to strengthen our fellow Christians and us. "When you have done everything you were told to do, you should be saying, 'We're just ordinary slaves, we have only done our duty' " (Luke 17:1-10). We may not always receive a reward as we use our God-given Holy Spirit infused gifts; yet we are to do what is right. "You [God] descended on Mount Sinai and spoke with them from heaven. You gave them right rulings and true teachings, good laws and *mitzvoth* (Nehemiah 9:13). I understand that doing good and right won't always feel good or benefit you; but if you don't do as your conscience [via the Holy Spirit] directs, you'll have to live with what you've done. Unless scientists finally do manage to contrive a potion, pill, or neural implant to erase memories completely with no side effects, now, in the meantime, there are *no* erase buttons. "We must all appear before the Messiah's court of judgment, where everyone will receive the good or bad consequences of what he [she] did while he [she] was in the body" (2 Corinthians 5:10). They're called rewards, and lack of rewards. No one knows what position in Heaven we'll receive depending on those rewards gained or lost. Whatever time you're living in, how do you want to live with the time you've got?

Like generations before you, you and people in the future will live life in cycles. The child developmental psychologist, Erik Erickson, postulated eight life stages. There's Trust vs. Mistrust; Autonomy vs. Shame; Initiative vs. Guilt; Industry vs. Inferiority; Identity vs. Role Confusion; Intimacy vs. isolation; Generativity vs. stagnation; and, Ego Integrity vs. Despair. We live, grow, change, and experience challenges throughout our lifespans. God calls these *seasons*. "Everything there is a season, a right time for every intention under heaven" (Ecclesiasts 3:1-8). In a recovery workshop I once participated in, I heard the phrase, when God closes one door He opens another. Sometimes, I imagine myself trembling and standing in a long, cold, lonely hallway. Behind me is a closed door. In front of me are locked ice-covered windows and a rock-solid steel door. *I can't. I can't.*

Then I remember how God manifested Himself to the Israelites around the Temple. "When all the people saw the column of cloud stationed at the entrance to the tent, they would get up and prostrate themselves, each man at his tent door" (Exodus 33:10). God is the open door. When we touch what we perceive to be cold fearful steel … we find the barrier not as cold and hard as we thought. God is responding … cracking open the door to let in His great light to flood that long lonely hallway. Then, we can step confidently into new territories and new beginnings that God has replaced with what's dead or has ended in our lives. In Jesus's great "Don't" speech in Matthew 7, at one point, he says: "Don't give to dogs what is holy, and don't throw your pearls to the pigs. If you do, they may trample them under their feet, then turn and attack you. Keep asking, and it will be given to you; keep seeking, and you will find; keep knocking, and the door will be opened to you. For everyone who keeps asking receives; he who keeps seeking finds; and to him who keeps knocking, the door will be opened" (6-8). Since Shepherd Jesus is stationed at *every* door and window, and dressed in regal clothes with outstretched arms, whom and what do we have to fear? In reality, He creates for us all opportunities. "There is one God, the Father, from whom all things come and for whom we exist; and one Lord, Yeshua the Messiah, through whom were created all things and through whom we have our being" (1 Corinthians 8:6). In any day or age, take the first step toward the open door, wipe the ice off the windowpane with the backs of your hand, and then go, with Him. My mom also had another phrase: you'll never know until you try.

At any time and in every season—through struggle, joy, or illness—God is with you. "*Adonai* is good, a stronghold in time of trouble; he takes care of those who take refuge in him" (Nahum 1:7). He is with you, protecting you, and guiding you through the Holy Spirit. He has a final destination for you—with Him forever.

"Meanwhile, through trusting, you are being protected by God's power for a deliverance ready to be revealed at the Last Time" (1 Peter 1:5). Your final cycle? Eternity with Him.

Which brings me to humanity's last absolute. I don't want to rattle you … I don't want you disabled with anxiety … but, I've got news for you. You're gonna die one day. "My life is but a breath," says Job (Job 7:7). David said, "Man is like a puff of wind, his days like a fleeting shadow" (Psalm 144:4). Maybe as you read this now, *I'm* dead-n-gone. Do a Bible search on the word, *die*, and you'll see so many phrases you can hardly count them.

"I'm old now, I don't know when I will die" (Genesis 27:2). It's true. We don't know when we'll leave this Earth, but pick any day on the calendar—January 1 to December 31. One of those days in the future you'll die. That'll be just a physical death. Jesus said: "In this age, men and women marry, but those judged worthy of the age to come, and of resurrection from the dead, do not get married because they can no longer die. Being children of the Resurrection, they are like angels; indeed, they are children of God. But even Moshe showed that the dead are raised; for in the passage about the bush, he calls *Adonai* 'the God of Avraham, the God of Yitz'chak and the God of Ya'akov.' Now He is not God of the dead, but of the living—to him all are alive" (Luke 20:34-38). We, believers, do not die. In any age or any cosmic date, we'll transition to eternity with Him. And we'll see one another and our Christ-trusting relatives. "Praised be God, Father of our Lord Jesus the Messiah, who, in keeping with his great mercy, has caused us, through the resurrection of Jesus the Messiah from the dead, to be born again to a living hope, to an inheritance that cannot decay, spoil or fade, kept safe for you in heaven" (1 Peter 3-4). We just need to remember to keep God in the center of every decision make and everything we do. "Unless God builds the house, its builders work in vain" (Psalm 127:1). By the resurrection power of Jesus, we will all, one day, share in His glory. May God's peace, grace, and strength be with you always in Jesus our Savior through the Holy Spirit. Amen.

THANKSGIVING AND EASTER WEEK BONUS

GOD DESIGNED

THANKSGIVING

Including the Good News that Jesus died for us, Psalm 100 gives us the most special message from God in the world. God made *you*. *You* are His. *You* are part of His Chosen community of people for eternity. For what do we thank Him on this day of Thanksgiving? Our great, holy, perfect Creator? We read in Psalm 100:

> Enter his gates with thanksgiving,
> enter his courtyards with praise;
> give thanks to him, and bless his name.
> For *Adonai* is good, his grace continues forever,
> and his faithfulness lasts through all generations (4-5).

God is love, John tells us (1 John 4:8). And God is good (Psalm 107:1). Love *and* goodness combined. That's an equation, equaling holiness. We can know the word "good" because of what is *not* good, wouldn't you say? As a child, my grandparents would order me, "Now, Joycie ... you *be* a good girl." The stern directive came with a shake of an arthritic-stricken finger usually.

Ouch if I wasn't good. The consequences of not being good appeared to extend into eternity.

However, God *is* good. God *is* grace. God is love, eternally.

What is grace? "The free and unmerited favor of God, as manifested in the salvation of sinners and the bestowal of blessings." When we didn't deserve His love, He died for us. He *always* loves me, *and* you. What is our problem? We might not *feel* His love. We can't physically see Him. We don't audibly *hear* His voice. Yet, He loves us enduringly, showers us with grace, and promises us faithfulness. He'll never leave you. "Be strong, be bold, don't be afraid or frightened of them, for *Adonai* your God is going with you. He will neither fail you nor abandon you" (Deuteronomy 31:6). He promises you, "I will *never* fail you or abandon you" (Hebrews 13:5). God *does* what He promises.

Are you feeling abandoned, alone, deserted, shaken, troubled, or wounded? "God supports all who fall and lifts up all who are bent over," David says in Psalm 145. One day, we will stand in God's presence through Jesus. We have so much to be thankful for today.

This day, we praise you Lord, and bless you. In everything, give thanks (1 Thessalonians 5:18). Amen.

J.P. OSTERMAN

PALM SUNDAY
MAKING WAVES

Talk about a change in tempo for Jesus. Palm Sunday is the day He vaults to Fame-in-a-Day and the beginning of His last week on Earth. Thereafter, he will endure an agonizing crucifixion. Then He will give us a promising new life on Resurrection Day. Of these seven days, you'd think Palm Sunday would Jesus would surmount a throne to proclaim himself King. He didn't. What can we learn from Palm Sunday?

On that eventful day, people lined up with palms and praised Jesus. He rode through the countryside on a donkey, thus fulfilling Zachariah's prophecy. "Rejoice greatly, O daughter of Zion! Shout, O daughter of Jerusalem! Behold, thy King cometh unto thee! He is just and having salvation, lowly, and riding upon an ass and upon a colt, the foal of an ass. And I will cut off the chariot from Ephraim, and the horse from Jerusalem, and the battle bow shall be cut off. He shall speak peace unto the heathen, and His dominion shall be from sea even to sea, and from the river even to the ends of the earth" (Zachariah 9:9-10). Jesus *has* and *owns* everything. This Exaltation Parade occurs after He raises Lazarus from the dead. People are believing His message of repentance, change, and salvation. "Hosanna!" they shout, which means, "save." Jesus was accomplishing His mission—saving souls.

This time is also Passover, another Jewish festival celebrating freedom from Egyptian tyranny. Jesus's children were pleading to Him: 'Lord, save us! Lord, grant us success" (Psalm 118:25)! You can imagine their cheering, and the hope on their excited faces as they wait for Jesus to assume His kingship and claim God's Nation. Powerful people, however, want to see our Lord taken down. "The Pharisees said to one another, 'See, this is getting us nowhere. Look how the whole world has gone after him' (John 12:19)!" Wow, "the whole world." People *are* believing. A chapter earlier, after Lazarus walks out of a sealed tomb, Jesus's enemies remark, "If we let him go on like this, everyone will believe in him" (John 11:48). Jesus couldn't assume a throne then because God sees the Big Picture across eternity. God knows us, and loves us infinitesimally. He knows *you*. He died for you ... for all humanity still unborn.

Lord, thank you for the day when we accepted *you*. Amen.

MONDAY
PASSION WEEK

After people overwhelmed Jesus with palm branches, worship, praise and thanksgiving, Jesus appears energized. Palm Sunday should have been the day when Jesus *should* have been proclaimed King of Israel. He was fulfilling the prophesy: "They quickly took their cloaks and spread them under him on the bare steps. Then they blew the trumpet and shouted, 'Jehu is king' " (2 Kings 9:13). An alternate reality occurs, however.

Jesus leaves Bethany, the West Bank city of al-Eizariya, which means, "Place of Lazarus," where he raised Lazarus from death to life. Bethany is located about 1.5 miles east of Jerusalem and south-east of the Mount of Olives. Little-by-little, Jesus travels the paved roads to his ultimate destination. His weighty cross. What might have kept His mind off that looming cross—the place which he will soon sweat blood? When we know hard times are coming, we begin to divert our attention elsewhere. He doesn't. He considers us.

"Every day he taught at the Temple. The head *cohanim*, the *Torah*-teachers and the leaders of the people tried to find a way of putting an end to him. But they couldn't find any way of doing it, because all the people were hanging onto his every word" (Luke 19:47). He had friends. He had rivals. He had worshippers. And then there were the powerful spies monitoring his every move. In these last days, two events show Jesus's mood.

As he approaches and overlooks Jerusalem, He cries. God had sent Him *for* His Jewish nation, but they don't accept His divinity. "If you, even you, had only known on this day what would bring you peace—but now it is hidden from your eyes" (Luke 19:42; Matthew 23:37). How will Jesus be hidden? He will soon be leaving this Earth. When He does, people won't have opportunities He's been giving them to accept Him as Messiah. Then, Jesus turns angry. See the seven woes He unleashes to "the teachers of the Law and Pharisees" (Matthew 23). That occurs around the same time He enters the Temple and "drives out" all the businesses (Luke 19:46). It would be like attending church and expecting to see people worshipping God, but instead they're buying and selling things as if it's Monday through Friday. Still, Jesus ceaselessly teaches. I see Jesus trying desperately to open blind eyes. Let us know Him today.

Lord, help us always see. Amen.

Tuesday
Hurdles

A few tragedies lately have left me crying. In a nearby city, a mother killed her three children. In France, a pilot drove his jet carrying 150 people into a mountain side.

Have you ever cried to God, asking him, "Why, Lord? Why!"

In many instances, when people die in an airplane crash, or a typhoon strikes, a tidal waves inundates a coastline, a fire decimates homes, or an earthquakes shatters buildings; a few people survive or escape injury free. Sometimes, we hear of people who "missed the fated flight," "left town just in time," or "were in another place" at that ill-fated space-time and survived. We have to ask: "God, why?"

Often times, those who escaped disasters experience survivors' guilt because they can't understand *why* they lived while others died. They're alive and breathing. People who boarded the plane are victims. How do we make sense of senseless tragedy? Does God pick who lives and dies?

On Tuesday during Passion Week, we find Jesus de-fruiting a fig tree and debating "experts" at the Temple. Judas prepares to betray Him. In our DNA, God endows us with free will. Why would Jesus kill a fig tree? He gives us a Faith lesson. "If ye have faith and doubt not, ye shall not only do this which is done to the fig tree, but also if ye shall say unto this mountain, 'Be thou removed and be thou cast into the sea,' it shall be done. And all things whatsoever ye shall ask in prayer, believing, ye shall receive" (Matthew 21:21-22). Then He debates priests and elders in the Temple. They demand to know: "Tell us, what *s'mikhah* do you have that authorizes you to do these things? Who gave you this *s'mikhah*" (Luke 20:2)? "S'mikhah" means *authority*, as when God told Moses to anoint Joshua "so the whole Israelite community will obey him" (Numbers 27:18-20). God imbibes Jesus with authority over *everything*, including miracles and resurrections. He is also Judge. "Those who reject me and don't accept what I say have a judge—the word which I have spoken will judge them on the Last Day" (John 12:48). I would not want to be Hitler, Andreas Lubits, or Jessica McCarty on that Last Day as the innocent who died at their hands are now glorified with our Lord, forever.

God, you care for your children, and will decide the final outcomes of *every* act of violence (Numbers 21:5). Amen.

WEDNESDAY
PASSION WEEK

King David once said: "Fools say in their hearts, 'There is no God.' They deal corruptly. Their deeds are vile. Not one does what is right" (Psalm 14:1). We're not talking about non-belief in Jesus, but non-belief in God. If you've heard someone say there is no God, they're a fool. A *fool* is: *a person who acts unwisely or imprudently.* How do we respond? I ask, "Have you ever died and returned to tell me God does *not* exist? What if you're wrong, and the 74% who *do* believe in God are right (Harris Poll, December 2013)?" Let's examine a few possibilities that might change someone's mind about God.

Wednesday of Passion Week appears to be a day of silence, until we look at Judas. Jesus walked with Judas for *three* years. Being omniscient, He knew Judas's character, his thieving ways as treasurer (John 12:6), and that he'd betray Him with thirty pieces of silver, fulfilling Zachariah's prophesy. "So they weighed out my wages, thirty silver *shekels* [twelve ounces]. Concerning that 'princely sum' at which they valued me, *Adonai* said, 'Throw it into the treasury!' So I took the thirty silver [shekels] and threw them into the treasury in the house of *Adonai*" (Zachariah 11:10-13). Thirty shekels is the value Jesus's enemies assigned to Him. Being God in the flesh, Jesus realized he was *daily* spending time with the person who would betray Him to the Romans for crucifixion (Matthew 17:5; 3:17). Now, I offer one proof of Jesus as God who walked among us.

Would you keep company *every* day for over three years with a person who dislikes you, steals from you, and who will have the motive, means, and opportunity to kill you? That's how Jesus lived, ate, and slept around Judas. Only God could handle such minute-by-minute falsehood. But get this; ultimately, Judas is sorry. "He was seized with remorse and returned the thirty silver coins to the head *cohanim* and elders, saying, 'I sinned in betraying an innocent man to death.' ... Hurling the pieces of silver into the sanctuary, he left; then he went off and hanged himself" (Matthew 27:3-5). We see a sorrowful repentant Judas. God is a loving, forgiving, merciful God.

Could Judas be in Heaven? There was another last-minute confession, the man on the cross next to Jesus. We can never judge unless we'll be judged as to who is saved or not saved.

God, your forgiveness and grace are for everyone. Amen.

J.P. Osterman

Maundy Thursday
"Do This in Memory of Me" (Luke 22:19)

There's nothing more nurturing than eating together. You can put cereal on the table for lunch, and I've made pancakes with chocolate chip eyes for dinner. Dining together is fellowshipping and creating bonding moments. The "set apart" time can also facilitate repairing relationships.

Have you eaten with family lately?

This same type of close-knit community Jesus nurtured with his disciples for over three years *ends* with a final meal. He also washes his disciples' feet, a lesson of service. What might have happened in the upper room that Jesus asked his followers to prepare (Mark 14:12-16; Luke 22:13)? We do know Jesus's urgency to share with them a meal which they have no idea of its importance in the tapestry of Christian faith. "I have really wanted so much to celebrate this *Seder* with you before I die" (Luke 22:15-16)! Jesus will become the lamb's blood for salvation. The priesthood began with these twelve chosen people—except Judas will be gone soon. And their instructional time with Him will end before the stroke of midnight, the beginning of His agony. "This very night, before the rooster crows, you will disown me three times," he tells Peter. This meal with Jesus probably lasted several hours as He prepared them for a drastic change in the fabric of the universe. How does this affect you?

They reclined at a long table (Mark 14:18), a symbol for the Jews escaping those worked-to-the-bone Egyptian days. And the meal they ate was a Passover Seder, a ritual performed by a community, or multiple generations of a family, retelling the story of God liberating them from slavery and claiming them for the Promised Land (Exodus 6:6-7). At Passover Seder, we drink four cups of wine, eat matza, mix parsley with salt water, and eat horseradish, all symbolic foods re-enacting that harsh desperate time when the Egyptians exploited the Jews as slaves, until God intervened and saved them. God's name is *Ehyeh Asher Ehyeh* [I am/will be what I am/will be], Exodus 3:14. As Jesus eats His last meal with his friends, we become aware of His urgency to save us *all*. He glances with intense eyes around the Seder table into the unsuspecting stares of his friends he will see no more. He knows what's about to happen—His death to secure our souls for eternity.

Jesus, give us fruits of your spirit to love people. Amen.

GOOD FRIDAY
ON THE CROSS

Several companies offer spit-in-a-tube genetic tests to run through their DNA databases and report back to us our genealogy.

Could you be a king's descendant? Magellan? Maybe Blackbeard! Ouch, do ya *really* wanna know? These companies have two markets. Inquisitive genealogists and people asking the question, "Who am I?" Let's look at our heritage and identity in Christ. Let's *know* we are reconciled to God and sealed into His heavenly kingdom, *forever*. We won't find our identities in the past, but in an exciting brilliant future.

We—*you* and *me*—belong to Jesus. "Yeshua [Hebrew for, *Jesus*, meaning, *safety*] said to them: 'We are now going up to Jerusalem, where everything written through the prophets about the Son of Man will come true. For he will be handed over to the *Goyim* [gentiles] and be ridiculed, insulted and spat upon. Then, after they have beaten him, they will kill him. But on the third day he will rise' "(Luke 18:31-33). You might ask, "How does Jesus's death make *me* His? Jesus is, "God's lamb. The one who is taking away the sin of the world" (John 1:29). Before Jesus, only shedding blood inside the Temple on an altar would God forgive sins. "If an individual commits a sin ... he is to bring as his offering [a lamb in Egypt] ... without defect ... lay his hand on the head of the sin offering and slaughter the sin offering. ... The *cohen* is to take some of its blood with his finger and put it on the horns of the altar for burnt offerings. All its remaining blood he is to pour out at the base of the altar. ... The *cohen* is to make it go up in smoke on the altar as a fragrant aroma for *Adonai*. ... Thus the *cohen* will make atonement for him in regard to the sin he committed, and he will be forgiven." (Leviticus 4). When drops of Jesus' blood dripped from his body—precious red elements *He* lost for you and me—God's demand for an unblemished sacrifice for our sins was met. "In union with him, through the shedding of his blood, we are set free—our sins are forgiven" (Ephesians 1:7). Halleluiah! Everything you've ever done apart from God is wiped out. You're His. On a Friday, over 2,000 years ago, Jesus became *our* lamb so we could be sin free before God and sealed to God for eternity. That's forever with Jesus. What now? "Have life, life in its fullest measure" (John 10:10)! God bless you.

Jesus, you willingly died for us. We praise you. Amen.

J.P. Osterman

HOLY SATURDAY
THE DAY THE WORLD STOOD STILL

I imagine the interim between Jesus' death and resurrection would have been stifling and dreary, with a global-wide eclipse. Strange phenomena occurred.

Venture with me as we encounter mysteries that brought skeptics to their knees. Jesus *is* Messiah.

In Matthew 2:2, the Wise Men search for Jesus, calling Him King of the Jews. And God made Him a special star in celebration of his birth, "His star in the east." Ironic how Jesus's last banner is the placard Pontius Pilate nails over Jesus's blood-beaten head. It is the charge against Him—the reason for His crucifixion. "This is YESHUA THE KING OF THE JEWS" (Matthew 27:37, Mark 15:2, Luke 23:38, and John 19:19). Then, the sky darkens. Do you hear the ground rumble and dirt crack? Inside the Temple, the finely-woven veil (parokhet) *rips-splits*, giving people preparing for Passover access to the Most Holy Place, the Tabernacle, God's presence in our world. "And they shall make me a holy [place], and I may dwell among them" (Exodus 25:8). Because Jesus shed His precious blood on the cross, God now dwells with you and me. He's here! His Holy Spirit talks to us and moves in our lives. And Jesus is our priest.

But that's not all that happened after His death.

Rocks split. Can you imagine a dark land, and low-hanging undulating clouds in a murky, light-twisting sky? "Graves opened, and the bodies of many holy people who had died were raised to life" (Matthew 27:52). God changed the universe that day. "When the Roman officer and those with him who were keeping watch over Jesus saw the earthquake and what was happening, they were awestruck and said, 'He really was a son of God' "(Matthew 27:54). Those astounded people experiencing those jaw-dropping miracles were the first post-crucifixion conversions. Every day since, our Christian numbers have been increasing in God's Book of Life. You ever wondered about Pontius Pilate? He orders guards to "secure" Jesus's grave. "So they ... made the grave secure by sealing the stone and putting the guard on watch" (Matthew 27:65-66, Mark 15:46, Luke 24:2, John 20:1). No stone, no amount of Earth's crust, dark energy or dark matter can stop God's power. He is *El Elyon*, who re-created Jesus's body for new glory. You'll have a new body as well.

God, we long for all knees to bend in worship to you. Amen.

GOD DESIGNED

EASTER SUNDAY
HE IS RISEN! ALLELUIA!

Can you imagine seeing someone you watched die, alive again?

Paul says: "The Messiah died for our sins ... and he was buried; and he was raised on the third day ... and he was seen by Peter, then by the Twelve. Afterwards, he was seen by more than five hundred brothers at one time, the majority of whom are still alive, though some have died. Later he was seen by James, then by all the emissaries [apostles] Last of all, he was seen by me, even though I was born at the wrong time" (1 Corinthians 15:3-8). More than 500 brothers, at one time, saw Jesus resurrected from the death. That's *not* including the women, such as Mary Magdalene, Mary the mother of James and Joseph, and the mother of Zebedee's sons (Matthew 28:1). Or all the dead people who rose up from their graves after Jesus's crucifixion to appear among the population.

Think of someone holy and famous who's been dead, for example, a pope, priest, Christian brother or sister. Now imagine them appearing right in front of you with a new body. Then Jesus! That would convince you that Jesus was Messiah for sure, right? That's why Jesus's Resurrection is so vital to our Christian faith. "After Jesus rose, they [holy people] came out of the graves and went into the holy city, where many people saw them" (Matthew 27:53). Right-and-left, soldiers, bystanders, spectators, Jewish elders, and commoners were proclaiming: "He really was a son of God" (Matthew 27:54; Luke 23:47). We, the Christian community, began growing into beautiful flowers, spreading seeds of faith, belief, and hope to advance God's Kingdom. How did God resurrect Jesus?

Jesus told people about His Father's power and capabilities. "I can ask my Father, and he will instantly provide more than a dozen armies of angels to help me" (Matthew 26:53). Those were the armies of Heaven in Joshua 5:15, 1 Kings 20:13, 2 Kings 7:6, 2 Kings 21:5, 2 Kings 23:5, Isaiah 40:26, Isaiah 43:14, and Jeremiah 8:2, only fragments. Brothers and Sisters, because we trusted in Christ as savior, God is now for us. His love and protection we *now* have at our disposal. Just trust Him. Jesus said: "Have you trusted because you have seen me? How blessed are those who do not see, but trust anyway" (John 20:28). We will see Him (1 Corinthians 15:50-56) one heavenly day.

Lord, we long to see your face through new eyes. Amen.

389

ABOUT THE AUTHOR

J.P. Osterman was one of five finalists in the 2015 Brevard Library Foundation's "Patrick D. Smith Literary Award." She won the prestigious Rupert Hughes Award at the Maui Writers' Conference for her novel, *The Matter Stream*, which she has been transforming into her **Nelta Series** of books. Her one-act play, *The Man Next to Me*, won First Place at the Southern California Writers' Conference and was published in the *San Diego Writer's Monthly*.

Including *God Designed*, her debut inspirational book, J.P. has written a total of ten books, from main stream fiction - to - a young adult novel - to - two collections of her short stories and finally her favorite genre - Science Fiction.

Her first published novel was the highly acclaimed young adult book entitled *The Screaming Stone,* which was followed by her whistleblower suspense novel *Corporate Revenge*, and *Pete's Crossroad* transformed from her award-winning play and short story, "The Man Next to Me."

While teaching high school English in the 1990s, she met with Ray Bradbury on more than one occasion, who inspired her to write science fiction. Her Science Fiction books include: a realistic look at colonizing Mars and the exploration of the far reaches of the universe in *Cosmic Rift,* contacting ancient aliens in *First Communication* (Book I, The Nelta Series). *Battlefield Matrix* (Book II) and *Astrocity Sagan* (Book III) continue the series. She recently compiled and released two short-story books, *Commuter Collection*: **Short Stories from the Edge** and *Pareidolia: Science Fiction Short Stories*.

J.P. Osterman was a reader and writer throughout her youth. She graduated from University of San Diego with a B.A. in English (with an emphasis in writing) and later a Master's degree from Azusa Pacific University. She is on the Board of Directors and is Secretary of the Space Coast Writers' Guild and a member of Brevard Scribblers. You will find a synopsis of all her books on Amazon.com: http://tinyurl.com/msb8uc7

www.ingramcontent.com/pod-product-compliance
Lightning Source LLC
LaVergne TN
LVHW051448080426
835509LV00017B/1699

* 9 7 8 0 6 9 2 5 5 0 9 5 3 *